Kafka and Noise

Kafka and Noise

*The Discovery of Cinematic Sound
in Literary Modernism*

✦

Kata Gellen

NORTHWESTERN UNIVERSITY PRESS
EVANSTON, ILLINOIS

Northwestern University Press
www.nupress.northwestern.edu

Printed in the United States of America

10 9 8 7 6 5 4 3 2 1

Library of Congress Cataloging-in-Publication Data

Names: Gellen Norberg, Kata, 1978– author.
Title: Kafka and noise : the discovery of cinematic sound in literary modernism /
    Kata Gellen.
Description: Evanston, Illinois : Northwestern University Press, 2019. | Includes
    bibliographical references and index.
Identifiers: LCCN 2018035292 | ISBN 9780810138940 (cloth : alk. paper) |
    ISBN 9780810138933 (pbk. : alk. paper) | ISBN 9780810138957 (ebook)
Subjects: LCSH: Kafka, Franz, 1883–1924—Criticism and interpretation. |
    Noise in literature. | Sound in motion pictures.
Classification: LCC PT2621.A26 Z73298 2019 | DDC 833.912—dc23
LC record available at https://lccn.loc.gov/2018035292

For Ezra and Esther.

The rest is noise.

CONTENTS

ACKNOWLEDGMENTS

Many colleagues, friends, and family members have supported me over the years as I wrote this book. I would first like to thank my dissertation advisers, Michael Jennings and Daniel Heller-Roazen, as well as Devin Fore and Thomas Y. Levin, who served as readers. My interest in and approach to modernism, sound, media, and form derive from the extraordinary training I received from these and other professors in graduate school.

I am extremely grateful to those individuals who read and gave me helpful feedback on drafts of my work: Yelena Baraz, Agnes Callard, Doreen Densky, Eric Downing, Ido Lewit, Mary Simonson, Aarthi Vadde, and Saskia Ziolkowski, who read all of it and then some. I would also like to thank a number of friends and colleagues who have supported and inspired me in numerous ways: Karen Auerbach, Paul Buchholz, Flora Cassen, William C. Donahue, Stefani Engelstein, Susanne Freytag, Natasha Gordinsky, Ruth V. Gross, Malachi Hacohen, April Henry, Jonathan Hess, Anton Kaes, Lutz Koepnick, Richard Langston, Michael Levine, Laura Lieber, Vivian Liska, Joseph Metz, Michael Valdez Moses, Jakob Norberg, Thomas Pfau, Henry Pickford, Inga Pollmann, James Rolleston, Claire Scott, Corina Stan, Margaret Swanson, Dorothy Thorpe-Turner, Gabriel Trop, Jacqueline Waeber, Ingeborg Walther, Tin Wegel, and Emma Woelk. Their companionship, encouragement, skepticism, and wisdom are greatly appreciated.

I am grateful to everyone at Northwestern University Press who worked with me to improve the book manuscript and see it through to publication, especially Nathan MacBrien, Trevor Perri, and JD Wilson, as well as the blind reviewers. Their attentiveness, rigor, and professionalism have been exemplary.

Duke University, which consistently encourages and supports innovative research in the humanities, has provided tremendous institutional backing for my work. I am proud to call it my academic and professional home. I am grateful for all my wonderful colleagues and students at Duke and in the Carolina-Duke Graduate Program in German Studies, and above all for the intellectual vibrancy, richness, and openness of these academic settings. Teaching, learning, and working within this community of scholars and students is the best part of my job.

Finally I would like to acknowledge and thank the Volkswagen-Mellon Foundation, which supported me through a fellowship at the Dahlem Humanities Center at the Freie Universität Berlin in 2013–14, and the Center for Philosophy, Art, and Literature and the Franklin Humanities Institute at Duke University for a generous grant to support Kafka events in 2014–15, which Saskia and I organized.

ABBREVIATIONS AND TRANSLATIONS

The following abbreviations are used throughout to refer to frequently cited works by Franz Kafka:

B   *Briefe, 1914–1917*. Edited by Hans-Gerd Koch. Frankfurt am Main: Fischer, 2005.

C   *The Castle*. Translated by Willa and Edwin Muir. New York: Schocken, 1995.

D   *The Diaries of Franz Kafka, 1910–1913*. Edited by Max Brod. Translated by Joseph Kresh. New York: Schocken, 1968.

DzL   *Drucke zu Lebzeiten*. Edited by Wolf Kittler, Hans-Gerd Koch, and Gerhard Neumann. Frankfurt am Main: Fischer, 2002.

KSS   *Kafka's Selected Stories: New Translations, Backgrounds and Contexts, Criticism*. Edited and translated by Stanley Corngold. New York: W. W. Norton, 2007.

L   *Letters to Friends, Family, and Editors*. Translated by Richard and Clara Winston. New York: Schocken, 1977.

M   *The Metamorphosis*. Edited and translated by Stanley Corngold. New York: Modern Library, 2013.

NSF I   *Nachgelassene Schriften und Fragmente I*. Edited by Malcolm Pasley. Frankfurt am Main: Fischer, 2002.

NSF II *Nachgelassene Schriften und Fragmente II*. Edited by Jost Schillemeit. Frankfurt am Main: Fischer, 2002

S   *Das Schloß*. Edited by Malcolm Pasley. Frankfurt am Main: Fischer, 2002.

T   *Tagebücher*. Edited by Hans-Gerd Koch, Michael Müller, and Malcolm Pasley. Frankfurt am Main: Fischer, 2002.

All citations appear in English in the body of the text. Where available and appropriate, I have used published translations, occasionally with modifications. These are marked as "trans. modified." Otherwise I have provided my own translations, marked as "trans. mine." Certain key words and phrases are given in the German original as well. The initial mention of all works includes the original title and year of publication or, if unpublished in Kafka's lifetime, composition. Some of these titles are not Kafka's own, but were assigned by Kafka's editor and friend Max Brod.

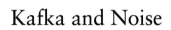

Kafka and Noise

Chapter 1

✦

Dreaming in Sound

Listening to Kafka Cinematically

> Kafka's novels are not screenplays for experimental theatre, since they lack in principle the very spectator who might intervene in such experiments. They represent rather the last and disappearing connecting texts of the silent film (and it is no accident that the latter disappeared at almost exactly the same time as Kafka's death); the ambiguity of gesture lies somewhere between sinking into speechlessness (the destruction of language) and the emergence from the latter into music.
>
> —Theodor Adorno to Walter Benjamin, 1934

Franz Kafka was preoccupied with noise as a literary object for his entire mature writing life, from 1912 until his death in 1924. Early on, Kafka described how everyday household sounds and city noise broke his concentration and prevented him from writing. Near the end, disruptive sounds were still invading and unsettling his creative process, but they had become inextricable from writing. Many of the central figures in Kafka's late works, from Josefine the singer to the burrowing creature, are defined by their struggle with noise. Though it originally stood in the way of writing, noise became the condition of his literary production.

Noise can be found both within and around Kafka's written works. It is the central theme of certain stories, such as "Great Noise" ("Großer Lärm," 1912) and "The Burrow" ("Der Bau," 1923), which depict acoustic disturbances directly. The experience of noise seems to have left its mark on Kafka's writings in other ways as well, inspiring a variety of literary endeavors. Works such as "The Silence of the Sirens" ("Das Schweigen der Sirenen," 1917) and "Investigations of a Dog" ("Forschungen eines Hundes," 1922) reveal an interest in the distinction between sound and silence, a borderland of elusive sonic quality. Other texts exhibit a fascination with distorted and ungraspable voices, which contain a kind of verbal noise. Examples include the squeaking sounds that transform Gregor Samsa's speech in "The Metamorphosis"

("Die Verwandlung," 1915) and Josefine's chirping, whistling song in "Josefine, the Singer or the Mouse People" ("Josefine, die Sängerin oder das Volk der Mäuse," 1924). Beyond the fictional works, Kafka's diaries and letters contain further reflections on the link between noise and writing, most significantly in his extensive reflections on the practice of literary recitation from the year 1912.

This book constitutes the first sustained study of sound in Kafka's writing.[1] Its central premise is that noise, a phenomenon with no apparent function, meaning, or value, presents a productive obstacle to modernist literary narration. Acoustic phenomena and events in Kafka's works produce various forms of inscrutability—not knowing what or how a sound signifies, as well as more basic uncertainties about its source, location, status, sonic qualities, and side effects. Noise also poses a problem for representation: how does silent written narrative capture or convey auditory effects? The attempt to tell stories about and through noise thus exemplifies two central "crises" of modernism: the crisis of knowledge and the crisis of narration. Kafka's works articulate and respond to these crises by grappling with noise. A variety of disruptive and indeterminate sounds are experienced as impenetrable and uninterpretable, but they also emerge as the basis for exploring certain aspects of narrative form, voice, and fiction. Noise is an absent center in Kafka's works: ungraspable yet ineradicable, it reflects a set of conditions, assumptions, and implications that govern literary writing.

"Great Noise"

One can discern an arc of noise in Kafka's literary career. The 1923 story "The Burrow," often read as Kafka's reckoning with death, represents its end point, while the early sketch "Great Noise" marks its beginning. In a surprising reversal, "The Burrow," unfinished and unpublished in Kafka's lifetime, has received much scholarly attention in recent years, whereas "Great Noise," one of Kafka's first publications, has been almost entirely ignored. Initially recorded in his diary in 1911, the latter appeared in 1912 in the *Herder-Blätter*, a Jewish student newspaper in Prague run by Willy Haas, who was to become an important screenplay writer and film critic in Weimar Berlin:

> I sit in my room in the Noise Headquarters of the entire apartment. I hear every door slam, and by these noises I am spared only the feet falling continuously between them, yet I still hear the stove doors snapping shut in the kitchen. Father barges through the doors of my room and crosses through, his nightgown trailing behind him, the ashes are being scraped from the oven in the next room, Valli, bellowing each word through the hall, asks if father's hat has been cleaned. A hiss that wishes to befriend me lifts the cry of a responding voice.

The apartment doors become unlatched and are blown open, and like the walls of a swollen throat open wider still with the singing of a female voice, and finally shut with a thudding, manly and most thoughtless jolt. Father has gone, now a gentler, scattered, helpless noise is invoked in the voices of two canaries. I had considered earlier, and now with the canaries I consider anew, if I shouldn't open the door a crack and slither snakelike into the neighboring room to beg my sisters and their governess, from the floor, for quiet.[2]

There are several senses in which noise is at a maximum in this short piece. The volume is high: sounds pile up on top of one another, and the decibel level rises steadily. It is also cacophonous: disparate noises produced by humans, animals, and objects mingle and clash, resulting in acoustic disarray. There is a tremendous sense of sonic dynamism—sounds moving, crossing paths, entering and exiting spaces—all within the confines of the bourgeois apartment. The acoustic registers also overlay one another, as when the wind blowing through the front door is compared to the wheezing that results from a "catarrhal" inflammation of the throat. The noise of family life is shaped by the spaces in which it is made and heard, and the sounds of the apartment are described in terms of human organs and ailments. This results in a feeling of acoustic plenitude, even confusion and excess. In addition to these semantic and rhetorical complexities, the style of the passage makes it feel noisy. The writing begins to feel a bit rushed, especially in the middle sentences, in which the sounds come in rapid succession: scraping, bellowing, hissing, crying, thudding. Thoughts are not completed, sentences are not finished, and proper punctuation is dispensed with, almost as though Kafka the writer could not keep up with Kafka the listener. Auditory impressions threaten to overwhelm his faculties of sensation as well as literary control.

In addition to the quantity and variety of noise, and the complex rhetoric and rhythm of its representation, this short work presents noise as maximally knowable: there are no acoustic mysteries. Every sound described in "Great Noise" is the sound *of* something that can be identified and named. Here Kafka does not try to depict sounds themselves. Instead he refers to them by their specific causes: the sound of a door slamming, ashes being scraped, a hissing voice, a shouting voice, a singing voice, birds chirping, and so on. He offers precise labels for all the sounds in his home, even if he feels at their mercy. The desire for silence that emerges at the end of the text adds to the rhetoric of submission and supplication. There Kafka figures himself as a snake-like creature with the modest but unfulfilled wish of creeping into the other room to ask his sisters and their governess for a bit of peace and quiet. This is a self-image with which readers of Kafka are familiar: the one who suffers because he is unable to speak out, and also the one who likens himself to an animal by virtue of his voicelessness and his strained relationship with his own body. In this instance, he is a passive earwitness to other people's (and animals') noisy habits and activities, who longs for silence but is power-less to bring it about. The density and rapidity of the middle sentences, which present the menace of auditory overload, contribute to this feeling of being a hapless victim.

As I have been intimating, though, this is a carefully orchestrated illusion. Kafka's writing is *not* breathless or frenzied, and certainly not desper-ate. Admittedly, it feels a bit rushed in the middle section, an effect Kafka achieves by presenting sounds in an unbroken series and replacing periods with commas. But overall "Great Noise" describes sounds according to their sources and effects in an organized sequence. It thus demonstrates Kafka's impressive verbal mastery of the noises surrounding him. Though he can do nothing to silence them, he effectively brings them under control by iden-tifying them, labeling them, organizing them, and wishing them away. The negative feelings associated with each sound should not obscure the linguis-tic and literary command Kafka demonstrates in describing the acoustic series. Notwithstanding Kafka's self-effacing image of himself creeping on the ground, begging for quiet from the only people who might actually listen, his text is characterized by a controlled, even masterful literary presentation of noise.

This is the most crucial sense in which "Great Noise" presents sound at a maximum. It is not simply that the text is rather noisy, though this is undeni-ably true, but that its sounds can be heard, identified, and explained through effective uses of literary language: rich descriptions, explanations of cause, rhetorical figures. The work thus presents noise in a condition of maximum knowability and representability. Here sound is never sound alone, but sound connected to a source or cause, and often to a function or task as well. Noise never gets out of control, which is to say, outside the bounds of understand-ing and representation. It is bothersome, but not cognitively or aesthetically overwhelming. Noise is part of the bourgeois order of the home, which is itself antithetical to the task of writing. Yet it also seems to have the potential for literary inspiration. "Great Noise" is, after all, a diary entry repurposed as a literary sketch. Here noise is a problem of quantity and variety; this is irritating and exasperating, but it does not fundamentally destabilize the listener's relationship to his environment by throwing him into a state of self-doubt. The text itself, in which disparate sounds are effectively named, organized, and explained, proves this point. Sensory overload does not flus-ter Kafka the writer, even if he assumes the posture of perturbation. "Great Noise" displays authorial mastery over noise.

At the other end of the spectrum lies sonic underload, the persistent encoun-ter with inscrutable sound. Minimally knowable noise puts a perceptible strain on Kafka's characters and narrators: these sounds cannot be identified or grasped, much less interpreted or evaluated. This experience dominates Kafka's later sound stories, especially "The Silence of the Sirens," "Josefine, the Singer," and "The Burrow," which lie at the heart of this book. Noise is as irritating and inescapable in these works as it is in "Great Noise," but it is also fundamentally unstable, uncertain, and indescribable. Sometimes its source cannot be determined, and frequently its status is ambiguous, since the noise cannot be distinguished from silence, music, speech, or other kinds of sound. In short, one hears without knowing *what* one is hearing. Thus minimal noise must often be described not only without knowledge of its source, meaning, or value, but even apart from its actual acoustic qualities. Yet it is present, indisputably *there*, and thus cannot be reduced to nothing. This persistent minimalism generates excitement and anxiety about these sounds and thereby fuels the narratives in which they appear. "Josefine" is motivated not by the beauty or efficacy of Josefine's song, but by the very indeterminacy of the sound she makes—its proximity to noise. "The Burrow" is propelled not by the burrower's wish for safety and solitude, which is satisfied in its opening sentence, but by the persistent but unidentifiable noise that invades his home. A central aim of this book is to uncover the literary significance of these tenacious, unaccountable minimal noises.

Literary theory, I contend, cannot supply all the tools needed for this project. Poetics can help explain aspects of sound in poetry, such as onomatopoeia and rhyme, but the representation of sound in prose narrative rarely involves this kind of direct inscription. Since prose narrative is governed by the convention of silent reading, the implications of its oral articulation—its status as audible speech—is largely peripheral. Narrative theory can help explain how noise propels or retards storytelling, but it cannot account for the specific significance of sound. In Kafka, noise has a special relationship to the structure and development of narrative, a relationship contingent on specific features of sound and its interplay with literary language. Sound studies, an emerging interdisciplinary field that considers both the technical and cultural dimensions of a range of acoustic and auditory phenomena, supplies useful concepts and terms, but it tends to focus on actual sound and hearing, whereas sound in literary narrative is represented in writing; it is apprehended with the mind, not the ears.

While all of these theoretical discourses—poetics, narrative theory, and sound studies—inform the present study in implicit and explicit ways, none of them proves entirely adequate to the task at hand. I work with a silent medium, literary prose, and yet with an object, noise, that is constantly pushing against the limits of that medium. Kafka's noises stage a struggle against the medium that both contains them and determines how they are represented, perceived, and understood. Neither literary theory, which has no means of theorizing sound, nor sound studies, which has shown little interest in literary narrative, can fully apprehend this struggle. In order to grasp how literary sound functions within a medium against which it is constantly pushing, I introduce another theoretical discourse: film studies. The role of sound in both silent and sound film has been the subject of a lively critical discourse since the 1920s. Various semiotic, aesthetic, and technical questions from the debates around film sound can be applied to the study of noise in Kafka's writings—not because film and literature are so similar, but precisely because their differences are so instructive. When concepts and tools that were developed to analyze sound in film are modified and reapplied to literature, the fault lines of each medium are revealed. This helps us understand not only noise in Kafka, but the limits and potential of representing sound in literary narrative more generally. Kafka's writing in turn exposes new dimensions of how sound is used in film and theorized by film scholars.

This intermedial methodology offers great insight into the problem of noise in Kafka. Since literary critics have developed neither the vocabulary nor the theoretical framework to conceptualize and explore how sound works in literary texts, and since sound studies has largely ignored literature, concepts from film theory and practice can be imported into literary analysis to understand the role sound plays in Kafka's works. As it happens, the study of the relationship between Kafka and cinema, and even the place of acoustic phenomena within it, is nearly as old as Kafka himself. In the 1930s, Walter Benjamin and Theodor Adorno debated whether theater or cinema provided a more apt analogy for Kafka's writing. In his famous essay on Kafka, Benjamin suggested that certain episodes can be characterized as "gestic theater," a term closely aligned with Bertolt Brecht's epic theater. "One of the most significant functions of this theater," he wrote, "is to dissolve events into their gestural components."[3] Indeed, for Benjamin "Kafka's entire work constitutes a code of gestures which surely had no definite symbolic meaning for the author from the outset; rather, the author tried to derive such a meaning from them in ever-changing contexts and experimental groupings. The theater is the logical place for such groupings."[4] Adorno disagreed not with Benjamin's premise—the significance of gesture in Kafka and the impossibility of assigning fixed meanings to them—but with his conclusion that this indecipherable gestural practice derived from the theater. In a 1934 letter he wrote, "If one were to seek out the origin of such gesture, one would look for it less in the Chinese theatre, so it seems to me, than in modernity itself, that is, in the extinction of language."[5] Adorno thereby posits that the inscrutability of gesture in Kafka is distinctly modern.

He also objects to the idea that Kafka's gestures are theatrical in the sense that they belong to the world of the stage and can thus be performed, visualized, and viewed by an audience from an outside position. Instead, Adorno asserts that Kafka's works are theatrical only in the sense of a "world-theatre" that "tolerates no standpoint external to itself." Indeed, for Adorno this absence of an outside position dissolves the tie between Kafka's writings and Brechtian theater.

> Kafka's novels are not screenplays for experimental theatre, since they lack in principle the very spectator who might intervene in such experiments. They represent rather the last and disappearing

connecting texts of the silent film (and it is no accident that the latter
disappeared at almost exactly the same time as Kafka's death); the
ambiguity of gesture lies somewhere between sinking into speechlessness (the destruction of language) and the emergence from the latter
into music.[6]

This provocative statement, which also serves as the epigraph to this opening chapter, is foundational for the small but growing group of scholars
who work on Kafka and film. It asserts for the first time an affinity between
gesture in Kafka and in silent film. What has gone largely unnoticed is the
significance of sound and silence in Adorno's account of this connection: he
invokes speechlessness, music, and the disappearance of silent film (which
also implies the advent of sound film). For Adorno, Kafka's gestures and
silent film gesture are linked through the loss of language, a modern condition, and the potential elevation of gesture to music. He also draws attention
to the nearly simultaneous moment that Kafka stops writing and silent films
cease to be made, thereby suggesting a link between unreadable physical
gestures and acoustic uncertainty. Kafka's modernist prose and silent film
use the body to evoke sounds that are both threatening and exhilarating in
their ultimate unknowability: ambiguous gestures can signal music, noise, or
silence, or perhaps even a suspension among these alternatives. Adorno thus
sets forth an idea that is a central premise of this book: that the line between
Kafka and cinema runs through sound. Moreover, he suggests that the fundamental inscrutability of sound in Kafka can be understood in connection
with developments in modern media and the disintegration of language in
modernity.

How do we apply Adorno's insights to a reading of Kafka? Given his
insistence on the ambiguity of sound in Kafka and its connection to the end
of silent film, one way is to examine Kafka's fiction alongside silent film. The
comparison I propose is between "The Metamorphosis," the famous story
in which Gregor Samsa is transformed into an insect-like creature, and the
silent film *The Artist* (2011), directed by Michel Hazanavicius. The fact that
the film explicitly thematizes the rocky transition to sound film, which is precisely the modern "moment" that Adorno sees playing out in Kafka's works,
makes for an illuminating comparison. Indeed, the reading I offer supports
Adorno's claim that Kafka's works represent the last connecting texts to the
silent film era. Moreover, *The Artist*, like Gregor himself, is a kind of hybrid:
it mimics silent film aesthetics but actually uses modern sound film technology, and it was made several decades after the death of the medium. The
belated resurfacing of a (pseudo-)silent film makes for a productive comparison with Kafka's own story of a monstrous mutation. In sum, *The Artist*
looks at early twentieth-century conditions of sound production, reproduction, and reception through a twenty-first-century lens, which is exactly what
I propose to do with Kafka's oeuvre.

Though the overt subject matter of the story and film is unrelated, their manner of presenting and engaging noise, voice, and music is mutually instructive. "The Metamorphosis" is about a traveling salesman, Gregor Samsa, who wakes up one morning to find himself transformed into a "monstrous vermin [*ungeheueren Ungeziefer*]," while the film chronicles the late 1920s transition to sound film through the story of two stars, Peppy Miller, who rises because she is able to seize on the potential of the new medium, and George Valentin, who seems unable to adjust to it (*M* 3; *DzL* 115). Acoustic disruption plays a central role in both works. In "The Metamorphosis," Gregor discovers early on that his voice has been invaded by a painful squeak that distorts his speech and ultimately forces him to cease verbal communication. In *The Artist*, new technologies for recording and reproducing sound create a demand for the voice in cinema, which renders George Valentin's silent film acting obsolete.

Gregor is forced into silence, and George is forced to speak or accept the end of his career. They seem to flounder under the acoustic exigencies of the worlds into which they awaken. Indeed, both works contain crucial scenes of waking up, where characters must negotiate new regimes of sound and silence. A comparative analysis of this process reveals how noise gives structure and meaning to the literary and cinematic representations of sleep, wakefulness, and the in-between process of awakening. Both Gregor and George are overwhelmed by their new acoustic realities but develop coping mechanisms to respond to them. Moreover, these works make differing uses of the technique of the acoustic close-up—a term originally used to describe an intense and focused representation of sound in cinema—to capture the process of transformation. The acoustic close-up expands and extends the moment of awakening, lending it depth, detail, and duration. The use of this technique in literature and film structures and informs my reading of the transformations that are so central to these works.

In the chapters that follow, I take two approaches to analyzing literature and film together. The first is instrumental: I call on terms and concepts from film theory and practice when they help explain something that literary ones alone cannot. The cinematic lens allows us to see, hear, and above all understand and conceptualize the literary text anew (chapters 2 and 4). The second is based on analogy: a previously unacknowledged parallel between cinematic and literary phenomena helps us grasp new dimensions and implications of each. Here the point is less to show that there is something cinematic at work in literature, and more to suggest that the side-by-side analysis of works of art that belong to different media reveals historical, aesthetic, and conceptual links, as well as telling differences (chapters 1 and 3). My use of the acoustic close-up to describe Gregor's and George's respective awakenings adheres to the second method. I do not, strictly speaking, need one work to speak about the other, but the comparison effectively demonstrates how the device of the acoustic close-up captures transitional states in both literature and film.

"The Metamorphosis": A Moment of
Awakening in Acoustic Close-Up

"The Metamorphosis" contains numerous transformations. There is, most prominently, Gregor's physical transformation, which involves a new but indeterminate insect-like bodily form.[7] There is also Gregor's more general transformation into a pariah, especially in the eyes of his family, and his death, the end point of his transformation. Then there is his family's transformation in class and lifestyle, which involves their diminishing economic means but rising social status. These shifts culminate in the sister Grete's emergence as a woman and the family's decision to move into a smaller apartment, both of which signal their new membership in the petite bourgeoisie. But there is another transformation, one which has received rather little, if any critical attention: Gregor's gradual silencing, his transformation into one who does not speak. It could be argued that the first of the three sections of "The Metamorphosis" is organized around this process of devocalization, which is itself triggered by Gregor's terrifying, estranging encounter with his own voice.

When Gregor wakes up to find himself transformed into a monstrous vermin, he is initially unfazed by this change. Gregor's calmness is nearly as jarring as the transformation itself, which ought to elicit surprise, indeed shock and fear. But Gregor simply acknowledges plainly and directly that his body no longer resembles that of a human being, at which point his thoughts wander off to concerns about finances, professional commitments, and family obligations.[8] Gregor's equanimity suggests that these personal and work-related woes have preoccupied him for some time now, and while his new animality might exacerbate them, it is probably not their cause. The double shock that the opening of Kafka's famous story delivers—a shock that eludes most readers because the story is so familiar (we seem to know it before we read it, even for the first time)—consists first in Gregor's fantastic transformation and second in his calm and relaxed response to this turn of events. As Theodor Adorno notes, "It is not the monstrous [*das Ungeheuerliche*] which shocks, but its self-evident nature."[9]

After the matter-of-fact description of Gregor's new body, the topic of his metamorphosis falls away and other matters dominate the pages that follow. The narrator thus presents a spectacular piece of information as simply as possible and then continues to play it down by demonstrating how little it concerns Gregor. He is distraught about his new physical form only to the extent that it is inconvenient: he cannot scratch himself, get up, or find a comfortable resting position. His thoughts do grow increasingly agitated, but this is due to long-standing problems at work and at home, not the fact that he seems to inhabit the body of a large beetle. His transformation, to the extent that it arouses this particular set of concerns, actually confirms the continuity between the old and new Gregor; it certainly does not cause an existential crisis. After all, the first line of the story describes not a feeling of alienation, but a moment of self-recognition. Gregor's body might look radically different than it did before, but what he realizes is that despite the transformation, he is still himself: "When Gregor Samsa woke up one morning from unsettling dreams, he *found himself* changed in his bed into a monstrous vermin" (M 3, emphasis added). Most readers, focused on Gregor's creatureliness, have overlooked the amazing fact that he awakens to a feeling of self-connectedness. Shifting the emphasis away from the "monstrous vermin" and onto the fact that Gregor "found himself," his relative composure comes into focus. To find oneself is to enjoy a kind of existential solidity that Kafka's characters rarely experience.

But Gregor does not remain calm and relaxed about his new physical state for long. He soon undergoes a second transformation, one that the reader witnesses—earwitnesses, to be precise—rather than simply learns about after the fact: the transformation of Gregor's voice. This change is preceded by a series of acoustic signals, irksome noises that disturb Gregor's relative composure. As he lies in bed, largely unconcerned with his debilitating bestial form, the ticking of the clock starts to unnerve him. Eventually its persistent reminder of the connection between noise and time brings Gregor to a state of heightened agitation:

> He looked over at the alarm clock, which was ticking on the chest of drawers. "God Almighty!" he thought. It was six-thirty, the hands were quietly moving forward, it was actually past the half-hour, it was already nearly a quarter to. Could it be that the alarm hadn't gone off? You could see from the bed that it was set correctly for four o'clock; it certainly had gone off, too. But was it possible to sleep quietly through a ringing that made the furniture shake? Well, he certainly hadn't slept quietly [*ruhig*], but probably all the more soundly [*fester*] for that. (M 5; DzL 118)

This passage complicates the relationship of silence, noise, sleep, and time. Time does not proceed on its predictable course when sleep occurs, perhaps because it is immune to the ticking of the clock. Sleep undermines the progression of time and thereby poses a serious threat to the regimented life that Gregor leads as a traveling salesman, since catching trains (which run on schedules) is so crucial to his job. Time is marked by one type of regular noise (the ticking of the clock), but it should also be restored by another kind of irregular but controlled noise (the alarm bell). Clearly this is where something has gone awry: either the bell did not ring or Gregor slept through it. In any event, noise was supposed to restore the rule of time and end the period of sleep, but this crucial shift did not take place.[10]

Stanley Corngold's translation of *ruhig* as "quietly" and *fester* as "more soundly" highlights the dialectic of sound present in the passage. Just as the ticking of the clock marks time and the ringing of the alarm bell is supposed to cause a shift from sleep to wakefulness (i.e., to restore time), there is a sense in which sleep, the antitemporal activity par excellence, is also governed by the relationship of sound and silence. After all, the ringing of the bell should cross the border from the conscious waking world into the realm of sleep; this is what triggers waking up. Given that this shift does not take place as planned, and that this failure to wake up seems to lie at the heart of Gregor's troubles, it is fair to say that there is something amiss in the acoustic economy of Gregor's sleep. Moreover, if sound and silence are off-balance in Gregor's sleep world, it is hardly surprising that the sounds of his waking life are also disturbed.

Gregor proceeds to grow increasingly anxious thinking about his next moves: will he be able to catch the next train, what will his boss think, and why does he feel so drowsy considering he has slept so much? These thoughts about time, work, and sleep immediately precede the moment of Gregor's acoustic alienation from within, the encounter with his own transformed voice:

> Just as he was thinking all this over at top speed, without being able to decide to get out of bed—the alarm clock had just struck a quarter to seven—he heard a cautious knocking at the door next to the head of his bed. "Gregor," someone called—it was his mother—"it's a quarter to seven. Didn't you want to catch the train?" What a soft voice [*sanfte Stimme*]! Gregor was shocked to hear his own voice answering, unmistakably his own voice, true, but in which, as if from below, an insistent distressing chirping [*Piepsen*] intruded, which left the clarity of his words intact only for a moment really, before so badly garbling them as they carried that no one could be sure if he had heard right. (M 6; DzL 119)

In addition to the persistent reminders of time (the ticking clock, the rushedness of his thoughts) the moment of Gregor's vocal transformation is also preceded by a series of acoustic signals: he hears his bedside clock strike, a knock at the door, and the soft sound of his mother calling, all in quick succession. The last of these sounds induces a change in Gregor, not because the mother's voice is itself alarming—it is in fact soft, gentle (*sanft*)—but because it brings Gregor to speech. What shocks and frightens him is the sound of his own voice, the strangeness of which is all the more apparent against the backdrop of the mother's. Gregor begins to speak, but we do not know what he tries to say or how long his effort lasts. We know only that he says enough to perceive a terrible change in his voice, which seems to be neither his own nor another's. It has been invaded by a foreign element, a *Piepsen* (chirping, squeaking, beeping) that produces a frightening and alienating effect. Gregor is unnerved by the uncanny mixture of familiarity and strangeness, as well as by his registration of an *internal* change. Indeed, he is jarred more by the perception of an alien element operating within than by the recognition of his insect-like exterior. Thus he loses his composure not when he realizes that he no longer *looks* like the self he knows, but when he realizes he no longer *sounds* like that self.

Why is the discovery of this *Piepsen* so distressing? The term itself, which designates a squealing or squeaking sound, is generally associated with small animals or young children, or with an automated machine sound. For a grown man to discover such a sound issuing from his body is understandably disconcerting, especially when it is also uncontrollable. One characteristic of typical human speech is that it is voluntary and controlled: one chooses one's words and how to speak them. The fact that Gregor cannot suppress the *Piepsen* in his voice suggests that his capacity for vocalization is becoming automated and instinctual, like that of an animal or infant. Gregor's regression to a state of linguistic powerlessness exacerbates the feelings of servitude and impotence that characterize his work and home life.

Moreover, the insidiousness of this *Piepsen* seems to derive from its tricky manner of sustaining itself: the effect of vocal disfigurement is delayed, which means that Gregor does not stop speaking until it is too late. The sound is figured as a parasitic foreign element, secretly embedded in Gregor's vocal apparatus. It feeds off the voice, emerging from hiding only at the moment it can maximally distort the spoken word. It thus sustains itself by postponing its mutational effect. This lag gives Gregor false confidence in his capacity for communication, so that he continues to speak, at least for a time. If Gregor's voice were completely unrecognizable to him or if the vocal disfigurement were immediately audible, presumably he would fall silent after a single word. Instead, the unsettling familiarity of his voice lures him to speak, yet what he produces is speech that both does and does not belong to him.

Nevertheless, this moment of acoustic alienation represents the beginning of Gregor's gradual descent into silence. After this point, Gregor's linguistic efforts proceed very cautiously. He forms words slowly and deliberately, in an effort to remain inconspicuous to the audience of family members and coworkers gathered outside his door. Growing increasingly comfortable with his new voice, he delivers a rather lengthy plea to the manager, who reacts by implying that he has not understood a word of what Gregor has said and referring to his "animal voice [*Tierstimme*]" (*DzL* 131). To Gregor's ears, however, his voice is becoming increasingly clear and familiar. The "chirping" is no doubt still present, but either he can no longer hear it or he no longer finds it strange. There seems to be a widening gap between how Gregor perceives his voice and how others do. Moreover, the reaction to his "animal voice" is described in distinctly sonic terms: the manager's soft tone, the mother's yelling, the rustling of skirts, the tearing open of the front door, and the conspicuous silence of the door left open: "The door could not be heard slamming; they had probably left it open, as is the custom in homes where a great misfortune has occurred" (*M* 14). Given that the story is focalized through Gregor, such a description reveals his remarkable sensitivity to sound and silence. On one level, this is not surprising: Gregor cannot see the reaction of his family and the manager, so it is natural that he would be especially attuned to the sounds they are making. He is simply being resourceful by gathering information through any available perceptual means. But the sensitivity of his auditory powers seems to exist in an inverse relationship to his capacity for vocal communication. The worse he speaks, the better he seems to hear.

The onset of Gregor's second period of calm can be explained both by his improved hearing and by the fact that "the others now believed that there was something the matter with him and were ready to help him":

> In order to make his voice as clear as possible for the crucial discussions that were approaching, he cleared his throat a little—taking pains, of course, to do so in a very muffled manner, since this noise, too, might sound different from human coughing, a thing he no longer trusted himself to decide. In the next room, meanwhile, everything had become completely still. Perhaps his parents were sitting at the table with the manager, whispering; perhaps they were all leaning against the door and listening. (M 14–15)

Despite the hopelessness of his situation, all but guaranteed by his ugly and ungainly animal exterior, Gregor is able to muster a feeling of confidence and safety on the basis of an acoustic exchange, even one that fails to communicate. All he wants now is to be *heard*. Since meaningful communication is no longer an option for him, he settles for a more basic sort of interpersonal exchange: the transmission of sounds, stripped of communicable content, which nevertheless provides assurance that someone is listening. For Gregor, this kind of empty conversation is the last resort of a half-human creature desperate to maintain a connection to his family and coworkers. He produces some manner of vocal noise, and he listens intently to the sounds and silences outside his door. These acts of making and hearing sound, no matter how basic and limited in content, reassure Gregor that he still belongs to the world of family and work.

The comfort of this acoustic exchange sustains Gregor for a time. He hears the manager speculate about his movements on the basis of the sounds he hears through the closed door, and the manager's words give Gregor new confidence. Though they are of no material consequence, Gregor gains support and strength from the knowledge that family members and colleagues are listening to him and talking about him. Part real, part imagined, Gregor's sonic sustenance reaches its climax at this moment:

> "Listen," said the manager in the next room, "he's turning the key."
> This was great encouragement to Gregor; but everyone should have

cheered him on, his father and mother too. "Go, Gregor," they should
have called, "keep going, at that lock, harder, harder!" And in the
delusion that they were all following his efforts with suspense, he
clamped his jaws madly on the key with all the strength he could
muster. (*M* 15–16)

Gregor thereby harnesses the tremendous acoustic energy of the moment,
generated by his own distorted voice, the agitating ticks and rings of the
alarm clock, and the auditory exchange with his family members and colleagues on the other side of the door. These sounds give Gregor a kind of
power and confidence that will elude him forever after but in this moment
help him open the door.

Depending on the progress of the key, he danced around the lock;
holding himself upright only by his mouth, he clung to the key, as the
situation demanded, or pressed it down again with the whole weight
of his body. The clearer click [*hellere Klang*] of the lock as it finally
snapped back positively woke Gregor up [*erweckte Gregor förmlich*].
With a sigh of relief he said to himself, "So I didn't need the locksmith
after all," and laid his head down on the handle in order to open wide
[one wing of the double doors]. (*M* 16; *DzL* 133)

Thus Gregor accomplishes a physical feat through energy generated by an
acoustic exchange. Simply hearing the others speak about him, and thus
knowing that they are in some way engaged with him and invested in him,
gives him the strength and drive to open the door. In short, the scene is pow-
ered by sound.

This act is significant not only because it allows Gregor finally to emerge
from his room, but also because it completes the act of awakening that
was begun in the first sentence of the story. This time it is brought on by
a "clearer" or "brighter" sound (*hellere Klang*), which "positively" awakened Gregor (*erweckte Gregor förmlich*)—the adverb *förmlich* functions as
an intensifier, so there is a sense of the comparative at work in this word
too. The sentence thus contains two indications that this act of awakening
should be thought of in relation to an earlier one, the comparative *heller* and
the adverb *förmlich*. The comparison, I contend, is to the story's beginning.
Thus, the *erwachte* (awakened) of the opening sentence is completed by the
erweckte (awakened) of this sentence.[11] In retrospect it is clear that the clock,
which insistently marks time but fails to bring Gregor fully from sleep to
wakefulness, has actually prolonged the moment of awakening. This explains
why Gregor's experience of sound and silence continues to obey the logic of
sleep, or at least that of an in-between state of consciousness, long after his
initial awakening. Until the moment Gregor opens the door, the second and
final awakening, he is in the process of waking up, a process that lasts at least

thirty minutes and probably quite a bit longer.[12] This period is characterized by a heightened sensitivity to issues of sound and hearing. The most prominent and frequently discussed signs of this sensitivity are Gregor's "animal voice" and the "chirping" in his speech, but in fact, as I have shown, the first twenty pages of the story are saturated with descriptions of voices, sounds, hearing, and silence.

Once Gregor is positively awake, there is little left for him to do but to fall silent. After he emerges from his room there is an initial uproar, consisting largely of the shrieks of the mother and the manager and the wild hissing noises (*Zischlaute*) of the father, who chases him wildly around the apartment (*DzL* 140). But by the closing words of the first section of the story, Gregor has been returned to his room and silenced, once and for all. The final sentence of this section reads: "The door was slammed shut with the cane, then at last everything was quiet [*still*]" (*M* 22; *DzL* 142). These words refer not only to the general onset of quiet, but also to the fact that Gregor has given up speaking for good. Once his parents are through screaming and hissing, the beast Gregor is ready to take his vow of silence.[13]

The opening of "The Metamorphosis" thus reveals a complex and unpredictable acoustic economy of awakening, which helps explain why Kafka calls it "the riskiest moment of the day," one that can easily go awry. The drawn-out process of waking up is characterized by a chaotic and unstable acoustic mélange, while the moment of definitive wakefulness brings silence. As Joel Morris has argued, Kafka's moments of awakening are "risky" because they demand quick-wittedness and decisiveness. Without these qualities, one runs the risk of failing to orient oneself, which might be the actual cause of Josef K.'s arrest in *The Trial* (*Der Proceß*, 1915) and Gregor's transformation.[14] Morris cites the following key passage, which Kafka deleted from *The Trial*:

> One is after all in sleep and in dreams at least seemingly in a state that is in its essence different from awakening, and to this belongs an infinite presence of mind or better a mental quickness, in order that with the opening of one's eyes one more or less finds everything at the same spot where one had left it in the evening. This is why the moment of awakening is also the riskiest moment of the day.[15]

One completes a crucial task in the moment of awakening, namely the linking of today's waking life to the memory of yesterday. It is crucial for the establishment of continuity; otherwise, one would begin a new life each day. Morris connects Kafka's ideas about the risky moment of awakening to a contemporary philosophical work by Kafka's friends Max Brod and Felix Weltsch, *Intuition and Concept: Outline of a System of Concept Formation* (*Anschauung und Begriff: Grundzüge eines Systems der Begriffsbildung*). According to them, the process of orientation relies on a store of memories that generate base experience or intuitions (*A*), with some additional input from immediate perceptual stimuli (x), which tend to corroborate the stored memories ($A + x$). But in Kafka's stories the perceptions undermine and threaten to undo the entirety of base experience ($x - A$).[16] The moment of awakening is thus a direct, unfiltered, and unbuffered encounter with the external world, which is why it is so risky: one perceives reality without the security of life's store of intuitions. Indeed, since it forces a reckoning with pure perceptions, the moment of awakening is not only more real than dream life, but also more real than waking life.

Remarkably, this moment of awakening extends over a period of more than thirty minutes, perhaps even an hour, in "The Metamorphosis." It is obvious why Gregor would need a long time to orient himself on this of all mornings, but the implications of this extended process are perhaps less clear.[17] Gregor experiences a drawn-out period in which intuition is suspended: he simply perceives his new reality and takes it at face value, instead of trying to add his store of experience to these new perceptions. The combination ($A + x$) would be jarring and ultimately irresolvable—after all, Gregor's new physical form is incompatible with past experience—whereas the perceptions alone (x) can simply be accepted on their own terms during this extended moment of awakening. According to Morris, this moment is "risky" because it threatens to undo intuition ($x - A$), which is indeed dangerous from the perspective of the fully conscious subject whose self-understanding is premised on existential wholeness and continuity: she assumes that experiences are cumulative, not that each day is a tabula rasa. But from the perspective of a subject undergoing an internal and external transformation, the absence of intuition is liberating. It allows her simply to take in the world as it presents itself to her perceptual and cognitive faculties at that instant, without expectations or preconceptions. Morris's account of "the riskiest moment" thus explains Gregor's relative equanimity throughout the opening pages of the story: he is operating without the constraints of base experience and thus lacks the intuition that would reveal the extreme irregularity of his situation. Gregor's suspended state of awakening therefore creates a circumstance that liberates rather than constrains his consciousness, at least for the duration of that extended "moment." The disorientation comes after that "moment" has passed, once the awakening is complete, for that is when Gregor must confront his new physical form with the full force of his present perceptions and past experiences.[18]

It is in the context of this extended process of awakening that the acoustic drama described earlier plays out. Had the process only taken a few seconds or minutes, as it generally does, Gregor would not have been able to inhabit and experience this state of acoustic indeterminacy. He might have fallen silent immediately, or he might have made full use of his "animal voice," thereby alienating his family and the manager in one stroke. Instead the gradual emergence of the chirping sound, the restrained use of speech, and the ticking of the clock combined with the mystery of its alarm bell constitute much of the story's opening drama, precisely because it takes Gregor so long to awaken fully. In this way, the literary text is able to draw out what is typically a momentary experience and represent sound with a newfound intimacy and intensity. A filmed version of these events might approximate them in a slow-motion sequence, but it could hardly contain the acoustic detail and reflection that Kafka gives. Gregor's metamorphosis is remarkable not only on account of his dramatic new bodily form, but because the "moment" of awakening in which it is apprehended produces an intense and concentrated attention to sound. The moment of awakening is given in "acoustic close-up."

The early film theorist Béla Balázs was the first person to offer a theoretically sophisticated theory of sound in cinema. While most others were debating the merits of the coming of sound—what it might add to or detract from the medium of silent film[19]—Balázs, already in 1930, was reflecting on the potential of sound film to change our faculties of perception, mostly on the basis of his exposure to silent film.[20] He offered the following speculation about what he called "the sound close-up [*Tongroßaufnahme*]":

> We may say of the sound close-up that it can transmit auditory impressions of which we are only in the rarest of instances aware with the unaided ear, even though we do constantly "register" them in some sense. We hear, but simply do not become conscious of these soft, intimate sounds, since they are drowned out by everyday noise as if by an avalanche of sound. They are the undertones, the minor events of the acoustic world that slip unawares into the unconscious, where their effect is often more powerful than any sound that penetrates our waking minds. The task of the sound close-up will be to raise for the first time to the level of consciousness this large and important sphere of auditory experience.[21]

Balázs was invoking the potential of sound film to make us hear in new ways. Through acoustic close-ups, film could emphasize sounds that were minor, peripheral, or quiet and thereby draw attention to acoustic phenomena that belong to film's sonic landscape but might otherwise go unheeded. For him, the acoustic close-up is useful for exploring the relationship among sounds in a film sequence. When a camera closes in and lingers on a sound, whether through acoustic or visual means, "we hear not just the sound close to us but also its relation and connection to the acoustic totality."[22]

Acoustic close-ups are possible in sound film as well as silent film, for example in a blown-up image of a sound source. They can also appear in literature, though admittedly through different means. Literature must represent sounds consecutively, which makes it difficult to capture the hubbub of overlapping sounds directly. Yet it has the advantage of not being constrained by the real-time duration of sounds, which might be very loud or dissonant or remarkable in some other way, but brief and hence difficult to linger on. Literature can "hold" a sound for as long as it wishes, potentially extending the representation of a short-lived sound across multiple pages. In film, a slow-motion sequence could draw out (but thereby also distort) a sound and thereby add a few seconds to its duration, but after a certain point the realism and recognizability of the sound would be compromised. The literary acoustic close-up can dwell on sound in a way that film cannot, but it can only do so by rearranging sounds sequentially that film is free to present simultaneously.

We can read the opening of Kafka's "Metamorphosis" as an acoustic close-up of the various sounds that constitute Gregor's "moment" of awakening. This is why sound and time, the two central features of this technique, play such a central role, and indeed seem engaged in a dialectical battle: sound (the alarm bell) is supposed to return Gregor from sleep to waking time (the ticking), but it fails to do so as planned, which is why Gregor is suspended for over thirty minutes in an in-between state in which disparate noises and voices flood his perceptions without really shocking him into silence and submission. But whereas in film time is a limiting factor to the acoustic close-up, in literature time can be manipulated in its service. Kafka's literary acoustic close-up slows time down, hence the drawn-out "moment" of awakening. It can also depict the relationship between noises (ticking, ringing), voices (Gregor's, the mother's), and silence with an otherwise impossible level of detail and attention. For Kafka, this technique is a way to capture and extend a momentary state on the border between consciousness and unconsciousness, as well as the perceptual conditions that govern it. Kafka thereby succeeds in isolating an instant in Gregor's transformation and exploring, in extremely close acoustic detail, how his perceptual faculties function at that instant. By understanding Gregor's relationship to the sounds he makes and hears at the "moment" of awakening, we gain insight into his transformation.

To conceive of the opening of Kafka's "Metamorphosis" as an acoustic close-up is not to suggest that Kafka was thinking cinematically when he wrote the story. He was certainly not thinking about sound film, which would not be invented for another ten years, well after Kafka's death. He might have been thinking about silent film, which played with ideas of sound and employed externally generated voices, noise, and music (lecturers, barkers, musicians, gramophones, etc.) even if it lacked the means to synchronize and integrate sound. But this is not my claim either. Rather, I am suggesting that the best way for readers to understand how sound works in the opening episode of "The Metamorphosis" is to apply the concept of the acoustic close-up to it, and specifically to consider how this cinematic technique plays out in a literary context. I am thus calling for a theoretical intervention, not a historical reconstruction. Applying the idea of the acoustic close-up to the literary medium gives us a deeper understanding of the role of sound in Gregor's transformation and refines our grasp of its function in the medium it was initially developed to describe, namely film. Removing the concept from film studies and refunctionalizing it for literature helps delineate its potential and limits, in both its old and new contexts.

The Artist: Another Moment of Awakening in Acoustic Close-Up

The Artist also offers an example of a cinematic acoustic close-up that features a state between sleep and wakefulness, a moment of awakening, and a man undergoing a personal and professional transformation. The film tells the story of George Valentin, a silent film star in Hollywood in the late 1920s, when sound film suddenly hit the scene and quickly threatened to make silent film obsolete. George's first reaction to the new medium is to dismiss it, as he simply cannot take it seriously. He watches a sound test with his studio boss and producer Al Zimmer, laughing superciliously. George seems to find the new medium ridiculous and embarrassing. Al admonishes George not to laugh: sound film is the future. "If that's the future, you can have it," George sneers as he exits the viewing room.[23] It is crucial to note that this entire scene—and nearly the entire film, with two significant exceptions—is silent. Like historical silent films, it is accompanied by music (for mood and pace) and intertitles (for dialogue), but seems to lack integrated synchronized sound. Of course the actual technologies used to create the nondiegetic soundtrack for this 2011 film are radically different, both in type and quality, from the methods employed to add musical accompaniment to silent film, but the effect is similar. *The Artist* poses masterfully as a silent film, reviving the very medium whose death its diegetic narrative chronicles.

This scene cuts directly from George's exit to a shot of him sitting in front of a mirror in his small apartment inside a Hollywood studio. George picks up his glass, takes a sip, and places it back down on the table. It emits an audible clink. George then looks quizzically at the glass, picks it up again, and puts it down again. It makes the sound again. Now George's face grows more serious. For him, this experience is disturbing and grave, not funny at all, even if the viewer perceives the humor of the event. Experimenting with his new sound world, George deliberately knocks over his shaving brush and drops his metal comb. Everything makes noise. Then George hears voices and laughter coming from outside, and he gets up to open the door. He appears to say something to himself out loud, but George's own voice is audible neither to him nor to the film audience. He looks in the mirror and touches his throat, as if to coax some sound out of his vocal cords, to no avail. Until George tries to speak, the relationship between sound and silence in this scene represents a simple reversal of the norms of silent film: synchronized noises are now audible. But George's soundless speech complicates matters, for it means that he does not simply find himself, all of a sudden, in a sound film. Instead, he seems to be caught somewhere in between silence and

Figure 1.1. George's mirrored soundless scream. Hazanavicius, *The Artist*, scene 5.

sound, literally in the transition from silent to sound film. The world around him is moving on, but he is stuck in a silent film, screaming soundlessly.

As the scene continues, the contrast between George's inability to speak and his noisy surroundings grows even starker. He becomes increasingly agitated by his voicelessness, and when he stands up, he knocks over a chair loudly, his dog begins to bark, and the phone starts to ring. The silencing of his voice is all the more dramatic in the context of the cacophonous world in which he suddenly finds himself. Moreover, the camera angle is askew, which adds to the feeling of disorientation and confusion. George screams at himself in the mirror, but no sound issues from him; the fact that his soundless scream is visible to George himself, and doubled for the viewer, compounds the distress (figure 1.1). Meanwhile the ringing, barking, and laughter from outside continue. Their combined effect is to emphasize George's acoustic powerlessness. He is increasingly overwhelmed by the sounds that surround him at the same time as he exercises decreasing control over his own voice.

The scene disturbs the viewer-listener as much as it does George, but our response takes place on a semiotic rather than an emotional level: the film has suddenly become a sound film in which objects and people emit audible sounds. Integrated synchronized film sound seems to take hold of the film *The Artist* at the same moment that it takes hold of the character George.

The shift can be explained as an externalization of George's own experience: as soon as his career is surpassed by the advent of sound film, his whole existence is surpassed by it, too. The film thus uses an extradiegetic technique (shifting from silent to sound film) to represent how dramatic and jarring this transition is for George.

The symbolic meaning of this disconnect between George's silence and his sonifying surroundings is clear—the world keeps moving while he is left behind, a silent film star stuck in a sound film world—but there is also a perplexing semiotic dimension to this disjunction. George loses his own voice completely at the moment that his world begins to sonify. It is not just that *we* cannot hear him, but also that he cannot hear *himself*. George thus simultaneously inhabits a sound film and impossibly defies a basic principle of all film, silent film included, namely that the actors inhabit a world of sound to which only the viewers are deaf. Silent film actors always spoke and communicated onscreen, even though the sound of their voices was not recorded and played back. They did not rely on sign language or pantomime, even if they developed an acting style with exaggerated facial expressions and gestures. Indeed, it is an essential premise of silent film semiosis that it takes place in a world of sound: the characters speak and sounds are audible within the diegesis, even if they are not audible to the audience; the characters are unaware, so to speak, that we cannot hear them. This is undeniably the conditions under which *The Artist*, a film in which the characters can hear each other even if the viewer cannot hear them, has been operating until this point. George's silent voice thus signals the radical undoing of silent film semiosis, including in the very film we are in the process of watching. *The Artist* thereby suggests that the advent of sound did not simply add a new element to a preexisting cinematic tradition; rather, it thoroughly undermined and reshaped the medium.

Until this point, every sound we have heard (the glass clinking, the dog barking, the telephone ringing, the girl laughing) can be described as an acoustic close-up. Not only are these sounds clearly heard, first in isolation and then together with the others, but the camera also zeroes in on the sound source. Thus the film achieves precisely what Balázs described when he first theorized the phenomenon of the acoustic close-up: it brings our awareness and attention to sounds that normally get drowned out, or simply ignored. Glasses always clink when we put them down, but how often do we actually *hear* this? We barely register such sounds, because they are so everyday, so insignificant, and so inconsequential. Yet they are part of our sound world, and hence something that concerns Balázs, who is interested in the expansion and refinement of our sensory apparatus. In the context of *The Artist*, the extreme audibility of this and other mundane sounds, their presentation in acoustic close-up, alerts us to the dramatic shift that George personally experiences and the film industry as a whole undergoes with the advent of sound film: suddenly everything sonifies. The acoustic close-up of George's absent voice, a powerful depiction of silence, also draws attention to the shift from silent to sound film. Balázs and others have noted that that the representation of silence first became possible with the advent of sound film.[24] It is only in contrast to sonification and vocalization that silence emerges as representable. Indeed, in *The Artist* George's scream registers as silent precisely because the scene is suddenly flooded with sound. Thus, the various acoustic close-ups in this sequence function on the figural, subjective level (they capture how George is perceiving the world) at the same time as they reinforce the film's broader narrative about cinematic transformation.

The scene's combination of acoustic excess and deficit reaches its climax in its closing shot, at once the film's most dramatic acoustic close-up and George's moment of awakening.[25] Overwhelmed by the sounds in his little apartment, George ventures outside, where the sound of the laughing girl grows ever louder as she approaches. She also seems to multiply inexplicably, first into three and finally into a whole gaggle of girls. This confirms that the problem with George's sonic world is not simply that it does not register or reproduce voice (as opposed to noise), since the girls' voices are audible, but that it is resistant to George's voice in particular. It also subverts other acoustic expectations, as if to confirm that George is suddenly inhabiting a topsy-turvy sound world. In the final moment of the sequence, George watches a feather float from the sky and hit the ground with a deafening thud; this is a subjective sound to which the viewer-listener is privy. Once again, an inverted acoustic situation—the feather's fall should be soundless, not excruciatingly loud—is accompanied by a visual double, the feather's shadow, in much the same way that George's soundless scream earlier in the sequence was visible as a direct and a mirror image. Nonmimetic sounds are marked by visual doubling, perhaps to draw attention to the sonic mismatch. Another silent scream follows the drop of the feather: the sound itself cannot be given in close-up, since there is nothing to hear, so instead the film presents George's face in a progressive close-up that emphasizes the inexplicable muteness of his voice—an acoustic close-up of silence (figure 1.2). The feather's deafening fall and George's soundless scream are complementary images, since they both invert acoustic realities. George *ought* to have a voice when he tries to scream, and the feather *ought* to fall to the ground silently, but the film refuses to conform to the natural sonic order. The inversion of this order, as presented in these acoustic close-ups, is evidence of the dramatic and playful potential of the new medium of sound film, which can create imaginary sound worlds. Verisimilitude is not everything, the film seems to say. The acoustic close-up can make us hear more fully what was already in our world—that is what it can contribute to verisimilitude—but it can also transform sounds in thoroughly fantastical, dreamlike ways for reasons beyond fidelity to the real.

Indeed, the moment that the feather lands with a loud thud is the moment that George wakes up from what we belatedly learn was a dream. The scene

Figure 1.2. An acoustic close-up of silence. Hazanavicius, *The Artist*, scene 5.

cuts directly from an image of George silently screaming and covering his ears to an image of his eyes opening as he lies in bed next to his wife. Thus the whole sequence, with its acoustic close-ups, unrealistic amplification of sound, and conspicuously silent voice, was a kind of dream, indeed a nightmare of the new sound film. In his waking life, George refuses to accept this new cinematic and professional reality, whereas in his dream he confronts it head-on; the unconscious seems to be the site where repressed fears play themselves out. The moment of awakening is thus doubled in this scene. It involves George both literally waking up (the shift from sleep to wakefulness) and opening his eyes and ears to the new sound film, in all its danger and excitement.

It seems that in *The Artist*, too, the moment of awakening can be "the riskiest moment," but for the opposite reason than for Kafka's characters. Gregor remains strangely free of intuitions and expectations during his extended process of awakening, which is why its conclusion—the actual awakening—is so jarring. Once he is truly and completely awake, he must fall silent. George, however, is disturbed and distraught throughout his dream, and the moment of awakening only heightens his fear and worry. It can still be described as "the riskiest moment," for with awakening comes George's realization that he can no longer deny the reality of the new sound film: he must either transform himself as an actor or accept the end of his career. His dream, specifically its acoustic exaggerations and reversals, has forced him to confront this fact in a way that realistic or conventional representations of sound could not.

The fact that George's moment of awakening seems to correspond to a loud noise offers another point of comparison to Gregor's. The uncharacteristically loud thud of the feather rouses the sleeper from his nightmare, but there is no indication that the thud associated with the feather in the dream has come from George's actual environment. George simply opens his eyes and slowly gets out of bed. We therefore have no reason to believe that the noise he hears in his dream derives from the real world, as is often the case with loud sounds that rouse us from sleep. Mladen Dolar references this point in his psychoanalytic reading of "The Burrow," where he also examines the "moment of awakening":

> Freud maintains that one crucial function of the dream is to be the guardian of sleep. Any external disturbance that might wake us up is integrated into the dream in order to keep us asleep. The dream protects the sleeper from the intrusion of reality. One eventually wakes up when the external disturbance becomes too intrusive for the dream to tackle.[26]

Contrary to this account and to general expectations, there is no mixing of dream images and real-world sounds in George's moment of awakening. To paraphrase Dolar paraphrasing Freud, actual sounds frequently invade our dream worlds, and our dreams can sometimes accommodate and incorporate them, at least to an extent; the point at which the merging of dream images and real-world sounds breaks down is the moment of awakening. In *The Artist*, however, the noise belongs entirely to the dream world. Its loudness and disruptiveness are the product of George's unconscious, but that does not stop him from looking for the source of the sound when he awakens.

This is not the only way to explain the thud of the feather at the end of the dream sequence. The fact that the *viewer* no longer hears the sound when George wakes up proves nothing, since with George's awakening the film has clearly returned to the mode of silent film. There can be sounds only in George's dream, which adheres to a sound film semiotic, and not in his waking life, which adheres to a silent film semiotic. Thus, we simply cannot know whether the thud of the feather that awakens George is contained entirely within his dream or whether it derives from the real world and seeps into George's dream world, because in *The Artist* the real world is silent and only dreams have sound. If we assume the sound is entirely dreamed and has no real-world correlate, *The Artist* seems to have found an ingenious way to represent the permeable border between silent film and sound film, via the permeable border between sleep and wakefulness. On the contrary, if we assume it comes from the outside, the film would still be probing and revealing these same boundaries, for it would be the only sound capable of crossing them. In fact, the issue is undecidable, which suggests that the film is using the acoustic close-up to represent not so much silent or sound film but the process of transitioning from one to the other. By capturing and complicating the moment of awakening through this device, in its visible and audible forms, the film represents the disruptive and destabilizing transition from sleep to wakefulness, and from silence to sound. The hybrid dream sequence in which sound worlds are inverted, undermined, and reconfigured in unpredictable ways is both an expression of George's subjective experience and a visualization and sonification of the experience of transitional states more generally.

In both "The Metamorphosis" and *The Artist*, the moment of awakening is brought about by a dramatic acoustic close-up that puts an end to "unsettling dreams" and returns the protagonists to consciousness. In both instances, these are dreams and realities whose acoustic orders have been radically altered and thus require reorientation in sound and silence. For Gregor and George the process of awakening, a crucial aspect of their transformations, is inextricable from a series of remarkable acoustic experiences, which are presented in acoustic close-up. In "The Metamorphosis," the literary acoustic close-up allows Kafka to dramatize and extend the "moment of awakening," which is essential to representing Gregor's transformation. *The Artist*, a film that uses sound selectively and strategically in its attempt to pose as a silent film, also employs the technique of the acoustic close-up to represent the moment of awakening. This signals the shift from dream to reality, from sound film to silent film, and from a realm of exaggerated and inverted sounds to a realm of predictable sonic absence. This shift restores a state that existed prior to George's dream, yet the dream of sound film has clearly also transformed his waking life. George will never really awaken from this dream, for it represents a cinema-historical transition from which there is no turning back, *The Artist* itself notwithstanding. In much the same way, Gregor wakes up from "troubled dreams" that do not permit a return to a predream state. In both cases, acoustic close-ups allows these characters to awaken to a previously unknown reality and at the same time to preclude the possibility of returning to their former worlds. Though stripped of their voices, they wake up with heightened powers of hearing and a new capacity to negotiate the sounds and silences of the worlds they now inhabit. Gregor immediately puts this sonically generated power to use, harnessing it to unlatch and open the door, though of course in the end no sound can save him. George, by contrast, needs more time to acclimate himself to the sound world, but by the end of the film he has done so with such success that his own voice breaks through to the audience. Gregor's and George's transformations, considered side by side and in acoustic close-up, reveal the power of sound to portray transformations—from sleep to wakefulness, from voice to voicelessness, and from silent to sound film. Because it can suspend time and thereby extend the duration of sound events, and because it can play with and invert sonic expectations, the acoustic close-up is uniquely capable of capturing moments of transition and transformation, which are otherwise fleeting and subjective.

Methodology and Overview

Kafka and Noise makes the central methodological claim that film sound—that is, sound as it has been used and theorized in the context of cinema—can be applied to Kafka's writing as a way of deepening and broadening our understanding of his engagement with noise. A series of concepts from film theory and techniques from film practice can thus be used to grasp the role sound plays in Kafka's writing. In addition to the acoustic close-up, these include "acousmatic" or disembodied sound, nondiegetic sound, implied sound, sound bridges, and voice-over. Additionally, certain aspects of the discourse surrounding early cinema, especially the period of transition from silent to sound film, resonate with Kafka's literary treatment of sound. Thus, various practical, theoretical, and historical dimensions of cinematic sound bear on Kafka's writings.[27]

By contrast, literary critics have only recently begun to develop the vocabulary and theoretical framework to conceptualize and explore the role of sound in literary narrative.[28] This delay can be explained in part by the fact that prose texts are silent: they can represent but not produce sounds.[29] To be sure, literature is not a visual medium either, but there is a substantial body of theory on literary optics and literary vision. Literary criticism has taken up the "visual turn" in a way that has not yet happened with the more recent "acoustic turn."[30] To the extent that they have been explored, literary sound and literary hearing have been treated largely as reflections of historical circumstances. In interpretations of modernist literature, this has included references to such developments as urbanization, mechanical warfare, technological innovation, and new media. The presence of sound in literary modernism has not gone unnoticed, but the vocabulary and concepts needed to analyze it thoroughly are still being developed.[31]

While it is undeniable that the acoustic realities of modern life seep into modernist literature, the significance of literary sound goes beyond its mimetic function. Thus, I turn to cinema for a new set of vocabulary and concepts to understand noise in Kafka. Given that film theorists and filmmakers have been examining and experimenting with sound for over a hundred years, even in the silent period, they have amassed a rich store of words and ideas to describe sound in film. Many of the acoustic techniques they have employed and auditory phenomena they have theorized appear in modified form in literature. Though film theory and analysis cannot be applied directly or wholesale to literary texts, the necessary adjustments and modifications actually help us specify how sound works in each medium.

I take a broad view of the cinematic medium, which includes but is not limited to films themselves. Petr Szczepanik proposes "vertical hybridity" as a way to speak about

> a medium's identity as a mix of technological devices, practices, discourses, and institutions. This implies that a medium cannot be defined as a purely technological invention or as any kind of delimited material device but can only be defined as a multilevel construct, which also includes purely discursive "inventions" and objects, assembled from values, expectations, projects, fictions, and dreams circulating within contemporary discussions about the nature of a new medium.[32]

Szczepanik demonstrates that only such an integrative approach allows us to grasp the significance of film sound in the transitional period from the late 1920s to the early 1930s. This includes the examination of literary and critical writing on film, adjacent technologies such as radio and gramophone, institutional factors such as censorship, and related artistic practices from the lowbrow (ventriloquy) to the highbrow (synaesthetic poetry). In other words, cinematic sensibilities emerge from a complex web of technological, social, cultural, and aesthetic phenomena, many of which precede the strictly cinematic techniques and theories in question. This idea of vertical hybridity also applies to my analysis of Kafka. The fact that he wrote about gramophones and telephones is evidence of an attunement to cinematic sound, even if the latter had not yet been invented in his lifetime in the form we know. By introducing sound recording and playback, enabling voices to be transmitted across wide distances, and normalizing the separation of voices from bodies, these earlier technologies created the conditions of a modern experience of sound.

One can also look at this issue historically: even during the period of silent film, radio and gramophones were used to popularize and market silent film stars, which means that these technologies form a crucial prehistory to sound film.[33] Kafka lived during the early days of radio, gramophones, and telephones—which is to say, in the era of reproducible and disembodied sound, technologized voices, and audio playback. His literary engagement with sound was certainly influenced by his experience of its technological mediation. Film helps us distill the central acoustic problems in Kafka's writing and offers a conceptual vocabulary for their expression, but both Kafka's lived experience and cinema itself were also shaped in crucial ways by earlier sound technologies.

On the surface, Kafka rejects these technologies for their dehumanizing, alienating effects. In the years 1912 and 1913 he writes to his lover Felice

Bauer on at least two occasions about her work with technologically mediated voices, first as a secretary in a gramophone company and then writing
sales letters for parlographs, an early dictation machine:

November 27, 1912

My idea of your company was more or less right, but I should never
have thought that the confounded din of 1500 gramophones would
emanate from it every day. How many people's nerves are you guilty
of shattering, dearest lady? . . . As for me, I don't even have to hear
a gramophone; their very existence I consider a threat. I liked them
only in Paris; Pathé have a showroom there on one of the boulevards,
with Pathephones, where for a small coin one can listen to a prodi-
gious program (chosen from a fat catalogue). You should do this in
Berlin, if it isn't done already. Do you also sell records? I shall order
1000 records with your voice, and all you need say is that you grant
me as many kisses as I need to forget all sorrow.[34]

Jan. 10–11 (or 9–10), 1913

I am fundamentally frightened of Parlographs. A machine with its
silent, serious demands strikes me as exercising a greater, more cruel
compulsion on one's capacities than any human being. How insignificant, how easy to control, to send away, to shout down, upbraid,
question, or stare at, a living typist is! He who dictates is master,
but faced with a Parlograph he is degraded and becomes a factory
worker whose brain has to serve a whirring machine. Think how long
a chain of thought is forced out of the poor, naturally slow-working
brain![35]

Kafka refers repeatedly to the fifteen hundred gramophones and their fifteen hundred shrieks: he finds the tremendous volume of sound produced by
these music machines jarring and overwhelming, even if he does not hear a
single one. The very thought of so many technologized voices, disembodied
and proliferating wildly, causes tremendous anxiety. His angst extends to
parlographs, even if he does not use one, as the very idea of giving one's
authorial voice to a machine is deeply unsettling: it feels like a submission,
a relinquishing of bodily and mental control to a mechanical apparatus. Yet
Kafka's remarks about the gramophone and parlograph also suggest a sense
of thrill about these technologies, not least because he associates them with
his beloved Felice. His agitated and excited tone reveals that he is eager to
reflect on the effects of mechanization and technology on the voice, their
implications for modern urban experience, and their potential influence on
writing.

Kafka and Noise considers Kafka's writing in connection to cinematic and precinematic sound technology in order to make arguments about the relationship of film and literature that are both theoretically sophisticated and historically informed. The readings are always motivated by Kafka's own literary engagement with sound and noise. I begin with noises in Kafka—the acoustic disruptions, unrecognizable voices, disembodied sounds, and inscrutable silences that pervade his works—and employ ideas from film practice, history, and theory to work through them. The application of film concepts to Kafka's writing sometimes doubles back on film itself. That is, having considered film concepts in a literary context, they can gain new meaning and relevance when returned to their original cinematic context, in part because their newly discovered literary potential exposes their previously invisible contours in film. The book thus argues for a model of intermediality based on continuous reciprocal interpretation and theorization across media, in order to demonstrate that noise is an object or experience through which Kafka explores the limits of writing. Precisely because noise upsets and violates aesthetic conventions and semantic norms, one must constantly seek to explain and justify its place in literature. Noise becomes a phenomenon through which to investigate not only what does and does not belong in literature, but also what literature can and cannot do. Each chapter thus shows how noise pushes literature to an extreme—of perception, of representation, and of cognition.

This approach to Kafka and noise, which takes inspiration from Adorno's idea about the link between Kafka and silent film, relates to recent criticism on Kafka, modernism, and intermediality. In her entry on "Film and Photography" in the 2010 *Kafka Handbook* (*Kafka-Handbuch*), Carolin Duttlinger notes that the

> subject area of film and photography points to two interconnected questions: on the one hand there are the actual films and photographs that Kafka came in contact with and which are either explicitly thematized or implicitly reflected in his texts. On the other hand however there is the question of the general influence of both media on Kafka's imagination and literary production—that is, of specific filmic or photographic modes of perception and writing in Kafka's oeuvre.[36]

To a point, Duttlinger is right to categorize the extant work on Kafka and cinema in the way she does. The first category is exemplified by Hanns Zischler's 1996 book *Kafka Goes to the Movies* (*Kafka geht ins Kino*), which reconstructs Kafka's moviegoing habits on the basis of autobiographical remarks and historical evidence.[37] An important work in the second category is Peter-André Alt's 2009 study, *Kafka and Film: On Cinematographic Narration* (*Kafka und der Film: Über kinematographisches Erzählen*). Alt's central thesis is that Kafka's novels are governed by a distinctly cinematic mode of narration, namely a sequencing of images without logic or causality.[38] The 2016 volume *Mediamorphosis: Kafka and the Moving Image* testifies to the growing interest in cinematically inflected readings of Kafka, as well as Kafka's influence on film. Moreover, the introduction to this volume offers a concise and useful summary of the current state of the study of Kafka and cinema.[39]

Critics working in both areas of scholarship that Duttlinger identifies are rightly concerned with historical and biographical circumstances. Whether one is documenting Kafka's moviegoing practice or arguing for influence and inspiration, it is necessary to establish what he saw, when, with whom, and under what circumstances. The historical fact of Kafka's exposure to silent film is as important as his experience of precinematic sound technologies. But there is a further link between Kafka's writing and cinema that Duttlinger's categories do not cover: the usefulness of film theory and practice to explain and interpret crucial aspects of Kafka's writings. By looking at how sound is used in film and theorized by film scholars, we can account for the presence and significance of a variety of difficult and elusive sounds in Kafka, ones that resist the interpretive methods typically applied to them. Critics could extend this field in two ways: by applying these film concepts to a broader range of literary texts, and by arguing for the relevance of other film concepts to Kafka and other writers. We already have a rich store of concepts for describing and theorizing film—from montage to cinematic time, from the offscreen to the gaze—that might have useful analogues in literature.[40] Yet these concepts cannot simply be imported "as is" from one media discourse into another. They must be analyzed, modified, and adjusted to the conditions of the new medium, and even then the fit is never perfect. It is precisely this misapplication and this imperfect fit that proves so productive and revealing, since it creates a kind of interpretive tension. The attempt to apply analytical concepts developed for one medium (film) to another (literature) creates friction and thereby exposes the assumptions we make about the media in question, their limits, and their possibilities.[41]

This study also capitalizes on the tension between sound and literature. Given its silence, literary narrative has no easy, direct, or self-evident way to represent sound. As noted, the norms and standards for writing about sound are less established than those for writing about visual processes and optical experiences. Sound is generally regarded as a secondary attribute or mere effect, whereas vision seems to give us direct access to an object or experience. Thus, purely acoustic descriptions always seem deficient, incapable of producing a complete picture. Indeed, to write about sound alone, without reference to causes and origins, is generally disorienting and ineffective. This is why it is so exasperating and challenging to account for literary sound, particularly noise, for it seems to lack both semantic content and aesthetic value. But sound is everywhere in modernist prose, and there is tremendous variety in how authors approach it. The possibilities range from the direct alphabetical inscription of noise (Joyce, Beckett) to virtuosic, melodious accounts of musical transcendence (Mann, Proust), and from jarring descriptions of the din of urban life (Woolf, Döblin) to inscrutable sounds with potentially metaphysical meanings (Benjamin, Rilke). Perhaps modernist writers have found myriad creative ways to write about voice, noise, and music because there is no obvious or prescribed way to do so. The absence of norms means that each attempt to write about sound is original and also contains a more or less hidden program for its realization.

Literature has not arrived at a standard for representing sound, least of all noise. The absence of a convention is crucial to modernist writers' attempts to engage with sound in literary narrative. Unlike a sound film, whose acoustic dimension might be highly absorbing, literary renditions of sound are always beset by the incongruous fact of their silence. Writers must devise means of representing sound, by working around or even against the silence of the medium. Until norms and practices are established, each work must confront this difficulty anew. Kafka never settled on one approach, which means that each story, letter, and diary entry on sound presents a novel attempt to reckon with this tension between the object—noise—and the medium of writing. Perhaps this representational friction was precisely what drew Kafka to noise.

The broader implication of this claim is that nonsounding media can reveal aspects of sonic modernity that are unavailable to sounding media. Radio, sound film, and television can be called "insider" media when it comes to sound, since they can convey acoustic content directly. Literary prose is an "insider" medium when it comes to psychological reflection, emotional exploration, and philosophical contemplation, since its primary tool is expressive language, which lends itself to the representation of thoughts and feelings. Conversely, painting can be considered an "outsider" medium when it comes to philosophical argument. Since painting generally works with images, and philosophy generally requires language, a painter would have to work extra hard—indeed, against her medium—to convey philosophical content. Literary narrative is an "outsider" to sound, since it does not lend itself naturally or easily to its representation. It has no acoustic means at its disposal, so it must either represent sound indirectly or apply it to the text externally, for example in the form of a dramatization or reading.[42]

The notion of an "outsider" medium lays the groundwork for a theory of intermediality that eschews any kind of technological determinism.[43] Whenever a work of art tries to reach outside its own medium—when it probes the limits of what can be done within a medium in order to expand its range—it reveals an intermedial impulse. This might seem uncontroversial, yet it challenges the Kittlerian model of cultural analysis that until recently dominated our understanding of perception and representation in modernism, especially in the German-language context. In his media-theoretical works *Discourse Networks 1800/1900* (*Aufschreibesysteme 1800/1900*,

1985)[44] and *Gramophone, Film, Typewriter* (*Grammophon Film Typewriter*, 1986), Friedrich Kittler argued that literature is fundamentally determined by the media conditions that govern its inscription.[45] It is not that literature and film simply represent or reflect changes in modernity (for example, psychiatry, modern warfare, and methods of education), but that works of art and the institutions of modernity are all constituted by these media practices. My argument broadens Kittler's in two ways: first, I claim not only that new media shape literature, but that media theory shapes our ability to read literature; second, I argue that changes in sensation and representation go beyond the technological innovations to which they are sometimes linked. The literary representation of sound, natural or machine-made, already contains a productive friction, which suggests the intrinsic intermediality of sound in Franz Kafka's writings.[46]

I am not the first to write about sound in Kafka, but I am the first to do so through the conceptual framework of film.[47] Several works of German literary criticism, by notable scholars such as Wolf Kittler,[48] Gerhard Kurz, Gerhard Neumann,[49] and Bettina Menke,[50] explore aspects of the relationship of Kafka and sound.[51] However, my work has much more in common with the cultural theorist and psychoanalytic critic Mladen Dolar, who has written penetratingly on Kafka and sound. He devotes the final chapter of his 2006 book *A Voice and Nothing More* to voices in Kafka, and a long essay from 2011 to the noise in "The Burrow." In the book on voice, Dolar argues that the decades-long debate about the law in Kafka—whether it is nothing or everything, whether it has no inside or rather no outside—finds a sort of resolution in Kafka's engagement with the voice. His stories offer three strategies for dealing with the problem of the law: the voice as pretense in "Silence of the Sirens," the voice as minimal difference in "Josefine," and the voice as the basis for a "science of freedom" in "Investigations of a Dog."[52] Dolar's essay "The Burrow of Sound" is one of very few works that deal explicitly with noise in Kafka. Though he focuses on one story, Dolar suggests that we view "sound and voice as the last most tenuous and tenacious red thread of [Kafka's] pursuit, something that goes, perhaps, straight to the core of his work, and something that has the value of a testament," a statement that seems to echo Adorno's comment to Benjamin discussed earlier.[53] Dolar argues that the noise in the burrow is "an entity of the edge": it allows Kafka to explore various fragile but charged liminal spaces and borderlands, such as the moment of awakening, the problem of causality, and the advent of modernism itself.[54] These ideas resonate with the present study, since my goal is to explore the work noise does in and for Kafka, rather than to posit its meaning or value.

Like Dolar, I am indebted to Gilles Deleuze and Félix Guattari's 1975 book *Kafka: Toward a Minor Literature* (*Kafka: Pour une littérature mineure*), which begins with the idea of the burrow—Kafka's oeuvre as a rhizomatic maze of tunnels—and moves quickly to note the various "scenes of sonorous intrusions" in Kafka's stories.[55] Deleuze and Guattari argue that sound interests Kafka precisely because it "escapes signification, composition, song, words."[56] Indeed, it offers a "line of flight" from given forms and meanings, since "sound doesn't show up here as a form of expression, but rather as an *unformed material of expression*, that will act on the other terms."[57] For them, noise in Kafka functions as a destabilizing, disarticulating force in the production of textual meaning. This point contributes to their overall theory of deterritorialization in Kafka—the notion, first applied to Kafka's specific brand of German,[58] that Kafka's mode of expression is defined by that which is incomplete or in-process (trial/process,[59] metamorphosis, "becoming-animal"), minor (genres such as letters and short stories), and revolutionary (the politics of the assemblage). Noise forms a kind of foundation for their entire reading: "Sound doesn't act like a formal element; rather, it leads to an active disorganization of expression and, by reaction, of content itself."[60]

Given how influential Deleuze and Guattari's theory of minor literature has proven,[61] it is remarkable how little attention has been paid to the role of noise within it. It is not so much that their book offers the first interpretation of difficult sounds in Kafka as that it reminds us again how impenetrable and central those sounds are, decades after Adorno's comment to Benjamin. All of these thinkers have planted the seeds out of which this book grows. They pose the problem of sound in Kafka and take it seriously enough to suggest that it warrants sustained close reading. They have collectively, if unwittingly, posited the nexus of Kafka, sound, and film as a fertile and worthwhile field of inquiry, but they have left the actual work of this scholarly endeavor to others.

The chapters that follow fill in the details of this relationship. I show how the application of film concepts to noise in Kafka allows us to see the "work" that noise does in and for Kafka's writing. As is apparent in "Great Noise," the early sketch discussed above, noise disrupts and even prevents the act of writing. But as I showed regarding "The Metamorphosis" and will demonstrate further in the following chapters, noise also allows Kafka to probe the perceptual, representational, and cognitive limits of literary expression. Noise becomes a figure through which to experiment with literary possibility—and to run the risk of literary failure.

Chapter 2, "Acts of Listening in Silent Media: Implied Sound in Kafka and Early Film," compares implied sounds in Kafka's writings and in silent film. Film can show sound sources and acts of hearing, and literature can describe these processes in terms of the physical movements, positions, and gestures they involve. In both cases, the nonaudible evocation of sound can trigger the process of mental hearing, but implied sounds have an additional crucial function: they help form and organize the space of narrative. By analyzing a series of "soundless" or acoustically indeterminate sounds in Kafka and silent film, I demonstrate the spatializing power of implied sound in both contexts. At the heart of this reading stands Josefine the singer, whose quiet power, like that of the silent film diva, derives not from her voice but from her physical presence. Josefine's singing creates an architecture of the body that fills in for an absent built environment. The bodily gestures and postures associated with her song, rather than the song itself, make literary space narratable, in much the same way that implied sound in early cinema sutures space to give coherence and intelligibility to silent film narrative. A work like "Josefine" thus operates at the limits of representational possibility: it replaces buildings with acoustically ordered space and thus suggests that noise can substitute for architecture in the spatial structuring of narrative.

Chapter 3, "The Vocal Supplement: Recitation in Kafka and the Advent of Sound Film," examines Kafka's attitudes toward the vocalization of literary works (readings, lectures, recitation, declamation, and acting) together with critical and cinematic reactions to the introduction of sound film. It juxtaposes a parallel phenomenon in seemingly unrelated contexts—the addition of the voice to two media previously experienced as soundless—in order to reveal a shared ambivalence about the voice in aesthetic modernity. The voice threatens to unsettle issues of authenticity, ownership, and authorship, but also promises to infuse old art forms with play, humor, and sociability. This ambivalence plays out in Kafka's diary entries on recitation and reading, as well as in films that engage with the transition to sound, including *The Blue Angel* (*Der blaue Engel*, 1930), *Modern Times* (1936), and *Singin' in the Rain* (1952). By juxtaposing Kafka's writings on recitation and the discourse of the new sound film, this chapter explores the power of the voice to destabilize the aesthetic norms of silent media. Finally, Kafka's "Lecture on the Yiddish Language" ("Rede über die jiddische Sprache," 1912) and "A Report to an Academy" ("Ein Bericht für eine Akademie," 1917) suggest that the orality of recitation can be considered primary, as opposed to derivative or supplementary, which implies a further expansion of literary potential through the "noise" of the voice.

Chapter 4, "Metaleptic Noise: Acousmatic Nondiegetic Sound in Kafka and Film," examines a series of disembodied sounds in Kafka's writings, most importantly the noise in "The Burrow," whose source is undiscoverable because it lies outside the fictional diegesis. It derives from a world that is inaccessible to the story's first-person narrator, yet it is audible to him. Here noise probes the border between reality and fiction, and enables Kafka to explore the possibility of a character that transcends the storyworld that ought to circumscribe his existence, a phenomenon known to narrative theorists as metalepsis. Noise, in short, is responsible for the burrower's intimations of other worlds. The chapter goes on to propose an analogy between narrative worlds and species worlds, both of which involve fundamental transgressions with existential implications. In "Investigations of a Dog," another first-person animal story that involves metalepsis, noise permits Kafka's characters to transcend not only narrative borders, but the perceptual and cognitive horizons of their species. Noise is the metaleptic figure through which Kafka explores the possibility of listening our way into animal worlds while remaining rooted in human environments.

The epilogue draws out the implications of these acoustic portals into other worlds by proposing a modernist epistemology of sound. It also reflects on the contribution of *Kafka and Noise*, and of literary study more broadly, to the growing field of sound studies.

Chapter 2

✦

Acts of Listening in Silent Media

Implied Sound in Kafka and Early Film

In the first lines of Franz Kafka's last published story, "Josefine, the Singer or the Mouse Folk," the narrator declares: "Our singer is named Josefine. Anyone who has not heard her does not know the power of song" (*KSS* 94). While the mice in the story, including the one who is narrating, seem to have heard Josefine's song, the reader must be denied this experience. She will never *hear* Josefine's song, only read about it. It will remain inaccessible as a direct auditory experience, because Josefine's song exists only as it is described in a work of literature, and literary writing has no intrinsic means of making sound.[1] Kafka's story thus opens by declaring that its readers will never understand the very thing it seeks to explain.

Given that Kafka's readers will never hear Josefine and must therefore remain ignorant of the power of song, why does Kafka choose literature as the medium through which to represent song, or song as an appropriate subject for literary expression? Why inscribe failure from the start, by declaring that readers can never know and appreciate the very thing that lies at the heart of the narrative they are about to read? The story begins by proclaiming an insurmountable handicap: Josefine might be capable of expressing the power of song, but readers will never hear it, for literal hearing is simply beyond the perceptual bounds of what a reader can do. We miss out on the wonder of Josefine not because we are in the wrong place at the wrong time, but because we are in the wrong medium.

At the same time, what makes Josefine's singing special, even for those who hear her, is its ungraspability and indeterminacy; its musical qualities cannot be identified, despite the narrator's repeated attempts. Every statement about it is eventually contradicted, each assertion ultimately proven wrong, or at least deemed unverifiable. It is impossible to make a true claim about Josefine's song because it is a self-contradiction: "What she is whistling here is no whistling [*Was sie hier pfeift, ist kein Pfeifen*]" (*KSS* 96, trans. modified; *DzL* 354). Josefine's song is not one with itself, and this internal inconsistency is its distinctive feature. This explains the song's endless capacity to elude our grasp, to evade all attempts at characterization and explanation. Indeed, we cannot even know whether it is Josefine's song or her silence that is so formidable. We know only the effect of her presence—her power to unify the mouse folk—but not the nature of her musical gift, which has the air of something impossible or unreal.

Given these facts about Josefine, it turns out that the *most* appropriate medium, indeed the only one that can adequately capture her singing, is one that does not present sound directly or completely. For if there is something ungraspable or impossible about Josefine's voice, no actual heard sound could convey these qualities. Any real sound would fall short of depicting the unreality of Josefine's voice. It appears, then, that Kafka did not after all choose the wrong medium for depicting Josefine's voice. The limits of literature do not close off possibilities; instead they allow Kafka to represent the voice in ways that sounding media do not. It turns out that literary writing is not obsolete in the modern age of technologically reproducible and mass communicable sound. Rather than a shortcoming, its stubborn silence is the necessary condition for representing a kind of music whose acoustic effect contains its contradiction. Josefine's voice can only be represented in a medium that, because it does not produce or reproduce actual sounds, is capable of invoking the hidden, ineffable dimensions of acoustic experience and expression. To transfer Josefine's song into a sonifying medium would be to destroy its most distinctive quality and the source of its power—its indeterminacy and impossibility.

In addition to literary writing, another prime example of a nonsonifying medium is silent film. Leaving aside acoustic accompaniment,[2] pre-1927 films could represent speech, music, and noise only through indirect visual means, namely intertitles and visualized sound. Here, too, the limits of the medium could be seen as a handicap, something that hindered its full expressive potential. But this view is anachronistic: silent filmmakers were surely more focused on what could be done within their medium than what couldn't be. It is only in retrospect that silent film seems to be "lacking" in some fundamental way (and only after the invention of sound film that it is even designated as "silent"). Instead of regarding silent film's silence as a shortcoming, we might see it as an asset, or at least a constitutive element: what does the silence of silent film allow it to express, and might this go beyond what could be expressed in a sonifying medium? Much as literature allows Kafka to posit a sound that can be represented but not heard, the very inability of silent film to sonify can reveal a secret, inaudible dimension of sound.

In a 1934 note that is as suggestive as it is incomplete, Walter Benjamin wrote: "Sound film as the limit for Kafka's and Chaplin's worlds."[3] His first insight was to link Franz Kafka, who was to become the most famous author of German-language modernist literature, and Charlie Chaplin, who was already at the time the most famous silent film artist in the world. The second insight was to identify sound film as a limit for two artists working in different media, a palpable border that informs and even structures every hint or idea of sound in their works. To be clear, this is a limit, not a limitation: it reveals the shared contours of two silent media, not their inadequacies. Benjamin's comment need not imply that Kafka's and Chaplin's diegetic worlds measured themselves against sound film. But it does suggest that new insights into the representational strategies and potential of their nonsonifying works emerge when they are read in conjunction with one another and retrospectively, from a time after the invention of sound film.[4]

Given that Josefine's voice cannot be heard, it is important to look closely at its textual presentation. In addition to the unstable and contradictory descriptions of her song, the narrator describes a series of gestures and bodily poses that express the act of singing. These gestures and similar ones in other works by Kafka—descriptions of bodies that signal the presence of sound— are the subject of this chapter. In his essay on Kafka, Benjamin also puts tremendous stock in Kafka's gestures. Though they have no fixed symbolic or allegorical meaning, Benjamin argues that Kafka "tried to derive such a meaning from them in ever-changing contexts and experimental groupings."[5] In a discussion of "Benjamin's thinking about . . . the gestural dimension of acoustic phenomena in Kafka," Michael Levine notes that "at a certain point these phenomena become less important for the way they sound than for what they do."[6] Indeed, they don't "sound" like anything, which is why one needs to rethink how this substitution works: gestures do not communicate the content, form, or feeling of the sounds they stand for; rather, they stand in place of sound. While it is important to think about what silent film and literary writing are trying to accomplish when they invoke sound, I want to focus less on what is absent and withheld (the sound, or the signified) than on what is present and given (the body, or the signifier), in order to explore the power and meaning of implied sounds for literary and filmic expression.[7] As Benjamin notes, "[The] greater Kafka's mastery became, the more frequently he avoided adapting these gestures to common situations or explaining them."[8] Gestures do not unlock mysteries in Kafka; they *are* the mystery.[9]

This chapter explores and compares how silent film and literary prose represent sound through silent gestures, whether given in images or words. Kafka's fictions and silent film are responding to the same challenge of representing sound in a silent medium, and they are doing so for related ends: the construction of narrative space through implied sound. The chapter centers on readings of four works by Kafka—"The Knock at the Courtyard Gate" ("Der Schlag ans Hoftor," 1917), "The Silence of the Sirens," "Eleven Sons" ("Elf Söhne," 1917), and "Josefine, the Singer or the Mouse Folk"—alongside examples from silent film, contemporary film theory on implied sound, and Kurt Pinthus's *Cinema Book* (*Kinobuch*), a 1913 compilation of film scenarios by the rising stars of German expressionism.[10] This transmedial analysis reveals the persistent and productive uncertainty of implied sound: bodies engaged in indeterminate acts of hearing and making noise shape the space of narrative, even as they defy acoustic resolution.

Implied Sound and Subception: Kafka's "The Knock at the Courtyard Gate" and Chaplin's *The Kid*

In his moving account of listening as a cultural and aesthetic mode, *Sinister Resonance*, the musician and critic David Toop writes that listening

> is a specimen of mediumship, a question of discerning and engag-
> ing with what lies beyond the world of forms. When sound, silence
> and other modalities of auditory phenomena are represented through
> "silent" media, this association of mediumship becomes more acute.
> Dwelling in every written text there are voices; within images, there
> is some suggestion of acoustic space. Sound surrounds, yet our rela-
> tion to its enveloping, intrusive, fleeting nature is fragile (a game of
> Chinese whispers) rather than decisive.[11]

In addition to drawing our attention to the sounds present in silent media, Toop raises the counterintuitive point that we are perhaps most attentive as listeners in situations where we are not in fact using our ears. Silent media force us to detect sounds where they cannot be heard and to conjure them, rather than simply to listen for them. This takes a good deal of perceptual and cognitive work, which is why we engage most intensively with acoustics and hearing when confronted with silent media. These acts of imagination and their consequences for how readers and viewers grasp narrative space are the subject of this chapter.

In a brief but illuminating article on F. W. Murnau's silent masterpiece *Sunrise* (1927), Melinda Szaloky sets forth an idea that is another basic premise of this chapter: there is "an acoustic dimension of the silent cinema that has been insufficiently recognized, one that does not originate from extrafilmic sound effects but, instead, issues from the images themselves."[12] She speaks of "visual acoustics" and "sounding images," terms comparable to my notion of implied sound. In a similar vein, the film historian Isabelle Raynauld notes that

> films produced between 1895 and 1929 have long been considered
> silent or without sound. If there is some truth to this statement, if
> only from a purely technical vantage point, it is nonetheless false
> from the vantage point of narrative. In fact, . . . even if films were
> projected without integrated synchronous sound, the presumed silent
> stories told were actually happening in a sound world and not in a
> "deaf world." In other words, silent stories took place, intra- and
> extra-diegetically, in a hearing world. The films not only represented
> sound, the act of hearing and of listening in many inventive ways, but
> also showed silence, as well as noisy and talky situations. It can be
> said with certainty that the writers and directors of early cinema used
> the dramatic potential of sound to create complex stories.[13]

Raynauld's article goes on to ask questions about the function and purpose of inaudible speech in cinema and to make an argument about early screen-writing practices and the role of speech therein. She draws attention to the fact that ideas of sound can be as powerful and significant as actual sounds in silent cinema. This is especially important given that the vast majority of research on sound in silent film deals with the presence of actual sounds—live or recorded music, barkers and talkers, audience noise, projector noise, and so on—and neglects to consider how early cinema represents sounds and hearing through the moving image.[14] Raynauld insists that "when we watch a film from the retrospectively called silent era, we are asked *to look at sound and to see voices*."[15] This, too, is part of the "mediumship of the listener," to speak with Toop. Szaloky, who also notes that silent films take place in sound worlds, goes so far as to suggest that we consider medium not in terms of what a given means of representation is technically capable of, but rather in terms of what it communicates to audiences:

> We may consider the silence of the silent film from the standpoint of the medium itself where the medium is defined not in terms of its material technology but as a representational practice directed toward reception by spectators. Were silent films populated by deaf and mute characters who moved about in a soundless space? Did spectators believe that silent films told stories of voiceless people in a soundless world? This was hardly the case.[16]

Szaloky's suggestion that we rethink what a medium is on the basis of what it can represent might leave us with notions of media so fluid and variable as to be unusable, but her impulse is valid: the technical limitations of a medium do not correspond in any neat and predictable way with its representational potential.

Some of the earliest critics of the silent screen also recognized and discussed the phenomenon of "visible speech." In his foundational work of film theory, *Visible Man (Der sichtbare Mensch*, 1924), Béla Balázs compares the speech of silent film actors to the gestural language of dancers and the speech of stage actors:

> The film actor speaks, exactly as does the stage actor. There is no difference in his gestures. We just do not hear him; but we *see* him speak. That's where the great difference lies. In the theatre, where we concentrate above all on the words, we do not notice speech as expressive movement, as an expressive play of the mouth or the entire face. For the most part, indeed, there is in theatre nothing of this kind to attend to. What counts there is the sound of the words, and mouth movements are merely the means to an expression; they have no meaning of their own.

> In film, however, speaking becomes immediate, visual, facial expression. To *see* speech is to learn quite different things from just hearing the words. The speaking mouth often shows more than actual words can convey.[17]

Together, the content of Balázs's claims about theater speech and silent film speech and the rhetoric of his juxtaposition capture their relationship brilliantly. On the one hand, these phenomena seem to be very similar, and from the actor's perspective they might even be identical. On the other, they are utterly different, since theater speech is perceived primarily as linguistic content and silent cinema speech is perceived largely as facial expression and bodily gesture. These forms of speech are thus closely related at their source, in the performer, but divergent in their effect on viewing audiences. The act of watching a silent film is what imbues the gestures and expressions that accompany speech with expressive potential, not least because the speech they accompany is no longer audible, and is thus typically inaccessible as linguistic content.[18] In fact, silent film actors probably modified their gestures and expressions to accommodate the soundlessness of the medium, developing an acting style somewhere between theater and pantomime. This resulted in expressionist film style, which was particularly suited to convey the *idea* of sound through moving images of actors' bodies and faces.[19]

Several decades after Balázs's early reflections on silent film speech, the filmmaker and theorist Michel Chion proposed replacing the term "silent cinema" with "deaf cinema," on the grounds that films made before the advent of sound were not actually silent—they were often accompanied by live or recorded music, speech, and noise in the form of sound effects, and they contained a host of "implied noises."[20] Sounds were frequently suggested visually, for example through images of bells or musical instruments. Filmmakers could either use repeated close-ups—Chion cites the example of Sergei Eisenstein's 1925 film *Strike!*, in which an image of a factory siren recurs—or "write and shoot scenes that included an active sound source as a pretext for having this kind of refrain-image around which to organize the sequence."[21] The source of the sound, given in an image, stood in for an acoustic effect. In addition to the visual suggestion of sound in "deaf cinema," sounds could be evoked through written intertitles. By manipulating typography, filmmakers could not only display the content of speech, but also represent such acoustic features as volume, tone, and emphasis.[22] Silent film evoked sound by making visual reference to its causes and offering written representations of its linguistic content.

The film scholar Dominique Nasta argues that implied sound in silent film triggers the act of "subception," or "subliminal auditive perception," a psychological phenomenon whereby a perceiving subject mentally compensates for or "fills out" an incomplete perception.[23] Like Toop, she claims that visualized sounds unaccompanied by actual sounds—"exclamatory titles,

visualized shouts, knocks on the door, eavesdropping, etc."—actually emphasize the act of hearing.[24] Nasta goes on to argue that sound events based on
"subliminal auditive perception" can have more "immediacy" and "brutality"
than those based on ordinary hearing precisely because they require the listener's active participation.[25] The absence of actual sound focuses the viewer
on the sound source, the effects of which she must imagine. This requires a
heightened alertness and more cognitive work on the part of the viewer. As
Michel Chion explains, in the silent film era these acts of imaginary audition
could call forth a wide variety of sounds, from dialogue to noise, "for just as
you could internally hear the actors' voices, you could also internally hear or
imagine all sounds suggested by the film. There are automatic associations of
perceptions that are not easily undone, and the silent cinema was swarming
with implied noises."[26]

Whether or not Kafka got the idea from silent film, it is worth considering
how subception is at play in his writing. Here it is the linguistic evocation of
a sound in literature rather than its visualization in cinema that inspires the
reader to complete or imagine the auditory sensation, but both cases involve
a form of mental hearing. There are significant differences between the silent
evocation of sound through images and words. Before addressing these, it is
important to note Kafka's tendency to destabilize acts of subception: he often
invites us to imagine sounds, and then partially withdraws the invitation.
Thus, in Kafka even the most seemingly straightforward instance of literary subception—a hand knocking on a gate—is full of unnerving twists and
turns. We are asked to imagine the sounds that typically accompany certain
gestures, and then forced to question whether this act of mental hearing was
warranted.

Kafka's short story "The Knock at the Courtyard Gate" depicts a sound
event that could in principle be visualized in silent film or verbalized in literary
prose. In the story, a great deal—a man's prosecution and imprisonment—
hangs on this fateful acoustic disruption, yet we cannot be sure it ever took
place. This is one of the first works that Benjamin mentions in the context
of his discussion of Kafka's gestures, and it is the example that illustrates his
claim that "the gesture remains the decisive thing, the center of the event."[27]
The story begins as follows:

> It was in the summer, a hot day. On the way home with my sister, I
> passed a courtyard gate. I don't know whether she knocked at the
> gate out of mischief or distraction or whether she merely made a
> threatening gesture with her fist and did not knock at all. (*KSS* 124)

Benjamin notes that the "very possibility of the third alternative puts the
other two, which at first seemed harmless, in a different light. It is from the
swampy soil of such experiences that Kafka's female characters rise."[28] The
first two options originally seem harmless not because the sister's motive is

irrelevant, but because they both allow the act to be judged and guilt to be determined. Moreover, the first two options invite and validate the act of subception: we are meant to imagine the sound of the knock on the gate, and then to consider questions of motive and guilt. Before the sentence is completed, however, the process of subliminal auditive perception is undermined, or at least rendered inconclusive, for if the sister only made the *gesture* of knocking without actually touching the surface of the gate and hence without producing noise, the literary description should only inspire a mental image of the knock, not its sound. Thus, the third option revises the first two not only on a moral level, as Benjamin suggests—is her culpability increased or diminished if she only *pretended* to knock? Is this more mischievous than knocking deliberately or more innocent than knocking absentmindedly?— but also on a perceptual and cognitive level, since the reader does not know what she is licensed to imagine. Should she be hearing a sound in her mind, or visualizing an empty, silent gesture?

The uncertain knock, which renders the status of the sound event undecidable and the act of subception incompletable, comes to serve as the basis for the outrageously incommensurable punishment that befalls the narrator at the end of the story: he is imprisoned, with no prospect of release, all on account of his sister's possible knock. This is the overt absurdity and horror, the typically "Kafkaesque" element, of the story. But there is also a more subtle acoustic uncertainty that I have been delineating, which can be related to the gestures of silent film. Kafka's knock could be visualized, but since silent film and literary prose are soundless media, both representations would leave open the possibility that the sister only made the gesture of knocking. The uncertainty that Kafka describes corresponds to the precarious situation of the silent film viewer, who cannot know the relationship of the sound-producing gestures viewed onscreen to either actual or imagined sounds. Thus Kafka's text draws out an ambiguity also present but generally unacknowledged in silent film. By raising the possibility that verbalized sound—and by extension visualized sound—might consist of empty gestures, Kafka destabilizes certain fundamental assumptions of silent film viewing.

These three opening sentences, when considered in the context of silent film, raise broad questions about the status of sonic gestures in that medium. Would a knock on a gate, in a silent film, refer to a sound that was once made but not recorded? Would it refer to a sound that never needed to be made, but only visually evoked, so that it could later be imagined by viewers, repeatedly and collectively? Or is it a purely visual event, which does not necessarily warrant an act of mental hearing?[29] These questions cannot be answered, which might be the point of "The Knock at the Courtyard Gate": the consequences of the sister's knock are outrageous not because her transgression was so minor, but because we cannot know whether there was a transgression at all. Like *The Trial*, the story revolves around a transgression that is asserted but cannot be explained.

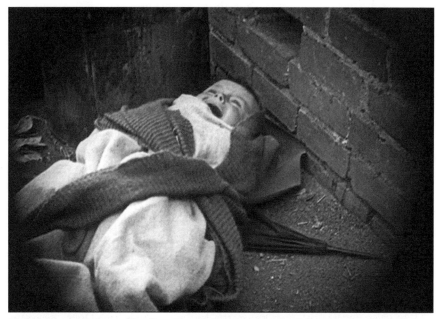

Figure 2.1. Implied sound in silent film: the baby's cry made visible. Charlie Chaplin, dir., *The Kid*, 1921 (Burbank, Calif.: Warner Home Video, 2003), DVD, scene 3, "His morning promenade."

Kafka thus reveals the indeterminacy of implied sound, which proves productively destabilizing for both literature and film. Now, it must be noted that there are countless implied sounds in silent cinema that are *not* indeterminate. They are soundless, but their signifying intention and effect are unambiguous; the viewer knows what she is meant to hear in her mind. In these cases the film provides sufficient visual clues to confirm that subliminal auditive perception is justified, even if the precise nature of the sound can only be suggested and will ultimately be subject to the viewer's imagination. Even in such cases, where the implied sound is *not* an empty gesture, Kafka's story helps show that other aspects of implied sound—for example its role in a narrative sequence, its temporality—might be less stable than originally assumed.

One such instance can be found in Charlie Chaplin's 1921 film *The Kid*, which Kafka certainly knew about and might have seen.[30] In an early scene where the tramp finds an abandoned baby on the street, an acoustic signal— the baby's cry—seems to trigger his discovery. This sound is represented in a close-up of the baby: mouth wide open, eyes narrowed, cheeks taut (figure 2.1). There is no question that the baby is bawling, and little doubt that this sound, rather than the inconspicuous sight of his small swaddled body, lying low on the ground next to a pile of trash or rubble, is what catches the tramp's attention. The visualized acoustic close-up allows the viewer to see what the tramp hears.

The crying baby seems to present a straightforward instance of visualized sound, one essential to a narrative triggered by the accidental discovery of the baby: the tramp will soon realize that the baby belongs to no one; his attempts to get rid of it are unsuccessful, leaving him no choice but to care for it himself. This scene clearly warrants an act of mental hearing, as the entire plot of the film is contingent on this moment, yet its temporality remains unclear: when does the baby start crying, and for how long does he cry? The first question arises because we cannot know whether the tramp initially sees or hears the baby: his initial glance in the baby's direction does not reveal whether he already hears it and, if he doesn't, whether he has seen the baby yet. The second question about the duration of the cry derives from the fact that visualized sounds must be presented sequentially rather than synchronic- ally: sounding images do not necessarily coincide with the onset or end point of the sounds they evoke. While these acoustic uncertainties do not affect the film's narrative development, they do render a central moment undecidable. Moreover, they reveal certain assumptions and projections that undergird how viewers perceive and grasp implied sounds.

The first uncertainty centers on the following question: Does the tramp discover the baby on the street through sight or sound? This is a question that the image of the baby's cry leaves unanswerable, even if, after the fact, it seems obvious that the trigger must have been acoustic. Right before the image of the crying baby is given, prior to any indication of a sound, the tramp looks down to his left; the viewer knows the baby is lying there, as it was visible in the corner of the screen a few seconds earlier (figure 2.2). However, since the baby is absent in this frame and since the look on the tramp's face is not one of obvious surprise, we cannot say whether he has actually spotted the baby yet. Nor can we know whether the baby is already crying at this point. How, then, do we explain this glance? One answer is aesthetic: it mirrors the glance he has just cast to the right, having tossed his ratty fingerless gloves into the trash can on that side. He looks to the right, he looks to the left; there is an appealing symmetry to the gesture, a sense of visual balance. Another answer lies in the character of the tramp: he is a scavenger, always on the lookout for other people's discarded belongings—indeed, this is probably the reason for his morning promenade—and thus constantly scanning the ground. A third possibility is that he does in fact hear the baby's cry, and the camera simply caught him before his expression changes to one of surprise. Had the film given a shot of him making a gesture of hearing—for instance, his hand cup- ping his ear—followed by the shot of the crying baby, the temporal sequence would have been clear. As it stands, the order cannot be decided.

The problem of sequence relates to the second ambiguity mentioned above, namely the question of acoustic duration. In a sound film, sounds can (but do not always) accompany the events they correspond to in a straightforward,

Figure 2.2. The tramp's initial glance toward the baby. Chaplin, *The Kid*, scene 3, "His morning promenade."

realistic way. Implied sounds in silent film are a trickier matter, since the beginning and end points of a sound event may or may not be visualized. In *The Kid*, we can ask whether the baby starts crying before the sounding image was shown, or whether the image correlates with the onset of the sound. We can also wonder how long the baby continues to cry after we see this image. The film itself cannot answer these questions, though we can fairly assume that the sound extends beyond the few seconds during which the baby's face appears onscreen, given that distressed babies generally cry for more than a few seconds. Thus it seems clear that the momentary image signifies a longer acoustic event. This reveals another feature of implied sound, namely that it is necessarily sequentialized, even when it is meant to be understood as accompanying certain events and actions in a film. By sequentializing that which is simultaneous, the film destabilizes certain elements of narrative development. Issues of cause and effect get muddled because the film must create a visual order for events that are not necessarily taking place one after the other. Since silent film viewers understand this exigency—we grasp that the order in which a visualized sound is given does not necessarily represent its place in the logic of the narrative—we are free to imagine various possibilities for the sound's duration, starting point, and end point.

These ambiguities do not necessarily disturb the narrative development of *The Kid*. What is significant in that regard is that the tramp discovers the kid, not these details about whether sight precedes sound or vice versa. In terms of narrative structure, what seems essential is that this act is delayed, which creates a mood of suspense as the viewer anticipates the discovery. When the tramp arrives at the location where the baby is lying on the ground, a series of events delay his discovery of the child: a heap of ashes is dumped on him from a window above, after which he brushes himself off, removes a cigarette case from his coat pocket, selects a butt, removes his gloves, lights the butt, and discards the gloves. As noted, the drawn-out nature of the scene has a clear narrative function: viewers are acutely aware of the child, who is even visible in the frame at certain moments in the sequence, and we know where this is all headed—that the tramp will find and raise the child. The delay is an effective mechanism for generating suspense. Yet this anticipation also means that once the tramp finally discovers the baby and we see it wailing, we reach for the most obvious explanation: the baby started crying, the tramp heard him, the tramp rescued him. This reveals the automatic but potentially unfounded cognitive acts that accompany visualized sound.

This scene therefore exposes an unsettling aspect of silent film viewing: the viewer must not only imagine visualized sounds in her mind, but also synchronize them with other images in the film. The process of mental hearing is both about imagining sounds that are not audible and about reordering what is visible onscreen. We automatically undermine the sequence of images that silent film presents, since we understand that certain things are meant to be grasped as simultaneous and since we want things to conform to a logic of cause and effect. In addition to questions of sequentialization, implied sound in silent film introduces problems of duration: we see an image momentarily, but might assume that the sound it signifies was meant to have started before we saw it and continued thereafter. The problem of duration is especially intractable in the case of background sound in silent film: its peripherality is difficult to represent, yet its duration is significant. In *The Kid*, the baby's cry is foregrounded through a close-up in order to confirm the tramp's discovery. Other types of sounds, especially ones that are more muted, less predictable, and function as background phenomena, are harder to evoke through silent film images. In other words, implied sounds in silent film have a certain dramatic quality that is hard to escape; they are generally not atmospheric.

Implied sounds raise questions about sequentialization, duration, and emphasis (background/foreground), even when there is no doubt that the sound is meant to be heard. Even if Kafka's possibly empty sound gesture has no precise cinematic correlate, "The Knock at the Courtyard Gate" hints at a broader instability about implied sound that relates to film. Any number of unacknowledged assumptions and projections structure our understanding of implied sound—not just their ontological status, but also their sequencing, duration, and relative significance. Hearing can be partial and subjective, and *imagined* hearing even more so. When we bring Kafka's literary experiments with implied sound to bear on silent film, it becomes clear that a related set of assumptions and projections are at work in how we imagine the sounds we see in silent cinema.[31]

The "Double Silence" of Visualized Sound: "The Silence of the Sirens"

Numerous scholars have noted the remarkable role that gesture plays in Kafka's works, starting with Walter Benjamin's and Theodor W. Adorno's essays on the author, which date from 1934 and 1953, respectively, and with their correspondence on Kafka from 1934, which I discussed in the opening chapter. One can consider the significance of Kafka's gestures in connection to a number of related topics: the body, movement and stillness, confinement, performance, communication, ritual, animals, and photography and film. The last of these is most relevant in this context.[32]

Peter-André Alt devotes a chapter of his book *Kafka and Film* to arguing that Kafka's gestures are cinematic, and more specifically that they are informed by the gestures of early expressionist cinema. Having argued that figural speech in Kafka's writings—for example, in the story "A Fratricide" ("Ein Brudermord," 1920)—can have an intertitular quality,[33] he proceeds to offer the following argument about cinematic gesture:

> Repeatedly the text depicts gestures that correspond to the body language of silent film actors. The list of examples is long and impressive: "but Schmar genuflected"; "looked at the knife against the moonlight"; "he presses . . . face and hands against the stones"; "he strokes his hair under his raised up hat"; "eavesdrops in the fateful side alley"; "he gazes down shaking his head"; "Pallas bends over deeply"; "standing on tippy toes, with an outstretched arm"; "the fur opens, she stumbles over Wese, the body clothed in a nightgown belongs to him"; "the mouth pressing on the shoulder of the guard." Comparable to the characters' exclamations, which, like light figures of writing, flare up in the form of imaginary intertitles, these gestures achieve an aesthetic independence that frees them from psychological connections.[34]

Alt concludes that the language of gesture in Kafka, much like the language of gesture in film, offers a model of nonsubjective or nonpsychological perception; it reflects "the phenomenology of seeing, of gestures, and of body language" rather than interiority.[35]

Alt's observations about the cinematic nature of Kafka's gestures are persuasive, yet his main point—about the links between early expressionist film and verbal and body language in Kafka—suggests a conclusion that Alt does not so much as hint at: that silent cinema's modes of expression, both verbal and corporeal, can be read in their relationship to the *absence of audible sound*. Intertitles need to be short, punchy, and dramatic, since they disrupt the visual flow of the film in order to clarify a narrative situation in which characters cannot speak for themselves and voices cannot be laid over images. Likewise, the exaggerated gestures, facial expressions, and movements of silent film actors forgo realism for the sake of expressivity: the actors cannot state in words what they think and feel, so their bodies are refunctionalized to silently express the fact that they are speaking. As Chion explains, "For modern spectators all the gesticulation in the earliest fiction films (between 1910 and 1915) has no other purpose. The idea was not so much to translate through coded, mimed gestures the content of what was being said . . . ; it was rather to show with the whole body that one was speaking."[36] Together Alt and Chion show not simply that "Kafka's expressionism is the expressionism of film," but that Kafka's expressionism is the expressionism of silent cinema's aesthetic of inaudibility.[37]

There is one example in Alt's list of cinematic gestures in "A Fratricide" that is worth dwelling on: "eavesdrops in the fateful side alley." Whether described in literature or viewed onscreen, this instance of implied hearing seems to require an act of auditory imagination. As in the case of the knock at the courtyard gate, it might be unclear whether there is actually anything to be heard, though silence here could have different implications. The gesture of eavesdropping could be empty (the eavesdropper is only pretending to listen) or simply unsuccessful (a sound was made, but the eavesdropper fails to hear it). That is, one can appear to be eavesdropping without actually hearing anything, without there even having been anything to hear. In both cases, the implied sound urges us to visualize the bodily pose and movements associated with eavesdropping, even though the acoustic event and auditory experience remain undecidable. In short, the act of auditory imagination is uncertain, but the act of visual imagination is not. This story thus presents a second example of an indeterminate literary representation of a sound event in Kafka, though one that is even further removed from any actual sound than the gesture in "The Knock at the Courtyard Gate." If that text describes the soundless gesture of making noise, "A Fratricide" could be said to describe the soundless gesture of hearing it. Indeed, more than the gesture of knocking, the gesture of eavesdropping can be thought of independently of its sonic dimension. One can imagine an eavesdropper in purely visual terms—the Dutch painter Nicholaes Maes's series of paintings from the 1650s that feature eavesdroppers in domestic interiors attests to this—whereas one cannot really imagine a knock without at least posing the question of sound. Thus, the link between the acoustic gesture and the process of mental hearing is even more tenuous in "A Fratricide" than in "The Knock at the Courtyard Gate."

One begins to wonder whether in Kafka the evocation of sound and hearing through body language can ever be trusted, or whether acoustic and auditory gestures always invite and at the same time undermine acts of mental hearing. If Kafka's sound gestures are empty, or "doubly silent," then they not only exist in a soundless medium, but soundlessly mimic sound-producing gestures. The skepticism that emerges from Kafka's representations of acoustic gesture can function as a critique of silent film in that it urges us to rethink its techniques of visualized sound: What if silent film, too, was only ever mimicking the silent gestures associated with sound, rather than inviting us to hear it in our minds? What if silent film is also "doubly silent"—silent not only to extradiegetic audiences but to diegetic ones too? Kafka's indeterminate sound gestures cast suspicion on the automatic, perhaps involuntary manner in which viewers internally hear the sounds implied by silent film images. By raising the possibility of acoustically empty sound gestures, Kafka unsettles the cognitive acts that undergird the processes of reading literature and watching film. He destabilizes the "mediumship of the listener."

The "double silence" of Kafka's visualized sounds finds its most complete and complex articulation in "The Silence of the Sirens," Kafka's retelling of the Homeric myth of Odysseus's cunning stratagem to enjoy the Sirens' beautiful song without succumbing to its deadly effects. In book 12 of *The Odyssey*, the hero orders his men to stop their ears with wax and tie him to the mast of the ship so that he alone can listen to the song while they row.[38] In Kafka's version, Odysseus's ears are also stopped, which means that he is denied the pleasure of their song. His pleasure is derived entirely from the sight of the apparently singing Sirens.

What is unique about Kafka's Sirens is that they "have an even more terrible weapon than their song—namely, their silence [*Schweigen*]. Though it has never actually happened, it is conceivable that someone could have escaped from their singing [*Gesange*], but never from their silence [*Verstummen*]" (KSS 128; NSF II 40). Since everyone's ears are stopped, including Odysseus's, neither he nor his crew can say whether the Sirens produce music or silence, or some combination of the two, so no one can judge how dangerous the situation really is.

Watching a scene of silent singing in a controlled environment, where images of beautiful and untouchable women flit before one's eyes—this describes both Odysseus and the silent film viewer. Whether he blocks out their music or their silence, Odysseus confronts precisely the problem of silent cinema spectatorship that I have been articulating: he is unable to determine the cause of silence—the Sirens' actual soundlessness or the wax in his ears—and hence whether they are mimicking the gesture of song or really singing. Indeed, the acoustic indeterminacy of Kafka's Sirens is analogous to the uncertain status of implied sound in silent film on numerous levels:

> But Odysseus did not hear their silence, so to speak; he thought they were singing and that only he was safeguarded from hearing it; first he glimpsed the turnings of their necks, their deep breathing, their

tearful eyes, their half-open mouths; but he believed that these were part of the arias that resounded, unheard, around him. But soon everything slipped from the gaze he was aiming into the distance; the Sirens literally vanished from his consciousness [*verschwanden ihm förmlich*], and just when he was closest to them, he no longer knew of them [*wußte er nichts mehr von ihnen*]. (*KSS* 128; *NSF II* 41)

Kafka's description of this acoustically indeterminate gesture recalls any number of melodramatic scenes from silent cinema, in which tremendous pathos and feeling are depicted through gestures that simulate vocal expression.[39] (These will be discussed in more detail below.) The Sirens also evoke the inaudible but visually vivid bodily practice of expressionist cinema, whose aesthetic and emotional effects are shaped by the silence of the medium. What matters in those works is the exaggerated and showy *appearance* of making sound. Like a silent film viewer, Odysseus assumes that actual sounds accompany the visual gesture of singing—the turned necks, the deep breaths, the tear-filled eyes, the half-open mouths—but that the music is simply inaccessible to him on account of the wax in his ears. This is false, the narrator tells us, explicitly undercutting the conceit of implied sound that was only implicitly challenged in "The Knock at the Courtyard Gate": "in fact, when Odysseus came, these powerful singers did not sing" (*KSS* 128). Kafka's Sirens are truly silent, which means that Odysseus was blocking out not their song, but their silence. Odysseus thus operates under the same assumptions as the silent film viewer, who reads sounds into acoustic and auditory gestures without realizing that they might be soundless at their source. Kafka's Sirens are simply "going through the motions" of making sound, and the same could be true of silent film actors.

Kafka's silent Sirens thereby disrupt the imaginative phenomenology of implied or visualized sound. His Odysseus exposes the unspoken assumption at the heart of silent film spectatorship—that implied sounds necessarily stand for actual sounds—and the misguided acts of mental hearing that might result from it. In sharper terms, one could say that Odysseus and the silent film viewer are duped: they assume they are deaf listeners in a sound world, whereas they might actually be witnesses to a silent pantomime, an ostentatious display of silence. Béla Balázs wrote that "pantomime is silent not just to the ear but also for the eye. Not a mute art, but the art of muteness: the dreamland of silence. [Silent] film, however, is merely soundless."[40] Drawing a line between silent film and pantomime helps initially, though that distinction begins to blur when applied to Kafka's Sirens. Pantomime makes silence its medium, whereas silent film pretends that it is making sound. Both art forms are mute, but pantomime works with this condition and silent film remains in denial about it. They both rely heavily on the body and its capacity for gestural language, but only pantomime acknowledges why it must do this. Pantomime exists in and through silence; with silent film, it is as though someone has simply pressed the mute button. These extrapolations from Balázs's claim are useful for conceptualizing the semiotic operations of these art forms; nevertheless, Kafka's Sirens reveal the murkiness of the distinction. One knows how to read the silence of the performers only if one knows whether one is viewing silent film or pantomime. Odysseus does not know what he is watching, which leaves him unable to interpret the Sirens' particular brand of silence and to judge the danger of the situation. He does not realize that he is at the wrong show.

There are other elements of this short text that evoke silent film, such as the role of movement and the status of the spectator. In the second sentence of the longer passage quoted above, Odysseus is presented as a passive viewer of a moving image that floats before his eyes. Even if he is surrounded by the rowers (the masses), his viewing experience is isolated. As his ship moves slowly across the water, Odysseus watches a scene unfold before him as his body is fixed to one spot. All of this captures the condition of silent film spectatorship. Though he is actually far more constrained than the typical film viewer, the description functions as an allegory of the silent film viewer's stasis, passivity, and isolation before the moving image. His ears are stopped, and both his body and head are bound, which forces his gaze in one direction; the speed, distance, and direction of the ship's movement determine the angle and duration of the "shot." The Sirens seem to pass soundlessly before Odysseus's eyes, similarly to how an image moves across a screen: it enters on one side and exits on the other, urges the silent film viewer to imagine accompanying sounds, and precludes the possibility of lingering on the image. The narrator reports that as soon as they were out of sight, "the Sirens literally vanished from his consciousness, and just when he was closest to them, he no longer knew of them" (KSS 128). This is remarkably consistent with the cinematic image's particular combination of vividness and ephemerality.

Kafka's cinematic retelling of Homer's myth does not end here. The description of bodily poses and movements continues, but without any reference to song—as if it were clear, by this point in the story, that the power of the Sirens lies not in their song or their silence, but in their gestures.[41]

> But they, more beautiful than ever, stretched and twisted their limbs, let their ghastly hair blow freely in the wind, spread their claws on the rocks; they no longer wanted to seduce, they wanted only to grasp the luster [Abglanz] of Odysseus's great eyes for as long as possible. (KSS 128; NSF II 41)

Much like the stars of the silent screen, the Sirens are a visual spectacle. This is the claim advanced in The Opera Singer and the Silent Film by Paul Fryer, who de-emphasizes the process of acoustic imagination triggered by singers on the silent screen and argues that their primary effect was visual.[42] His focus on celebrity suggests that the phenomenon of stardom did not line up in any direct way with the actual talents of the star or the medium in question. This is how opera stars, originally celebrated for their voices, could turn into silent film stars—not because people necessarily imagined or knew what their voices sounded like, but because their celebrity derived as much from visual cues, popular media, the press, advertising, and rumor as from actual musical performance. Moreover, the growth and mass distribution of sound recordings coincided with the period of silent film. Stars were thus manufactured out of disembodied voices (mostly in the form of phonograph cylinder records and gramophone records) and silent singers (in the form of photographs and moving images), though not necessarily in a coordinated or complementary way. The distinctness of these media meant that early stardom, itself a product of mass entertainment, might have had a fusing function: it created a persona out of fragments of technologically mediated performing bodies.

Kafka's Sirens also seem to comment on the status of divas and the phenomenon of stardom. The treacherous beauty of their twisted limbs, turning torsos, wild hair, and sharp claws conforms entirely to the image of the mid-1910s silent film diva—melancholy, dangerous, self-destructive, and above all a *sight* to be *seen*. When the narrator states that the Sirens no longer wanted to seduce Odysseus, but rather to catch a glimpse of the luster of his eyes, this indicates a desire to be seen. The word *Abglanz* is translated as "luster," but it actually indicates a mirroring effect: they want to see the sparkle of Odysseus's eyes, as well as their own luminous reflection in them. There is an element of vanity here, the idea of being a witness to your own performance of yourself. Wishing to be an object of his mirroring gaze, the Sirens put on a show of tortured and tempting corporeality—not to seduce Odysseus, but so that they can witness their own performance in his reflecting eyes. To imagine Odysseus's eyes as a mobile mirror of themselves is not unlike imagining him as a movie camera. The Sirens desire stardom, their own commodification as image. This explains why they long to see a shining moving image of their own bodies in Odysseus's gaze: in Kafka's retelling, he is the first silent film viewer—or perhaps the silent film camera—and they are the first silent film divas.[43]

In one sense, this text seems to settle a matter that remains undecided in "A Fratricide" and "The Knock at the Courtyard Gate," namely the acoustic status of the sound gesture. Those texts raise the *possibility* that such gestures are empty, or "doubly silent," whereas the gestures of the Sirens are definitely soundless: they strike a singing pose but emit no sound. Their acting is in fact a pantomime, the soundless simulation of sound-making gestures, postures, and movements. Kafka's Odysseus only saves himself from this deadly pantomime by mistaking it for a somewhat less dangerous silent film.

Though this aspect of the text—reflected in its title, "The Silence of the Sirens"—is definitive, Kafka does not forgo his characteristic "final twist," that technique of undermining the work's apparent narrative logic or figural certainty through a last-minute intervention or deviation. The question raised is not whether the Sirens sing or remain silent, but whether or not Odysseus *knows* that their gestures are sonically empty in the double sense. It is assumed until the final paragraph of the story that Odysseus is ignorant of the fact that his earplugs are shielding him from the Sirens' deadly silence, rather than their less lethal but still dangerous song. This puts the reader in a position of greater knowledge than Odysseus, which in turn allows us to appreciate the instability of implied sounds and to question the acts of imaginative hearing they seem to demand. This seems to make sense, since the Sirens' musical gestures can only have the proper effect if Odysseus believes that they signify music that he cannot hear, much as the moviegoer must assume that implied sounds stand in for real ones. This assumption is overturned in the last minute. In Kafka's myth the Sirens' gestures are in fact empty (i.e., soundless), and it turns out that Odysseus secretly knew this all along:

> Odysseus, it is said, was so full of tricks, was such a fox, that not even the goddess of destiny could penetrate his innermost self; perhaps, although this can no longer be grasped by human reason, he really did notice that the Sirens were silent and held up to them and the gods the semblance of the events above only as a kind of shield [*den obigen Scheinvorgang nur gewissermaßen als Schild entgegengehalten*]. (*KSS* 128; *NSF II* 42)

The meaning of Odysseus's ruse, his private knowledge about the silence of the Sirens, is devastatingly opaque. He is pretending to think the Sirens are singing while knowing all along that they are silent; he responds to the Sirens' pretense (to singing) with a pretense of his own (of believing in the song)—but why? What could this proliferation of posturing mean? If we continue to read the story in terms of implied sound in silent film, we can understand Odysseus's *cognitive* posture as a response to the *bodily* posture of the silently "singing" Sirens. Odysseus pretends to think they are making music for the same reason that the Sirens themselves pretend to make music: because this is the necessary conceit of the media in question, myth and silent film. The actors (or Sirens) and the viewer (or Odysseus) are both engaged in a silent show: they are pretending to sing, he is pretending to be blocked from hearing their song. Both act as though there were actual sounds at play, which under less constrained circumstances might have been made and heard, and which must therefore be imagined or mentally conjured. These acts of subception are fundamental to cinematic experience, whether or not they are justified (in the sense that the viewer or reader is warranted in imagining sounds). They are the necessary fiction, the myth, on which silent cinema sound is founded. Everyone—Sirens and actors, Odysseus and viewer—is implicated in this myth, according to which sounds that nobody makes and nobody hears demand attention, cognitive work, and imagination.

This myth also explains why reflection and reciprocal exchange figure so centrally in this text: what matters is not whether silent gestures represent sound or silence, but whether Odysseus can maintain "the semblance of events . . . as a kind of shield." This shield is not, as one might assume, further protection against the deadliness of the Sirens' silence; it is not a shield used for self-defense. Rather, it is a kind of sign that Odysseus holds up to the Sirens and the gods, the guardians of mythology, as a way of showcasing his own cleverness and guile. It signals that he is consciously playing along, just like the Sirens do with their silent cinematic song. Odysseus is showing that he recognizes and accepts the necessary fictions of mythology and of silent film in which he is implicated; he is in on the game. Unlike "The Knock at the Courtyard Gate" and "A Fratricide," "The Silence of the Sirens" does not present a position of radical skepticism toward imagined sound. Such texts are conceptually intriguing, and as I have shown they allow us to question the phenomenological processes that accompany the presentation of implied sounds in verbal and visual images—this automatic "hearing in the mind." However, such skepticism also threatens to undermine the semiotic structure of implied sound. Once the act of imagining visualized sound has been so radically undermined, it is unclear what to make of silent film speech, singing, and noise. We are left wondering how the story—or the show—can go on. Thus, to assume a stance of radical skepticism toward implied sound in silent film would ultimately prove very disruptive and distracting for the viewer.

The enlightened silent film viewer must have license to engage in subception, but should do so critically and skeptically. She should not assume that all implied sounds ought to trigger acts of mental hearing, but neither should she assume that none of them ought to. Odysseus's pretense, his final cunning, the "shield" or "sign" (*Schild*) that maintains "the semblance of the events above," is the conceit that allows the Sirens to serve as silent film actresses and Odysseus to function as a silent film spectator; it is what allows the show to go on. It is the sign that announces his willingness to play the game of silent film, but not to be fooled by it. Kafka's myth thereby reveals the instabilities and illusions of silent spectatorship, but keeps them firmly in place so that we can all keep watching and listening—for the silence.

Visualizing the Voice of the Singer: *Tonbilder*, Kafka's "Eleven Sons," and Kurt Pinthus's *Kinobuch*

Kafka's singers, it would seem, are seen and not heard. This situation is over-determined in "The Silence of the Sirens" because of the emptiness of the acoustic gesture, or what I have called its "double silence." The silence of the medium conceals a deeper silence, one as invisible as it is inaudible. But we do not need to consider such an extreme example to recognize that for Kafka singing tends to be more a bodily posture than an acoustic event.

Even in situations where a text explicitly evokes sound, Kafka emphasizes visual rather than sonic qualities, especially the appearance of the body of the singer. Thus, the visible gestures of singing dominate even those instances where acts of mental hearing are warranted. The presence of "actual" sound does not diminish their participation in a semiotic of silent film.

The *Tonbild*, which reached its height of popularity around 1908 can be seen as a contemporary cinematic correlate to Kafka's literary presentation of singing voices. *Tonbilder*, or "sound pictures," consisted of audio recordings of singers, usually performing famous songs from operas and operettas, which were shown in cinemas with film clips of actors pretending to sing, in order to create a simulacrum of cinematically recorded sound. Though the technical limitations were significant (the clips had to be short, and the visuals and vocals frequently fell out of sync), *Tonbilder* anticipated true sound film technology by nearly twenty years and shared in its ambitions. Nevertheless, it would be wrong to think of the *Tonbild* as an early version of sound film, not least because it clearly looked like a silent film with sound tacked on—it lacked naturalism and verisimilitude. One critic offered the following description in 1913:

> The only German industrial sector of cinematography is the *Tonbild*. These monsters are produced thus: A singer (or several) records a "vocal" on the gramophone disc. As rhythm for this mostly dreadful singsong, an actor then mimes the movements of a singer; a cheap decoration is placed alongside and all of this is recorded cinematographically. Then, in the cinema, the playback of the vocal is ruined by the simultaneous projection of the mime with his mouth agape and his arms waving. And this tastelessness the cinema playbills call a *Tonbild*.[44]

The idea of the *Tonbild* as a "monster" is useful for thinking about Kafka and noise: the form is an awkward, artificial, and rather contrived attempt to merge separate recordings of sound and image. While audiences seem to have been entertained by *Tonbilder* for a few years, interest died out fairly quickly. They were also quite expensive to produce. In 1913 they were abandoned altogether and the film industry returned exclusively to the production of conventional silent films.[45]

For our purposes, *Tonbilder* are interesting because they represent another instance of acoustic ambiguity in silent film. Sound is explicit and audible rather than implicit and imagined, yet it does not align naturally with the onscreen image. Indeed, in *Tonbilder* the music was primary and the image supplementary—that is, the image was synchronized to the music, not the other way around. It is thus wrong to associate them with "implied sound": they present audible sounds, and these sounds dictate the images displayed. If anything, *Tonbilder* represent the inverse phenomenon: they actualize the "implied images" evoked by recorded sound.

Tonbilder are also important because they demonstrate that the addition
of sound to silent cinema does not undo the gestural language that Kafka's
literary singers and silent film singers share. Whether they are "doubly silent,"
contain implicit sounds, or actually sonify (as in the case of *Tonbilder*,
through a carefully orchestrated pseudo-naturalism), physical bodies play a
substantial role in the presentation of these singers. In fact, their gestures and
movements speak louder than the sounds they make. This is the fundamental ground for linking the representation of sound in Kafka's writing and
silent cinema, and it is why implied sounds in both media take on a crucial
relationship to space. In Kafka's works and in silent film, bodies producing
and hearing sounds—not the acts of mental hearing, but the bodily gestures
and movements that trigger them—demonstrate the spatializing function of
visualized sound.

Like "The Silence of the Sirens," Kafka's story "Eleven Sons" was written
in 1917, but it was published in the 1919 collection *A Country Doctor* (*Ein
Landarzt*). In this short work, each of the eleven sons is described in contradictory or at least inconclusive language. Each is admirable or likable in some
respects but also possesses unfavorable qualities. In describing the sons, the
narrator repeatedly uses the words *aber*, *doch*, and *allerdings*, grammatical
particles that undermine statements in minor, tentative ways. These words,
which can be translated as "but," "yet," "still," or "however," serve to emphasize that each of the sons is in some sense at odds with himself: he is this, *but
also* that; he has these qualities, *yet* he has others too; he is one thing, *though
admittedly* he is something else as well. Perhaps as a result of these perceived
inconsistencies in character, a suspicious and slightly accusatory tone slips
into the father's narration, even when he is describing supposedly admirable
qualities. He says, for example, about the fifth son: "He is innocent. Perhaps
all too innocent. Friendly to everyone. Perhaps all too friendly."[46] The tenth
son appears to most to be "a boundless hypocrite," but is sensible and careful
in his speech.[47] The father passes no explicit judgments, but it is clear from
the eleven short descriptions that these sons cannot be trusted, or maybe that
the father simply cannot decide whether or not they can be trusted.

The final sentences of the last description (of the eleventh son) confirm this
skepticism and typify Kafka's practice of inserting a final, destabilizing twist
at the end of his stories: "Sometimes he looks at me as if to say: 'I will take you
with me, father.' Then I think: 'You are the last person I would trust myself
to.' And again his look seems to say: 'Then at least let me be the last.' "[48] In
one sense, the father's use of the phrase "the last" is hyperbolic: "You're the
last person *in the world* to whom I would trust myself." But in the context of
a narrative about eleven sons, each of whom has been described in turn, the
phrase "the last" could be understood within this subset of people: "You are
the last *of my eleven sons* to whom I would trust myself." Or it could be that
the father's thought means one thing, and the son's response (itself imagined
by the father, and expressed in a look) means another. The openness of this

matter—the eleventh son as the least trustworthy person in the world, or the least trustworthy of the eleven sons, and the entanglement of assumptions and projected thoughts on the matter—reinforces the instability of judgment in the story. The sons are not simply complex and multifaceted. They are fluid; they cannot be pinned down; any attempt at definite characterization seems to elude the narrating father.

It is against this background of figural uncertainty that one can read the account of the third son, whose relevance to the general argument about visualized musical voices will soon become apparent.

> The third son is similarly good-looking, but he has not the kind of good looks that I admire. His is the beauty of the singer: the curving lips; the dreamy eye; the head that asks for a background of drapery to achieve its effect; the exaggerated swell of the chest; the hands that swiftly flutter up and far too swiftly fall; the legs that move in a mincing way because they have not the strength to carry. And what is more: the tone of his voice is lacking in fullness; it deceives momentarily; makes the connoisseur prick up his ears; but trails away soon after.[49]

The third son possesses the beauty of a singer, yet his status as a vocalist is described primarily in visual terms and with reference to bodily features and gestures. The reference to the "drapery" behind the son's head, a backdrop to his performance, suggests that his singing practice is theatrical, and maybe even cinematic (curtains were present in cinemas as well as the theater). In any event, the son's appearance must be grasped as a musical performance whose effects are predominantly visual. This recalls Kafka's silent Sirens, for whom singing is a pose, not a sound-producing event. In both works, an ostensibly musical phenomenon is manifested in certain conventions of bodily artifice—appearances, gestures, movements, postures—given primarily to the eye. In the case of the Sirens, the trickery or deceit lies in the fact that there is no actual music or song, only the optical *and* auditory illusion thereof: had Odysseus simply stopped his ears, he would have been like a silent film viewer; given that the Sirens are (probably) not even singing, he is more like a viewer of a silent film whose implied sounds have undergone a Kafkan destabilization. In "Eleven Sons," the third son has a voice that can be heard and described, but it is thoroughly inadequate: weak, incomplete, deceptive, it attracts the listener's attention but quickly dissolves into mere breath. Like his appearance, his voice is alluring and attractive, but ultimately proves to be an empty display. Despite this vocal deficiency, the temptation to showcase the son is strong, which reveals the degree to which Kafka conceives of vocal performance as artificial and false. The third son is a mediocre singer who has only the appearance of an extraordinary one, but this is enough to want to make him a star—of the stage, and perhaps especially of the silent screen, where actual vocal ability is irrelevant because all voices manifest silently. Vocal performance is not only *possible* in the absence of vocal talent; here it seems to be constituted by this absence.

Critics have argued that the eleven sons refer to stories on which Kafka was working at the time. In his biography of Kafka, Max Brod claims that his close friend told him as much—" 'The eleven sons are quite simply eleven stories I am working on this very moment' "—and Kafka's marginalia confirms this reading.[50] Both Malcolm Pasley and Breon Mitchell have worked out the details of this self-professed conception of literary paternity along comparable lines, but have arrived at different conclusions. The former argues that the third son corresponds to "An Imperial Message" ("Eine kaiserliche Botschaft"), the latter that he refers to "A Country Doctor" ("Ein Landarzt"). Neither reading, however, accounts for the third son's musicality as an instance of vocal performance, silent or otherwise. Pasley refers to "the lyrical quality of [the] story"[51] and Mitchell to the country doctor's theatricality.[52] He also notes that "A Country Doctor" is the only story among the eleven Kafka listed in the margins of his manuscript in which there is any actual singing.[53] A more compelling reading of the third son's musical posturing emerges when we abandon the rigid schema to which Pasley and Mitchell are both committed—one son, one story from the collection *A Country Doctor*—and look more broadly to Kafka's oeuvre for ways to comprehend and contextualize this figure. The third son prefigures the singer Josefine, whose physical bearing also governs the perception of vocal effects, which is not to say that Kafka had already conceived of "Josefine, the Singer or the Mouse Folk" in 1917. My point is not to find the "right" story, but to suggest that Kafka had been interested in vocal performance—its pretenses, its artificiality, its manifestation as a language of gesture rather than sound—long before he wrote his mouse story.

Before returning to "Josefine," it is helpful to consider the characterization of the third son alongside a contemporary work that evokes the visualization of sound in the cinema, Kurt Pinthus's *Cinema Book* (*Kinobuch*). The work contains a collection of film skits or scenarios (*Kinostücke*) and was published at the end of 1913 by Kurt Wolff, who also published Kafka's stories "The Stoker" ("Der Heizer") and "The Judgment" ("Das Urteil") that same year. Max Brod contributed to the collection, as did numerous other acquaintances of Kafka, and Kafka himself might also have been invited to do so.[54] It is likely that Kafka was familiar with the book.

The opening paragraphs of Pinthus's introduction present a polemic against the conflation of theater and cinema. He explains that the essence of theater is "the dialogue, the word," whereas the main content of movies is "animated nature, unfamiliar settings, surprising tricks, highly moving scenes."[55] Thus, he continues, cinema is at its weakest and least effective when it relies too heavily on speech and dialogue: "A powerful finale, for example the revelation of a terrible fact which shocks the actors and audience, will produce only a soundless rattling of the lower jaws and a few horrified gestures on the film screen, and even the explanatory title card remains ineffectual."[56] Whether or not Kafka would have agreed, the vivid descriptions of visualized sound are remarkable: they confirm that the status of soundless speech and dialogue was central to early discussions of silent narrative film. It could not have escaped a reader as attuned to the question of performative gesture and posture as Kafka that the main object of Pinthus's critique of silent cinema was the continued presence of visualized speech. The very thing that was being deemed ineffectual and artless in silent film—the "soundless rattling of the lower jaws"—would press increasingly on Kafka's literary consciousness.

The *Kinobuch* lies at the crossroads between film and literature, since the scenarios it contains are meant to be filmed, but they can also be read as free-standing works of literature.[57] Moreover, many of the contributors—Max Brod, Walter Hasenclever, Else Lasker-Schüler, and Franz Blei, to name just a few—were to become important and prolific writers, poets, journalists, and publicists in Prague, Vienna, Berlin, and beyond. The film scenarios they produced are works of literature that must be read cinematically. They were written to be filmed, whether or not this actually happened. This is significant for Kafka's cinematically inflected literary writing, since it offers a historical basis for thinking about cinematic modes at work in literary writing. Moreover, the film skits present ways of visualizing sound that align with, derive from, contribute to, and complicate cinematic experience. Pinthus's project of creating a literature *for* the cinema introduces questions of intermedial translation and adaptation that pertain to Kafka.

The problem of visualizing sound silently emerges clearly in Brod's own contribution to the *Kinobuch*, "A Day in the Life of Kühnebeck, the Young Idealist" ("Ein Tag aus dem Leben Kühnebecks, des jungen Idealisten"). After briefly outlining the merits of writing in a way that will maximize the potential of the new medium, the text begins: "The young idealist wakes up. He is twelve years old, a high school student. Since he's had a terrific night's sleep, he is immediately in the best of moods, a fact he expresses by grinning heroically and stretching out his arms."[58] Until this point, the situation can be easily visualized and potentially filmed. Not only would facial expressions and gestures effectively transmit the character's mood and disposition, but location, clothing, and the actor himself would allow a film director to set the scene as Brod describes it. He continues:

> The whole world is a brilliant dream to him. For what twelve-year-old would it have been otherwise! Now, Kühnebeck must be on his way to school, and he has to hop to it, since it's getting late.—*On the way he hears a street organ.* At once his sailor's face perks up blissfully. He steps into the courtyard of the building where the street organ is playing. *Ecstasy over the beautiful melodies.* Presently the street organ transforms into a small orchestra, the organ grinder

himself into the conductor. The walls of the courtyard remain, the orchestra sits on a makeshift podium. Earlier the audience will be informed: "The appearance of the street organ in Kühnebeck's imagination." Finally the music lover runs around the violinist's stand and flings his arms around the conductor's neck. Right away: "Reality": the shocked organ grinder watches as the student runs off.[59]

The second scene of Brod's silent film scenario revolves entirely around sound, and also contains remarkable ideas for evoking music and listening through cinematic images. The sentences in italics contain Kühnebeck's subjective auditory experiences for which a visual expression must be found. They refer to sound content that cannot be conveyed directly but must instead be evoked onscreen. The descriptions that follow are the visual solution, given in language; they delineate the cinematic form that these sound events will take. In other words, the italicized sentences contain the auditory signified (the sound that is implied, and to some extent the subjective reaction to it) that silent cinema is unable to depict through an acoustic signifier (actual sound). The sentences that follow lay out the process of visual signification through which silent cinema can evoke the sound indirectly.

The first instance of visualized sound is straightforward: the facial expression of the boy will demonstrate that his auditory attention has been captured by the sound of the street organ. The second instance is more complex and highly creative: the sudden presence and mise-en-scène of the orchestra will visually represent the boy's ecstatic reaction to the music. It is unclear whether the visually striking replacement of the street organ by the orchestra is meant to correspond primarily to the boy's feeling or to the music itself, but this uncertainty marks the vision as subjective. It matters little whether seeing the street organ enhances the music and thus spurs the boy's visual imagination, or whether an actual intensification of the music triggers the vision. Brod has conceived of an ingenious way to represent a heightening of musical sensation through cinematic imagery, and he has also hit upon the inherent ambiguity of silent film sound. On the level of acoustic detail, much remains unknown: when Kühnebeck steps into the courtyard, should we understand the music as getting louder, faster, more rhythmic, more melodic, or more musically complex? The dramatic change in image signifies an intensification, but the nature of this intensification remains unclear. More fundamentally, what does this wonderful music actually sound like? Clearly Brod's film scenario, written for the silent cinema, cannot present audible sound. Nor should it rely on the text's verbal descriptions of sound, since the fully realized work is not literary but cinematic. The point is to translate the musical encounter into filmable images and thereby provide a visualized sound for the silent moviegoer, and all this must be represented, provisionally, in literary form. This comes rather close to the translation of vocal experience into literary gesture, posture, and movement via silent film aesthetics and semiotics in Kafka, since in both cases the literary work must translate sound into image before it can translate it into words. It seems the visual dimension of implied sound in literature can be linked to its silent cinematic correlate in multiple ways.

In a new introduction written for the 1963 edition of the *Kinobuch*, Pinthus redescribes the original motivation for the work. Once again the task of distinguishing cinema from other art forms, here theater and the novel, proves central. Referring to the original contributors, he writes:

> We all knew there were already great film actors who could make themselves understood very eloquently without words and who could express themselves comically or poignantly simply through pantomime and body movements, such as Asta Nielsen, whom we regarded so highly and whose silent film acting was never reached again. We also knew that some playwrights and novelists had already said they would permit their works to be adapted for the screen by people unknown to them. But we knew of no authors or writers who had written a piece directly and explicitly for the cinema.[60]

For Pinthus there is a world of difference between the soundless motions of the mouth and jaws supplemented by an intertitle, which he views as an artless and ineffective substitute for speech, and the evocative gestures and movements of talented silent film stars.[61] Writing for the cinema should ideally obviate the former and aspire to the latter.

Whether Kafka deemed the gesturing and posturing of the Sirens or the third son to be closer to "soundless rattling" or to Asta Nielsen's virtuosic acting, Pinthus's distinctions seem to inform his silent evocations of sound. In truth, Kafka probably felt torn over how exactly to judge these visualized voices. He portrays the singing of the Sirens as *both* artful and false, the performance of the third son as *both* poignant and cheap, and, as I will show, Josefine's voice as *both* truly musical singing and merely commonplace whistling. If in silent cinema the ambivalence toward the visualized voice derives from a sense that there are good and bad ways to evoke sound through images, for Kafka this ambivalence is not so much programmatic as a constitutive feature of the silent evocation of sound. It is not that he approves of one practice and disapproves of the other, but rather that visualized voices *as such* are both enticing and distasteful, powerful and false.

Creating Auditory Space through Visualized Sound: "Josefine, the Singer or the Mouse Folk"

Not all of Kafka's visible voices are silent. The third son actually sings, though not very well. Josefine does as well, though it is unclear whether the sounds she makes fall into the category of music, noise, or silence. In any event, it is clear that the visual gesture of singing *can* be accompanied by "actual" sound, that is, sound inaudible to the reader but audible in the diegetic world of the fiction. More simply, in "Josefine" the mouse singer sings and the mice hear her song. The situation is anything but simple, however, for two central and intertwined reasons: the nature of Josefine's song cannot be determined, and the gestures, postures, and movements that accompany her singing, which are in fact the locus and source of her effect, must be grasped in their relationship to cinema. The impossibility of conveying Josefine's effect through literary means is not a shortcoming, but an opportunity to express something entirely new, an aspect of music that exceeds audible sound and is therefore drowned out in sonifying media.

For Kafka, a sound event can be ontologically fixed—we know we are meant to understand it as an actual sound—but still acoustically indeterminate. Such a sound is audible within the fiction, yet defies the reader's attempts to understand and imagine it. "Josefine" is structured around a series of failed attempts to capture the musical distinction of her vocal production, whose existence remains largely unquestioned. Is it "singing [*Singen*]" or "whistling [*Pfeifen*]"? Does her power lie in her song, or rather her silence, which would make it a repetition of the siren problem? Does her song perform a kind of work? Is it embellished with coloratura, a kind of operatic vocal ornamentation, as she asserts at one point? The point about coloratura illustrates the general problem of making definitive statements about Josefine's song. She does not so much claim to use it as threaten to withhold it, and in any event it is unclear whether anyone can tell the difference. In his typical self-effacing style, the narrator explains:

> I know nothing about coloraturas, and I have never noticed any sign of coloratura in her song. But Josefine intends to shorten the coloraturas, for the present not eliminate them but simply shorten them. She has allegedly carried out her threat; as for me, I have, of course, noticed nothing different from her previous performances. (*KSS* 106)

The only thing that can really be said about Josefine's song is that it eludes definition. The narrator raises a series of questions about it, none of which can be answered. He makes no secret of this, given his open declaration that Josefine's song is a self-contradiction: "What she is whistling here is no whistling." Given that Josefine's song is not even identical to itself, we can hardly expect to identify any lasting features, qualities, or effects. Yet this is what the narrator persistently attempts, for the entire length of the story. This radical acoustic indeterminacy means that even though the story begins by distinguishing Josefine as the lone singer among an unmusical folk, her status as a vocalist slowly unravels over the course of a narrative that repeatedly tries but always fails to sustain any claims about the distinctiveness of her song. Indeed, the story can be read as a series of unsuccessful attempts to establish the difference between Josefine's singing and the mouse folk's whistling.[62] Though the title presents two options—Josefine the singer or the mouse folk—the difference implied in this choice grows increasingly illusory.

The question, then, is whether it is possible to understand Josefine's distinctiveness in nonacoustic terms. My previous efforts to destabilize notions of visualized sound in silent film come into play here. Josefine resembles a silent film singer, whose effects are based on the gestures, postures, and motions of singing, rather than its sound.[63] This is why her song can only be grasped as distinctive when her performance is seen, not simply heard. From a great distance, her voice emits "only an ordinary squeak, at most a sound somewhat striking in its delicacy or weakness. But if you stand in front of her, it really is not just a squeaking: to understand her art, you must not only hear her but also see her" (KSS 96). The fact that Josefine's art is as much visual as it is acoustic itself suggests an affinity to silent cinema: in what other medium was the most recognizable feature of a singer her visual appearance, not her voice? Indeed, what distinguishes Josefine from the other mice is not the sound of her song, but the body language that accompanies the act of singing. When Josefine gives her "squeak of triumph," she is "in total ecstasy, her arms stretched out and her neck extended as high as it would go" (KSS 97). The whistling of the other mice is "the very same thing that we were hearing from Josefine"; "it would have been impossible to specify the difference" (KSS 97). Their whistling is the same, but their appearance is not. Josefine's dramatically outstretched arms and taut throat are *visual* signs that make her whistling into art, performance, and public spectacle.

Given how frequently the narrator invokes Josefine's bodily posture as the locus of her effects, it is remarkable that scholars have generally failed to see Josefine's appearance as her distinguishing feature.[64] We are so attuned to thinking of her as a singer—it is stated in the title, after all—and to thinking of the predominant dimension of singing to be audible music, that we readily overlook the fact that the real debate involves not whether her vocal activity should be called singing or whistling, but whether it is primarily a visual or acoustic phenomenon. In fact, what distinguishes Josefine from the other mice is her appearance. The posture of singing has a unique power to unite the mice, to make a unified whole out of an otherwise scattered mass of individuals. Josefine is responsible for this feeling of warmth and togetherness, "the sensation of the crowd as, body warmly pressed on body, breathing with awe, it listens" (KSS 98). When she sings, the mice halt their busy activity and are, for a moment at least, unified in the act of listening—or, more precisely, the act of watching Josefine sing.

> And to gather around her this crowd of our people, who are almost continually in motion, shooting off here and there for purposes that are often not very clear, Josefine generally needs to do no more than assume that stance—her little head tilted back, mouth half-open, eyes

> turned toward the heights—that indicates that she intends to sing
> [daß sie zu singen beabsichtigt]. (KSS 98; DzL 357)

The mice are unified not by Josefine's singing, but by her *intention* to sing, which is conveyed through silent but visible bodily signs: a reclined head, a half-open mouth, an upward gaze.

The image of Josefine poised to sing is strongly reminiscent of female singers in silent films from this period, for example in early Italian melodramas and adaptations of operas and operettas. Kafka certainly encountered this image of the female singer, defined by her bodily presence and dramatic affect, at the movies.[65] Whether or not they were depicted in the act of singing, audiences were invited to read these female characters as divas. Indeed, several opera singers such as Geraldine Farrar, Mary Garden, and Lina Cavalieri became silent film actresses, and their identities clung to them through this transition. Postcards, posters, and other publicity materials also advertised them as singers regardless of what they were doing onscreen.[66]

Josefine adopts the typical pose of such a singer: "head tilted back, mouth half-open, eyes turned toward the heights." Peter Delpeut's 1999 film, *Diva Dolorosa*, a documentary about early Italian film melodrama that splices together clips from a series of films from the mid-1910s, offers visual evidence for this claim (figures 2.3–2.6). The significance of the singer is divorced not only from actual music and sound, but even from the visualized act of singing. What comes in its place is the patent visibility of her body—particularly the bared throat—which guarantees her identity as a tortured singer. In scene after scene in Delpeut's documentary, gloomy, dark-eyed women tear open their dresses, grope their heaving bosoms, and writhe, stretch, and twist their newly exposed necks—much like Kafka's Sirens and Josefine. It almost seems that the true protagonist of these films is not the diva, but her bared throat.[67] In addition to its erotic drama, this image is a cipher for singing: the exposed throat reveals the source of sound, the bodily locus from which the voice originates, which can be made visible but not audible in this medium. In the era of silent film divas, the singer's throat substitutes for the dramatic aria, the musical climax.

There is further cinematic evidence that Kafka associated Josefine's song with the image of the bared female throat. *A Thief of Hearts* (*La broyeuse de coeurs*), a French melodrama Kafka saw with his sister in mid-March 1913, shows numerous images of a jilted consumptive fiancée who clutches at her bared throat. In one scene, the distressed young woman walks out onto her balcony, dramatically sheds the gauzy scarf and cardigan she was wearing to expose her neck and shoulders, and proceeds to clutch her breasts and chest as she has a coughing fit (figures 2.7 and 2.8). The other main female figure, the voluptuous dancer who is the "heartbreaker" named in the film's title, makes a related display: she wears rich velvety dresses with plunging necklines, which give her bared chest plenty of screen time, too. Indeed, as with the

Figure 2.3. The diva clutching at her throat. Peter Delpeut, dir., *Diva Dolorosa*, 1999 (New York: Zeitgeist, 2008), DVD, chapter 7, "Punishment."

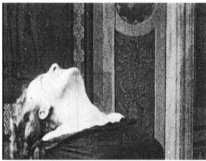

Figure 2.4. The diva's outstretched throat. Delpeut, *Diva Dolorosa*, chapter 7, "Punishment."

Figure 2.5. The diva's bared throat. Delpeut, *Diva Dolorosa*, chapter 6, "Power Upheaved."

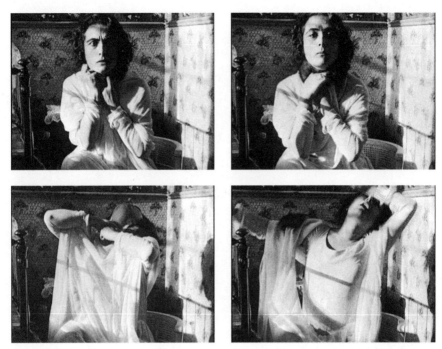

Figure 2.6. The diva baring her throat. Delpeut, *Diva Dolorosa*, chapter 8, "Shattered and Defeated."

fiancée, there are multiple scenes of unveiling: the chest and neck are initially covered and we watch as they are repeatedly exposed. Whether as a display of illness or seduction, these scenes showcase the visibility of the throat.

For the musicologist Michal Grover-Friedlander, it is precisely the absent voice in silent film that makes the medium so apt for opera adaptations:

> Silent film is uniquely suited to revealing opera's tendency to go beyond song in its fascination with and anxiety about silence. The way the voice is "absent" in silent film is exactly the way opera attempts to "transcend" voice. Introducing the voice of opera into silent film does not change the universe of silence, as voice in opera functions in the condition, or under the constant threat, of the loss of that voice, of disintegration into the cry, and into silence.[68]

For Grover-Friedlander, the excessive visuality of the silent film diva correlates with the excessive sonority of the diva's death cry in staged opera. Neither medium can contain the intensity of this moment. What results is a kind of monstrosity, a noise that signals the limits of representation. Silence in silent film is not something that needs to be compensated for; rather, it is

Figure 2.7. Exposing the throat. Camille de Morlhon, dir., *La broyeuse de coeurs*, 1913, in *Kafka geht ins Kino / Kafka va au cinéma / Kafka Goes to the Movies*, DVD 2, comp. Hanns Zischler (Munich: Edition Filmmuseum, 2017), DVD.

Figure 2.8. Clutching the throat. Morlhon, *La broyeuse de coeurs*.

the only way to capture the monstrous excess of the operatic voice.[69] The silent visualization of the throat is thus a fitting rendering of the diva's impossible voice, which must be presented through nonacoustic means.

Josefine looks and acts like a silent film diva, and her singing functions according to the logic that Grover-Friedlander describes. Like those silent singers, her effect derives not from any acoustic quality but from her dramatic presence, which is itself a product of gesture, posture, and positioning. For my purposes, it is less important to establish the story's specific relationship to opera than to think about how Josefine, like these silent film divas, can be said to signify in her soundlessness. Grover-Friedlander shows how such a reading of silent musical gestures is possible: gestural excess in silent film corresponds to vocal excess in opera. Without drawing on silent film, others have made a related argument about Josefine. John Hargraves notes that she "sings to 'tauben Ohren' (deaf ears) and does not think her people understand what they hear."[70] Indeed, there is no evidence that the mice hear anything at all, only that Josefine sings: she sings to deaf ears not because the mice do not understand, but because there is nothing to hear. Hargraves unwittingly describes "Josefine, the Singer" in a manner entirely consistent with silent film, in which the actress/diva uses her voice but the medium silences it. There is, or might be, sound on the level of production but not on that of reception. The indeterminate gesture or posture of singing is, I have argued, an uncertainty that characterizes many of Kafka's implied sounds. Here it is less important to know, or even to ask, whether Josefine is actually singing and what her voice might sound like, than to recognize that her impact on the other mice derives from her physical presence. Her body validates her as a singer. As with silent film divas, Josefine's silence might seem to reflect the limits of the medium in which she is presented, but actually shows that her powers transcend hearing.

Despite the uncertainties of her voice, Josefine's diva-like pose has a forceful unifying effect on the mice. The precise nature of the exchange between Josefine and her audience is impossible to ascertain, not only on the semiotic level just discussed but also in terms of power relations: Does her song protect the mice, or do they act as her guardians?—who is helping whom? Despite this question, there seems to be one incontrovertible fact, perhaps the only one in the entire story: temporarily at least, a community is formed around Josefine's body when she gestures as if to sing. Almost every attempt the narrator makes to explain Josefine's effects devolves into doubts and contradictions. Only her physical bodily presence gives a clear image of her power. At one moment there is a palpable shift from uncertain interpretations of her influence to certain descriptions of the physical conditions from which it derives. Josefine, we learn,

> rarely has anything to say, she is silent among the blabbermouths, but it flashes from her eyes, you can read it off her tightly shut lips—among us only a few can keep their lips shut, but she can. Whenever we get

bad news—and some days it rushes in pell-mell, falsehoods and half-truths included—she rises up immediately, although normally she is drawn wearily to the ground, rises up and cranes her neck and strives to oversee her flock like the shepherd before the storm. (*KSS* 99)

Again, what is at play is not an acoustic quality but visible gestures—the flash of Josefine's eyes, the appearance of her closed mouth, her outstretched body. Like the divas of silent cinema, Josefine also seems to vacillate between a limpness and lethargy that causes her to sink to the ground with fatigue, and moments of wide-eyed alertness accompanied by an erect body and stretched throat, which signal a readiness to lead the mice and perform for them. It is in these moments of verticality and tautness that Josefine produces a community of viewers, not listeners, who take refuge from their political and economic worries in her performance. This resonates not only with received ideas about the "escapist" function of cinematic experience, but with the notion of collective as opposed to atomized spectatorship: if Josefine is a silent film diva, the mouse folk is the cinemagoing audience, collectively mesmerized by her visual performance. By emphasizing the unifying function of Josefine's visualized gestures of song, Kafka both taps into conventional explanations of the social function of silent film spectatorship and suggests that this function is itself contingent on collective spectatorship. The "escape" is achieved communally, through the visual sign of singing.

Thus, the source of Josefine's unique power to unify the mice is not the sound of her music, but the gestures and postures that accompany and precede her performances.[71] Indeed, Josefine's special status derives from her capacity to produce an architecture of the body. What the mice see when Josefine sings, or prepares to sing, is a fixed structure, a stable if temporary object: her verticality constitutes spatial form. This is highly significant in the context of a story that otherwise lacks any markers of space. There are no buildings, rooms, walls, gates, or other architectural markers; there is not so much as a stage or podium for Josefine to stand on. Nor are there institutional spaces (schools, offices, factories) that would help situate mouse activity, or topographical details (hills, trees, or ravines) that might produce spatial contour and thereby facilitate orientation. I am unaware of any scholarship that has noted this peculiar feature of "Josefine"—that it seems to take place in a kind of spatial vacuum—even though this spacelessness is, so to speak, everywhere. Consider, for example, the explicit absence of schools:

We do not have schools, but countless crowds of our children come rushing out of our people at the shortest possible intervals, cheerfully squealing or peeping as long as they cannot yet squeak, tumbling or rolling away from the pressure at their backs as long as they are too young to run, clumsily tearing everything along with them in their mass as long as they cannot yet see—our children! (*KSS* 101)

This mobile, expanding mass of mice defies any principle of physical containment or spatial organization. It perfectly reflects architectureless space: unbounded, drifting, amoeba-like. In "Josefine," then, there is no such thing as spatial form, only the undifferentiated and seemingly bare space in which the mouse folk scurries about and performs an unspecified variety of work. Even when the mice seem to emerge from somewhere, as in this passage, it is not a place—a location, a building, a site—but rather the group of mice. Thus, at the moment when Kafka's story most explicitly negates the existence of architecture, it also suggests that the mice themselves can be a source of spatial definition.

This absence of delimited space is especially remarkable considering that Kafka's writing is otherwise densely populated with built structures. Indeed, one of Kafka's main modes of literary expression can be termed "architectural narration." Buildings, houses, and castles, as well as various architectural features associated with them (walls, staircases, towers, gates, and rooms of all sorts, including barrooms, bedrooms, and courtrooms) play an important role in so many of Kafka's works: they structure the space of narrative and the process of narration. These buildings and sites are often incomplete or labyrinthine—there is too much or too little architecture—which means they both require endless elucidation and resist conclusive answers. It is out of this architectural struggle that so many of Kafka's narratives emerge. Architectural narration, then, is the act of narrating through and against architecture, and its potential is infinite precisely because Kafka's edifices are often elusive, as in *The Castle*, or provisional: "The Great Wall of China" ("Beim Bau der chinesischen Mauer," 1917) names a structure that is under construction and incompletable, and "The Burrow" presents a negative edifice, an intricate underground cavern that is deconstructed over the course of an unfinishable narrative. Kafka's buildings are never really there, or really done, or really what they seem to be; they are usually unwieldy, difficult to navigate, and far from transparent. His characters build, and they explore built spaces, often with anxious zeal, but rarely if ever are they able to complete or comprehend an architectural construct.[72]

Strangely, none of these claims about architectural narration seems to apply to "Josefine, the Singer," a story in which buildings are not elusive, labyrinthine, or dilapidated, but simply absent—that is, unless we think of Josefine herself *as* the missing architecture. Josefine does not occupy space (like Gregor Samsa) or look for space (like K. in *The Castle*) or build and destroy space (like the burrower). Rather, she creates space through her body, indeed she *is* space. When she strikes a pose—to sing, or as if to sing—the mouse folk stops and pays attention not because of what they hear, but because of what they see: a stilled body. The mice, who spend their days running about in all directions, are stunned into stillness by this piece of murine architecture. Kafka emphasizes the contrast between their random, aimless movement and the stillness of Josefine's body. Her corporeal steadiness halts their formless

activity; it freezes them, literally giving shape to the community. Her calm
and motionless stance imposes order and direction on the disorderly mass.
All the mice look toward her, and, like so many works of architecture, she
channels their gazes upward. A pillar, a simple column pointing to the sky,
Josefine embodies the basic principle of all building.[73]

John T. Hamilton develops a related idea about music in a reading of
Kafka's "Metamorphosis." He argues that "music plays a privileged role in
Kafka's writings . . . because of its capacity to modify perceptions of space.
It is precisely music's qualification of spatial experience that gives rise to
its thorough ambivalence, as either an occasion for ecstasy or a cause for
despair."[74] Hamilton thus invites us to understand music in Kafka as a
function of space. This is consistent with my argument that the process of
community formation only *seems* to hinge on sound in "Josefine," whereas it
is actually driven by an architecture of the body. Josefine strikes a pose and
suddenly all the mice stand frozen before her: her body, quite like a building,
configures the space of narrative, though only provisionally. This explains
why the only descriptions of space the story offers are corporeal ones—space
as it relates to the gestures, postures, and movements of the body. Music
provides the pretext for the body, which is in turn the condition for the production of space.

In her article on implied sounds in silent film, Raynauld argues that silent
film is not only full of "sound occurrences," but that in some ways sound is
more complex and more significant in silent cinema precisely because "sound
is not only present, it is *represented* in novel and unique ways. Instead of
doing away with sound entirely, the early cinema writers and filmmakers
found a chorus of strategies to make sound be *heard inside* the story and
be seen on the screen."[75] It is precisely this "hearing inside" and "being seen
on the screen" that bear on Kafka's silent representations of sound—for
example in the case of "Josefine," where the act of singing must be accessed
primarily through visual rather than auditory means. Granted, the story's
first lines, quoted at the beginning of this chapter, seem to undermine this
reading; there the emphasis is on actual hearing, not the visual perception of
vocal performance. But a closer analysis once again reveals the twisted logic
of implied sound. A verbal evocation of sound that seems to demand an act
of mental hearing actually serves an altogether different purpose. "Our singer
is named Josefine. Anyone who has not heard her does not know the power
of song" (*KSS* 94). The second sentence is written as a negative statement:
anyone who has *not* heard her, *cannot* grasp the power of song. But this does
not mean that those who *have* heard her *do* grasp it. Indeed, knowing that
Josefine's effects derive from her bodily architecture and not from any quality
that can be discerned by the ear, one could read the opening as a declaration
of this lack of knowledge: those who *have* heard Josefine's song are as ignorant of the power of music as those who have *not*, either because her song
is ineffectual as an acoustic experience or because those who have access to

it are incapable of appreciating it.[76] This might seem like a roundabout way of making this rather simple point—that to hear Josefine is *not* necessarily to know the power of song—but it is entirely consistent with the presentation of Josefine as a diva. Like a silent film star, Josefine needs to be treated with tremendous care. The narrator must nurse her sense of uniqueness and entitlement; he must play into her sense of her own celebrity. He must sustain the myth of her song in order for her to assume her role in the story as "Josefine, *the singer*." At the same time, he must choose his words carefully so as to avoid spreading lies about Josefine, since in truth Josefine's acoustic powers are nonexistent. The narrator's careful phrasing achieves precisely this goal: sound seems to be of utmost significance, whereas in fact it is unclear whether any sound is ever made or heard. This makes noise a kind of absent center in the text.

As in the case of so many of Kafka's opening lines, the simplicity and straightforwardness of these two sentences are deceptive. They make a claim about Josefine's exceptionality in the same breath that they undermine this claim, and indeed cast doubt on the possibility of making such claims at all. Much as silent film sound is the product of a carefully constructed cinematic myth, Josefine's song is the product of a carefully constructed narrative myth: they employ the same tactic of presenting the unpresentable (sound), whether in words or images, and investing tremendous but unspecifiable significance in this sound precisely through its nonpresence. Both situations hinge on the conceit of audible effects (i.e., bodily gesture masquerading as vocal performance). What is remarkable is that "Josefine" both sustains and exposes this conceit. Time and again the story speaks as if Josefine's song were remarkable, whereas the only thing it can really assert is that her bodily gestures have a unifying effect on the mouse folk. This disjunction can be compared to a related conceit at work in silent film sound. This is not to say that silent film divas performed the same unifying function as Josefine, but more generally that their power derives not from the sounds they make (they are silent) or even from the ones we imagine them to be making (mental hearing does not and should not necessarily take place), but from the dramatic physicality of their bodies. One can of course speculate about what the divas' power consists in—the ability to seduce, to devastate, to overwhelm with feeling and desire?—but in any case their bodies, like Josefine's, give a powerful performance, regardless of the sounds they might also evoke.

Verbal Cues: The Distinction of
Implied Sound in Literature

As in "Josefine," visualized sound in silent film has a spatial function. In his article, "The First *Transi-Sounds* of Parallel Editing," Bernard Perron offers a prehistory to the phenomenon of transition sounds. Known consciously or unconsciously to anyone who has ever watched a sound film, these are sounds of any kind (music, dialogue, voice-over, etc.) that serve as an acoustic bridge between sequences in a film; they connect locations or times within the film's diegesis. Perron argues that "from 1907–1908 on, the visualization of sound and listening played an important part in the suturing of space."[77] Even if silent film did not call on viewers to actually listen, it certainly required them to understand that acts of listening were taking place. Indeed, what he calls "amplified sound communication"—onscreen displays of acts of making and hearing sound, such as a hand cupping an ear or a character holding a telephone—is arguably even more essential to connecting and transitioning between spaces in silent film than in sound film, where the presence of actual sound normalizes and thus de-emphasizes the sound event. The realism of actual sound makes it susceptible to being overlooked (or "overheard"), whereas the exaggeration and emphasis of visualized sound amplifies it: silent sound is "louder" than actual sound.

But the heightened drama of visualized sound can also be explained as a function of its *inability* to transmit actual sound. Perron's central example of a "transi-sound" in silent film involves several scenes from the 1908 film *The Physician of the Castle* linked together by visible acts of concerted listening, where the location of the sound source remains unfilmed. First, this creates a sense of the "offscreen" in cinema, parallel to the offstage in theater. Second, the distinct spaces of listening are connected through "amplified sound communication": the sounds in which these listeners are interested are both acoustically and visually inaccessible, but this very absence guides the viewer's attempt to understand the events of the narrative. Though the viewer can neither see nor hear what everyone else does, the spaces of the film are sutured by multiple related shots of listening, which suggest an inaudible and invisible acoustic center.[78] "Through its spatial range, which exceeds visible information, and the attention given to the localization of its source, sound makes it possible to bridge the gaps separating diegetic spaces. Most of all, it permits the realization of intelligible transitions between these spaces."[79]

Josefine's gestures function analogously to the visualized sounds in silent film. Indeed, the story revolves around an inaccessible acoustic event or phenomenon that is suggested through her bodily architecture, or, to speak with Perron, the "amplified sound communication" of Josefine's singing gestures and poses. Her song is the inaudible and invisible center that commands the mice's and our attention and thereby creates a sense of coherent narrative space. Yet we neither see nor hear Josefine, we only read about her—which is to say, her song is given not in sounds or images, but in words, as text. Thus the final analysis of Josefine must come down to language, for the story appeals only indirectly to our eyes and ears, but makes direct demands on our linguistic faculty. Two words in particular, at once simple and overdetermined, unlock the relationship between implied sounds and the formation of space in Kafka's "Josefine." These two words, *Auditorium* (auditorium) and *mäuschenstill* (quiet as a little mouse), capture the mutual implication of sound and space in Kafka's text.

The word *Auditorium* should immediately raise eyebrows, given my earlier claim that "Josefine" is strangely and anomalously free of architecture. This word, which appears twice in the space of one sentence in the sixth paragraph of the story, seems to undermine this claim.

> Since squeaking is one of our unconscious habits, you might imagine that there will be some squeaking among Josefine's audience [*Auditorium*] as well; her artistry gives us a sense of well-being, and when we feel well, we squeak; but her audience [*Auditorium*] does not squeak, we are as quiet as mice [*mäuschenstill*]; as if we were partaking of the peace we long for, which at least our own squeaking prevents us from attaining, we keep quiet. (*KSS* 96; *DzL* 354)

The German word *Auditorium* can refer either to a group of listeners (audience) or to a physical space (auditorium). Stanley Corngold's English translation does well to use the same word, audience, for both instances, since this reflects the repetition in the original German and makes sense in both contexts. Nevertheless, the translation gives the impression that the story is in fact completely bereft of architecture: "audience" lacks any spatial dimension, whereas *Auditorium* signifies precisely this, a space of listening. If Josefine is the sole source of spatial form in Kafka's story, as I argue, how can we account for the presence of the word *Auditorium* in the narrative?

Josefine's *Auditorium* can be grasped in a way that acknowledges the spatiality inherent in this term without insisting that it names a physical site of listening. *Auditorium* refers to a space for hearing, but not a specific location or structure. Instead, it signifies spatiality itself, the condition of possibility of literary acoustics, which take the form of implied sound. Josefine's auditorium is the "space" in which the "sounds" of her voice can be "heard": none of this is actual hearing, but all of it revolves around the *idea* of hearing. This constitutes the conceit or myth of implied sound. The Latin root of the word points to this abstract spatiality: *Auditorium* literally means a "space for hearing," but in an abstract rather than a concrete sense; this is why the German word can actually mean two things, a space and an audience. Josefine's *Auditorium* is suspended between these meanings. It functions simultaneously as an acknowledgment of the spatial requirements of acoustic and auditory experience in literature and a sign that these conditions can be met only in the most tenuous way—first through the momentary configuration of space through Josefine's body and second through this verbal abstraction. The term designates a kind of spatiality, constituted by the listening mice, that enables an articulation of literary sound.

The fact that *Auditorium* is one of very few non-Germanic words that appear in the story[80] and is used twice in one sentence highlights its importance and exceptionality. Kafka could have used the word *Publikum* (audience) or *Zuhörer* (listeners), as he does a few sentences later, but then the spatial connotation would be entirely absent. Alternatively, he might have used the word *Hörraum* (listening room), but then the primary or denotative meaning of an audience of listeners would have disappeared. Moreover, the Germanic compound *Hörraum* would have invoked a concrete space, a location, a site. Only the Latinate word *Auditorium* allows Kafka to mean one thing but imply another, indeed to imply the very thing that is otherwise banished from the story, physical space. In fact, because the second instance of the word *Auditorium must* mean an audience and *not* a place, this word is uniquely capable of banishing architecture from the story while simultaneously calling forth the idea of architectural structures. The word urges us to search for spatial coordinates in a story that persistently withholds them; it attunes us to what is absent and needed. Indeed, sound and space are both evoked in their absence, which showcases literary language's brilliant power to capture the story's dual absent centers in a single word. The inability to transmit audible sounds and visible images is not a weakness or shortcoming of literature, but the basis of a modernist literary narrative engaged in a semiotic game in which perceptual experiences are simultaneously presented and withheld.

The second word that captures how implied sound both exposes and compensates for spacelessness in Kafka's story is *mäuschenstill*, an adjective used to describe the silence of Josefine's "Auditorium." The importance of this word is clear not only from its proximity in the text to "Auditorium," but also from the fact that it performs Kafka's (in)famous literary maneuver, the so-called literalization of the metaphor. Much has been said about this process of making metaphorical language come alive in Kafka: some have argued it is at the heart of Kafka's uncanny, and hence of the "kafkaesque," while others have deconstructed this claim and the assumptions that undergird it. In the case of "The Metamorphosis," calling or treating a human being like vermin seems to get literalized—it transforms from figure to reality—when Gregor Samsa wakes up one morning and discovers that he has become a "monstrous vermin [*ungeheuren Ungeziefer*]."[81] In the case of "Josefine," the German expression *mäuschenstill*—quiet as a little mouse—gets literalized when it is used to describe the mouse folk: they are not quiet *as* little mice, but are simply quiet little mice. What does this imply, given that the story seems to drive the point home that neither Josefine's nor the mouse folk's sonic effects can actually be verified? These are fictional mice whose sound level is uncertain, guided by a mouse singer whose vocal production is radically indeterminate. If we know nothing for sure about murine acoustics, how can it serve as the grounds for metaphorical discourse?

Whether or not one supports the literalization thesis, Kafka is surely inviting the reader to think about how rhetorical language is transformed—and possibly even deformed, degraded, and rendered illegible—when metaphors appear to be literalized. To be confronted with a "metaphor come alive" reveals the instability and indeterminacy of rhetorical language. If Gregor (as the embodiment of the quality of being vermin-like) exposes the fraught and contaminated relationship between monsters and humans, then Josefine (as the embodiment of the quality of being *mäuschenstill*) exposes the crucial but elusive nexus of sound and space. The term that is meant to explain and clarify an acoustic phenomenon—a particular kind of silence (*Stille*)—is undermined and possibly contradicted by Josefine's vocal practice, whose effects derive exclusively from her static physical pose, her stillness (also *Stille*). Josefine may or may not be as *quiet* (*still*) as a mouse, but she is in fact as *still* (*still*) as a mouse: we know this from her statue-like physical stance, the only verifiable feature of her musicality and the source of her unifying power. *Mäuschenstill* thus refers not to silence, as we had assumed, but to the absence of movement, to stillness. We cannot know whether Josefine embodies the acoustic quality described by this word, and hence whether she literalizes the metaphor. We do know, however, that it describes the gestural quality of her song and reveals the secret of her musicality, but not in the way we originally expected. The idea of stillness is hidden in plain sight, behind the more obvious meaning of *still* as "quiet." The word must be read against itself, and above all against the apparent grain of the story, in order for this secret to be exposed. Thus, an act of verbal dissection is required to expose the source of Josefine's power, namely that it is not acoustic but based on an architecture of the body. The word must be read not as a literalized metaphor, but as a literal term whose predominant metaphoricity conceals its truth.

As with the word *Auditorium*, the secret of *mäuschenstill* is concealed on its surface: one must isolate and analyze these words to grasp the fundamentally spatial and bodily character of auditory experience and acoustic expression in the story. These words, overripe with meaning, trigger a drive to interpret that distracts us from their actual significance. *Auditorium* seems to promise architecture in a spaceless story, and *mäuschenstill* seems to invite metaphorical thinking as a means of understanding sound. Neither of these statements is exactly true, but the act of dissection reveals a truth about the spatial principle that undergirds the conceit of sound and listening in Kafka. Rather than serve as the space through which narrative is organized, the word *Auditorium* confirms the absence of architecture in "Josefine" and posits the need for Josefine's body to fill the spatial void. And rather than inform us about the acoustic condition of the audience, the word *mäuschenstill* confirms the significance of stilled bodies. Taken together, and considered alongside the story's numerous descriptions of Josefine's corporeal architecture, these words represent the foundation of an acoustic discourse of spatiality in Kafka's late story. They reveal that the struggle to determine literary space via sound takes place in the cracks of language.

Much as Perron argues about early silent film, the central acoustic event in Kafka's story does not need to be presented or even represented in order to structure the narrative around it; it can be a negative presence. If enough ears and eyes and minds are directed toward the sound in question, even if it is acoustically indeterminate or inaudible, its spatial effects can be suggested and its linguistic form can be analyzed. In Kafka's story, visualized sound may not "suture" space in order to lend coherence to narrative in the way Perron claims for silent film, but it is a successful instance of spatiality in the context of a story that repeatedly tries and fails to make assertions about sound. Together with words such as *Auditorium* and *mäuschenstill*, visualized sounds map the story's ostensible acoustic discourse onto space. If a central problem of "Josefine, the Singer or the Mouse Folk" is the use of language to generate spatiality out of a silence that gestures toward sound, it has much in common with early film. Indeed, this act—the production of space through the silent evocation of sound—lies at the heart of Kafka's affinity with silent film.

By shifting the interpretation of "Josefine" from sound (the apparent signified) to spaces and bodies, and more precisely the words used to describe them (the signifier), we draw attention to the mouse narrator. After all, the story consists of his descriptions, words, and images, yet he consistently underplays his individual identity: he tends to speak in the first-person plural rather than the first-person singular, as if to affirm a commitment to collective identity. Even when he expresses thoughts and opinions, he usually attributes them to the mouse folk or one of its subgroups. There is, it would seem, only one individual in this story, and her name is Josefine.

Nevertheless, the narrator's voice belongs to a single speaker, not a chorus.[82] "Josefine" represents a prime instance of the phenomenon of "speaking for" in Kafka, when one individual's voice speaks in the name of a group.[83] Thus what appears to be a kind of modesty—the narrator stays in the background and pushes Josefine into the limelight—actually betrays his presumptuousness: he assumes the power and right to speak for the mice as a whole. He is, moreover, the *only* mouse who claims this right. Even Josefine does not presume to speak on behalf of the others: she makes requests of the mice, and desperately wants to be acknowledged and appreciated by them, but never asserts control or ownership of them. By contrast, the narrator's very practice of narration represents a claim to exceptional status, since as a rule the mice do not engage in storytelling or historicizing. As he states in the final sentence of the story, Josefine will be forgotten, "for we practice no history [*da wir keine Geschichte treiben*]" (*KSS* 108; *DzL* 377). This sentimental conclusion, delivered almost as an afterthought, forces a revision of everything that has come before. The mouse folk is defined by activity and work, not contemplative thought; they lack a tradition of self-reflection and representation. Given that they do not "practice history," what can be made of the storytelling zeal of the narrator, who presents himself as a typical mouse?

In fact, the narrator's voice succeeds precisely where Josefine's voice fails, namely in proving its distinction. His seemingly self-effacing narration is a performance, a calculated if quiet manipulation. Josefine makes an explicit show of her voice, which proves to be nothing at all: it is empty, the show of a silent film diva, as full of drama as it is lacking in substance. By contrast, the narrator inconspicuously runs the show that is the story of Josefine. His powers of narration are a secret in plain sight: she may have the body, but he has the voice. If Josefine's song represents difference with no content, the narrator's story represents content with no difference—a demonstrable exception to the mouse folk that lacks an explicit claim to exceptional status. The narrator mouse uses his voice effectively, and there is certainty about its existence. It is the one voice that proves itself to be powerful and different, even if he does not make a show of his uniqueness and claims to speak on behalf of others. Indeed, the narrator withholds the essential piece of information that confirms his exceptionality—the fact that the mice are not in the business of telling stories, but that he has just told one nevertheless—until the story's last breath. These final sentences contain the story's great surprise, a basic but shattering truth about the central narrative puzzle. All along we were paying attention to the content of the story, rather than its form. Now we see that in "talking Josefine up" the narrator was secretly valorizing not her voice but his own.

"Josefine, the Singer or the Mouse Folk" presents a competition of voices between Josefine and the narrator, in which the narrator is victorious. This victory is clear for the reasons just given: he can distinguish his voice and demonstrate its effects, whereas she cannot. By implication, it is also a victory of language over music, for he can do something distinctive with words that she cannot do with song. Josefine's uncertain attempts at coloratura and other musical flourishes can be contrasted with the narrator's brilliant verbal gems; as I have shown, words such as *Auditorium* and *mäuschenstill* simultaneously conceal and reveal the secret core of Josefine's power, namely her bodily architecture. These are *his* coloraturas. The narrator's triumph is also a triumph of voice over body, writing over orality, and recording over live performance. For Josefine and her song will fade into oblivion—"she will enjoy the heightened redemption of being forgotten"—whereas his story has been preserved in writing (*KSS* 108).

The narrator's vocal victory casts doubts on his apparent attitude toward Josefine: was it ever his intention to glorify her, or were his motives self-serving? Perhaps he was purposefully failing in all his attempts to distinguish Josefine, for his goal was always to distinguish himself through acts of virtuosic narration that showcased his own voice, not Josefine's. Maybe his aim was never to prove how special Josefine's song was, but to win the battle of voices himself. The pretense of trying but always failing to describe her vocal distinction enables his own display of vocal mastery, a brilliant narrative ploy. Much as in "The Silence of the Sirens," masters of the voice prove to be cunning tricksters, sly foxes.

Conclusion: A Suspended Semiotics of Sound

"Josefine" is a story that is in some sense written against itself. It seems to put sound center stage, whereas in truth there is no sound and no stage, only Josefine's body. It uses the word "Auditorium," but this only emphasizes the absence of architectural structures and the need for acoustic substitutions. It describes the silence of the mice with a literalized metaphor, only to upend the literal meaning of the metaphor. This chapter has shown that Kafka frequently engaged in a kind of sound writing that undid itself, resulting in a suspended semiotics of sound.[84] "The Knock at the Courtyard Gate" and "The Silence of the Sirens" both appear to present sounds with serious, even fatal consequences, but they actually reveal the basic instability of representing sound in silent media. They undermine the text's seemingly straightforward invitation to engage in acts of mental hearing. By shifting the focus away from what is absent in these works (the sounds implied) and toward what is present in them (gestures, poses, movements), and by drawing parallels to the visualization of sound in silent film, I have sought to present an intermedial semiotics of silent sound. Kafka's use of implied sounds reveals certain assumptions that undergird silent film viewership, especially with respect to acoustic gesture, the role of sound in silent film production, and acts of subception or mental hearing. Conversely, implied sound in silent cinema opens up new avenues for thinking about gesture in Kafka, especially its spatializing function.

In her book *Franz Kafka and the Silent Film* (*Franz Kafka und der Stummfilm*), Anna Brabandt claims to offer an intermedial reading of Kafka's work through the lens of silent film, by focusing on the significance of visuality in Kafka. She devotes a section to "Mute Speaking with the Body," in which she analyzes Kafka's gestures in terms of various silent film techniques, such as the close-up, the visual representation of figural relationships, and what she calls the "Optical Conversion of Speech."[85] But she does not focus on the absence of sound and its resultant acoustical ambiguities as the crucial link between Kafka and silent film. Instead, she formulates the issue in terms of speech and communication—the capacity for gestures to signify specific content—a paradigm in which Kafka inevitably falls short. While the surface similarities between Kafka's gestures and silent film gestures are striking, she argues that they are in fact incomparable: in silent film these gestures "are the means of communication and are supposed to transmit the characters' thoughts and feelings to the viewer," whereas "in Kafka these inner realms are often inaccessible."[86] Brabandt calls "the readability of signs in film . . . a basic requirement," while Kafka's gestures are opaque and resistant to interpretation.[87] Having established a surface connection between Kafka's gestures and silent film gestures, Brabandt claims they serve a distinct purpose in film (communication, narrative coherence, characterization) but none in Kafka. His gestures are empty references to a silent film aesthetic, mimicking silent film semiosis to no discernible end.[88]

Even Theodor Adorno, who first suggested the link between Kafka's gestures and silent film in his December 17, 1934, letter to Walter Benjamin,
does not clarify why this link is so important, but he seems to get further than
Brabandt. This key passage, in which Adorno responds to Benjamin's invocation of the theater in reference to Kafka's gestures, served as the epigraph
to my opening chapter. There Adorno identifies the powerful expressivity of
Kafka's gestures, but also draws attention to their ambiguity, which reflects
the essential mystery of sound in Kafka: its suspension between silence and
music. Ambiguous gestures are an expression of this vertical tug-of-war,
pulling downward toward muteness and upward toward music: the words
Versinken (sinking) and *Sicherheben* (self-raising) lend a clear up-down
tension to Adorno's characterization. His claim thus hints at the spatial
dimension of Kafka's discourse on sound that is at the heart of my reading (recall that Josefine's taut uprightness is the key to her effects). Without
referring explicitly to architecture or space, Adorno seems to characterize the
ambiguity of Kafka's acoustic gestures through a vertical tension that keeps
sound in a state of suspension: the dangerous gravitational pull of silence,
muteness, and noise versus the potentially lofty ascension to music. Kafka's
gestures are always drawn in these two directions, and so the ambiguity of
gesture is expressed as the dual vector of music and noise. The suspension in
space, which I have figured in architectural terms, is what Kafka and silent
film share.

Adorno thus demonstrates in two sentences that the link between Kafka
and silent film runs far deeper than Brabandt suggests.[89] I have delineated the
semiotic basis for this link and elucidated its consequences for interpretations
of both Kafka's writing and silent film. The result is a model for intermedial
analysis that goes beyond the identification of similar themes and modes of
viewing, which is what Brabandt and Alt offer. Their studies begin and end
with the question of perception; they demonstrate that Kafka's vision was
influenced by silent film, but only in one specific sense—the transposition of
cinematic viewing onto writing. My reading shows that the analysis of sound
deepens the discussion of gestures in Kafka and in silent film. Kafka's stories
demonstrate that implied sound consists not in what is *not* there, namely
sound, but in the struggle for representation, in representation as a struggle.
The unreadable gestures and linguistic curiosities that constitute this struggle
are the material of implied sound, and their impenetrability is its essence, not
its dark side. To return to the idea that first motivated this chapter, implied
sound exists not as a poor substitute for actual sound, but to capture its hidden, ineffable, and—most crucially—inaudible character.

Chapter 3

The Vocal Supplement

Recitation in Kafka and the Advent of Sound Film

According to a popular anecdote, Franz Kafka periodically broke into fits of laughter when he read his stories aloud. His close friend and earliest biographer Max Brod notes that Kafka, while reading the first chapter of *The Trial* to a group of friends, "laughed so much that there were moments when he couldn't read any further."[1] What strikes most people about this anecdote is the laughter: did Kafka really have such a good sense of humor, what exactly did he find funny about the opening of *The Trial*, and what does this say about the comedic dimension of his writing? These are important questions, but I want to take a step back from them and dwell on another aspect of the story—not the laughter, but the act of reading for an audience, the vocal performance of literature.[2]

By now it is widely known and well documented that Kafka read his works aloud to friends and family and attended recitations, including several by two of the most prominent reciters of the day, Ludwig Hardt[3] and Alexander Moissi.[4] What is less well understood, however, is Kafka's precise attitude toward this practice: what did he get out of recitation, as a performer and as a spectator? It is clear that Kafka was fascinated by the experience of hearing a literary work recited.[5] For him, literature was fundamentally if temporarily transformed by the act of recitation, and the effects of this transformation were both exhilarating and troubling. The addition of the human voice and body to the literary text made it come alive and endowed it with new powers to move, excite, and possibly even seduce the listener. Yet it was not clear to Kafka that these effects were positive. First, vocal performance might be no more than a cheap thrill that did not add substantially to the written work. Second, it consistently stirred feelings of self-satisfaction and vanity in the reciter, which were largely misplaced, given that the work actually "belonged" to the writer, not the reciter. Recitation could blur matters of artistic creation and reception; effects of the written text could be misappropriated by the reciter and misattributed by the listener. Thus, the practice of recitation, for all its delights, threatened questions of literary integrity and authorship. There is a direct line, in Kafka's imagination, from recitation to plagiarism.

In Kafka's writings on the topic, the allure of recitation is always mixed with his misgivings about the practice, an ambivalence that contributes to the eloquence and complexity with which Kafka wrote about the topic. His attempts to describe the voice and its effects are frequently intense, breathless, and convoluted, and this heightened reaction to the voice relates to its shameful allure. A note from 1917 reads:

> Always first draw fresh breath after outbursts of vanity and self-satisfaction. The orgy while reading the story in *Der Jude*. Like a squirrel in its cage. Bliss of movement, desperation about constriction, craziness of endurance, feeling of misery in the face of the calm of the external. All this both simultaneously and alternatingly, still in the filth of the end a sunray of bliss [*Glückseligkeit*]. (*NSF II* 30)[6]

Here Kafka is describing a reading he gave of his story "Jackals and Arabs" ("Schakale und Araber," 1917). Kafka's self-criticism is consistent with his general critique of the reciter, who is motivated by self-love and a desire for attention and praise. Moreover, the passage shows how the experience of recitation is both orgiastic and wrenching. Kafka likens himself to a squirrel in a cage, with alternating feelings of bliss, desperation, madness, and misery. For the squirrel, these mixed sensations and emotions derive from its frenetic movement, its indefinite confinement to a small space, and its perception of a calm and peaceful world beyond its cage.

Kafka also explores the link between performance and encagement in two famous stories, "A Report to an Academy" ("Ein Bericht für eine Akademie," 1917) and "A Hunger Artist" ("Ein Hungerkünstler," 1922). The former was also published in *Der Jude*, just one month after "Jackals and Arabs." In all of these texts, the cage is also a kind of a stage: it transforms its contents into a performance, a show, a spectacle. What takes place within the metaphorical cage Kafka describes in his notebook is a literary recitation that rises to the heights of bliss (*Glückseligkeit*) and sinks to the depths of dirt and excrement. Over and over in his diaries Kafka invokes the thrilling entrapment of vocal performance, as well as the bodily delights, emotional degradation, sublimity, and self-hatred that accompany it. He works through his ambivalence toward recitation, but nowhere else does he express with such precision and directness how recitation associates him, "simultaneously and alternatingly," with bliss and filth.

This chapter pairs Kafka's reflections on the voice as a medium for literary transmission with films and film theory that reflect a related ambivalence about the voice in cinema. While the voice is live in one case and technologically mediated in the other, in both situations it is perceived as supplemental. As Philip Auslander argues, the distinction between live presence and technological mediation, which structures much of performance theory, breaks down on close analysis of actual performances, many of which contain some degree of each. Moreover, there are multiple forms of mediation, only some of which are technological: everything that puts distance between the performer and the audience counts as a kind of mediation.[7] The films analyzed in this chapter all depict live performances (varieté, song-and-dance, ventriloquism) through a technological medium, meaning both live and recorded voices play a part in them. In the case of Kafka's reflections on recitation, no technology is involved, but the vocal organ itself complicates the question of mediation: for him the written text is immediate, and vocal performance adds a layer of distance. The voice is a mediating tool and hence inherently technologized. The chapter closes with readings of two important works by Kafka, his "Speech on the Yiddish Language" ("Rede über die jiddische Sprache," 1912) and the story "Report to an Academy," which challenge the idea of vocalized literature as derivative and mediated and suggest a potentially "pure" recitation at work in Kafka's writing.

The Transition to Sound Film and
the Debate over the Voice

The introduction of sound film was a contentious moment in film history, but it seems there was one point that nearly everyone agreed on: the new medium would be completely different from everything that had come before. Critics debated whether sound film was good or bad art, natural or artificial, effective or confusing, entertaining or annoying, but everyone seemed to agree that sound was not a minor adjustment or addition to silent film. Sound promised to change everything about how films were produced, distributed, and experienced by viewers. It was going to be a revolution.

From our contemporary perspective, in which sound film appears whole and silent film incomplete, it can seem as if the addition of sound was simply completing an art form that had remained in a state of infancy since its invention three decades earlier. It can seem to us that sound film is the "natural" state of cinematic art toward which silent film was always striving. This is not how contemporary audiences experienced the transition, and certainly not how early filmmakers and film theorists viewed it. As the film scholar Robert Spadoni writes, in the early days of sound film

> viewers were aware of a connotation of *synchronization* that the word no longer carries today. During the silent eras, as James Lastra notes, the word in the context of moviegoing had referred primarily to live musical accompaniment. *Synchronization* in this context suggests something extratextual pieced onto the whole for effect rather than something intrinsic to the profilmic world that has been drawn

out of it and captured on film or disc. Synchronized voices are understood to accompany moving lips rather than to issue from them.[8]

In short, audiences perceived sound film as anything but natural. Film had
always been a silent medium, so there was nothing obvious, given, or predictable about the addition of sound. The fact that in its day silent film was just
called "film" attests to this: only after the invention of sound film did the
earlier form appear to be lacking in some way and was it renamed to reflect
this "deficiency."
     Filmmakers adjusted to the introduction of sound in numerous ways.
Acting styles became more muted, shots got significantly longer, and plots
grew more sophisticated. As audiences had to reckon with new cinematic
conventions, sensations, and techniques, and as viewers' eyes and ears were
retrained accordingly, they became "medium-sensitive."[9] In this transitional
period, "[synchronized] speech registered, unambiguously, as a major change,
and viewers for a time lacked the cognitive training to process this new constitutive element of cinema as routinely and transparently as they had the
silent film intertitle."[10] The early German filmmaker and film theorist Walter
Ruttmann understood this already in 1928: "It would be utterly wrong to see
it [sound film] as a simple augmentation of silent film. It is not sound film's
task to give voice to silent film. It must be clear from the outset that its laws
have almost nothing to do with those of soundless film. A completely new
situation is evolving here."[11]
     According to Spadoni, the earliest sound film audiences found voices,
not music or noise, particularly jarring. Moreover, what disturbed them was
not imperfect synchronization, but rather the fact that all the sound came
from one spot behind the screen even though the characters appeared to
be speaking from various locations.[12] Thus, it was specifically the problem
of connecting visible bodies to audible voices that initially unsettled them.[13]
"As audiences grew accustomed to the loudspeaker-screen configuration, the
bodies on the screen merged with the voices. Until then, even perfectly synchronized and acceptably natural-sounding speech might strike the viewer as
an obviously mechanical contrivance."[14]
     The first reactions to sound film included feelings of wonder, exhilaration,
uncanniness, and confusion. Whether audiences reacted positively or negatively, they knew that they were dealing with something completely new, and
possibly transformative.[15] Some were very enthusiastic, others highly critical,
but almost no one remained neutral. The German film critic Rudolf Arnheim,
one of the harshest critics of the new medium, admitted in a 1928 essay
that sound film "gets under your skin far more than silent film," but found
this intensity to be disadvantageous: sound can make the cinematic experience so thrilling and powerful that it detracts from and even degrades the
visual dimension of cinema, which is where Arnheim located film's essence
and power.[16] Sound could add "a great deal to the amusement of the public

at large," but it would damage the experience for those with a true sense of cinematic art.[17] The filmmaker G. W. Pabst was also initially skeptical about the new medium, writing that sound would only bring "unsustainable half-measures to a self-contained art form that is in its liveliest stage of development."[18] Many, including Pabst and Arnheim, wrote that despite its seemingly spectacular effects, sound film was just a gimmick that offered cheap thrills. In contrast to these voices, there were others, such as the film theorists Sergei Eisenstein and Béla Balázs, who were early defenders of the new medium, provided certain principles were upheld. They believed sound film had the potential for aesthetically revolutionary effects, though it would take time to develop the requisite technical and stylistic mastery to achieve them.[19] In 1928, Ruttmann took a more distanced view of the matter: "Sound film is the talk of the town. Sound film ruffles feathers, excites discussion, and has endured premature judgments, both hostile and enthusiastic."[20]

The initial excitement and the bold statements it inspired were a short-lived reaction to something novel, thrilling, and even threatening. While the evolution of sound film is ongoing, audiences quickly adjusted to the new medium. After a few years, or maybe even months, viewers no longer found it magical or disturbing that onscreen bodies could speak. Having grown accustomed to the conventions of sound film, they had one of two basic reactions:

> Synchronized sound film . . . could strike audiences as a dazzling reproduction of a preexisting unity or it could entertain them as a thrilling approximation and reassembly of that unity. It could take viewers straight to the speaking person or, afresh, to the cinema as a technological medium. The cinema was, according to the latter sense, less a window that had always been clear (and now had been opened to let the sounds through) than it was a noisy attraction busily cranking out sensory delights before a house of astonished patrons.[21]

Spadoni is suggesting that after the initial period in which talking pictures seemed uncanny and wondrous, audiences were still "dazzled" and "thrilled" by them, but not for the same reasons. They could either indulge in sound film's powers of verisimilitude or appreciate its technical sophistication—in other words, they could focus on the representation itself or the process of representation. Audiences did not naively believe that cinematic sound was "natural" or "real," or that it was supernatural or magical, and they had moved past the initial stage of giddy delight or knee-jerk aversion.

In an essay from 1932, by which point sound film had established itself as the norm in Germany, Arnheim offered a rather bleak assessment:

> We met the arrival of sound film with distrust. It seemed, after all, that it would have to destroy all the exceptional qualities of silent

film that we had loved. Then we became more hopeful, because we admitted that sound film would be able to replace the attractions that it destroyed with new ones of its own. Since then, it has become apparent that sound film desires to make as little use of these new possibilities as possible. It has destroyed, but without replacing anything.[22]

G. W. Pabst, writing in 1929, revised his earlier view, which had been highly skeptical and dismissive, in a far more radical way: now that "sound film has learned to reproduce human voices and environments completely, . . . it can transcend the limitations and constraints of both theater and silent film"; "sound film complements the poignancy of the visible with the magic of the word."[23] Nevertheless, Pabst stands by a part of his earlier statement: "Like so many technical inventions, what was magic yesterday is today merely a gimmick and tomorrow may become a vital necessity."[24]

At the end of this essay Pabst goes a step further by declaring that sound film "forges such a strong connection between the two [the visible and the magic of the word] that it can escape even the bonds of national linguistic specificity—perhaps it is even a step on the way to creating a universal world language."[25] For different reasons, Béla Balázs, probably the most fervent early advocate of sound film, also championed its powers. He wrote that "sound film should not merely contribute sound to the silent film and thus make it even more like nature, but . . . should approach the reality of life from a totally different angle and open up a new treasure-house of human experience."[26] He commented extensively on matters of technique and style: sound should not be mere accompaniment, "but the subject, source and mover of the action"; it should lead to discoveries that would otherwise not have been possible.[27] Just as silent film helped us see things that were previously invisible, sound film would allow us to hear things that had been inaudible.

> The sound film will teach us to analyse even chaotic noise with our ear and read the score of life's symphony. Our ear will hear the different voices in the general babble and distinguish their character as manifestations of individual life. It is an old maxim that art saves us from chaos. The arts differ from each other in the specific kind of chaos which they fight against. The vocation of the sound film is to redeem us from the chaos of shapeless noise by accepting it as expression, as significance, as meaning.[28]

Balázs's hopes were also dashed. Twenty years after his initial optimism, he declared sound film a disappointment; it had not fulfilled its redemptive promise.

Balázs, Arnheim, Ruttmann, and Pabst were among the most prominent voices in the German-language debate over the introduction of sound into cinema, and their contributions resonate with Kafka's writings on recitation. Both situations present a silent medium, silent film or literature, which must reckon with the addition of sound, particularly voices. Cinema audiences seem to have had an easier time assimilating music and noise than human speech, which was disruptive, confusing, and uncanny, much as it is in Kafka's descriptions of literary recitation. It seemed to come from without and upset an internal order and logic that film had been cultivating for thirty years. In Kafka's writing, too, the addition of the voice upsets the order between author, work, reciter, and listener. The voice is not "natural" or "real" in any simple or direct sense. It does not *restore* cinema to a natural state for German filmmakers and film theorists, and it does not *restore* literature to a natural state for Kafka. Instead, the voice is a supplement: it comes from the outside and is potentially corrosive and distorting, but also thrilling and vibrant. Once introduced, filmmakers and audiences cannot do without it, even if everyone is aware that its tricks can be cheap and its appeal superficial. Kafka had similar misgivings about the voice, and he also found himself repeatedly drawn to it. The two art forms are linked by a persistent ambivalence toward vocal effects: a feeling that the voice degrades and heightens aesthetic experience, that it is excessive but necessary, and that it damages art but brings an undeniable and irresistible degree of fame and recognition to the artist.

Recitation, Performance, and Vocal Training: Proper and Improper Uses of the Voice in Kafka and *The Blue Angel*

Ever since the invention of the printing press and the advent of widespread literacy, reading has been primarily a solitary and silent practice, yet literature can "sonify," or make sound, through various means.[29] In addition to the obvious case of theater, it is possible to make operas out of stories, set poems to music, adapt novels for film and television, perform radio plays, listen to audio recordings of books, and, quite simply, read literature aloud. There are thus numerous ways to draw literature out of its modern condition of silence and solitude and make it into an experience that is both oral and aural, and sometimes social. One of these practices, literary recitation, was very important for Franz Kafka.

Lothar Müller's *The Second Voice: The Art of Speech from Goethe to Kafka* (*Die zweite Stimme: Vortragskunst von Goethe bis Kafka*) provides a historical reconstruction of Kafka's numerous encounters with recitation, both as listener and performer, in early twentieth-century Prague and Berlin. Reinhardt Meyer-Kalkus's cultural history, *Voice and the Speaking Arts in the Twentieth Century* (*Stimme und Sprechkünste im 20. Jahrhundert*), includes a chapter on animal voices in Charles Darwin and Kafka, and detailed accounts of the theatrical, musical, and literary contexts in which various forms of vocal art emerged and resurfaced in the first decades of the twentieth century. The existing scholarship on Kafka and recitation thus focuses on historical and cultural context rather than the rhetoric of recitation in Kafka's writings. How does Kafka describe the human voice? How does he figure the relationship between written text and spoken word, between author and reciter? How does the act of recitation transform the written text? What is its impact on listener and performer?

There is no extant sound recording of Kafka's voice, but there are recordings of readings and performances by famous actors and reciters whom Kafka heard and wrote about, such as Alexander Moissi (1879–1935), and who performed Kafka's works, such as Ludwig Hardt (1886–1947).[30] These recordings, while fascinating, cannot serve as a basis for understanding Kafka's ideas about the speaking voice: first, because we can only hear with our own ears, not Kafka's, and second, because for us these voices are technologically mediated, whereas Kafka heard them live. The written record Kafka left in his diaries of the informal readings he gave for his family and friends and the professional recitations he attended, mostly in Prague and Berlin, are better grounds for understanding his attitude toward the practice. These writings offer a picture of the complexity and ambivalence of Kafka's feelings about recitation—that is, the various pleasures, anxieties, misgivings, and dangers he associated with it.

Kafka thought a great deal about what happens when a literary text is read aloud or recited—to the reciter and listener, the author, and the text itself. The nature and implications of these reflections are the main subject of this chapter section and the two that follow. Each section will focus on a diary entry from 1912 that bears on the topic of literary recitation: in the first, Kafka compares the experience of reading his work aloud to his sisters and colleagues; in the second, he relates an encounter with an amateur reciter named Oskar Reichmann; in the third, he gives an account of a reading by the actor Alexander Moissi. These texts reveal a profound discomfort and deep fascination with recitation, particularly with how this practice upends and transforms the status of authorship by reconfiguring the relationship between writer, work, performer, and audience. The lines between them are constantly being blurred, a source of frustration and suspicion for Kafka, who claims to be committed to the clarity of effects and impressions. Recitation seems incapable of producing "a pure impression," making it an inherently noisy or messy act; it thereby undermines the supposed purity of the written text. At the same time, Kafka is seduced by the prospect of achieving intimacy with and power over his listeners, a skill he admires in the virtuoso reciter, and he also enjoys the sociability and play that recitation entails. Kafka's ambivalence toward the practice thus stems from its potential to confer on the performer a dubious but enormously seductive power.

The fifth book of Kafka's diaries opens with a remarkable comparison of two modes of recitation: reading to his sisters and reading to his colleagues.

This contrast between the personal and the professional represents the first point of tension in Kafka's characterization of recitation.

> January 4 [1912]. It is only because of my vanity [*Eitelkeit*] that I like so much to read to my sisters (so that today, for instance, it is already too late to write). Not that I am convinced that I shall achieve something significant in the reading, it is only that I am dominated by the passion to get so close to the good works I read that I merge with them, not through my own merit, indeed, but only through the attentiveness of my listening sisters, which has been excited by what is being read and is unresponsive to inessentials; and therefore too, under the concealment my vanity [*Eitelkeit*] affords me, I can share as creator in the effect which the work alone has exercised. That is why I really read admirably to my sisters and stress the accents with extreme exactness just as I feel them, because later I am abundantly rewarded not only by myself but also by my sisters.
>
> But if I read to Brod or Baum or others, just because of my pretensions my reading must appear horribly bad to everyone, even if they know nothing of the usual quality of my reading; for here I know that the listener is fully aware of the separation [*Sonderung*] between me and what is being read, here I cannot merge completely with what I read without feeling myself to be ridiculous, a feeling which can expect no support from the listener; with my voice I flutter around what is being read, try to force my way in here and there because they want me to, but don't intend this seriously because they don't expect that much from me at all; but what they really want me to do, to read without vanity [*Eitelkeit*], calmly and distantly, and to become passionate only when a genuine passion demands it, that I cannot do; but although I believe I have resigned myself to reading badly to everyone except my sisters, my vanity [*Eitelkeit*], which this time has no justification, still shows itself: I feel offended if anyone finds fault with my reading, I become flushed and want to read on quickly, just as I usually strive, once I have begun, to read on endlessly, out of an unconscious yearning that during the course of the long reading there may be produced, at least in me, that vain [*eitel*], false feeling of integration with what I read which makes me forget that I shall never be strong enough at any one moment to impose my feelings on the clear vision of the listener and that at home it is always the sisters who initiate this longed-for substitution. (D 212–13, trans. modified; T 345–46)

Kafka delineates two types of recitation here: one mode is self-indulgent and narcissistic while the other adheres to standards of propriety and professionalism. He practices the first for the benefit of his sisters and on account of his "vanity [*Eitelkeit*]," a word that appears four times in the space of this entry; the adjective "vain [*eitel*]" appears once too. He imagines it to be a somewhat dramatic mode of recitation, with varied accents, intonations, and inflections. It achieves a kind of union, albeit false and deceptive, between reader and work. This is why Kafka uses verbs like "to push oneself onto [*sich herandrängen*]" and "to penetrate [*eindringen*]," and repeatedly invokes ideas of unity and flow. This model of reading is one in which qualities of performance such as voice, gesture, and facial expression merge with textual effects, which makes it difficult to tell what exactly is causing the reaction in his sisters—the text, the performance, or some combination of the two. Kafka finds the prospect of wielding influence and power over his audience alluring, not least because it can elicit praise, but he also feels some shame and embarrassment over this aspiration, which explains the aggressive, even sexually predatory undertone of his account.

What exactly is Kafka's problem with reading aloud to an audience? To blur the line between reader and work is to take personal credit for an achievement that is textual. This is what Kafka means when he explains that he "can share as creator in the effect which the work alone has exercised." Literary sonification thus involves a kind of theft, or at least a modicum of dishonesty. It also implies a distasteful lust for fame or recognition, and precludes the possibility of a clear literary impression. This is even a problem when author and reader are one and the same, as when Kafka would read his own works to his sisters and friends. At issue, first, is that Kafka the reader is producing effects beyond what Kafka the author achieved in writing the text, which compromises the status of the written word. Second, Kafka the reader seems to be enjoying recognition and praise that really belong to Kafka the author: the addition of the voice makes him parasitical on himself.

The second model of recitation outlined in the diary entry from January 4, 1912, is dictated, Kafka suggests, by the expectations and demands of his friends and colleagues Max Brod and Oskar Baum. It is characterized by calmness and distance and upholds a strict division between reader and work. The word "separation [*Sonderung*]" distinguishes this practice from the mixing and muddling of effects, the "flowing together [*in eins verfließe(n)*]," that occurs when reading to his sisters. In the presence of Brod and Baum, Kafka claims, he should not attempt to forge a union between reader and text through vocal effects or emotional ploys, lest he become "ridiculous [*lächerlich*]" to himself and others and turn red with shame. Instead, the proper distinctions—between work, performance, reciter, and author—should be maintained. Kafka projects this demand for sober performance and the maintenance of boundaries onto the rigid standards of other authors, the guardians of professional norms. This is why he refers repeatedly to what is expected, required, and wished for from him.

The supposed advantage to this affectless reading is that it allows the text to shine through more clearly, and thereby enables the listener to grasp the literary work as text—literally as "that which has been written [*das Geschriebene*]"—without the interference of anything superfluous and distracting. In the final breathless clause of the passage's last sentence, though, Kafka complicates this dichotomy with several twists. First he suggests that authorial expectations would dictate not that he read without *any* feeling, but in a generally calm and distant way, "and to become passionate only when a genuine passion demands it." This, Kafka states, he cannot do: he can read in a cold and neutral mode—this is "bad," but it is the recitational style he adopts for everyone other than his sisters—but he cannot adjust his presentation to the demands of the work. This seems to suggest that for Kafka the dramatic flair of recitation is a function of the relationship between reader and audience, rather than something that comes from the work itself. Second, Kafka indicates that even though he has resigned himself to the distant uninflected mode of recitation in professional contexts, as soon as he senses critique or disapproval, he feels tremendous embarrassment and is spurred on to read, "to read on endlessly, out of an unconscious yearning that during the course of the long reading there may be produced, at least in me, that vain, false feeling of integration with what I read." Thus, Kafka cannot in fact keep apart the two recitational styles, a failure that is triggered by the feeling of being censured. If the appeal of reading dramatically to the sisters lies in the recognition and admiration he accrues, what disturbs and undermines the straightforward style is the sense that his audience is dissatisfied with his performance. The feeling of critique produces a powerful if unconscious longing for unity with the text, which results in a relentless, even frantic reading, even though Kafka is aware of the deleterious effects of this style. The final lines of the quoted passage capture his resignation: his feelings of unity with the text will never produce "a clear overview" for the reader, and at home only the sisters' muddled impressions await him. Ultimately Kafka feels ambivalence about both recitational styles: the drive toward dramatic performance is powerful, even irresistible, because of his desire both for unity with the text and for audience approval, yet its results are neither satisfying nor respectable.

Kafka's ambivalence toward literary recitation can be understood in the context of historical and contemporary practice. As Müller explains in *The Second Voice*, there is a long and rich tradition of literary recitation, which does not, as some might think, die out in the twentieth century. If anything, it becomes increasingly differentiated, with distinctions drawn between reading aloud (*Vorlesen*), recitation (*Rezitieren*), declamation (*Deklamation*), and acting (*Schauspielerei*). These practices represent, at least in theory, a spectrum of vocal performance that ranges from strictly text-bound, straightforward, affectless, and gestureless reading to increasingly interpretive and dramatic performance.[31] Kafka thinks that Brod and Baum expect him simply to read aloud in a neutral style, perhaps punctuating his reading with a bit of recitational flair when the text demands it. At the same time Kafka seems to wish he were capable of some measure of theatricality, which would allow him to commune with the listener and the text to achieve a powerful emotional bond. But in his anxious excitement and fear of reproach he probably imagines, with fear and delight, that he is treading much riskier ground, perhaps even indulging in the liberties of *Schauspielerei*.

The actual place of Kafka's recitational practice on this spectrum cannot be known, but his *sense* of where it belongs is revealing. This feeling is determined by the norms, desires, and expectations at work in Kafka's imagination, which represent a complex web of projected and internalized rules. Thus he depicts the cold and distant manner of recitation as something imposed from without, though he also admits that these are subjective impressions. The expression "according to my feeling [*meinem Gefühl nach*]" appears twice, as if Kafka were trying to remind himself that the strains and pressures he perceives all come from *within*; indeed, the second time he uses this phrase he modifies the word "feeling [*Gefühl*]" with the clause "which can expect no support from the listener [*das keine Unterstützung vom Zuhörer zu erwarten hat*]." Kafka seems to recognize that the issue is not that others will find him ridiculous if he adds dramatic flourish to his recitation, but that he will find himself ridiculous. Kafka feels trapped by this internal sense of an external pressure to perform in a prescribed way. The expectation comes at once from without and from within.

This attitude and the rhetorical gesture that accompanies it are also at work in Kafka's famous *Letter to the Father* (*Brief an den Vater*, 1919). There his assumptions about his father's unreasonable expectations and his own inability to live up to them make his failure inevitable: the conflation of external and internal pressures guarantees disappointment. For example, early in the letter Kafka describes himself as "weak" and attributes to his father the qualities "strength, health, appetite, loudness of voice, eloquence, self-satisfaction, worldly superiority, stamina."[32] It is not this polarity alone that makes them incompatible, but its existence in the context of a father-son relationship:

> In any case, we were so different, and in our differences such a danger to each other that, had anyone wanted to predict how I, the slowly developing child, and you, the fully-grown man, would behave towards one another, they could have presumed that you would simply trample me underfoot until nothing of me remained.[33]

Convinced of his weakness and powerlessness in the eyes of his father, Kafka can only imagine complete domination by him. He thus projects a certain vision of himself onto his father, the necessary outcome of which is personal failure. Indeed, Kafka practically confesses his reliance on a logic of inevitable failure at the end of his letter, where he speculatively ventriloquizes the father's defensive and accusatory retort, to which he then provides a hypothetical counterresponse: "This whole reproach, which can in part be turned back against you, comes not from you but rather from me. Not even your mistrust of others is as great as my mistrust of myself, instilled in me by you."[34] Kafka recognizes that the demands and expectations of others originate in him, yet even his "mistrust of myself," which Kafka claims is stronger than the father's mistrust of him, is expropriated. By blaming the father for this, Kafka demonstrates the ultimate inextricability of inner guilt and outer pressure in matters of rules, conventions, and expectations.

The *Letter to the Father* is relevant to the discussion of Kafka's diary entry on recitation not only because they share a logic of inevitable disappointment, but also because they both invoke the idea of parasitism. In the letter, Kafka twice uses the word "parasite [*Schmarotzer*]" in his act of imaginative ventriloquism—that is, while speaking to himself in the father's voice:

> "Fundamentally, though, in this as in everything else, you have only proved to me that all my reproaches have been justified, and that one especially justified reproach was still lacking, namely reproach of your insincerity, your fawning, your feeding off me [*Schmarotzertums*]. If I am not sorely mistaken, you are feeding off me [*schmarotzest du*] even with this letter."[35]

The *Letter to the Father* shows that the logic of inevitable failure and the expropriated self-critique are closely linked. It also shows how tortured Kafka was by issues of artistic integrity. Writing, in Kafka's articulation of the father's critique, is itself a kind of parasitical activity—not simply because Kafka lives at home and relies on his parents for various practical aspects of life, but because his writerly praxis draws a great deal from his vexed relationship with his father.

The diary entry on recitation also expresses an internally generated critique from without. Kafka is torn between his own shameful desires and the supposed demands of others. This is clear not only from his subtle admission that much of his thinking about recitation derives from subjective feeling rather than explicit rules, but also from the use of the impersonal "man" and the passive voice. Kafka's concern with "what is wanted [*was man will*]," "what is expected [*was erwartet wird*]," and "what is permitted [*was ich darf*]" reflects a deep sense of obedience to the standards and expectations of others. This extract from the long entry quoted above is revealing:

> With my voice I flutter around what is being read, try to force my way in here and there because they [*man*] want me to, but don't intend this seriously because they [*man*] don't expect that much from me at all.

The first *man* (literally "one," but in this translation "they") refers not to an outside force but to Kafka himself: Kafka is the one who wants to use his voice to become one with the text, to penetrate it to the point where virtuoso performance completely overtakes the written word. By extension this "they [*man*]" also implicates a certain kind of listener, less sophisticated and more eager for entertainment than Kafka's literary crowd, such as his sisters: they too want Kafka to read in a certain way. The second "they [*man*]" refers to the invisible master—some amalgamation of Brod, Baum, professional strictures, and Kafka's bad conscience—who demands that Kafka's voice restrain itself, that it allow the text to act alone on the thoughts and feelings of the reader, without the artificial and supplementary effects of vocal ornament.

The conflict Kafka sets up between professional norms and personal vanity also reflects a degree of parasitism, even if it is not called that here. In the *Letter to the Father*, Kafka imagines that the father would consider even the writing of the letter a parasitical act, since the father-son relationship is itself a source of literary inspiration. In a famous letter to Max Brod from June 1921, Kafka states that the contemporary German-Jewish writer's "inspiration" comes from rejecting the father, rather than from any specific content or attitude, which seems to confirm that writing is predicated on a stormy and stressful father-son relationship.[36] This in turn implies that even this epistolary gesture toward reconciliation or self-justification is yet another literary act that feeds on the tensions and disagreements between father and son. The relationship exists for the sake of writing, not vice versa. His writing, Kafka imagines his father would charge, is parasitical on life.

The conflict between the speaker and the written text in Kafka's diary entry reflects a related misgiving or suspicion about sonification: recitation purports to amplify and enhance the written text, but actually feeds on it. This is why recitation is a parasitical activity, even when Kafka is reciting his own text. The reciter can never remain neutral and straightforward, becoming impassioned only in response to textual demands, but will instead always seek to delight and dazzle the audience, and thereby muddle impressions and take personal credit for textual effects. Recitation puts the performer in the spotlight, making it seem as though the work exists in order to be recited. According to Kafka, the relationship of dependence is in fact reversed—the act of vocalization is parasitical on the text—which makes the entire procedure of literary sonification even more distasteful. It is not plain scrounging, but *dishonest* scrounging, a sly reversal of the positions of parasite and host.

To summarize, the diary entry from early January 1912 posits an impossible ideal with regard to the prospect of literary sonification. There are two models of recitation, and neither is adequate, even if Kafka calls one of them "good" and one of them "bad." The "good" kind tries to create a union between the reader and the written word, but is false and vain. It is an attempt to be more than what one truly is, and to convey the benefits of this act of posturing onto one's work. The "bad" kind is cold and dry and gives little satisfaction, though it aspires to a clarity of effect. In the end Kafka cannot pull it off even when he tries, so the pure literary effect is compromised.

Despite these problems, the passage is shot through with a sense of the tremendous power of literary recitation: the feelings of pride and joy that presenting one's work can bring; the thrill of holding an audience captive; the hope of achieving a union between speaker, work, and audience; and the promise of a clear vision derived from the vocal transmission of a literary text. There remains a hope that bringing the literary text into the auditory dimension might breathe new life into it. This effect is enhanced by the breathless, convoluted, even pathetic style of the passage, especially toward the end, which might even function as a kind of textual substitute for a dramatic oral performance. Kafka achieves a kind of intimacy and union with the written word that is forbidden when it comes to reading aloud. This is a seepage of excess performative energy into the realm of personal writing: what Kafka cannot permit himself in an actual recitation, for reasons of shame and propriety, finds an outlet in the genre of the personal diary. Kafka's written description does not literally sonify, yet the writing is infused with the energy and drive of dramatic recitation. The winding prose, endless modifications and qualifications, and excited desperation of this passage reflect a compromise between the conflicting modes of recitation it describes. Perhaps, it suggests, a bit of drama, excess, and linguistic writhing and turmoil are permitted, provided they remain in the controlled (i.e., soundless) territory of the written word.

In much the same way that Kafka is drawn to the voice but unsure how to judge its effects, early film critics and audiences found the voice magical but confusing; they were unwilling to trust their ears, yet they simply could not stop listening. One reaction to this dilemma was to try to train the voice for the new art form at hand. A 1928 *New York Times* article on the advent of sound film stated:

> According to reports from Hollywood, voice culture is becoming the most popular exercise in town. It is said that vocal instructors have sprung up like flowers in the sunshine, or weeds in the rain, as the case may be. Doubtless there are competent teachers among them. Certainly charlatans will reap a harvest, at least for a time. That's the way things go in Hollywood.
>
> All of which is eloquent of the fact that many movie stars are vocally unfit. A few who have had stage experience, and still fewer blessed with natural tone and timbre of voice, are ready to step before the sound-recording machine without fear of unfavorable results. But the majority are not so lucky. They are indigenous to Screenland. They have grown up in the studios. Their voices have never been trained, and many of them, exceptionally endowed with personality and appearance, are markedly deficient in voice.[37]

Two movies that engage with this moment in film history are the 1952 musical *Singin' in the Rain*, which will be discussed below, and the 2011 film *The Artist*, which was discussed in chapter 1. These two films, one made about twenty-five years and the other about eighty-five years after the period they portray, depict silent film actors' unpreparedness for the new sound film, as well as possible remedies, such as voice lessons. An earlier film, Josef von Sternberg's 1930 *Der blaue Engel* (*The Blue Angel*), also reflects the problem of vocal training in the early sound film era.[38] This film both belongs to and thematizes the transitional moment in cinema history, and it presents a dual model of vocal training, both idealized and failed, which resonates with Kafka's dual model of recitation.

Sternberg's film can be read as an allegory for the advent of sound film, even though technologized sound is not an overt theme.[39] Still, the narrative centers around the topic of training voices and the obsolescence of old forms of vocalization in the modern entertainment industry. There are two main characters in *Der blaue Engel*, both of whose professional lives involve the training of voices. Professor Rath is an imposing schoolteacher who seems to have complete control over the sounds in his classroom. In an early scene he gives his pupils a writing assignment that they are to complete in silent concentration. He opens the classroom window, and a gentle, melodious chorus of girls' voices comes wafting in through the window. Rath enjoys the music until he discovers that one pupil has a sexy postcard of Lola-Lola, a singer from the local variety show; he promptly snatches it away and shuts the window, thereby restoring the order of silence and asserting control over the youth. This is an indication of Rath's acoustic authority, but it is also a demonstration of cinematic mastery on the part of the director and sound editor. When Rath closes the window, he blocks out external sound completely, a symbolic rather than realistic exercise of acoustic control that is as much a statement about the power of the new sound film as Rath's power. The film's thematization of the voice is closely linked to its new technical apparatus.

In another early scene, Rath gives a lesson in English pronunciation (figure 3.1). A student recites Hamlet's "To be or not to be" soliloquy, but he repeatedly pronounces the word "the" as "ze." Rath, a guardian of vocal perfection, tries hard to get the pupil to say the word correctly; he even places a pencil between the pupil's teeth. The humor of the scene, perhaps lost on German audiences, derives not only from the physicality of the pencil in the mouth, the bodily proximity of Rath and the pupil, and the deterioration of the lesson into a literal spitting contest, but also from the fact that Rath himself, played by the German actor Emil Jannings, cannot pronounce the word "the" correctly either. He is playing a vocal expert, but he is himself an amateur—at least according to the standards of the new sound film, in which Jannings is appearing for the first time. Jannings was also enlisted to play Rath in the English-language version of the film, a challenging role given his poor command of English. In *The Blue Angel*, Jannings's thickly accented

Figure 3.1. Vocal training in *Der blaue Engel.* Josef von Sternberg, *Der blaue Engel*, UFA, 1930 (New York: Kino on Video, 2001), DVD, disc 1, scene 3, "To be or not to be."

English signifies his Germanness, which excuses his imperfect English but undermines his position of mastery and demands for perfect pronunciation from his pupils.

The subtle undermining of Rath's vocal mastery prefigures the far more dramatic and violent undoing of his voice over the course of the film. Though Rath is generally a quiet type, in Lola's presence his silence is a sign of submission. Her voice, a synecdoche for her presence as a whole, overpowers him. In his classroom he controls voices, music, noise, and silence, but in the nightclub he is submissive and mute. Later, this setting turns him into a performer too: he uses his voice to entertain audiences by belting out "Kikirikiiii," the rooster's crow. Rath thus goes from being a respectable schoolteacher who controls and helps to refine the voices of others to someone who makes animal sounds for cheap laughs. In the film's dramatic climax, he is dragged onstage and forced to make his signature noise for the audience's amusement. He is stunned, silent, horrified, and terrified, but eventually emits a desperate, quivering, unmodulated, and seemingly endless crow, a kind of pure noise. Rath stumbles offstage, wanders through the streets, and returns to his old desk in his former classroom to die.

The noise Rath makes in his final onstage appearance is jarring, frightening, and dissonant. Not only is he unable to speak and prevented from remaining silent, but the only sound he can make seems entirely out of his control. His shrill and violent vocalization functions as a death cry. On the level of performance and production, however, this process of vocal demise demonstrates considerable training and practice, as well as masterful execution, since Rath's crowing is not actually babble or noise, but a carefully executed act of vocalization performed and recorded for the benefit of cinema audiences. When Rath's voice is at its absolute nadir, Jannings gives his most virtuosic vocal performance.

The voice of Rath/Jannings represents one model of vocal training in *Der blaue Engel,* and the voice of Lola/Marlene Dietrich another. The story of Lola's voice is one of endless repetition. In fact everything about her—including her nickname "Lola-Lola," which at one point appears written over and over on the blackboard in Rath's classroom—suggests an unbreakable cycle. Lola might seem to be a figure of upward mobility, since as the film progresses she commands increasing respect from others, assumes greater authority, and wears nicer clothes, but in fact she is hopelessly stuck. This is perhaps most evident in her final song, a repetition of her signature number "Falling in Love Again (Can't Help It)" ("Ich bin von Kopf bis Fuss auf Liebe eingestellt"), which she sings on the same stage where she first appeared, with an air of familiarity and resignation. In this scene her troupe has returned to the small-town dive where she met Rath: she is literally right back where she started. Her voice can only prolong the status quo; it can never raise her out of the lowbrow world of cabaret performance. Like Rath, she ends up where she began. But while his story is one of decline and death, hers is one of ineluctable vocal sameness and stasis.

The relationship between the character Lola and the actress Marlene Dietrich is also telling. Much as Rath's vocal nadir coincides with the apex of Jannings's vocal talent, Lola's tragic vocal fate—being doomed to sing the same song endlessly, a song that announces that she is no good for anything but giving her body for "love"—is actually what elevated Dietrich to stardom. The song was a huge hit, and its endless repetition was not only a sign of Dietrich's fame and success, but its very condition: endless repeatability is the premise of mass-market entertainment, perhaps especially when it comes to popular music. Moreover, everything that seems simple and degraded about Lola's voice was actually a product of extensive vocal training. In her autobiography, Dietrich explains that even though she had come out of Max Reinhardt's elite acting school and was from "a good family," she could speak the Berlin dialect (*Berlinerisch*) and teach it to others. Sternberg thus used her as a local expert and voice trainer for all the actors who had to speak in this dialect.[40] Dietrich clearly takes pride in her role, but she is also unsettled by the fact that this training requires her not to refine but to coarsen her voice. She thus insists on her cultivation and expertise—the elite acting school, her upstanding background—in the same breath that she asserts qualifications as a native speaker and teacher of the Berlin dialect. Once again the voice is involved in a productive disjunction: to depict vocal decline and degradation requires careful vocal training.

The English-language version of the film presents further complications. Unlike Jannings, Dietrich actually spoke English very well and went on to a successful career in Hollywood. For *The Blue Angel*, she received vocal training from Sternberg himself (who was born in Vienna but had lived in the United States for a long time before returning to Germany to make this film) and from his American editor, Sam Winton. Dietrich claimed in her autobiography that she was meant to play "an American floozy" who speaks a "vulgar American," whereas everyone else was supposed to be English and to speak British English.[41] These accents and their connotations do not fully come through in the English-language version of the movie, but it is a logical adaptation of the situation presented in the German original. Moreover, it shows that Sternberg wanted to use the new technology of sound film not simply to communicate the content of speech, but to convey precisely those aspects of speech that silent film cannot, such as pronunciation, intonation, and accent. He hoped to represent national and class differences as well as physical and emotional dimensions of speech and silence through a studied and careful use of the voice.

Der blaue Engel and *The Blue Angel* thus present two models of vocal training: one is aligned with tradition and respectability but is now obsolete, and the other is aligned with modernity and mass popular entertainment but is doomed to endless repetition. Neither model is ideal: the first is dignified but outmoded, and the second is current but degraded. However, the issue of sound looks very different when seen from the perspective of the film's production history and its multiple language versions. The process of vocal training and techniques of acoustic recording and playback are the film's condition of possibility. Thus any simple dichotomy between "good" and "bad" models of vocal training and sound use comes undone. Rath's dignified and professional manner at the start of the film is undermined by Jannings's actual vocal abilities, whereas the subsequent breakdown of his voice proves Jannings's skills as a sound film actor. Similarly, the apparent denigration of Lola's singing is undercut by Dietrich's rise to stardom, as well as the fact that she can play her part so well only because she has undergone rigorous vocal training for both versions.

The dual model of vocal training in *Der blaue Engel* / *The Blue Angel* is as fraught as the dual model of recitation in Kafka's diary entry from early January 1912. In both, ideal uses of the voice are posited and repeatedly undermined, and problematic ones are revealed to be practical and necessary, as well as penetrating and powerful in their own right. The voice can be put to the most dignified and lofty uses or it can be distorted and corrupted, but in any event outcomes do not seem to conform to given standards and expectations.

In each case a binary is set up—two types of recitation, two kinds of vocal training—but vocal realities only emerge in their interplay, in the disjunction between ideal forms and practical realities, between "good" and "bad" uses of the voice. Kafka's ideas about the voice in literary recitation and Sternberg's treatment of the voice in the new sound film show that the modern voice is a contested object, indeed that the voice in modernity is constituted by this contest. It takes the form of pitting vocal models against one another; these models gradually break down and thereby reveal the fault lines of the debate. The voice can still be idealized in the face of modern performance culture and the mass entertainment industry, but it is also fundamentally transformed by this encounter. The struggle over the voice, rather than any single position or attitude, is what defines its place in and for modernity.

Recitation, Plagiarism, and Dubbing: Borrowed Voices in Kafka and *Singin' in the Rain*

Less than two months after the diary entry that compares reading to his sisters and friends—during which time he holds his famous lecture on Yiddish at the Jewish Town Hall (*Jüdisches Rathaus*) in Prague, which will be discussed below—Kafka returns to the topic of recitation in a series of diary entries on Oskar Reichmann, a paranoid bank employee, aspiring reciter, and amateur writer whom Kafka meets by chance. In entries on February 27 and 28, 1912, Kafka relates Reichmann's predicament as an ambiguous, irresolvable parable about originality and imitation, performance and publication, and intellectual property and plagiarism. He examines the tension between the written and oral presentation of literature, and exaggerates the dangers of the reciting voice to the point of farce.[42]

According to Kafka's diary account, he meets Herr Reichmann during an evening stroll on Prague's Zeltnergasse. Reichmann approaches Kafka and begs for advice: he is a victim of plagiarism, he alleges, and this act of literary theft has occurred at the hands of a certain Frau Dürège, a woman who runs a literary and musical salon in Prague in which Reichmann and his brother take part: Reichmann recites, the brother, "a virtuoso," plays piano. After performing one evening—a detailed rundown of the program is provided—Reichmann offers to show Frau Dürège an original work of his, an essay called "Lebensfreude," or "Joy of Life" (*T* 385). As she is too busy to read it then and there, Reichmann leaves the manuscript with her. Two days later he wakes up to find "his essay, word for word his essay" printed in the morning paper (*D* 240). At first Reichmann is thrilled, and he runs to his mother to share the news of his success: "One son is already a virtuoso, now the other is becoming an author!" (*D* 240). In Reichmann's eyes, the development from reciter to author represents a rise in status: recitation is derivative, whereas being a musician or author is creative. (Reichmann's view is not entirely coherent, given that reciting literature and playing music both involve acoustic performances of works written or composed by others.) Now that Reichmann has finally created something of his own, he too will count as a "real artist," at least in his mother's eyes.

From the very beginning, Kafka's account gives the reader progressive cause for doubt. While it is relayed in a neutral and direct tone, without overt judgment and with minimal commentary, Reichmann's claims are subtly undermined over the course of the diary entry. For example, what Reichmann describes as an original work of literary essayism, Kafka paraphrases as "an appeal to youth not to be sad, for after all there is nature, freedom, Goethe, Schiller, Shakespeare, flowers, insects, etc."—in other words, a trite sentiment followed by a series of clichés and commonplaces (D 239). Kafka simply recounts Reichmann's tale and does not pronounce judgment, but the ridiculousness of the story speaks for itself.

After Reichmann's initial excitement about seeing his work in print, his mood quickly changes: his work has been published without his consent and without remuneration, and he is outraged and determined to right the wrong. Of course, the supposed literary theft would not matter if the only thing that counted was the work itself, but this is a selfless artistic ideal to which no one can really adhere—not Josefine with her demand for recognition, not Kafka with his desire to delight and impress his sisters, and certainly not the delusional and self-aggrandizing Reichmann. Reichmann's case is especially absurd because he has no legitimate claim to authorial credit, since he cannot prove that Frau Durège plagiarized his work. The title of the published essay is "Das Kind als Schöpfer," or "The Child as Creator," which is different from the title of the essay Reichmann claims to have given Durège (T 385–86). More damningly, he cannot identify any individual sentences or even words that have been lifted from his essay:

> In reply to my question whether he would not show me the passages which correspond, because that would interest me especially and because only then could I advise him what to do, he begins to read his essay, turns to another passage, leafs through it without finding anything, and finally says that everything was copied. (D 240)

The entry goes on:

> I read aloud a few of the more striking passages from the paper. Is that in the essay? No. This? No. This? No. Yes, but these are just the interpolated passages. In its spirit, the whole thing, the whole thing, is copied. But proving it, I am afraid, will be difficult. (D 241)

Kafka is humoring his new acquaintance; he is obviously incredulous. Reichmann has no proof against the patroness and he comes across as evermore unreasonable, even paranoid. He goes on to describe his confrontation with Frau Durège—accusing her outright of plagiarism—and the increasingly desperate, frantic, and far-fetched suspicions he harbors against her and the newspaper that printed his essay. He suggests, at the climax of what is possibly a mental breakdown, that a Zionist media conspiracy is colluding against him to steal his work. Reichmann marches into Durège's office, repeatedly shouts "J'accuse!," and then proceeds to the office of the newspaper that has published the essay. There he asks the editor if he is a Zionist, after which he declares, again, "J'accuse!" He rings up another newspaper—"I want to give them the story for publication"—but when he cannot get through, he becomes convinced it is because the telephone company and the press are conspiring to silence him and cover the crime up (D 243). He thinks he hears voices on the line whispering about him, thwarting his plans for justice and revenge. Persecution, conspiracy, Jewish media collusion, suspiciousness toward technology, and hearing voices all play a part in Reichmann's story. These are the hallmarks of paranoid thinking.

Despite Kafka's detached and even tone, the absurdity of Reichmann's actions and claims could hardly be more apparent. His references to Zola and Dreyfus, Zionist conspiracy, and tapped phones and media cover-ups only exacerbate what is already a ridiculous situation. Reichmann may or may not have actually written an essay, and if he did he may or may not have given it to Frau Durège, but it is quite clear that the essay published in the newspaper two days after this alleged encounter is most certainly not his own. Kafka says none of this to Reichmann, and there is no need to spell it out in the diary either. Two weeks later he writes a laconic postscript: "The reciter, Reichmann, landed in the insane asylum a day after our conversation" (D 250).

While the interest in Reichmann lies largely in his literary delusions and paranoid thinking—his fantasy, on some level, to inspire outrage against his enemy, win adherents for his cause, and stand at the center of a public scandal—Reichmann's role as reciter and how it shapes his misconceptions about literary property are also significant. Kafka references Reichmann's recitational practice when trying to convince him to let go of the matter with Durège. His text is a lost cause, Kafka admonishes, but his vocal performance can still be salvaged; in fact, if he drops the claim against Durège and the newspaper, he can still participate in that evening's recitation. Kafka's tactic is thus to distract Reichmann from his ambitions as a writer and to get him to focus instead on his role as a reciter. He even encourages him to take acting lessons.

Though writing and reciting seem opposed in this account, in Reichmann's case they are related instances of derivative expression. Reichmann wants to transition from being a reciter, a performer who uses his voice to present literature written by others, to being a writer himself, who pens his own works. But the transition fails: Reichmann can only recite the works of others and implausibly accuse others of stealing his words; there is no possibility for original creation, and little understanding of where his work ends and the work of others begins. For instance, he is convinced that "his" essay is renamed "The Child as Creator" as a sly reference to him, which displays the narcissism of paranoid thinking: not only does the paranoiac discover meaning in everything, he discovers that the meaning of everything has to do with him. Reichmann's delusions are about authorship (he is convinced he is in fact a creator) and deception (he is convinced he has been deceived and his creation has been mishandled). Thus, his paranoid thinking reveals that he still thinks like a reciter—that is, like someone whose art is fundamentally parasitical on the creative work of others.

If Kafka thinks that even his own readings blur the lines between author, work, and performer, and that recitation thus precludes clear impressions, these undesirable effects would apply even more to Reichmann's recitational practice, the very style of which is imitative: "He is a good reciter, he was not nearly as good in the past as he is now, now he can already imitate Kainz so that no one can tell the difference. People may say he only imitates him, but he puts in a lot of his own too. He is short, to be sure, but he has mimicry, memory, presence, everything, everything" (D 237–38). Reichmann's recitational practice is thus doubly derivative: he not only recites the work of others, gaining prestige and fame for himself which is due to the authors and works he is reciting; he also imitates the style and technique of other prominent reciters.[43] He can copy the famous actor Josef Kainz (1858–1910), he first boasts, only to retract the statement partially. Reichmann wants to be associated with this famous fin-de-siècle Austro-Hungarian vocal performer, though he does not want to be accused of pure mimicry and idolatry. The comment about Kainz, notwithstanding Reichmann's attempted backtracking, contributes to the growing sense that Reichmann is only capable of imitation.

In his paraphrased monologue to Kafka, Reichmann compares himself not only to Josef Kainz, but also to another reciter and actor in his mold: "Then [Goethe's] 'Prometheus' is on his program too. There he isn't afraid of anyone, not even of Moissi, Moissi drinks, he doesn't" (D 238). Alexander Moissi (1879–1935) was a remarkable figure who captured the imagination of numerous authors, not to mention countless audiences in his lifetime. Robert Musil, Karl Kraus, Stefan Zweig, Max Brod, and other contemporaries wrote descriptions or reviews of his virtuoso performances.[44] By all available accounts, Moissi was able to use his voice, face, and body in extremely evocative, if strange ways. A recording of him reading "Prometheus" is remarkable in its breathlessness, intensity, melodiousness, and clarity of articulation.[45]

According to Meyer-Kalkus's history of vocal art, Josef Kainz was the most prominent practitioner of a new style of recitation that emerged around 1900, and actors like Moissi were successful adapters of a method Kainz invented and popularized.[46] It was characterized by a modern interest in the physiology of the voice, and especially in testing its limits and possibilities.[47] This differs greatly from the upsurge of interest in vocal art around 1800, the aim of which was the standardization of accents and pronunciation.[48] Early twentieth-century recitational practices witnessed a turn to increasingly musical and dramatic interpretations and relied on various exaggerated acoustic gestures (overaccentuation, overmelodization) for their effects. Still, unlike the performative strategies of later schools, such as the Berlin "Sturm"-Kreis and Dada sound poetry, Kainz and Moissi represented an oratorical practice above all committed to the transmission and enhancement of textual meaning.[49]

With this in mind, it is interesting to return to Reichmann's references to these two reciters in describing his own vocal art. He claims to be able to imitate and even surpass Kainz, and not to *fear* Moissi—specifically, the comment implies, Moissi's rendition of Goethe's "Prometheus." Now, given that Moissi was a student and follower of Kainz, his recitational style was itself imitative. And Goethe's "Prometheus," originally written in 1774, first appeared in an anonymous and unauthorized edition published by the philosopher Friedrich Heinrich Jacobi in 1785,[50] making Goethe prey to precisely the sort of plagiaristic crime of which Reichmann considers himself a victim: Durège, in other words, is Reichmann's Jacobi. Such comparisons are absurd on one level, but they situate Reichmann's vocal art firmly within a set of vexed questions about literary production, performance, and ownership within the German literary tradition. They also exhibit Reichmann's delusions of grandeur: the touchstone for his literary work is Goethe, the most revered German writer of all time, and the touchstones for his vocal art are Kainz and Moissi, two of the most prominent living German-language reciters. All evidence suggests that Reichmann is a mediocre writer (the essay seems banal, regardless of whether he wrote it) and an unexceptional reciter (his style is derivative). His excessively dramatic presentation of his situation is what turns his story into farce.

Reichmann's claim to be a victim of plagiarism relates to the questionable status of his recitational practice. He is trying to produce something original—first by developing a unique style, then by writing an original work—but his plans are thwarted. As soon as he has written something, it gets snatched away and published without proper attribution or compensation. Moreover, what allegedly happens to Reichmann is much worse than anything he has done, since plagiarism is a far more sinister form of imitation than recitation, as it involves deception. For all the pretense and vanity of the reciter, he does not in general claim authorship when it is not due to him; he blurs the lines between author, reciter, text, and audience, but this is an unintended side effect of performance, not a deliberate theft. Thus, the intellectual crime of which Reichmann claims to be a victim seems graver than the one he himself perpetrates. Yet we must not forget that Reichmann in all likelihood only imagines that someone has plagiarized his work. This shows he is delusional and paranoid, but it also suggests a fine attunement to questions of intellectual property and artistic adaptation. One can see this fantasy of victimhood as a projection of Reichmann's (or Kafka's) own guilt, an expression of bad conscience. It signals the unpleasant, nagging feeling that he, "the reciter Reichmann," is nothing but a fraud, that his art is not really his own, and that he himself is precisely what he imagines Frau Durège to be: a thief and a copycat.

Reichmann's accusation and the conviction from which it stems can be seen as a compensatory gesture. In an attempt to counterbalance or draw attention away from his own dishonest artistic practice—or simply because the issue of artistic authenticity is never far from his mind—he indicts another person for an obviously worse one. The attempt at mental redirection involves a likening of plagiarism to recitation, or at least a suggestion that they exist on a single spectrum of artistic imitation. We need not believe Reichmann's absurd accusation or understand exactly what is wrong with him to see how Kafka's diary narrative presents both recitation and plagiarism as two possible outcomes of a certain set of unsavory tendencies and pretensions with respect to literature: dishonesty, lack of originality, and lust for fame. The discomfort with recitation rests in the distorting effects of vocalization, which can lead to the misapprehension of textual effects and the false assignment of credit. These are, in more obvious ways, also the consequences of plagiarism. As literary "practices," recitation and plagiarism are related in their divergence from some ideal of true and original art—literature that speaks for itself, silently—and differ perhaps only in their degree of deviation.

More than either the diary entry on reciting to friends and family discussed above or the one on Alexander Moissi that will be discussed below, the account of Reichmann seems to present a straightforward condemnation of the practice of recitation. Even if it is disreputable or unsavory on some level, the judgment of recitation is otherwise mixed with a sense of thrill, excitement, and dramatic potential. Kafka's reflections convey the feeling that, for better or for worse, recitation might be the most powerful mode of literary transmission available. When it comes to Reichmann, however, recitation seems beyond redemption. The fact that it is placed on the same spectrum as plagiarism seals this point; once recitation can be viewed as an instance of stolen words, it is beyond defense. Perhaps Kafka's position on recitation is so extreme here because he only hears Reichmann talk *about* recitation—he never witnesses an actual performance—and recitation is always less appealing as an idea than as a lived practice that can exert a seductive and powerful force over listeners. In theory, recitation is easy to condemn; in reality, it is hard to resist.

Another way to read Kafka's condemnation of Reichmann is to understand the whole diary entry as farce, a genre characterized by its deliberately exaggerated, comical representations and its depictions of improbable situations. The victims in farce are incapacitated in some way—for example, they are drunk or mad—which is crucial to their comic effects. These characters are two-dimensional and thus garner little sympathy, and the improbable, often impossible situations in which they are caught induce laughter. Farce suspends the laws of cause and effect in the service of an ulterior artistic motive, the inducement of laughter. According to one psychoanalytic theory of the genre, the immediate cause that unleashes this laughter is aggressive action, physical or otherwise, toward the victim. We can take pleasure in brutality against the victim because the world he inhabits is in some basic sense unreal and impossible. In a dialectic between id and superego, the chaos and lawlessness of farce finds satisfaction in aggression and punishment and release in laughter.[51] This theory usefully emphasizes the proximity of laughter and pain in farce.

Farce is not, generally speaking, a genre to which Kafka inclines, probably because it does not allow him to express the ambivalence and indecision he tends to feel about many things. But farce's physical humor and bodily gags, its slapstick and buffoonery, are arguably very present in a text like "Blumfeld, an Elderly Bachelor" ("Blumfeld, ein älterer Junggeselle," 1915). Farce frequently involves unwieldy objects and out-of-control machines that go berserk in ways that are very funny to witness. Blumfeld's celluloid balls take on a manic and uncontrollable life of their own. The wild and futile hunt for a document in an overstuffed room in *The Castle* derives its humor from a similar source. Man is subjected to the chaos and whims of the objects he once created, and this produces ironic laughter.[52] The Reichmann story is less obviously physical, but it contains many other premises of farce: improbable situations, exaggerated reactions, and incapacitated victims who are laughed at and arouse no sympathy. The diminished physicality of Reichmann's story results from the fact that it is a prose narrative, whereas farce is most palpable in the theater. A performance of Reichmann's story, which contains readily visualizable episodes that could be staged or filmed with little alteration, would certainly be hilarious. It is a melodramatic story, in which a minor, indeed imagined injustice is treated as a major transgression and a sign of widespread conspiracy; all of this lends itself to ridicule. Whether we believe that the diary narrative really happened as Kafka tells it or that Kafka made the whole thing up hardly matters. Either real life or Kafka's imagination has served up the material of farce. More precisely, Reichmann gives Kafka melodrama—because from his perspective he is a tragic victim, not a buffoon—and Kafka transforms it effortlessly into farce: he gives it a different emotional charge through his dry and detached tone. As one scholar notes, the difference between melodrama and farce is that with the former one feels sympathy for the character, whereas with the latter one feels "amused contempt, or affectionate contempt."[53] Kafka needs only to present Reichmann's story, without commentary, to elicit precisely this response. The transformation from pathos into bathos is automatic and effortless.

In much the same way that the topic of vocal training in and for *Der blaue Engel* runs parallel to Kafka's ambivalence about recitation, the farcical treatment of the voice in *Singin' in the Rain* contains numerous parallels to

Kafka's account of Reichmann. In both cases, there is a formal connection between the literary and filmic treatment of the voice that does not depend on direct influence or adaptation. In Kafka's Reichmann story and in Stanley Donen and Gene Kelly's musical about the dawn of the sound film era, voice stands at the heart of farce. One presents recitation as farce, and the other presents sound film, specifically the practice of dubbing, as farce, yet neither work entirely dismisses the vocal practice in question. The point of the exaggeration is not to disqualify and discard these uses of the voice, even if they are critiqued to the point of ridicule, but to show that vocal performance is *always* compromised. It is involved in a series of substitutions, imitations, and ploys, which suggests that there is no such thing as a "pure" voice in modernity. The power of the voice lies in these negotiations and compromises.

Singin' in the Rain is, quite overtly, a film about trying and failing to train the voice for modern mass entertainment culture. The American musical portrays four actors in the late 1920s who try to make the difficult transition from silent to sound film. Jean Hagen plays the ditzy starlet Lina Lamont, who steals the show precisely because her voice is so awful: she speaks in a piercing, high-pitched squeal, she has horrible diction and awkward pronunciation, and she sings terribly. None of this stops her from being a silent film star, but it presents a serious obstacle when her studio must transform a silent film she has acted in into a sound film and initially tries to do so by having her speak her own parts. Lina's voice, which is both grating and deeply funny, brilliantly encapsulates and parodies the fears that accompanied the advent of sound film. In a hilarious scene with a diction coach that recalls the schoolroom episode in *Der blaue Engel*, the coach repeatedly tries to get Lina to say "can't" in a proper (i.e., quasi-British) accent, but she can only reproduce her crass Brooklyn wide-mouthed, diphthonged "can't," in ever louder and more exaggerated tones. As in the scene where Rath tries to train the student's voice, Lina and the coach become increasingly agitated over the course of their vocal contest, as the pupil proves unable to repeat after the teacher. Lina's voice, it turns out, is untrainable. Nor can she speak into the microphone, which causes other technical problems with sound recording. Her unruly voice threatens to write her out of the acting profession. Lina's voice also embodies the film's farcical element: its awfulness is hilarious, not tragic. Though it spells the end of her career, to feel sympathy is the farthest thing from any viewer's mind.

To solve the problem, the film's jolly trio—Don (Gene Kelly), Cosmo (Donald O'Connor), and Kathy (Debbie Reynolds)—invents the process of sound dubbing.[54] Since Lina's voice cannot be used for the film in which she has acted, *The Dancing Cavalier*, Kathy's substitutes for it. Now, Kathy is an aspiring theater actress who initially considers herself above the silly and predictable formulas of Hollywood cinema. She fancies herself part of a world in which the voice is dignified, artistic, Shakespearian—that is, until she has to sing and speak Lina's part in the schmaltzy musical. The dubbing of voices is a vocal performance that requires a substitution: it is like recitation in that one voice (Kathy's) speaks and sings for another (Lina's), but also like plagiarism in that it involves an act of deception, as audiences are unaware of the substitution and Kathy receives no credit for her contribution. The vexed matter of vocal creation and ownership thus reflects both models of literary borrowing present in Kafka's Reichmann story, recitation and plagiarism.

Who owns a voice, who owns the sounds associated with it, and does it really matter as long as the audience is entertained? These would be the central questions to ask about *Singin' in the Rain*, from the perspective of Kafka's anxieties about vocal performance and its blurring of lines between author, reciter, text, and voice. But perhaps they are not the right questions for a light-hearted musical farce about Hollywood's transition to sound film, especially one in which Kathy emerges so clearly as the heroine and Lina as the clown. The musical, it seems, is too joyous, comical, and earnest to get mired in these issues of authorship and ownership. After all, the film depicts dubbing as a clever solution to a pressing problem, not a viable long-term practice. Eventually the hoax is revealed and Kathy emerges as the new star, on the basis of her vocal performance. *Singin' in the Rain* thus celebrates the idea that cinema cultivates the voice and that voice dominates the new sound film—real voices connected to real bodies, without tricks and substitutions.

Indeed, as the last scene of the film demonstrates, sound film will only succeed if it switches out actors, not voices: Lina walks offstage, shamed and ridiculed, and Kathy takes her place as the new star. It is worth reviewing how the film arrives at this point. After the success of the dubbed film, Lina is to perform a number on stage in front of a live audience. Panicked, she insists that Kathy stand behind the curtain and sing while Lina silently mouths the words to the song. Kathy reluctantly agrees, and in the middle of the song her friends, listening from backstage and finally ready to give Kathy the credit she longs for and deserves, raise the curtain: the audience can immediately see that it is Kathy who is singing, not Lina! This comedy of exposed voices turns to farce when Cosmo starts to sing, since at that point a man's voice appears to issue from Lina's body. Vocal substitution has transgressed a border, one constituted by gender, and this deepens the farce. The humor is physical and the victim is incapacitated, trapped in the act of exposed lip-syncing. We feel the "amused contempt" that Bermel described as the affective hallmark of farce.[55]

This reading makes sense within the film's diegesis: *Singin' in the Rain* is a celebration of real singing, the unity of body and voice, and the promise of the new sound film; dubbing is an amusing detour, the unviability of which ultimately confirms the triumph of the authentic voice. As the critic Peter Wollen puts it, "The core issue in the film is that of the relationship between sound and image. Things can only end happily when, so to speak, a properly 'married print' is produced, in which voice and image are naturally joined together. The underlying theme is that of nature as truth and unity, versus artifice as falsehood and separation."[56] Accordingly, Kathy's voice is the one that is worthy of our attention and admiration, from beginning to end, whereas Lina, with her ridiculous and inadvertently funny voice, is the object of ridicule, brutality, and laughter.

Yet there is much more to the story of *Singin' in the Rain* than what happens onscreen. Indeed, farce transcends the diegesis. The "endearing irony" of *Singin' in the Rain*, as Wollen puts it, is that Debbie Reynolds, who played Kathy, could *not* in fact sing; her character stands for the pinnacle of vocal talent and respectability, but her voice was actually terrible, indeed untrainable. Her voice had to be dubbed, and it was dubbed by none other than Jean Hagen, who played Lina, the character who embodies vocal crassness and disrepute.[57] This means that the character Lina Lamont, who cannot sing, has the character Kathy Selden sing for her (the diegetic act of dubbing), but since Kathy is being played by an actress who cannot herself sing, her voice must be dubbed in order for the film to be made (the nondiegetic act of dubbing). This self-dubbing indicates, first, that Lina's irritating high-pitched squeal is a voice that Hagen cultivates for the part: she plays someone whose voice cannot be trained, whereas in fact her vocal virtuosity lies in having learned how to speak and sing so poorly so well. Like *Der blaue Engel*, this film demonstrates that voices can be trained to sound bad. Second, the neat chiasmus of vocal substitution deepens the film's farcical treatment of voice. Hagen sings for Reynolds, but Kathy sings for Lina, but since Hagen is playing Lina, the substitutions come full circle: Hagen ends up singing for Lina, which is simply what sound film actors and actresses typically do—they speak and sing for their characters! Self-dubbing, a technical trick that artificially reconstructs the natural unity of voice and body, makes a joke out of vocal naturalism.

The film's production narrative thus undermines the straightforward glorification of vocal authenticity and the unity of voice and body that the diegetic narrative seems to advance. Hagen's voice in Lina's mouth is anything but natural and direct; it must pass through other bodies and machines before it emerges as speech and song. The film thereby deepens the farce that is introduced when Cosmo's voice suddenly seems to issue from Lina's mouth. Here the diegetic critique of dubbing is not only disingenuous and easily unmasked, but reliant on a successful act of dubbing. The moment of apparent vocal triumph and honesty—when Kathy's face and voice are finally united—is in reality the moment of separation, since the actress Jean Hagen is now singing not for her own character, Lina Lamont, but for another, Kathy Selden. The direct contradiction between what the film is saying and doing creates another kind of farce, in the more colloquial sense of the term: a joke, a hypocrisy. The production narrative, which relies on dubbing, makes a farce of the film's diegetic narrative, which presents the unity of voice and body in a triumphant return to dignified filmmaking. What had seemed a rigid ideology of the voice turns out to be marked by compromise, ambivalence, and play. Any number of beautiful voices could have been chosen for Kathy

Selden's, but *only* Jean Hagen's could subvert the film's apparent critique of dubbing so ingeniously, by adding a layer of comic irony to the vocal farce. Its simultaneous critique of and reliance on dubbing is the punch line to the film's inside joke.

In closing, it is worth remembering that dubbing is rejected in the film's diegesis for the same reasons that Kafka casts doubts on recitation: borrowing words, speaking in another's voice, and seductive performances preclude clear impressions and do not allow credit to be given where it is due. But dubbing and recitation are also appealing for the same reasons: they make for a good show and they allow stars to be born. The titillating problem of stolen voices lies at the heart of both practices. They compromise artistic originality and ownership, at the same time that they reveal how fraught these concepts are. Beneath the fraudulent, derivative voices of Oskar Reichmann and Lina Lamont lies not something authentic and true, but more vocal trickery. Since we are dealing with farce, though, we respond to these narratives with laughter, not despondency. Kafka's Reichmann story and *Singin' in the Rain* use comedy to explore the instabilities and risks surrounding voices in modernity. This does not undo the critique, but it does puncture it in a particularly Kafkaesque way. For once recitation and dubbing are presented as farce, they can be neither rejected nor embraced, but serve as evidence that the modern performing voice is defined by its compromised and contradictory operations.

Recitation, Ventriloquism, and the Singing Tramp: Vocal Magic in Kafka and Chaplin

On March 3, 1912, a few days after Kafka recorded his encounter with Reichmann, he wrote another remarkable diary entry about the actor and reciter whom Reichmann claimed "not to fear." Kafka had attended a reading by Alexander Moissi on February 28, 1912, at the Prague *Rudolfinum*, a magnificent performance hall, only two days after his alleged encounter with Reichmann. Moissi's recital included Goethe's "Prometheus" and began with a poem that Hugo von Hofmannsthal had written to commemorate Josef Kainz, who had died in Vienna in September 1910. Kafka, having just told Reichmann's tale, which made reference to both Goethe's poem and the reciter Kainz, was primed for Moissi's performance. He listened with rapt attention.

> March 3. February 28 to hear Moissi. Unnatural spectacle. He sits in apparent calm, whenever possible keeps his folded hands between his knees, his eyes on the book lying before him and lets his voice pass over us with the breath of a runner.—The hall's good acoustics. Not a word is lost, nor is there the whisper of an echo, instead everything

grows gradually larger, as though the voice, already occupied with something else, continued to exercise a direct aftereffect, it grows stronger after the initial impetus and swallows us up.—The possibilities one sees here for one's own voice. Just as the hall works to the advantage of Moissi's voice, his voice works to the advantage of ours. Shameless tricks and surprises [*Unverschämte Kunstgriffe und Überraschungen*] at which one must look down at the floor and which one would never use oneself: singing individual verses at the very beginning, for instance, "Sleep, Miriam, my child"; wandering around of the voice in the melody; rapid utterance of the May song, it seems as if only the tip of the tongue were stuck between the words; dividing the phrase "November wind" in order to push the "wind" down and then let it whistle upward.—If one looks up at the ceiling of the hall, one is drawn upward by the verses.—Goethe's poems unattainable for the reciter, but one cannot for that reason find fault with this recitation, for each poem moves toward the goal.—Great effect later, when in reciting the encore, Shakespeare's "Rain Song," he stood erect, was free of the text, pulled at his handkerchief and then crushed it in his hands, and his eyes sparkled.—Round cheeks and yet an angular face. Soft hair, stroked over and over again with soft movements of his hand.—The enthusiastic reviews that one has read are a help to him, in our opinion, only until the first hearing, then he becomes entangled in them and cannot produce a pure impression [*reinen Eindruck*].—This sort of reciting from a chair, with the book before one, reminds one a little of ventriloquism [*Bauchreden*]. The artist, seemingly uninvolved, sits there like us, in his bowed face we see only the mouth move from time to time, and instead of speaking the verses himself, he lets them be spoken over his head.—Despite the fact that so many melodies were to be heard, that the voice seemed as controlled as a light boat in the water, the melody of the verses could really not be heard.—Some words were dissolved by the voice, they were taken hold of so gently that they shot up into the air and had nothing more to do with the human voice until, out of sheer necessity, the voice spoke some sharp consonant or other, brought the word back to earth and completed it. (D 245–46, trans. modified; T 393–95)

Aside from naming a few authors and texts, Kafka does not comment on the literary works Moissi recites, which is consistent with the tendency, in recitation, to subordinate written text to performance. His voice, gestures, breath, and gaze, as well as the physical space his body occupies, rather than the texts he recites, shape the listener's experience. This focus on performance over text suggests that Moissi's style of recitation is closer to acting (*Schauspielerei*) than reading aloud (*Vorlesen*). It is thus unlike the distant and sober method Kafka associates with professional conduct and closer to the emotional and dramatic recitation he undertakes for the benefit of his sisters.

Moissi's recitational style was in all likelihood far more theatrical than Kafka's, not least because Moissi performed for sizable and anonymous audiences, whereas Kafka's dramatic flair was displayed only for family members and close friends in the privacy of his home. Kafka was clearly impressed by this histrionic style and by the power it gave Moissi over his listening public. For instance, he describes how Moissi's voice "pass[es] over us with the breath of a runner," and how it seems to exert an almost unnatural control over linguistic content. Not only is each word audible, but no excess sound is discernible. Moreover, Moissi's words seem to have a power that extends beyond the moment of articulation: they grow bigger, stronger, and even take on an aspect of threat. Moissi's recitational practice also infuses the written word with a sense of urgency and importance. It infuses the text with sound and body and endows the voice with gravitas and duration.

Almost every feature of Moissi's performance is overdone: it contains too many melodies, forced onomatopoeias, overaccentuated syllables and words, exaggerated facial expressions, and melodramatic hand gestures. The result, however, is not that Moissi seems ridiculous, but that he seems omnipotent; unlike Reichmann's story, Moissi's performance is not the material of farce. He commands the audience's auditory, visual, intellectual, and emotional attention in a way that is almost supernatural, though not absurd. His vocal dynamism relies on a complete subjugation of text to recitation, such that the spoken words seem to come alive in the voice of the reciter. At the end of the passage, Moissi appears to achieve a kind of union of voice and text, or perhaps the dissolution of the text *in* the voice. The speaking voice animates but also endangers the written word, which, dissolved in the act of recitation, begins to float away, until the voice regains control by uttering a sharp consonant. This act of release and seizure is a sign of vocal virtuosity. Moissi's ability to decompose and reconstitute the word at will indicates the reciter's total command of the works recited. It signals the triumph of performance over text.

From Kafka's perspective, the disadvantage of these vocal manipulations is that the listener cannot tell where the text ends and the voice begins. Nor can the listener determine where he or she ends and others begin, for Moissi's voice encloses individuals—"swallows us up"—and unifies them, transforming them into a community of listeners. This is clear from Kafka's use of the word "we" and "our": "His voice works to the advantage of ours." The ability to unify the audience and convey a sense of vocal empowerment to its members is familiar from several other works by Kafka. Josefine's vocal performance, whether it is singing or piping or nothing at all, brings the mice together to form a community and enables at least one of its members, the mouse who narrates the story, to speak. In much the same way that Moissi's voice makes "our" voice possible, Josefine's voice allows another voice to shape and speak for the community.[58] Kafka makes a related move in his "Lecture on the Yiddish Language," which I will discuss below: there he attempts to persuade the audience of German-speaking Prague Jews not only that they can understand the Yiddish of the East European Jews (*Ostjuden*), but that their languages belong to the same linguistic family.[59] The lecture represents another example of vocal artistry in which individual expression has a collectivizing function. Moissi's performance fits the pattern: it forges a sense of unity between audience and performer and instills confidence in listeners about their collective vocal powers.

Kafka appreciates Moissi's performance not only for the effects it has on listeners, but also for what it offers him as a practicing reciter. Moissi's voice is inspiring, emboldening, and empowering. But Kafka also sees its disadvantages in terms that clearly recall the internalized (and possibly invented) critique of his writer friends. In Moissi's performance, text, voice, body, and space are all mutually constitutive. This is a messy, if exhilarating predicament. Moissi's voice presents irresolvable contradictions behind a smooth surface. For example, Kafka remarks that despite the lyrical qualities of his recitation, the poetic melody that inheres in the work remains inaudible. Something is lost in the excessive emotion, drama, and rhythms of Moissi's performance, namely the music of the text itself. It is unclear whether Moissi's voice damages or defiles the work, or whether the voice is simply unable to transmit the written text. Though he cannot quite access Goethe's poems, Kafka does not blame Moissi for trying. What is clear is that the spoken and written versions of literature cannot be reconciled, and that the former is a potentially harmful deviation. Kafka confirms this point in the closing words of the entry, where he describes the dissolution of words in Moissi's voice: this is a threat to textual integrity, even if it inspires awe and reaffirms Kafka's initial impression of Moissi's supernatural powers. As Rüdiger Schaper writes in his biography of the actor: "Does it not seem that Kafka too could barely withstand the experience of an Alexander Moissi onstage? For on the one hand he felt this recitation artist to be gimmicky and mannered, and on the other hand he was overwhelmed by his presence?"[60]

Kafka explicitly critiques Moissi's use of vocal tricks. What appears to be a higher power in Moissi—words that seem to float freely above the speaker and his voice—is exposed as a special effect of Moissi's novice ventriloquism. Kafka calls these illusions "shameless tricks and surprises" that one would be embarrassed to use. Here again the use of the pronoun *man*, translated as "they" or "one," is complicated: Kafka's comment must mean that one *ought* not employ such vocal tricks, that no self-respecting person would do so, since we know from his diary entry from January 4, 1912, that he *does* in fact try to impress his sisters through similar vocal ploys. This *man*, then, represents the looming presence of Kafka's social and professional conscience. It explains Kafka's awkward confession of shame on behalf of another: in one sense he disapproves of Moissi's behavior, but in another sense he admires his free spirit, his willingness to engage in dramatic and flamboyant public recitation, something that Kafka barely permits himself in intimate circles. Kafka discovers in Moissi a reciter who boldly and shamelessly achieves what Kafka secretly desires—to infuse his recitations with emotion and drama, and to relish the recognition and fame that such performances bring. This explains the simultaneous sense of superiority and awe in the tone of Kafka's diary entry. Moissi is bold and shameless, two things that Kafka is not. But he is also a fraud.[61]

Kafka's most revealing comment about Moissi's performance is the reference to ventriloquism, yet another vocal practice that can be considered alongside recitation, sound film acting, and dubbing. Ventriloquism is a form of direct vocal substitution that requires no technological manipulation but a good deal of skill and training: one must speak without moving one's mouth, with lips slightly parted, so that the sounds appear to be coming from somewhere else, usually a handheld dummy. "To ventriloquize" literally means "to speak from the belly," which is reflected in the German word *Bauchreden*. Though Moissi is not actually ventriloquizing, this is the impression he makes:

> This sort of reciting from a chair, with the book before one, reminds one a little of ventriloquism. The artist, seemingly uninvolved, sits there like us, in his bowed face we see only the mouth move from time to time, and instead of speaking the verses himself, he lets them be spoken over his head.

In this description, the ventriloquist's dummy is replaced by the book, a telling substitution in light of Kafka's misgivings about the relationship between the reciter's voice and the written text. Moissi does not speak for an inanimate other, but for literature itself: his ventriloquism gives voice directly to the text; indeed, it purports to *be* the voice of the text. If Moissi seems uninvolved, not even fully present as a reader, this speaks to the fantasy of a self-vocalizing text. The use of the passive voice supports this idea: the verses *are spoken* over Moissi's head, as if the text had its own vocal will.

This is probably Kafka's most idealized articulation of the powers of recitation, since it imagines the elimination of the reciter, and thus of his body, his gestures, and his physical presence. All that remains is a seemingly disembodied voice, which can appear as the "natural" voice of the text. If the text can "speak itself," questions of theft, appropriation, and the usurpation of credit and fame fall away. But we should not forget that for Kafka this kind of recitation is as repellant—"antinatural [*widernatürlich*]"—as it is magical. This adjective captures a sense of the supernatural and the wondrous, the abnormal and the degenerate. More than any other instance of vocal borrowing in Kafka's diaries, Moissi's ventriloquism treads the fine line between charlatanry and transcendence.

Kafka objects to Moissi's vocal gimmicks not only on aesthetic grounds, but because his performance, despite its thrills, is ultimately unsatisfying: "The enthusiastic reviews that one has read are a help to him, in our opinion, only until the first hearing, then he becomes entangled in them and cannot produce a *pure impression* [*reinen Eindruck*]" (emphasis added). The idea of the "pure impression" seems to belong to the same semantic field as the "clear vision of the listener [*klare Überblick des Zuhörers*]" of the earlier diary entry, which literary recitation also precludes. In Moissi's mouth, melodies become inaudible and words are "dissolved by the voice": this is precisely the muddying of effects that Kafka finds dangerous and unsettling in all recitation. Regardless of what it achieves for the listener, including sensations of pleasure and power, the practice of reading a work aloud blurs the listener's impression of it. It provides for a literary experience that is more intense and intimate, but also less clear and distinct. Since the listener is unable to draw sharp lines between reciter, author, text, and voice, the impression remains impure.

It is difficult to give a precise account of the "pure impression" in Kafka's thinking, since it is generally presented as an unrealized goal, a negative ideal, from the perspective of both performer and listener. Kafka uses the phrase on a few other occasions in his diaries to refer to the effect that certain recitations, lectures, and theater performances have on him. In the first, he describes his own reaction to a reading by Baum of several recently published works: "I was indifferent, in a bad mood, got no clear impression [*reinen Eindruck*] of the whole" (*D* 221; *T* 357). Here Kafka attributes the failure to produce a pure impression to his own mood, rather than to Baum's reading style, which suggests that the attitude of the listener is crucial to achieving this effect. In the second, he gives an account of his reaction to a theatrical performance: "For this first time on this fourth evening my distinct inability to get a clear impression [*reinen Eindruck*]. Our large company and the visits at my sisters' table were also responsible for it. Nevertheless I needn't have been so weak" (*D* 107; *T* 96). Here he uses the phrase "a pure impression" to describe his reaction to a performance of *Kol-Nidre*, a recent play by the Jewish writer Abraham Scharkansky that Kafka saw while the Yiddish theater troupe was in town. Kafka blames not only the actors and the audience, but his own feebleness for his failure to produce a pure impression.

It is clear how the first of these references to the "pure impression" relates to the description of Moissi, since it is also made in connection with a recitation. The second instance is further removed, but still relevant. The title of the play, which Kafka does not think is very good, is revealing: it names the evening service on Yom Kippur, the Jewish Day of Atonement, and the prayer with which that service opens. The Kol Nidre prayer, sung in Aramaic rather than Hebrew, is among the most moving, intense, and melancholy of the Jewish liturgy. Traditionally, this sad melody is chanted first in a soft and subdued voice, then repeated in increasingly loud and confident tones. Kafka writes about Kol Nidre—not the play, but the service and prayer—elsewhere in his diaries, after attending a Yom Kippur service at the Altneu Synagogue. That entry is from October 1, 1911, just three weeks before he comments on Scharkansky's play. He also describes the religious service as a failed acoustic experience: it leaves the listener "without the slightest conception of it all and without the possibility of orientation" (*D* 72). Like the theatrical *Kol-Nidre*, the religious service renders him incapable of forming "a pure impression." Whether literary, religious, or theatrical, these instances of vocal expression all reflect the inability of voices to generate a distinct, complete, and satisfying auditory effect.

The "pure impression" thus refers to an unattainable auditory ideal. In Kafka's experience, vocal performances leave the listener disoriented, confused, or simply uneasy, due to the fleeting quality of spoken language and its uneasy relationship to texts and authors. The words, dislodged from their textual foundation, seem to come and go according to the will of the reciter. Kafka suggests that there is a kind of deception built into the act of recitation: the reciter acts as though the work is only born in the act of recitation, and thus conceals or at best ignores its original textual status. It is telling that Kafka originally refers to the texts he recites as "that which is read aloud [*das Vorgelesene*]" or "that which is to be read aloud [*das Vorzulesende*]," as if the text's *raison d'être* were to be recited and it only came into being in the act of vocalization. Only later does he call them "works [*Werke*]," and thus shift the emphasis to the written artifact. Having questioned the seductive appeal of recitation, he insists on prioritizing the textual status of the literary work.

These performances also fail to produce "pure impressions" because they rely too heavily on extralinguistic dimensions of speech and voice. In addition to the reciter, the listener must also employ her body and its entire affective apparatus to take in the spoken word. She must grasp linguistic content, as well as vocal effects, facial expressions, hand gestures, and body movement. Her task is complicated by the fact that the rules for this kind of corporeal and emotional listening are not clearly defined and its yield not fully apparent. This contributes to the sense of vulnerability, even threat that Kafka feels at Moissi's performance. He cannot grasp precisely what is required of him, yet he knows he must do more than simply sharpen his ears.

Finally, the various acoustic events which fail to produce a "pure impression" all have an indeterminate relationship to music. These performances are not strictly musical,[62] but they do draw on certain features of music: they are characterized by elusive melodies, dissolved words, wandering voices, chanting, whistling, and humming. They are disturbing and intriguing because they cannot be pinned down; they play with both language and music, and thus occupy an acoustic borderland. This explains the disorientation Kafka feels as a listener and the discomfort he feels as a reciter: "With my voice I flutter around [*umfliege*] what is being read," he writes about himself; "wandering around [*ein Herumirren*] of the voice in the melody," he writes of Moissi. Kafka associates the voice of the reciter with circling, meandering movement.

It is a voice that floats, flows, and never settles down, its task unclear and its effect murky. It comes as no surprise, then, that recitation fails to produce a "pure impression" in the listener. It is a practice defined by commotion and confusion, one that relies on blurring the very distinctions that Kafka would like to uphold—between creator, work, and audience; between physical, cognitive, and emotional reactions; and between the methods and materials proper to each form of artistic expression.

However, Kafka's diaries do contain one example of a successful "pure impression." In December 1913, after attending a talk by his friend Hugo Bergmann, Kafka writes: "Lecture by Bergmann, 'Moses and the Present.' Pure impression [*Reiner Eindruck*]" (*D* 323–24; *T* 616). Kafka proceeds to offer a rather dry and direct paraphrase of the lecture—which was apparently about the historical person Moses and the relationship of freedom and slavery—and dismissively notes, "In any event I have nothing to do with it" (*D* 324). Despite this summary disavowal, the description that follows demonstrates that the lecture has *everything* to do with Kafka:

> There am I. I cannot leave. I have nothing to complain about. I do not suffer excessively, for I do not suffer consistently, it does not pile up, at least I do not feel it for the time being, and the degree of my suffering is far less than the suffering that is perhaps my due. (*D* 324)

When Kafka claims that the lecture has "nothing to do" with him, he clearly does not mean that its content is irrelevant to him. This diary entry comes from the first major period of Kafka's interest in Jewish issues (theology, Eastern Jewry, Yiddish, Zionism), so the topic is clearly interesting and pertinent to him. Moreover, the existential situation he describes—of suffering, stasis, and guilt, which nevertheless preclude self-pity—is obviously one that preoccupied Kafka for much of his writing life. It thus seems that he is commenting not on the lecture's topical relevance for him but on his emotional distance from it: it cannot touch him, cannot reach him. This is precisely why it can leave a "pure impression": the listener does not get sucked into the affective or psychological aspects of acoustic performance, but remains grounded and is therefore able to grasp the spoken words distinctly and completely. In short, to have "nothing to do" with the lecture is a good thing. It means that the seductive powers of acoustic performance are kept at bay, and Kafka can focus instead on the lecture's substance and meaning.

Kafka's remark about Bergmann's lecture suggests that the "pure impression," more than just a negative ideal, is something that can, under rare circumstances, actually be attained. It is a product of neutral, uninvolved, unemotional listening, which is itself enabled by a sober and direct presentational style. It is not a coincidence that Bergmann is neither performing theater or recitation, but giving an academic lecture. "Pure impressions" are possible when there is a clear and simple relationship between voice and text.

Then there is no room for "vocal magic," as practiced by the likes of Alexander Moissi, which artfully twists and embellishes words such that content and meaning are subordinated to feelings of wonder, play, and exhilaration.

As in the case of the first two diary entries on recitation, the description of Moissi can be productively related to the anxieties about voice that accompanied the introduction of sound film. Kafka's suggestion that the vocal performer was a kind of magician, or that the effects of his vocalization were supernatural, would resurface two decades later in early sound film: James Cruze's *The Great Gabbo* (1929), starring Erich von Stroheim, and Charlie Chaplin's *Modern Times* (1936) illustrate this point. In the former, ventriloquism itself is a cipher for the new sound film: disembodied and reembodied voices require mechanical manipulation and vocal trickery to achieve their effects. The latter makes a limited, cautious, and belated use of sound, tinged with both skepticism and a sense of wonder. Stroheim's ventriloquist and Chaplin's tramp emerge as Alexander Moissi's long-lost cinematic brothers.

The Great Gabbo tells the story of a virtuosic but cantankerous ventriloquist, Gabbo. He is a textbook misanthrope and bully, except when he is speaking through his dummy, Otto, who is capable of kindness, warmth, gratitude, and humility, and who functions as an externalization of certain "soft" qualities that Gabbo is otherwise unwilling or unable to express. Otto thus signifies its homophone "auto" (self): he is Gabbo, he completes him. The fact that most of Gabbo and Otto's banter revolves around the topic of identity—of sameness and difference—seems to confirm their oneness. Yet Otto sounds rather different from Gabbo, in terms of content and affect as well as accent, tone, and pitch. Though they both speak an "Austrian"-accented English (like the actor Stroheim)[63] interspersed with moments of English-accented German, Otto's German accent is more pronounced, his voice higher, and his speech more rhythmic. Otto's voice distills and embodies all that is playful, light-hearted, and childlike in Gabbo.

As Spadoni notes, "*The Great Gabbo* exploits, rather than resists, the transparently ventriloquistic nature of early sound film."[64] The acts of ventriloquism depicted in the film thus function as an allegory for the new sound film. Gabbo's ventriloquism not only *appears* magical, it is in fact impossible: he eats, drinks, and smokes while Otto speaks and sings, and he often neglects to manipulate Otto's jaw and head while Otto speaks or sings. In general ventriloquism seems at least a little bit magical—this is why we are impressed by it—but here it is in fact a film trick. The character Gabbo is not actually speaking for Otto while he is eating, drinking, and smoking, or probably ever. The actor Stroheim speaks for both of them, though not at the same time, which means that the film's central diegetic performance requires cinematic manipulation. What is presented as Gabbo's virtuoso ventriloquism, a kind of vocal magic, is really a product of sound recording, editing, and dubbing. Given that this situation is obvious to any viewer—that Gabbo is not speaking or singing for Otto is plain to see, and his arrogance and non-chalance only confirm this—this is not a "fail[ure] to convince," as Spadoni suggests, but the film's overt and self-conscious contradiction.[65] It simultaneously showcases and deflates the idea of virtuosic vocal performance by exaggerating a practice to the point of impossibility or magic. The very thing that is impressive about real ventriloquism becomes a joke and a fraud in the film's presentation of illusory ventriloquism. This might be an indictment of the new sound film, as it is based on tricks and deception, or it might be a celebration of its extraordinary powers of vocal manipulation and display.

The scene at the end of the film that expressionistically depicts Gabbo's mental breakdown functions according to a similar logic. Gabbo's mind becomes inundated with an excess of sounds and images that derive from earlier moments in the film, which is conveyed through a cacophony of sound and multiple exposures pieced together in an onscreen collage. The onset of Gabbo's decline is clearly the film's moment of technical triumph. As with the other films analyzed in this chapter, there is a disjunction between the diegetic attitude toward sound, which is largely negative, and the actual function and manipulation of sound on the level of production and audience effect. This ambivalence, which ultimately renders the status of vocal performance undecidable, links *The Great Gabbo* to Kafka's depiction of Moissi. These vocal contradictions point to the contested status of the voice in modernity.

Modern Times was made in 1936, nearly ten years after the introduction of sound film, and at least four years after the medium of silent film was all but abandoned. It is a direct and explicit rejection of the new sound film, yet it makes a limited use of sound, though not the technology of integrated synchronized film sound that had revolutionized filmmaking around 1927. The film is a self-conscious relic, and a masterpiece—indeed, it illustrates the phenomenon of the relic *as* masterpiece. Still, a very limited amount of speech is included in the audio track that accompanies the silent film, which consists mostly of music and sound effects, such as factory and city noise. Certain figures of authority and power (the factory owner, the prison warden) speak, though their speech is almost always technologically mediated (they communicate through radios, televisions, or phonographs) and their message is always one of control and repression. Technologically mediated sound is negatively coded.[66] In contrast, the film's two stars, Charlie Chaplin and Paulette Goddard, are masters of gesture, facial expression, and body movement; they laugh, grimace, dance, and roller-skate their way through the movie—which is to say, they communicate with their bodies and have no need for spoken language. *Modern Times* not only resists what is by 1936 the established norm of sound film, but also finds ways, within the bounds of silent film, to critique the use of sound.[67]

But there is one episode near the end of *Modern Times* that complicates this clear-cut picture: the famous scene in which the tramp sings his gibberish song. Even those critics who emphasize how the film aligns sound with the other forms of technological and industrial oppression that it critiques cannot account for this episode. For instance, one critic who makes the point that the film only uses sound to convey "negative messages . . . that relate either to social or industrial oppression," must offer this parenthetical caveat when it comes to the singing scene: "The tramp's comic song is not like these moments, obviously. But it is only necessary here to point out that it too ridicules socially oppressive codes in its nonsensical language that yet manages to relate a smutty story."[68]

In fact, the tramp's song contradicts every other use of sound the film has made until this point: it is illogical, liberating, playful, and funny. His voice is everything that the harsh, rationalizing, authoritarian voices in the film are not. The song he performs is nonsense but it communicates a story; it resembles Italian and French without actually being any single language or even a combination of languages; and it contains a mishmash of speechlike sounds that can be enunciated and intoned as if they were words, without actually being language. In short, the tramp's voice produces broadly comprehensible gibberish with a superficial resemblance to speech. This is the voice that the patrons of the restaurant are waiting for, and that audiences the world over have been excitedly anticipating for nearly a decade: Chaplin's voice onscreen. Nine years after the invention of sound film Chaplin's tramp has finally learned to speak and to sing. The debut is tremendous and shocking, for his voice defies all norms and expectations.

The tramp's performance is brilliant and foolish, sublime and ridiculous. We know it is entertaining, but is it art, and does it even matter? Like Moissi's performance, it seems to defile and distort language, yet the "words" become more, not less powerful and evocative in this disfigurement. Like recitation in general, the tramp's song denies the audience a "pure impression": one does not know what to call it or how to evaluate it, except to say that it is amusing, enjoyable, and memorable. In fact, this might be precisely what bothers Kafka so much about recitation—it is pleasing in ways that cannot be identified, because its effects are so muddled—whereas this muddling of effects is precisely what appeals to Chaplin. Rational, direct, normative uses of the voice are highly suspect, since they represent so many attempts to control others: this is true within the diegesis of *Modern Times*, but it is also a comment about conventional uses of sound in film, which manipulate the viewer into thinking and feeling in prescribed ways. Chaplin's resistance to sound is consistent with film theorists such as Arnheim and Balázs, who call for a disruptive, even "contrapuntal"[69] use of sound, rather than a realistic one. The nonsense song is a clever critique from within: Chaplin's voice can finally be heard onscreen, and not a word of it makes sense. Entangled in tricks and games, his is a voice that breaks the mold—of language, of meaning, of cinematic convention—and in so doing surprises, shocks, and delights the viewer. Chaplin bursts onto the sound film scene with a voice whose effects lie somewhere between magic and noise.

As a point of comparison, it is worth considering the film Chaplin made after *Modern Times, The Great Dictator* (1940). This is his first actual sound film, and it is here that the multiple voices of Charlie Chaplin make their appearance. If the singing scene in *Modern Times* combines the ridiculous and the sublime in a single delightfully undecidable vocal performance, *The Great Dictator* separates out these effects. Charlie Chaplin plays both Adenoid Hynkel, a parody of Adolf Hitler, and a poor Jewish barber who is also a World War I veteran. There are numerous scenes where Hynkel speaks a mock German that could be compared to the mock-French/Italian song of the earlier film: it sounds like German, and even contains a few German words—mostly food-related ones, such as sauerkraut and Wiener schnitzel—but it is definitely not real German. Hynkel's speeches are pure comedic gold, precisely because he can mimic and exaggerate the sounds of German so well, particularly Hitler's Austrian accent and intonation, while actually talking nonsense. This works as both slapstick and a critique of Hitler's propagandistic speeches, which are as nonsensical as Hynkel's German. The title *The Great Dictator*—as in, the one who dictates—refers not only to Hitler's tyrannical behavior, but to the power and significance of his voice, his live speeches, and his radio addresses; as one critic puts it, he is "the great dictaphone, so to speak."[70] Hynkel, the antagonist of Chaplin's first real sound film, embodies the worst vices of the reciter.

In the final scenes of the movie Hynkel has been accidentally arrested and the down-and-out Jew, having escaped from captivity dressed like an officer in Hynkel's party, is mistaken for the dictator. He is brought to a stage to speak before an enormous gathering of people, where he gives a clichéd but touching speech about human compassion, tolerance, and democracy. This speech is held in Chaplin's true voice, in every sense of the word. If the mock-German speeches represent Chaplin channeling Hitler with extraordinary humor, scorn, and powers of imitation, the second speech represents Chaplin's voice laid bare.[71] As Adrian Daub notes, the film's final speech can be read as "insisting that if real communicative speech were to take the place of Hynkel's half-hysterical, half-cynical ejaculations, those cheering him would somehow be roused from their mindless devotion."[72] Chaplin no longer wants to use sound to critique sound film, nor is he interested in using it to enhance silent film's gestural language, which is arguably its function in the gibberish song and in Hynkel-speak. The barber's speech is Chaplin's direct address to the camera and his worldwide audience. Here sound film is the platform for making a mass-media appeal to human reason and compassion.

In *Modern Times* there is a single vocal act, ridiculous and sublime, that redeems the voice from baseness and oppression. In *The Great Dictator*, this unity of the voice is no longer possible, and Chaplin must speak in two distinct, even opposed voices in order to distinguish the ridiculous—which is now also associated with the dangerous and murderous—from the sublime.[73]

In other words, the stakes are incomparably higher. One voice can no longer contain a multiplicity within it, since what is multiple contains contradictions that spell the difference between life and death. Rather, one body is capable of speaking in multiple voices, depending on whether the situation calls for comedy or sobriety. Once his political message takes center stage, Chaplin is no longer willing to merge the ridiculous and the sublime in the manner of *Modern Times*, an aesthetic choice dictated by dark times. Thus, the nonsense of Hynkel-speak turns out to be less complex than the nonsense of the gibberish song, whose indeterminate status allows it to straddle the line between magic and noise. Nevertheless, the relationship between Hynkel's and Chaplin's recitations, like that between Gabbo's cynical speech and Otto's cheerful performances, testifies to the significance of vocal masks in aesthetic modernity: single bodies make multiple, sometimes contradictory uses of the voice. For Kafka, Moissi was the fullest embodiment of this phenomenon.

Yiddish Voices: The Lecture as Recitation

In general, Kafka's accounts of recitation treat the voice as supplemental: the foundation of literature is written, and the act of speaking produces a derivative form. There are certain advantages and disadvantages to recitation, to be sure, but it is clear and unavoidable that bringing literature into the acoustic dimension detaches it from the written word. This is why Kafka's accounts of recitation are always pulled between the thrilling flight away from the text and the nervous insistence on remaining close to it. His descriptions of recitation probe what can get lost, confused, or distorted by the act of vocalization.

One work in Kafka's oeuvre, his "Speech on the Yiddish Language," complicates this pattern of excited ambivalence toward vocalization. Like the instances of recitation described in his diaries, the speech is delivered orally before an audience, but unlike them it is not based on a written text. The published version derives from the vocal performance, not the other way around. Kafka delivered the lecture from notes that are now lost, and the available text is a transcription by Elsa Taussig, Kafka's friend and Max Brod's future wife.[74] Kafka's lecture on Yiddish thus presents a precise inversion of the situation I have been describing—not a literary work that is potentially compromised in the act of recitation, but a vocal performance that is potentially compromised in the act of being written down.

Kafka's lecture on Yiddish has received a great deal of critical attention in the last thirty years, since it stands at the heart of many readings of "Jewish Kafka." Already in the 1970s and '80s, critics such as Ritchie Robertson and Giuliano Baioni recognized the significance of this work for Kafka studies, and it received much more attention after Gilles Deleuze and Félix Guattari published their work on Kafka and minor literature, which emphasized his relationship to Yiddish. More recently, the literary scholars Iris Bruce, David

Suchoff, Dan Miron, and Vivian Liska[75] have offered compelling though divergent readings of the lecture on Yiddish. I wish not to contribute another perspective on the vexing and fascinating question of Kafka's attitude toward Yiddish and Eastern Jewry (how much he really knew, how much he really cared, how much it influenced his life and writing, etc.) but to ask something new about the lecture: what can it tell us about his attitude toward recitation?[76]

To answer this question it is less important to look at the lecture's text—which, as noted, is supplemental and subsequent to the event—than to examine Kafka's accounts of the performance: his diary entries about preparing for the event, from February 8 and 13, 1912, and another long entry in which he gives a postlecture report, from February 25, 1912. These accounts reveal that Kafka thought about the lecture in terms similar to the ones in which he thought about recitation. Its effects could move and impress listeners, but also deceive them; it makes him feel powerful in a way that cannot be trusted, since this power seems to rest on a kind of magic or trickery; and it raises the possibly unrealistic hope of making a pure impression.

As he prepares for the lecture, Kafka is full of nervous excitement and energy, which is simultaneously debilitating and empowering. He describes himself as anxious, weak, and restless: "An incessant excitement has been oppressing me for days"; he is "overpowered by uncontrollable twitchings, the pulsing of my arteries sprang along my body like little flames" (D 232). But he also feels confident:

> I shall, of course, give a good lecture, that is certain, besides, the restlessness itself, heightened to an extreme that evening, will pull me together in such a way that there will not be room for restlessness and the talk will come straight out of me as though out of a gun barrel. But it is possible that I shall collapse after it, in any event I shall not be able to get over it for a long time. (D 232)

Kafka's anxious energy wracks his nerves, but it also guarantees a successful performance. This intensity and exhilaration is precisely what Kafka will associate with Moissi's recitational style less than three weeks later, a span of time that also contains the actual lecture and the encounter with and report on Reichmann: "Cold and heat alternate in me with the successive words of the sentence, I dream melodic rises and falls, I read sentences of Goethe's as though my whole body were running down the stresses" (D 232–33). The dreamy melody, the undulation of words, the way that spoken language becomes corporeal and sensuous—all of this prefigures Moissi's vocal magic. Moreover, the juxtaposition of opposite sensations (anxiety/confidence, weakness/power, cold/heat) and the resultant ambivalence are consistent with Kafka's reflections on recitation, which are often marked by the feeling of being pulled in two directions.

A week after he holds the lecture in the Jewish Town Hall in Prague, Kafka assesses the event. On the one hand, his account is structured and focused, as each paragraph begins with a topic related to the lecture: preparations, people consulted and places visited in advance, "Excitements [*Aufregungen*]," and "Benefits [*Nutzen*]." On the other hand, the description betrays the same frenzy and exhilaration of the previous accounts. The extensive list of preparations shows that vocal performance is not simply a matter of inspiration and luck, but of knowledge, foresight, and attentiveness to detail. Kafka truly takes responsibility for the event, which is why it goes off so well. "For two weeks I worried for fear that I could not produce the lecture. On the evening before the lecture I suddenly succeeded" (*D* 233). Though it comes together "suddenly," it is not entirely a surprise, since Kafka has in fact prepared extensively.

The list of "excitements" contains all of Kafka's negative experiences and feelings relating to the event: delays, distractions, obstacles, nervousness, anxiety, and "a great deal of indifference toward Löwy, almost disgust [*Abscheu*]" (*D* 234; *T* 378). Immediately following, the list of "benefits" contains all that is positive and promising about it:

> Benefits: Joy [*Freude*] in Löwy and confidence in him, proud, unearthly consciousness during my lecture (coolness in the presence of the audience, only the lack of practice kept me from using enthusiastic gestures freely), strong voice, effortless memory, recognition, but above all the power with which I loudly, decisively, determinedly, faultlessly, irresistibly, with clear eyes, almost casually, put down the impudence of the three town hall porters and gave them, instead of the twelve kronen they demanded, only six kronen, and even these with a grand air. In all this are revealed powers to which I would gladly entrust myself if they would remain. (My parents were not there.) (*D* 234–35; *T* 378)

For all the polemics about Kafka's relationship to Löwy and Yiddish—critics such as Beck, Isenberg, and Casanova claim deep and warm identification, whereas Miron argues for disdain and even revulsion[77]—this passage provides unmistakable evidence of Kafka's self-conscious and explicit ambivalence: he embraces and rejects the world of Yiddish at the same time. One section ends with the word "disgust [*Abscheu*]," and the very next one begins with the word "joy [*Freude*]"; both describe his feelings toward Löwy. There could hardly be a clearer expression of ambivalence than this juxtaposition. Just before "disgust" Kafka offers a milder negative affect, "indifference [*Gleichgültigkeit*]," and immediately following "joy" he names a milder positive feeling, "confidence [*Vertrauen*]" (*D* 234–35; *T* 378). Kafka is clearly torn: for every extremely positive feeling there is a correspondingly extreme negative one; for every mildly positive feeling there is a correspondingly mild negative one. The truth does not lie exclusively on either side.

It is not only with respect to Löwy that these two sections of the diary entry, "Excitements" and "Benefits," are perfectly contrasted. In general, all the feelings of doubt, frustration, worry, and displeasure in the first list are counterbalanced by the feelings of calm, strength, and power in the second. There is a strong father-son dimension to this description: all the positive attributes Kafka assigns to himself are the ones he believes his father thinks are sorely lacking in him. It is no coincidence that Kafka ends the paragraph with the parenthetical note about his parents' absence. Either he is suggesting that he can only muster this kind of confidence and strength when his father is not there, or he is expressing disappointment that his father does not see his moment of triumph. In any event, the absence of the father goes hand in hand with his sense of success.

Kafka evaluates the lecture in terms similar to his assessment of Moissi's recitation. Kafka's "proud, unearthly consciousness" prefigures the description of Moissi as an "unnatural spectacle." These vocal performances seem to approach the supernatural or magical, to go beyond what is earthly and natural to achieve their powerful effect. Thus, in both cases the union of voice, words, and audience produces a nearly transcendent experience. Moissi's "apparent calm" is also reminiscent of Kafka's "coolness," and both voices are characterized as strong, commanding, and decisive. Kafka the lecturer and Moissi the reciter are definitely in control. But Kafka imagines that Moissi feels this power and exhibits this poise all the time, whereas Kafka wavers between triumph and defeat. For instance, fear and anxiety permeate his account of the lecture preparations: "Wrote . . . to Löwy ('I won't be able to give the talk, save me!')" (D 234).

While there is no reference to the "pure impression [*reine Eindruck*]" in this passage, there is one phrase that comes close: "with clear eyes [*mit klaren Augen*]." Kafka uses it to describe not his lecture but how he puts the three porters in their place, which is actually the most triumphant moment in the account. While this might seem unrelated to the act of vocalization, it falls into the category of "powers" that are "revealed" to Kafka in the course of preparing and holding the lecture. Kafka may or may not have thought that he achieved a "pure impression," but he seems to associate a kind of clarity, as well as a good deal of decisiveness and strength, with the end result.

Given Kafka's interest and investment in recitation as a vocal practice, and that his descriptions of his lecture on Yiddish are so close in time, content, affect, and tone to his accounts of recitation, it is fair to examine the "Speech on the Yiddish Language" in terms of the discourse on recitation. The same two feelings, thrill and fear, govern Kafka's account of his lecture and his description of Moissi. Moreover, the fact that the lecture was meant to introduce and supplement an evening of readings and recitations—a contemporary review is titled "Eastern-Jewish Recitation Evening" ("Ostjüdischer Rezitationsabend")[78]—links it to the practice of recitation. Kafka even refers to his intention of "striking up a kind of recitative here as though in an opera" (*D* 232). Though a recitative in opera is not the same thing as literary recitation, they both involve a musicalization of speech that stops short of song (think Moissi's elusive melodies), and in this context mentioning one automatically evokes the other. Yet despite everything that invites us to consider Kafka's lecture in the context of recitation, it actually presents the opposite phenomenon: not a written work that is potentially enhanced or distorted through vocalization, but a work whose written form is based on a prior vocal performance. Here writing is derivative and speech is original.

In the case of Kafka's lecture on Yiddish, this written transcript has come to take precedence over the vocal performance, simply because writing was, at the time, far more easily preserved than acoustic events, and because literary scholars have a preference for written texts.[79] One must work against these factors to understand the significance of Kafka's lecture as a vocal performance. This is not to say that the content and meaning of the lecture are unimportant, only that they need to be understood alongside its conditions and manner of presentation. What the lecture on Yiddish communicates above all is the importance of *listening* to Yiddish—its words, its sounds, its melodies. Kafka encourages his audience of German-speaking Czech Jews, many of whom would have been resistant to the strangeness and foreignness of Yiddish, to let down their guard and truly listen. He tells them to abandon translation and not to put stock in explanations. Instead they should overcome their distance and let the language enter into them through the voices of the East European Jewish actors. This point about language and listening must have been far more powerful when recited than in the written form in which we encounter it. The medium of speech supports the message, whereas the written transcription undermines it.

Kafka's lecture on Yiddish might have been the closest he ever came to a "recitation" that achieved a "pure impression," because it was a vocal performance that owed nothing to writing. It could dispense with the worry, present in all of Kafka's reflections on recitation, that the voice was parasitical on the written text, and that its effects were powerful but false, entertaining but cheap, seductive but damaging. It was a vocal performance unfettered by issues of authorship, ownership, and the attribution of credit, which seemed to vex all instances of literary recitation, for all of these anxieties rest on the notion that the text is primary and the voice is secondary—an unexpected prefiguration of Derrida's grammatology—whereas the lecture on Yiddish reverses this situation. It thus challenges Kafka's basic pattern of parasitical relationships between closely connected but nonidentical phenomena, such as Josefine's singing and piping, the German and Yiddish languages, and written and recited literature. The second item in each of these pairings is usually presented as derivative, impure, and inferior, and it threatens to overtake the first, even though it owes its entire existence to it. This is why it is apt to call piping, Yiddish, and recitation "parasites," and why they are figured as such in Kafka's writing: they suck the life and energy out of their stronger, more stable and legitimate "hosts," yet they also offer a kind of delight, exhilaration, and distraction that proper singing, proper German, and proper writing do not. Moreover, these pairs of related but nonidentical phenomena are the narrative motors for the texts in which they appear: the endless struggle to define their relationship frustrates readers and fuels the literary work.

Josefine's piping, the Yiddish language, and the art of recitation all attest to Kafka's fascination with compromised forms, and specifically with the voice as a compromised organ. Kafka's search for a "pure impression" always fails because the voice itself is never pure. The lecture on Yiddish, a nonderivative act of vocalization, offers a possible alternative. It has the status of an original, spontaneous verbal creation. But even here the "pure impression" is aspirational: "clear eyes" are not, in the end, the same thing as a clear voice or a clear impression. Perhaps this is unsurprising, given that the lecture is so closely tied to both Yiddish and recitation, compromised vocal forms; it cannot escape their parasitical pull. Still, it is the closest Kafka ever came to entrusting himself fully to the powers of vocal performance. The productive tension of contradictory feelings (fear and self-confidence, weakness and power, disgust and pleasure) and the sense of transcendence (either of nature or oneself) make the lecture the most significant and possibly most successful recitational experience of Kafka's life.[80]

Reciting to an Academy

In addition to the lecture on Yiddish, one further work—his 1917 story "A Report to an Academy"—helps articulate a recitational ideal to which Kafka might have subscribed. The ape Red Peter (Rotpeter) tells the story of the birth of his speaking voice, which allows for the narrative we read. The story thematizes vocal performance and draws on issues related to Kafka's reflections on recitation: vocal distortion, clear versus muddled speech, gesture, mimicry, and spectacle. Moreover, the written text of Kafka's story masquerades as speech, which produces a reversal of primacy similar to the one discussed in the "Speech on the Yiddish Language." The discourse of the story resembles spoken language, which might represent the achievement of that elusive ideal union of the spoken and written. In "A Report" the written voice takes on certain desirable qualities of the speaking voice, meaning that recitation—speech, performance, spectacle—infuses and enriches writing, rather than parasitically drawing on it.[81]

Red Peter's skillful and repeated imitation of his human captors links the story to a set of concerns that arise in Kafka's reflections on recitation: mimicry, virtuosity, performance, and spectacle. He acts according to a principle of imitation: he learns to spit, smoke a pipe, drink alcohol, and even mimic the signs of pleasure that humans make while engaging in these activities. Indeed, he states, "even after throwing away the bottle, I do not forget to rub my belly brilliantly and grin" (*KSS* 82). These movements and gestures are what make Red Peter such a good performer: he grasps that the spectacle requires not simply a coarse imitation of general human behaviors like drinking and smoking, but an attunement to and reenactment of all the details of their performance. Moreover, Red Peter makes clear that he had no inherent wish to imitate humans—no independent desire to be like them—but was instead motivated exclusively by a desire to attain a goal: finding a "way out [*ein Ausweg*]." This is a conscious and deliberate act, a show put on for the benefit of others, in order to achieve a specific end.

The most significant element of Red Peter's acts of mimicry, performance, and spectacle is his cultivation of the voice. This is what makes him most humanoid, and what enables the report. He relates that when he was first brought into human company, he was said to have "made unusually little noise. . . . Glumly sobbing, painfully searching for fleas, wearily licking a coconut, knocking my skull against the wall of the crate, sticking out my tongue whenever someone came near me—these were the first occupations in my new life" (*KSS* 79). He thus remained mostly quiet, despite fairly clear signs that he was in distress. If anything, the humans around him seemed to make more noise than he did, in the form of laughter, coughs, grunts, and indistinct speech. This was the setting, so to speak, for the eventual birth of Red Peter's voice, which he calls "a victory" (*KSS* 82). Standing before "a large group of spectators," a phonograph playing in the background, Red Peter emptied a bottle in one masterful swig "like a professional drinker, . . . like an artist," and then uttered his first word (*KSS* 82, trans. modified):

> Because I couldn't help it, because I felt the urge, because all my senses were in an uproar, in short, I shouted "Hello!," broke out in human speech, with this cry leaped into the human community and felt its echo, "Just listen to that, he's talking!" like a kiss on my whole sweat-soaked body. (*KSS* 82)

The music, the spectators, the nervous thrill, the formation of community, the audience's audible response, and the feeling of accomplishment—no doubt this is a successful performance. As Wolf Kittler and Gerhard Neumann have pointed out, the initial moment of speech in this story is technologized, not only on account of the gramophone but also because Thomas Edison is reported to have said "Hello!" into the first phonograph in order to demonstrate its capacity to record and play back sound; according to another legend, he introduced the word "hello" as an internationally recognized telephone greeting.[82] Red Peter's linguistic birth is thus bound up with the advent of new sound technologies, which might suggest that his voice can never be "pure" or "clear," since it is mediated and performing from the start. His voice belongs in the company of Kafka's reciting voices, which are also transmitting (or mediating) written texts via vocal performance.

Neumann also claims that this is the moment when Red Peter "mutates into a human being," and he identifies this transformation with the act of performance itself.[83] In Neumann's ingenious reading, the significance of this event, the act of speaking, derives from the performance. To make this point, he must return to an earlier passage in the story, which contains what Neumann calls "one of the strangest sentences that could have been written in the European discourse on knowledge":[84]

> No one promised me that if I became like them, the cage door would
> be raised. Promises of that kind, for seemingly impossible fulfill-
> ment, are not given. But if fulfillment is achieved, the promises also
> appear subsequently, just where they had earlier been sought in vain.
> (*KSS* 81)

For Neumann, this description of a promise that appears as such only after the fact, because it is unthinkable and hence inarticulable in the moment prior to its fulfillment, reveals a new epistemological category: "the form of thought in which something is born into the present belatedly."[85] This means that a performance lies at the heart of Red Peter's transformation: indeed, the performative act rather than its content defines his speech. Red Peter's transformation is not about gaining academic knowledge, but rather learning to engage in speech acts.

In Neumann's reading, the voice and performance are not simply impor-tant themes in "A Report to an Academy." Rather, the story performs its own kind of orality; this written text contains its own recitation, even if that fact can only be discerned belatedly. Certain features of the text make its affinity to spoken language quite evident, most obviously the address with which it begins:

> Exalted Gentlemen of the Academy!
>
> You have granted me the honor of summoning me to submit to the
> Academy a report on my previous life as an ape. (*KSS* 76)

Clearly such an address only makes sense in the context of a speech. One can also look to earlier versions of the story that Kafka had sketched to confirm this point. In one fragment, a reporter describes and speaks to the trainer ("Impresario") who has taught Red Peter his tricks; in another, the reporter interviews the ape directly (*NSF I* 384–88). The third version, the one pub-lished in 1917, is the one in which "Kafka allows the ape to speak for himself before the academy."[86] This suggests that Kafka had always conceived of the ape as speaking, and he presented that speech in decreasing degrees of mediation. In the first version it is not even the ape's speech but the trainer's, as given by the reporter, that constitutes the narrative. In the second it is the ape's speech, but still embedded within the interview format. And in the published version, it is the ape's speech presented directly by him without the conceit of an interlocutor. Kafka thus tries to produce a written work infused with qualities of the voice, one that resembles—or at least invokes—aspects of recitation. This kind of performance is consistent with the overt theme of the story, an ape masquerading as a human through a written text masquerading as speech. The two levels of narrative discourse, the thematic and the performative, converge in written orality.

The exact status of Red Peter's voice is less clear. He has a narrative voice, and, if we believe his account, a speaking voice. Moreover, we have good reason to believe that these voices are one and the same—the narrative voice *is* the voice that speaks—but we cannot know this for sure. Indeed, the nature of this voice is uncertain, not least because it is given as a written voice. There is a further ambiguity: on the one hand, the paratextual account just offered would seem to indicate direct access; Kafka brings us, with his versions, progressively closer to Red Peter's true and unmediated voice, which we access in his self-presentation. On the other hand, as I have shown, Red Peter's voice is mediated from the start, from the moment of his first utterance. The fact that Kafka gestures toward both possibilities, immediacy and mediation, is what brings Red Peter's report into the same orbit as the other acts of recitation in Kafka.

Recitation is not only a practice that arouses ambivalent feelings (attraction and repulsion, praise and derogation), but also one that Kafka wants to invest with the hope of achieving "a pure impression." Red Peter's written spoken voice expresses this hope and also dashes it, which is precisely why it deserves to be considered alongside Kafka's reciting voices. A voice that actually recites cannot avoid the pitfalls of recitation: its confusions, obfuscations, falseness, and cheap thrills. Kafka prefers to invest imaginative energy in the prospect of a voice that recites *in writing*. The lecture on Yiddish and the story about the talking ape offer "ways out [*Auswege*]" of Kafka's irresolvable ambivalence toward recitation. The former does away with writing altogether (or at least makes it secondary), which eliminates the worry that speech is parasitic on writing, and the latter infuses writing with the spoken word, which dissolves the issue of primacy. With his primate-cum-human, Kafka has imagined a new literary form: recitation *as* writing.

Conclusion: The Role of the Voice for Kafka's Legacy

The East European German-Jewish writer Soma Morgenstern (1890–1976) was an early admirer of Franz Kafka. In June 1924, days after Kafka's death, Morgenstern agreed to write a review of an evening of readings given by Ludwig Hardt in Vienna in commemoration of Kafka.[87] By Morgenstern's own account, the editor of the newspaper was interested primarily in Hardt's recitations, not Kafka's writing, since Hardt was by that point a famous reciter and actor, whereas Kafka's name and works were barely known. (This interest in the reciter rather than the author of the works recited confirms Kafka's worst fears about the practice: his body is barely cold and his words are already being appropriated and his authorship overshadowed by acts of recitation.) Morgenstern, however, was mostly interested in paying his respects to Kafka, whose published works he had read and admired. Morgenstern would eventually come to be known for his novels, but during his time in Europe he wrote reviews of theater, film, and literature. His early interest in Kafka is relevant here, because he immediately recognized the significance of recitation for Kafka's legacy.

About thirty years after the review, Morgenstern wrote an essay in his diaries in which he tried to explain the "Kafka legend." It is not true, he claimed, that Kafka died a complete unknown. He had a small coterie of readers, and an aura had already developed around him. Morgenstern compared Kafka to a Chassidic Rebbe who garners the devotion and awe of a few believers. This grew and grew after his death, thanks largely to Max Brod's efforts at editing and publishing Kafka's works as well as his biography of Kafka, but also in part to another unrecognized factor: Ludwig Hardt's recitations.

> One man in particular, who was friends with Kafka and with whom I was also close at the time, contributed to the oral dissemination of the legend. It was the recitation artist Ludwig Hardt. Since he didn't live in Prague, he doesn't play a major role in Franz Kafka's biography. For this reason it seems fitting to me to emphasize here that among the few individuals who went out of their way to [promote and] spread [Kafka's] work and name during [his] lifetime, Ludwig Hardt would have to rank second after Max Brod. . . . Ludwig Hardt was a careening rhapsode, as he liked to call himself. Right after the First World War he incorporated short prose texts from Kafka's oeuvre into his programs and recited them by heart in many cities in Germany, Czechoslovakia, and Switzerland, most notably in Vienna. In many cities one heard the name Franz Kafka for the first time in the auditorium of Ludwig Hardt. In many newspapers Franz Kafka was first mentioned as a writer whose prose Ludwig Hardt recited. Since no one had taken notice of his works at the time.[88]

Morgenstern's insistence on the significance of recitation and particularly of Hardt's performances for Kafka's legacy is worth noting not only because it revises the received and accepted history that Max Brod was the sole person responsible for "making" Kafka after his death, but also because it serves as the final chapter in this account of Kafka and recitation. As I have argued, Kafka's diaries and letters frequently take up the topic of recitation, and his attitude toward it is highly ambivalent: Kafka is seduced by the reciter's vocal powers, which can confer fame, recognition, and praise on the reciter; at the same time he is profoundly unsettled by the power of recitation to reconfigure and indeed disturb the "proper" relationship between work, author, reciter, and listener. These worries turn out to be entirely justified: according to Morgenstern, the audiences have come for Hardt's voice, not Kafka's words.

Ludwig Hardt was himself fully cognizant of the discomfort that Kafka would have felt at the popularity of his recitations. Even if he had no way of knowing Kafka's private misgivings about recitation, he understood that Kafka "certainly would not have been happy to see that I am reciting his works. For him there was too much seduction in recitation. And seducing is precisely what his work absolutely will not and should not do."[89] Hardt grasped the problem perfectly: for Kafka the written word had a kind of purity or authenticity that was compromised in the act of vocalization. This is why he sometimes characterized the reciter as a charlatan who relied on cheap tricks and false impressions to impress his audiences. Hardt was right to suspect that Kafka would not have wanted to gain fame in this way. He had instructed Brod to burn his writings, and other means of securing his legacy were likely just as undesirable.

While Kafka disdains the reciter for his counterfeit art that damages and undermines the written word, his reflections on the practice are also always marked by feelings of excitement and wonder. Recitation is powerful, seductive, and thrilling, and the reciter is a kind of magician. Morgenstern picks up on this dimension of Kafka's attitude too. Morgenstern supposedly met Kafka twice, through Hardt. He reports having said to Kafka, "'Ludwig Hardt must interest you. He is not a bloated *artiste*. Ludwig Hardt is a servant of the word."[90] Morgenstern presents himself as someone who grasps what Kafka finds distasteful about the practice of recitation, namely the self-satisfaction of the reciter and the misplaced attention and credit he garners from the audience. The only acceptable reciter is the one who is a "servant of the word"—that is, someone who values the word itself, the basic building block of literature, above the audience's pleasure and the performer's vanity. When Morgenstern asks how Kafka met Hardt, Kafka responds by explaining that Brod introduced them ten years earlier and that he immediately found his recitations magical:

> "He's an enchanting person. So free, unburdened, powerful. . . . I saw him for the first time, and it was as though I'd already known him for a very, very long time. He's a magician."
>
> "Why a magician?"
>
> "I don't know. But he can elicit a strong feeling of freedom. That's why he's a magician."[91]

Morgenstern's account of Kafka's reaction to Hardt reflects his sense of vocal magic. We know from the description of Moissi that magicians must be approached with caution, but they do inspire wonder and provide entertainment.

Morgenstern continues to probe the question of Kafka and Hardt's relationship, and even doubles down on the earlier claim that Hardt was the second-most-important person after Brod in securing Kafka's legacy.

> No one did for him [Kafka] as much as this reciter, whom he rightly calls a magician. I think it is in the spirit of both masters if I try to describe this magic here. In that time there were still professional reciters in central Europe. Most of them were actors who hadn't made it because they only had voices. Compared to other reciters Ludwig Hardt had three voices, not one.[92]

Morgenstern goes on to explain that "[Hardt] had the power of conjuring things, which seemed like magic to Kafka."[93] This remarkable ability to make absent things present exclusively through the voice—from real and imagined animals to gestures and movement—is what Kafka finds magical, and this identification of vocal magic is, in turn, what Morgenstern finds significant about Kafka's relationship to Hardt. Morgenstern had probably read Kafka's diaries by this point, and was thus consciously or subconsciously channeling Kafka's own reflections on recitation.

Morgenstern begins the following section of his essay with a sentence that is, in the present context, both revealing and confusing: "Kafka was one of the few writers who spoke the same way that he wrote."[94] Following on the heels of a long section about the magic of Hardt's voice, itself undergirded by an awareness of Kafka's ambivalence toward recitation, this statement is at once perfectly fitting and thoroughly confounding. After all, recitation is the practice of giving voice to literary works that were written for the page. By definition, it destabilizes the relationship between the written and spoken text. But according to Morgenstern, this uncertainty is also one of the most distinctive features of Kafka's own literary voice. For if Kafka is one of the few authors who writes as he speaks, then the written and spoken are already inextricable in the work itself, before the question of recitation is even raised. What could it mean, then, to recite a work that is written in a language that resembles speech? It might mean that the reciter mimics the author's voice and thus ventriloquizes him. But it could also mean that the reciter effaces the author's voice: his reciting voice covers over the authorial vocality present in the text, and indeed threatens to eliminate the written work altogether. The reciter has no choice but to speak over the original voice, which was as present in writing as it had been in speech, but which could only be copied or destroyed in the act of recitation.

Morgenstern is thus suggesting that the situation that explicitly characterizes the lecture on Yiddish—a work that is primarily spoken and only secondarily written—implicitly characterizes *all* of Kafka's writing, and this goes a long way in explaining Kafka's ambivalence toward recitation. His claim also aligns with my reading of "A Report to an Academy," since it suggests the possibility of a written language infused by speech, what I called recitation as writing. Morgenstern goes a step further and claims that *all* of Kafka's writing exhibits this kind of written orality, indeed this is its distinctive feature. In the context of the argument of this chapter, Morgenstern's claim implies that the written word is not necessarily more authentic or pure *as such*, but rather that its special status derives from its direct connection to the author's voice. Recitation can never achieve a "pure impression" not because it covers over writing, but because it covers over the speech that is present in all writing, at least in all of Kafka's writing. It adds a vocal layer to writing that is already infused by the spoken voice of the author, and it is this vocal substrate that threatens to be silenced or effaced—though perhaps in some cases set free and revived—by the act of recitation. Such a vocal palimpsest is both thrilling and terrifying to Kafka, and when performed well, it is pure magic.

Chapter 4

Metaleptic Noise

Acousmatic Nondiegetic Sound in Kafka and Film

In his classic work of narratology, *Narrative Discourse: An Essay in Method*, Gérard Genette theorizes the concept of metalepsis, which he defines as a transition from one narrative level to another within a work of fiction.[1] Often metalepsis involves a shift in voice: either the nondiegetic narrator inserts himself into the diegesis, or he speaks in the second person, and thereby inserts *you*, the narratee, into it. In either case, it involves a transgression, since a nondiegetic narrator is, by definition, external to the storyworld he is describing. For Genette, the unsettling effect of this metaleptic crossing is either comical or fantastic.[2] Others have fleshed out this theory to delineate other possible functions of metalepsis, including metalepsis as a form of escapism, metalepsis as a demonstration of narratorial power, and metalepsis as a way of creating mutual understanding and solidarity, either between narrator and character, narrator and narratee, or narratee and character.[3]

But none of these explanations gets to the heart of what is so deeply unsettling about metalepsis, which has to do with the implications of its transgressions. The "functions" of metalepsis—what it accomplishes in and for a work of fiction—do little to help explain its metaphysical consequences, which include the possibility of turning reality into fiction and fiction into reality. After all, if an external narrator can cross over into a story, must we perhaps reckon with the idea that every storyworld, including the one we call reality, has a narrator that is not only in control but liable to barge in at any moment? Must we consider the possibility that there is an audience to our reality, that we too are being watched, listened to, or read? Metalepsis raises the unsettling possibility that there is an outside to every world, a nondiegesis to every diegesis, and that the borders between these worlds are not as impermeable as they seem.

In a single brief statement, Genette himself acknowledges that this is the truly uncanny feature of metalepsis: "The most troubling thing about metalepsis indeed lies in this unacceptable and insistent hypothesis, that the nondiegetic is perhaps always diegetic, and that the narrator and his narratees—you and I—perhaps belong to some narrative."[4] Genette and his followers have focused on *moments* of metalepsis, individual statements that transgress narrative levels or worlds. I call this "local metalepsis": for example, when a narrator discusses his own power to manipulate the events of a story, or when he speaks directly to the narratee. It is a technique employed in isolated moments for specific effects and often linked to character and plot development. In contrast, "global metalepsis" characterizes works that raise broader philosophical questions about reality and fiction: the existence of worlds embedded within other worlds, the notion that our reality is the work of a nondiegetic narrator, and the idea that an audience might be reading us—that we might, as Genette puts it, "belong to some narrative." This type of metalepsis has come to be associated with the postmodern novel, though it has significant precursors in modernist writers such as Kafka and Jorge Luis Borges.[5] Unlike its local variant, global metalepsis takes place not on the level of individual utterances and subtle linguistic shifts, but rather on that of character, major plot devices, and narrative form as a whole. It is not simply a technique but a broad theme and a structuring principle.

A second important feature of global metalepsis is that it encourages analogical thinking: we witness a transgression of storyworlds within a text, and we infer that further transgressions are possible, including ones that would compromise the status of the world that we as readers and viewers inhabit. In other words, once metalepsis is no longer a technique that is used locally within a work but something that shapes our understanding of the work as a whole, we tend to take a broader view of the existential crises of the characters we watch and read about. The more our situation as readers and viewers resembles the situation of diegetic readers and viewers, the more this identification takes place. To put the matter somewhat differently, once we see narrative worlds transgressed, we can no longer be certain that the world we inhabit is not also susceptible to this kind of transgression. Frequently the central event that marks global metalepsis is a character's realization that she is being narrated, and hence that her world is not the only world, but the product of another, perhaps even one world among many. The implication is that the reader, too, must ask this question about her own reality.

Woody Allen's 1985 film *The Purple Rose of Cairo*, which contains a film within a film, serves as an instructive example. Let us call Allen's film "film 1" and the film within it "film 2" (they are both titled *The Purple Rose of Cairo*). Early on, a character steps out of film 2 and begins to live his life offscreen, in the "real world," which is to say, the world of film 1. When Tom Baxter exits the black-and-white film he has been inhabiting, he is amazed by the bright colors of the "real world." Immediately a question arises: Is there always a more vibrant world beyond the one we typically inhabit? Not only does Tom exit and reenter film 2, but he brings Cecilia, the moviegoer, in for a visit, so that she temporarily inhabits a fictional world. Cecilia and Tom are in love, but Tom's defection is causing problems. Other characters from film 2, even other Toms, are now also trying to step offscreen and leave their fictional worlds. Eventually Gil Shepherd, the actor who plays Tom, is brought in to try to solve the problem, and a love triangle develops. Cecilia must choose between the "real" actor and the "fictional" character. She chooses reality, but this comes back to bite her: Gil leaves her, and she is left, once again, with nothing but the movies.[6]

The situation of a fictional character in the real world or a real person in a fictional world destabilizes the categories of "fiction" and "reality." *The Purple Rose of Cairo* presents multiple levels of reality: the diegesis of the film-within-a-film (film 2), the diegesis of Allen's film (film 1), and *our* diegesis (what we call reality). The fact that we are in the same exact situation as Cecilia—we are both watching a movie called *The Purple Rose of Cairo*—makes it all the more likely that we will entertain the idea that what happens to her could also happen to us. If the world of film 2 cannot be contained, if it seeps or bleeds into film 1, what is to say that we are not characters in yet another a film called *The Purple Rose of Cairo*? And who could prove that this does not continue ad infinitum? According to this mise-en-abyme logic, the terms "reality" and "fiction" must be dispensed with, as there are no fixed ontological categories. Rather, there are worlds that contain other worlds within them and worlds that are themselves contained within other worlds.

In Kafka, noise is the conduit into other worlds—narrative worlds and species worlds, as I will show. This chapter looks at a series of disembodied or "acousmatic" sounds in Kafka, including the mice that disturb sleep and writing in the famous "Mäusebrief" ("Mice-letter"), the telephone calls in *The Castle* (*Das Schloß*, 1922), the noise in "The Burrow," and music in "Investigations of a Dog." These sounds indicate the presence of other worlds, and sometimes even give direct access to them, on account of their peculiar status: in these late works by Kafka, noise is both acousmatic (its source cannot be found) and nondiegetic (its source lies outside the fictional diegesis). In point of fact a noise cannot be both of these things at once, since acousmatic sounds are audible to the characters in a storyworld and nondiegetic sounds are not; they belong to different worlds. Yet such "impossible" noises are precisely what Kafka presents in "The Burrow" and "Investigations of a Dog." These sounds can be conjured only in a medium like literature, which does not sonify but which can theorize and play with acoustic phenomena in ways that exceed actual human experience. This chapter examines metaleptic sounds that transgress narrative worlds and species worlds, and the existential instabilities they create.

Acousmatic Listening in "The Burrow"

To hear and depict sound in itself, without reference to a cause—this is what the French composer and sound theorist Pierre Schaeffer sought to achieve for musical listening. He unearthed the ancient story of the Acousmatics, the disciples of Pythagoras who listened to his teachings from behind a curtain so that they could concentrate entirely on the voice of their master.[7] Schaeffer cites this story from the Larousse dictionary and offers the following definition: "'*Acousmatic, adjective: is said of a noise that one hears without seeing what causes it.*'"[8] Schaeffer focused on the positive consequences of acousmatic listening: if one can listen to sounds without being distracted by how they are produced or transmitted, one can presumably hear more distinctly, clearly, and accurately, and thus focus on the character of sound itself. This kind of "pure listening," unencumbered by the other senses, allows a listener to treat sound itself as an object of reflection and study, rather than focus on its source or cause. He calls sounds that are dissociated from the other senses "sonorous objects":

> In listening to sonorous objects [*objets sonores*] whose instrumental causes are hidden, we are led to forget the latter and to take an interest in these objects for themselves. The dissociation of seeing and hearing here encourages another way of listening: we listen to the sonorous forms, without any aim other than that of hearing them better, in order to be able to describe them through an analysis of the content of our perceptions.[9]

It is easy to see how acousmatic sound can be useful for training the musical ear and for bringing a degree of objectivity to encounters with acoustic phenomena. Schaeffer wanted to examine sound as an independent phenomenon, and for him "the sonorous object is never revealed clearly except in the acousmatic experience."[10]

Schaeffer, born in 1910 and trained as a radio engineer and announcer, developed an early interest in the possibility of separating sound from its source. The radio, phonograph, and telephone were among the earliest technologies to record sounds and transmit them to other times and places. It had always been possible to hear a sound without seeing its source, but this was due to physical constraints—for example, the walls of a house that separate a listener from the chirping of a bird in a tree outside. Technologies of acoustic reproduction and transmission changed the fundamental nature of sound and hearing, and the cognitive process of reckoning with sounds whose sources were absent. Suddenly there could be a sound whose cause was not simply blocked from view, but was truly not there. A voice recorded and played back on a phonograph was therefore acousmatic in a stronger sense than the chirping bird. No matter how hard one looked, the source of the sound could not be found, since the singer belonged to another time and place.[11]

The phenomenon of producing synthetic sound, which began with near simultaneous experiments with sound inscription in the United States, the Soviet Union, and Germany in the 1920s, offered an even more radical experience of acousmatic sound. Synthetic sound represented the first acoustic experience that was not *of* something, "a sonic event whose origin was no longer a sounding instrument or human voice, but a graphic trace."[12] These sounds seemed to come from nowhere; they had no discernible physical origin. Synthetic sounds do not follow the expected sequence of events whereby sounds are made, heard, recorded, and played back. Instead, their inscription is primary, a first cause, so that when they are played they are in fact being heard for the first time, rather than being played *back*. Rainer Maria Rilke's "Primal Noise" ("Ur-Geräusch," 1919) poses the question of what sound would be generated by a phonograph needle tracing the coronal suture of a human skull. As media theorist Friedrich Kittler notes, this thought experiment encourages us to imagine the possible consequences of playing sounds that had never been recorded, "the decoding of a track that no one had ever encoded."[13] Rilke's text testifies to the modernist fascination with uncoupling acoustic effects from causes. Kittler saw a parallel in other modern thinkers such as Georg Simmel and Sigmund Freud, who proposed methods to "track traces without a subject. A writing without the writer . . . records the impossible reality at the basis of all media: white noise, primal sound."[14] Kafka, I will show, also conceived and inscribed a sound without a source.

In the 1980s, the French filmmaker and theorist Michel Chion seized on Schaeffer's definition of acousmatic sound and built a theory of cinematic experience around the notion of disembodied sounds, the *acousmêtre*. He argued that the power of sound film to withhold visually what it presents acoustically is its most distinctive and provocative feature. Other media present acousmatic sound, but only film can play with the concealment and revelation of sound sources, which makes acousmatic sound an agent of narrative propulsion. Sounds that "wander the surface of the screen, awaiting a place to attach to" are ghostly and unsettling; they awaken the viewer-listener's natural impulse to localize and identify the source of sounds.[15] For Chion, the thrill of cinematic experience derives from not knowing if, when, and how the sound sources will be made visually manifest, a process he calls "de-acousmatization."

If the cinematic *acousmêtre* was so disturbing, actual encounters with disembodied voices and unidentifiable noises at the dawn of the era of sound reproduction must have been even more so. Voices that seemed to come from nowhere were associated with the ether, a realm of the dead and undead.[16] Other sounds, even if they did not seem ghostly, eerie, or netherworldly, could still pose the threat of unknowability. Once the gramophone, telephone, and radio could sever sound from its source, the process of deacousmatization was no longer guaranteed. A sound could remain forever unlocated and unidentified. This is precisely the scenario that Kafka's story "The Burrow" presents. It expresses not only the fear induced by a sound whose cause cannot be discovered, but the even more unnerving idea that if noise in modernity can be said to derive from an unidentified elsewhere, could it not also come from an unknowable nowhere?

As I argued in the first chapter, "The Burrow" presents noise at a minimum. We have very limited information about it: we do not know who or what is making the sound, where it is coming from, if and when it will cease, and what, if any, purpose it serves; we do not even know what it sounds like. The noise in the burrow is disturbing first and foremost because its source cannot be identified and located, despite the burrower's intimate knowledge of his home: "I have the advantage of being in my own house, of knowing every one of the routes and where each one leads" (*KSS* 163). Given his accounts of his wanderings, exploratory tours, surveillance measures, and incessant inspections, there is no reason to doubt his knowledge of the burrow. If the noise cannot be located, it is not because there is some remote, concealed corner of the burrow of which the burrower is unaware, but because its cause is not present within the space of the burrow.

Immediately after he begins to hear the noise in the burrow, this "hardly audible hissing," the burrower resolves to find out where it is coming from (*KSS* 177). He begins confidently, given his intimate knowledge of the territory. The burrower formulates a logical plan, the first step of which is to locate the source of the noise: "I must first determine the location of the disturbance by making experimental excavations while listening attentively at the walls of my passage, only then will I be able to eliminate the noise" (*KSS* 177). The burrower conducts numerous investigations and excavations, in an attempt to find "the spot where intervention is called for" (*KSS* 177). By looking and listening, he hopes to connect the sound with a source, so that he can besiege the enemy. His efforts are in vain: "However much I search, I find nothing, or rather, I find too much" (*KSS* 178).

Indeed, the noise cannot be located because it seems to come from *everywhere*, which makes it impossible to hunt down. In which direction should the burrower pursue the noise, if it is coming from all sides? As he states four times in the passage below, he hears the very same sound from every point in the burrow:

> It is really nothing, sometimes I think that no one except me heard it; I hear it now, of course, more and more distinctly with an ear grown more acute by practice, *although in reality it is exactly the same noise* [*das gleiche Geräusch*] *everywhere*, something I can prove to myself by the comparative method. Nor is it growing louder, as I realize when I listen attentively at the center of the passage without pressing my ear to the wall. At that point it is really only by dint of straining— yes, of total submersion—that I divine rather than hear the breath of a sound now and again. But it is exactly *this steady equivalence* [*Gleichbleiben*] *at all spots* that bothers me most, for it cannot be squared with my initial hypothesis. Had I guessed the reason for the noise correctly, it would have had to emanate most audibly from one definite spot, which merely had to be located, and from there the noise would

have grown fainter and fainter. But if my explanation was not on target, what was I dealing with? The possibility remained that there were two noise centers, that up until now I had been listening only at some distance from both centers, and that as I approached the one center, its noise increased, but as a result of the decreasing noise from the other center, *the net result to the ear remained about the same [ein annähernd gleiches]*. And already I was close to believing that if I listened very carefully, I could make out differences of tone, even if very indistinctly, that agreed with my new hypothesis. In any case, I must extend the scope of the experiment much farther than I have done so far. And so I head down the passage to the castle court, where I begin to listen. Strange, *the same noise [das gleiche Geräusch] here as well*. (*KSS* 178–79; *NSF II* 608–9, emphasis added)

This remarkable account of the process of auditory orientation presents two possibilities: either the sound has one source (a hypothesis the burrower is forced to dismiss, given its nonvariability), or there are two "centers" from which the sound emanates, which creates a situation of stereophonic hearing in which sound comes from multiple sources and fills up the space of the burrow. But even this would produce some acoustic variation, which the burrower cannot confirm. As he moves about the burrow, he gets only an "indistinct" sense of any "differences of tone"; the emphasis is clearly on uniformity, hence the repeated use of the word *gleich* (same). Though there is no paragraph break, this is when the burrower abandons his attempt to locate the sound.

The problem of locating the noise is not a problem of excess, even though it seems to be everywhere at all times, but of lack—a lack of difference or variation that results in absolute sameness. The fact that the burrower hears the same noise everywhere means that he cannot gauge distance or position; he cannot orient himself with respect to it. As Mladen Dolar notes, "[There] are no clues or too many clues, which amount to the same, and the even distribution of clues makes them useless."[17] Verifiable difference would give him a starting point from which to search, whereas ineluctable sameness proves uninformative, disorienting, and threatening. This situation exemplifies the problem of noise at an absolute minimum: sound that stubbornly remains the same cannot reveal anything about where it comes from. It doggedly conceals its cause, and thereby prevents deacousmatization.[18]

The nonlocalizability of the noise in the burrow is the first of several clues that it is a sound without a source.[19] The many names assigned to it further confirms this status. The act of naming the noise, a linguistic process, could be seen as a way around the problem of localizing it, which is an audiovisual matter. If the cause of the sound cannot be discovered and confirmed by visual means, it might be posited by linguistic ones—or so the burrowing narrator might think. For Chion, who has spent much of his career theorizing the relationship between sound and image, the process of deacousmatization is visual.[20] He contends that film presents the most interesting acousmatic sounds because it is always engaged in the "play with showing, partially showing, and not showing."[21] Radio, for example, can present an acousmatic sound, but its source will never be revealed—that is, revealed *by visual means*. Thus, according to Chion, the medium itself precludes the possibility of deacousmatization.

I want to challenge the idea, suggested by Chion and adopted explicitly or implicitly by other theorists, that deacousmatization is always a visual process. There are ways to "know" sound, even to reveal and discover sound sources, aside from seeing them. Once acousmatic sound is wrested from the exclusive domain of cinema, these alternatives become clear. Various forms of sensory substitution might allow us to hear and to discover sound sources in new ways.[22] Moreover, one can *name* sounds, which is the primary means available in literature, which means that deacousmatization can be a linguistic process.

In the next section of the story, the burrower abandons his attempt to locate the noise and embarks on a linguistic project: finding a name for it. This is not a conscious undertaking, but one that is clear from the series of verbal designations for the noise that the narrator gives. The first hint of this process of linguistic deacousmatization comes in the unwieldy sentence that follows directly after the long passage quoted above:

> It is a noise produced by the digging of some trivial creatures, who have infamously exploited my absence, whatever it is, they are far from harboring any sort of hostility toward me, they are completely preoccupied by their own work, and as long as they encounter no obstacle in their path, they keep on in the direction they started in, I know all that and yet the fact that they have dared to come as close as the castle court is incomprehensible to me and disturbs me and muddles the intellectual clarity that is crucial to my work. (*KSS* 179)

This passage shows a remarkable degree of personification, consistent with Kafka's tendency to grant animals human traits and humans animal traits. It is assumed that the sound comes from an activity (digging), that it is performed by creatures (animals), and that these creatures possess a number of discernible characteristics (worthlessness or triviality, determination, brazenness, but not hostility or aggression). As the story progresses, this apparent intimacy with the sound deepens, though it is never substantiated. Though the burrower gets no closer to discovering the source of the noise, he grows increasingly comfortable describing it as if it had a discernible cause. In fact, the burrower constantly changes his mind about what he thinks is making the noise, which raises doubts as to whether he has any real knowledge of it at all. Still, though, he nurtures his linguistic relationship to the noise by continuing to name and describe it, as if it had a knowable, yet-to-be-discovered cause.

Throughout "The Burrow" the narrator uses a broad range of words to describe the noise he hears, from the most direct designations of the sound itself (hissing, whistling, noise) to the most concretized and personified—or rather animalized—names for the creaturely agent presumed responsible for the noise (opponent, enemy, persecutor, assailant, etc.). At one end of this spectrum the noise is treated as a Schaefferian "sonorous object": the sound alone is described and nothing about its source or effects is assumed or extrapolated. At the other end, the names given are the result of speculation, imagination, and personification; sources and origins are posited, embodied, and animated. Taken together, these designations represent the full metonymic progression from noise as a sensory impression to noise as a living creature. The problem with the latter extreme is that it involves assumptions and guesses that do not conform to the burrower's perceptions. And the problem with the former extreme is that it seems incomplete or vague: if there is a sound, it must be a sound *of* something. Either we must defy the rules of fiction and project something external onto the text, or we must defy the rules of reality and accept the presence of a sound without a source.

The spectrum of nomenclatural deviation in "The Burrow" goes from literal to metonymic naming. (1) The first category of names, which refer to the sound itself as a purely acoustic phenomenon, can be called "noise words." The burrower uses these terms when trying to identify the sound itself, for example "hissing [*Zischen*]," "whistling [*Pfeifen*]," and "noise [*Geräusch*]." The last of these three words is the least specific, but they all correspond directly to the perceived acoustic effect: they name the sound itself, without making any assumptions or implicit claims about what could be causing it. Of these designations, the word *Zischen* is the most literal, since it contains a degree of sound symbolism: its onomatopoetic quality makes it coextensive with the sound it designates; the sonic qualities of the signifier are continuous with the signified.[23] (2) The second nomenclatural category includes expressions that invoke activities commonly associated with the sounds in question. These terms for noisy operations take a small step away from sound itself and posit a noise-producing event or behavior (scraping, digging, drilling, sniffing) that is closely linked to the sound in question. In this sense they already begin to deviate from pure perception, though minimally. Nevertheless, these designations contain a degree of speculative thinking, since the burrower cannot confirm, visually or otherwise, that any of these activities is actually taking place. (3) From here it is another small step to the identification of body parts involved in these noisy operations. Thus the third type of name consists of references to creaturely limbs and organs. In practice, these designations often appear in conjunction with the noise-producing activity: the rustle of scurrying feet, the scraping of claws, the sniffing of snouts.

(4) The next degree of nomenclatural deviation is the most significant, since it involves the "animalization" of the noise. With these designations, the burrower goes beyond naming the noise, the activity that produces it, and the body parts implicated in the activity, in order to posit the existence of a noisy agent—a "noise-maker [*Lärmmacher*]" or a "hisser [*Zischer*]." It might seem that there is little difference between identifying a noise and a noise-maker, but to posit an agent on the basis of a single perceptible attribute is in fact a presumption, a speculation. The terms "noise-maker" and "hisser" assert the presence of an agent where there is actually only a sound, even if this imagined agent is reduced to its sound-producing function: it has no characteristics or features beyond the sound it is presumed to make. These names graft an abstract idea of agency onto a perceptible sound, even if such a being cannot be visualized on the basis of these words alone. They designate a pure embodiment of the process of noise-making, and thus remain in the realm of abstraction.

(5) Finally, there are terms that posit a recognizable creaturely identity, generally hostile and dangerous. These names give the noise enemy status. They assume the presence of an agent, assert his involvement in noisy activities, and endow him with identifiable motives, thoughts, desires, and feelings. This is certainly the most varied and probably the most common way of representing the acoustic disturbance in the burrow. It invokes neither the noise nor the activity that makes it, but a creaturely agent responsible for it. These words include "opponent [*Gegner*]," "enemy [*Feind*]," "persecutor [*Verfolger*]," "attacker [*Angreifer*]," "destroyer [*Verderber*]," "intruder [*Eindringling*]," and "digger [*Graber*]." Though these terms are general, they clearly communicate the presence of a treacherous adversary. When he decides that the sound cannot have a single source and so he must be facing not one but numerous enemies, the burrower adds the following names to his repertoire: "a busy people [*ein tätiges Volk*]," "the little people [*das kleine Volk*]," "the small fry [*das Kleinzeug*]," "the little diggers [*die kleinen Bohrer*]," "worthless creatures [*nichtige Tiere*]," "unknown creatures [*unbekannte Tiere*]," "strange creatures [*fremde Tiere*]," "very tiny creatures [*ganz winzige Tiere*]," and "a large herd of small creatures [*eine große Herde kleiner Tiere*]." These terms, which say nothing of sound and noise, elide the fact that the burrower's only direct knowledge of the disturbance is auditory. Indeed, they reveal the degree to which verbal designations of perceptual phenomena can diverge from empirical evidence. Accordingly, these words represent the greatest degree of abstraction from the burrower's actual perceptual experience, but are the most plausible cause for a disturbance. Unlike the semantically narrow linguistic rarities "noise-maker" and "hisser"— words with short histories and few connotations—and even more unlike the words that refer to sound alone or even to a sound-producing activity, the terms in this fifth category conform to human expectations about acoustic disturbance. They refer to enemies, intruders, and attackers and assume

that these are creaturely, foreign, threatening, and abundant. Of the various modes of naming noise, these terms conjure the most credible cause, even though they are the most speculative.

This final type of designation completes the metonymic leap from noise as a sensory impression to noise as a living beast. Most readers are quick to accept these inferences, given that all sounds have causes; if they cannot be located and identified, then they must be guessed at. The burrower's willingness to speculate seems entirely reasonable; indeed, it is a natural response to disembodied sound. After all, it seems far more likely that the burrower's home is being disturbed by a menacing horde of subterranean diggers than by disembodied whistling or uncaused hissing.[24] But no matter how reasonable this extrapolation from a bare auditory perception might seem, the story gives no indication that the noise is a symptom, effect, or consequence of something else. It offers no basis for the established pattern of interpretation, namely that all sounds must have external causes. Rather, it leads consistently to the conclusion that what is present in the burrow is a noise and nothing more, a sound without a source.

While other critics have picked up on this issue, I am the first to describe the interpretive bind of the noise in the burrow in this way. Both J. M. Coetzee's reading of time, tense, and aspect in "The Burrow" and Mladen Dolar's psychoanalytic reading of the story reveal their attunement to this problem. Coetzee flatly rejects readings that assume there must be a creature behind the noise: "It would be naive to think that the whistling is a warning and that 'the enemy' is some beast whom the reader does not get to see."[25] Though it is not central to his argument, Coetzee thereby articulates his conviction that the noise in the burrow cannot be deacousmatized and thus cannot be the sound *of* something. Dolar's reckoning with this issue is more anguished, as he articulates (but does not give in to) the temptation of assuming the presence of a noisy agent. After identifying "an enigma pertaining to causality" at the heart of the story, he suggests that "the impossibility of pinning down the cause to a locus and of unraveling its source, of discerning the indiscernible, offers a crack where fantasy comes in."[26] One must *imagine* a sound source, given that the story so persistently defies our attempts to discover one. In my reading, uncaused sound can exist in fictional worlds, whereas for Dolar "the dislocation of natural causality" sparks "fantasy," which in turn "unifies the absent cause of sounds into a single beastly creature."[27] On the one hand, Dolar's "beast" gives form and flesh to the source of the sound, which is in its essence uncaused and hence disembodied; it lends coherence and plausibility to something that is incoherent and impossible, at least outside fictional worlds. On the other hand, it gives form and flesh only in name, not spirit, for Dolar's "beast" is just another name for the impossibility of an uncaused noise:

> The impossibility of finding a univocal location of the sound in reality opens up a crack where fantasy comes flooding in. . . . By virtue

of its dis-location, the sound has the structural propensity of leading
to the assumption of the beast. Only the beast can straighten out its
crooked causality and provide it with being, location, oneness, stabil-
ity, duration, meaning—all those things that one was incapable of
achieving. With the mere supposition of the beast, by a single stroke,
it all makes sense, if beastly sense. It displays the beastly part of making sense—the part where the sense fills in the crack, underpinned by
fantasy.[28]

For Dolar, "fantasy" posits the "beast." This is the only way to rationalize a
situation that does not conform with human experience.

If we take a broader view of how deacousmatization works, we can grasp
the seemingly fantastical situation that "The Burrow" presents—the unreal
but thinkable situation of an uncaused sound, an autonomous acoustic
presence—without needing to imagine its cause as a "beast." Indeed, Kafka's
story suggests other modes of deacousmatization, which means that the noise
can be grasped in language even if it cannot be visualized. Simply to accept
the burrower's inferences about the noise—that any sound has a cause—is to
normalize a situation that Kafka's story presents as distinctly abnormal. It is
to impose the standards of our world onto another, one we have little reason
to think resembles ours so closely. Indeed, if we are to take the story's evidence at face value, we must recognize that it gives no grounds for assuming
that there is an object, activity, or agent causing the noise, notwithstanding
the burrower's acts of speculative naming. The plain but unlikely fact about
Kafka's story is that the disturbance in the burrow is noise alone, akin to
Schaeffer's "pure sonorous object" and Rilke's "primal noise."

Such an acoustic object is fictional in two senses. First, it is unreal: there
is no such thing as a sound without a cause (synthetic sound, too, is caused
by the machines and programmers that create it, even if it has no referent).
Second, it can only "exist" in art forms that are capable of producing fictional
worlds, such as film and literature. Through acts of playful manipulation,
these art forms can undo the necessary link between a natural sign and its signified: they can present smoke without fire, color without object, and sound
without a source. One cannot encounter an uncaused sound in the real world,
because such a sound cannot exist. There is no scenario in which one could
hear the noise in the burrow. It can never be made present to our perceptual
faculties, since heard sounds always have causes. But one can imagine and
represent such a sound, under the right conditions. Fiction can defy nature.
If we identify a cause, no matter how ghostly or beastly, we elide this truth
about the noise in the burrow.

There is a further possibility that every interpretation of the noise in the
burrow must entertain—that it is merely imagined or otherwise internally
caused, that it comes from within, which is why it is always there and yet cannot be found.[29] While it is true that Kafka's fictions take place at the border

Metaleptic Noise   151

of dreams, fantasies, or hallucinations, they remain *at* this border; they do not transgress it definitively. Kafka can present such peculiar and uncanny situations because his characters and events are real, and not merely imagined, dreamed, or metaphorical. After all, strange dreams are far less strange than strange realities. In addition to attributing the inexplicable in Kafka to dreams, some psychological and physical conditions can also be called on to normalize and rationalize the inexplicable. In the case of seemingly uncaused sounds, one could argue that certain psychological disturbances cause auditory hallucinations (such as the phenomenon of hearing voices), as do certain physical conditions (Kafka suffered from tinnitus). Yet these explanations of the noise in the burrow eliminate the presence of the incommensurable, which is the hallmark of the Kafkaesque. We are better off embracing the profound strangeness of Kafka's fictional scenarios than appealing to external rationalizations, which inevitably flatten Kafka's worlds, even if they make them more palatable. As Dolar notes, "There is a moment of phantasmagoria when the sound wavers, if ever so minimally, between its reality and unreality."[30] Even if there is reason to think that the noise is imagined, this wavering prevents us from settling on this reading, just as the nonlocalizability of the sound prevents us from isolating its source. We can be certain neither that the noise is audible in the burrow, nor that it is not. The work's only guarantee is its unending capacity to destabilize readers, its refusal to allow us to settle comfortably on one interpretation or another.[31] It would be a mistake to content ourselves with the version of reality that conforms with our lived experience, simply because the reality that Kafka's fictions present poses too much of a cognitive strain.

Coetzee's essay on the paradoxical temporality of "The Burrow" is instructive in this regard too, as it contains a revealing moment of hesitation. For him, the central problem of time lies in the iterativity of the first (prenoise) part of the narrative, which seems to be followed by the onset of noise. Yet the issue is more complicated than this: the noise returns continually, and there are clues that this return is familiar, even expected. Coetzee describes what he sees as the pivotal moment in the text:

> The shift from *ich* to *man* is maintained for much of the rest of the paragraph, in conformity with the new hypothetical mode of the narrative. It seems impossible to square this mode with a non-iterative understanding of the narrative unless one grants to the narrator the effective position of a fictional creator, someone toying with sequences which may or may not be inserted into the narrative. While this possibility cannot be dismissed absolutely, there is nothing else in the text to support the notion that the operations of writing are being so radically unmasked. On the other hand, if one understands the narrative as iterative, then the hypothetical sequence fits in as one which may or may not occur in a given iteration.[32]

Coetzee hints tentatively at a reading that he is ultimately unwilling to advance, because he does not believe there is enough textual evidence to support it—that the burrowing narrator is not fully "in" or "of" the story, but rather is himself a literary creator. I am more comfortable with this reading than Coetzee is; in fact this is the main point of my reading of "The Burrow," that Kafka's burrowing narrator *does* transcend the limits of his fictional world. This does not necessarily make him a "fictional creator," but it does mean he is a fictional character with the extraordinary ability to access a world beyond the one in which he exists, the world of his creator. Though nothing suggests that the creature is in a position of control or mastery, he possesses a consciousness that transcends the limits of the fictional work, "The Burrow."

In other words, unlike Coetzee I think there *is* something else in the text, something very central and crucial, which suggests that "the operations of writing are being so radically unmasked": the metaleptic figure of noise. Kafka's burrowing narrator hears a sound from another world—a nondiegetic sound, to use the language of film analysis—which means he participates, perhaps unwittingly, in the transcendence of narrative levels or worlds. In film, nondiegetic sounds come from a space outside the narrative and are inaudible within the narrative; they belong to a world unknown within the filmic diegesis, and are added by the director or sound editor for the benefit of the viewer-listener. The noise in the burrow, I argue, may be thought of as acousmatic on the one hand and nondiegetic on the other. For if the burrower hears a sound with an unknown source, that sound is acousmatic, whereas if the sound comes from another world, it is nondiegetic. Yet there is no possible intersection between these kinds of sounds: an acousmatic sound must have a source within the diegesis, even if it is never discovered, and nondiegetic sound can never be heard by characters within the fiction, if the storyworld is to remain whole and unbroken. Kafka not only imagines this impossible intersection, he realizes it in literary form. The noise in the burrow is a nondiegetic acousmatic sound. This means that the burrower, in listening, unknowingly transcends the boundaries of his created world. He hears acoustic intimations from beyond. To grasp the noise in the burrow as both acousmatic and nondiegetic is to begin to understand its status as a figure of metalepsis, a point to which I will return at the end of this chapter.

Chion's classic account of the unlocatable source of acousmatic sound in film is applicable to Kafka's literary text to a point. More interestingly, Chion himself raises the idea that I claim Kafka realizes—an acousmatic sound that cannot be deacousmatized, and which therefore hovers between the acousmatic and nondiegetic:

> For the spectator . . . the filmic acousmêtre is "off-screen," outside
> the image, and at the same time *in* the image: the loudspeaker that's

actually its source is located behind the image in the movie theater. It's as if the voice were wandering along the surface, *at once inside and outside*, seeking a place to settle. Especially when a film hasn't yet shown what body this voice normally inhabits.

Neither inside nor outside: such is the acousmêtre's fate in cinema.[33]

One could describe the noise in "The Burrow" in similar terms: it is both inside the text (in the sense that the burrower hears it, it is part of his world) and outside the text (in the sense that its source cannot be located). It is not quite nondiegetic in the cinematic sense, for then it would be clearly and explicitly part of the reader's world but not part of the fictional world of the work. Nondiegetic sounds are not perceptible in the storyworlds under scrutiny, whereas the noise in the burrow is very clearly audible *in* the burrow. Much like the filmic acousmêtre in Chion's description, the noise in the burrow is perpetually looking for a place to settle and reveal itself. The story is unfinished, however, and this process of revelation or deacousmatization will never happen. The noise will never be attached, once and for all, to a visible, nameable body, yet the story must operate under the illusion that it will. This infinite postponement of the moment of deacousmatization is how the story generates suspense through sound.

The act of withholding is crucial for Chion as well, for despite his investment in the process of deacousmatization, he is fascinated by cinematic sounds *without* a verifiable source. This explains why his first and most compelling example of acousmatic sound is the voice of the so-called Chief that speaks from behind a curtain in Fritz Lang's *The Testament of Dr. Mabuse* (*Das Testament des Dr. Mabuse*, 1932/33). This voice turns out to be a mere machine recording of a certain Dr. Baum, who, we are led to believe, has been hypnotized by Mabuse. As Chion cleverly demonstrates, the process of deacousmatization is itself an illusion, as we can confirm neither that the voice is Baum's nor that Mabuse has ordered him to speak in his place.

> Two scenes, then, involve a de-acousmatization process, revealing unexpected things behind the curtain and the door. In both, instead of the Chief we find an assemblage of equipment for vocal projection. The scenes actually function to conceal, in two senses. First, they put off until another time and place—i.e., to forever and nowhere—the true unveiling of the acousmêtre. Second, and above all, they conceal from us the fact that this elsewhere does not exist.[34]

Deacousmatization does not and cannot take place, because the voice is not coming from anywhere. There is no body to which the voice can be attached: "this elsewhere does not exist." Still, we are compelled to keep searching for this source, this place, this body, for the drive to deacousmatize is very powerful, even when the quest is futile.

"Ultimately it would appear that Mabuse is nothing"—this is how Chion begins the final paragraph of his tremendous reading of the film.[35] Recall how the burrower began to speak about the noise in the first long passage quoted in this chapter: "It is really nothing" (*KSS* 178). Mabuse is nothing, the noise in the burrow is nothing; uncaused sounds are nothing: they are all mere noise. There is no visible or nameable being or cause behind the acousmatic sound. No such thing is seen, and the attempts at naming are ineffectual: the burrower's multiple designations do not succeed in assigning a true cause, and the revelation of the recording device and naming of the voice in *The Testament of Dr. Mabuse* do nothing to prove that it is Mabuse who speaks. The film and the story compel us to look for and name an acoustic source, but in the end neither work can produce such a thing. Each presents a sound caused by nothing.

Chion eventually names this type of sound that is distinctly audible but not locatable or nameable the "acousmachine." These sounds are undeniably present but their sources cannot be found, as they do not exist:

> Ultimately, it would appear that Mabuse is nothing—nothing more or less than what people construct him as—and that he can exist at all because none of his properties is fixed. If there is a Mabuse, he is in this name without an identity, this body without a voice, this voice without a place; in the general madness of these disassembled elements, he is all possible acousmêtres and none at all, and when all is said and done, an *acousmachine*.[36]

We could also call the noise in the burrow an *acousmachine*, as the story does not so much deacousmatize it as posit the impossibility of that process. Kafka and Lang both produce a minimal noise—not simply a sound whose source is hidden (the acousmatic voice) or hidden and then revealed (the deacousmatized voice), but a sound that invites a relentless, fruitless attempt to reveal its source. Chion's acousmachine is a name for this minimal noise, a sound that comes from an elsewhere that is nowhere, caused by nothing.

Chion's reading of *The Testament of Dr. Mabuse* begins to get at my idea of a noise that is both acousmatic and nondiegetic. Chion does not himself argue this, since for him the sound in *Mabuse* is clearly diegetic. Yet its non-localizability—it is "nothing" and comes from "nowhere"—suggests that its source is not simply offscreen, but outside the diegesis. This is why the sound *cannot* be deacousmatized: no amount of searching would ever reveal its source, because it is inaccessible to the characters in the fiction. The cause of the sound and its acoustic effect lie in different worlds. Chion does not state this, but his analysis has inspired others to move in this direction.

In an essay on surveillance cinema, Thomas Y. Levin offers an account of precisely this metaleptic phenomenon—a diegetic sound whose source lies beyond the fictional frame. Levin accounts for the growing interest in surveillance as a theme in late twentieth-century film and as a mode of cinematic narration by treating it as a response to the loss of photochemical indexicality that results from the advent of digital film technology. Cinema used to be a "trace of the real"—or so André Bazin led us to believe—but in the age of digital manipulability this idea collapses and cinema seems to lose its hold on the real. According to Levin, surveillant narration, especially real-time footage, makes us feel that we are recapturing the real. The "semiotic appeal" of surveillance images lies in their "seemingly unproblematic, reliable referentiality."[37] In this context, Levin offers a powerful reading of Francis Ford Coppola's *The Conversation* (1974), a film that both thematizes surveillance and employs surveillant narration.

The Conversation is about a private audio surveillance man, Harry Caul, who gets involved in a case that ends in murder. In the final scene of the movie, Caul receives a phone call telling him that his apartment has been bugged. Wracked with guilt, paranoia, and anxiety, he tears apart his once tidy home in an attempt to find the device.

> Desperate to find the technological implant that has made it possible to do to him what he normally does to others, he literally deconstructs his place object by object, floorboard by floorboard, until finally, having failed to locate the device, we find him sitting, exhausted, amidst the trashed ruins of his violated privacy. Although he has dismantled every single artifact, tested every appliance, and ripped down every piece of wallpaper, the "bug" he so desperately seeks has eluded him. But it is right "there" in the film's final sequence, an extended high-angle shot, that slowly surveys the extent of the futile damage. Beginning in an empty corner, it pans slowly and methodically to the left until it captures the broken, saxophone-playing man, and then continues on past him until, having hit another corner, it suddenly and somewhat jerkily reverses itself and pans back, and then back again. Just as the sound is a semiotically confused blend of the diegetic (Harry's sax) and the extra-diegetic (the piano which is "accompanying" him), the structure of this shot itself stages a similar blurring in that its formal signature—the mechanical back-and-forth pan—reveals it to be the surveillant device that Harry is so desperately trying to uncover. But where "is" this thing located? It can't be "in" his apartment since the veteran expert would have long since discovered it: indeed Harry will never find the surveillant camera because it resides in a space that is epistemologically unavailable to him within the diegesis: surveillance has become *the condition of the narration itself*.[38]

According to Levin, Caul cannot find the bug not because he has not looked hard enough, but because it is not present in the diegetic world of the film.

It is located not simply outside his apartment, but outside the diegesis of the film, just like the source of the noise in Kafka's story is located not simply outside the burrow, but outside the burrower's diegetic world. There is a parallel between Levin's reading of the surveillant gaze in *The Conversation* and my interpretation of the noise in "The Burrow": both Harry Caul and the burrower are looking for something they are not capable of finding because the object of their search is "epistemologically unavailable" to them—it lies beyond the diegetic worlds they inhabit.

It might be possible to draw a further and more specific parallel between these works, namely between the noise in "The Burrow" and the mixture of diegetic and nondiegetic sound in this scene in *The Conversation*. Levin's description about how music works here is suggestive, yet it is not clear that Harry himself hears the piano accompanying him, or if only the viewer-listener does. If he does hear it, the link to Kafka's story is even stronger than previously suggested, for then Harry and the burrower both possess the fantastical ability to hear nondiegetic sounds—that is, sounds that come from other worlds. If this is the case, both characters perceive sounds that must, from their perspectives, be described as uncaused. From a broader perspective these sounds can be called metaleptic, as they transgress narrative levels or worlds: their cause lies outside the diegesis, but their effect can be felt within it. The viewer-listener or reader can access both worlds, but the characters, for whom the limits of the diegesis are the limits of their world, cannot. Here metalepsis is not a technique, such as a shift in voice (local metalepsis), nor is it the central and overt theme of the work (global metalepsis). Instead, in these works sound is a *figure* of metalepsis, a rhetorical phenomenon whose existence disturbs the integrity of narrative worlds.

Acousmatic Sounds in Kafka's Letters

Kafka's interest in sounds with invisible or nonexistent sources is not limited to his late story "The Burrow," but rather something that preoccupied him for many years. This experience was crucial to his sensibility as a writer, and particularly to his understanding of the troubled relationship between noise and work, especially the work of writing. On the one hand, noise that cannot be localized and labeled is an irritant, and thus a distraction from the task of writing. On the other hand, Kafka's works are propelled precisely by such disturbances, parasites, and intruders, and the noise in the burrow is the paradigmatic example. Thus, the presence of acousmatic sound in both real and fictional work environments suggests that noise is a migratory phenomenon in Kafka—it moves from reality to fiction and fiction to reality, enabling and disrupting both—as it becomes a figure of metalepsis.[39]

In two letters to his friend and colleague Felix Weltsch, from November 1917 and early July 1922, Kafka describes acts of listening that demonstrate the persistent provocations of acousmatic sound. In the first, the so-called "mice letter," Kafka describes a sleepless night in his room in the Bohemian village of Zürau, where he is recovering from a recent bout of illness. The letter exhibits neither the mastery over sound of "Great Noise," nor the exasperation that will characterize the burrower's inexplicable acoustic encounter. The sound Kafka hears is definitely acousmatic, but still more accessible than the noise in the burrow:

> Dear Felix, The first fatal flaw of Zürau: a night of mice, a frightful experience. I myself came through unscathed and my hair is no whiter than yesterday, but it was still gruesome. Here and there previously (I may have to stop writing any minute, you will learn the reason), here and there in the night I had heard a delicate nibbling, once in fact I started out of bed all atremble and had a look around and it stopped at once—but this time it was an uproar. What a frightful mute noisy people [*ein schreckliches stummes lärmendes Volk*] this is. (L 168, trans. modified; B 365)

This is an instance of disembodied sound where the source is known but it is still disturbing. The problem is not identifying the cause or even catching sight of the mice—here Chion's principle of visual deacousmatization is inoperative—but dealing with its variations: munching, rustling, gnawing, whistling, and silence. Kafka is unsettled by the unanticipated fluctuation of sound and silence, a reaction he expresses with a wonderfully concise series of adjectives: "frightful mute noisy." The silence and the noise, taken separately, are each disconcerting, but it is their unpredictable alteration that Kafka finds truly horrifying. After all, noise means actual disturbance (of sleep, of work), but silence indicates something even more agonizing: the anxious anticipation of disturbance.

Kafka's "mice letter" also introduces one of the central problems of "The Burrow": the challenge of locating, even if not necessarily seeing, the source of a disembodied sound. In fact, this feature of the letter almost prefigures the burrower's anxieties and efforts:

> Around two o'clock I was wakened by a rustling around my bed, and from then on the rustling did not stop until morning. Up the coal box, down the coal box, across the room they ran, describing circles, nibbling at wood, peeping softly while resting, and all along there was that sense of silence, of the secret labor of an oppressed proletarian people to whom the night belongs. To preserve my sanity [*Um mich gedanklich zu retten*], I decided that the noise was concentrated around the stove, which stands at the other end of the room, but it was everywhere, and reached its peak when a whole swarm of them leaped down together somewhere. (L 168, trans. modified; B 365–66)

This attempt at acoustic localization—tracking the sound, following its movements—also characterizes the activity of the burrower. In both instances there is a strong impulse to find the point from which the sound emanates. The burrower wants to locate the noise so that he can identify and eliminate it. In the letter, however, Kafka describes the frenzied path of the noise neither because he wants to find its source (he knows the mice are to blame) nor because he means to eliminate it (he has no intention of combating his mouse problem, beyond letting the detested cat into his room to help). Instead, he tries to localize the sound, he states, to preserve his sanity—literally, "to save myself mentally."

Why does the sound of the mice cause such mental anguish? Their constant unpredictable movement contributes to a sense of vulnerability and constraint. The mice move about with freedom and abandon, taking over the nighttime space of his room. Kafka refers to the "secret work" of this "proletarian people," "to whom the night belongs." The night had once belonged to Kafka and his writing, but his illness and convalescence forced him to give up his nocturnal habits. The scurrying of mice not only prevents Kafka from sleeping, but reminds him of the writing he once did in the nighttime space of his room. By describing the movement of the mice as a kind of work, Kafka expresses his disappointment and frustration at his own unproductivity as a writer. It is from this thought in particular that Kafka wishes to be rescued.

The narrator of "The Burrow" responds to the acoustic disturbance in his home with one of the most virtuosic streams of narrative excitement and agitation that Kafka ever produced. In his short account of his "night of mice," Kafka responds only with screams: "I was completely helpless, could find nothing in my whole being to cling to. I did not dare get up, light the lamp, all I could manage was a few screams, with which I tried to intimidate them" (*L* 168–69, trans. modified). He tries to counter noise with noise, perhaps in an effort to induce the same reaction in the mice that they have induced in him—fear, intimidation, loss of confidence—or perhaps because he is too startled and disturbed to respond more coherently. His inarticulate cries are thoroughly ineffectual, though they indicate the degree to which disembodied sounds bring out animal urges in human listeners.

The only effective antidote to mouse noise is the pet cat. Kafka must overcome his hatred of this animal and tolerate its presence, given the relief it will provide. This does not stop him from chasing the cat away when it tries to sit on his lap. It disrupts his writing, he tells Weltsch, making it another creature that simultaneously disturbs and enables his literary work. In the end Kafka tolerates the cat because it is an effective mouse hunter; indeed, it is his only defense against the noisy nighttime creatures.

About a week later, Kafka returns to the topic in a letter to Max Brod. Though he seems to have gained a modicum of affection toward the cat and recognizes his dependence on it, he still feels burdened by its presence: "I must always be on guard while I am reading or writing, lest she jump into my lap, or be ready with the ashes when she does her multiple jobs, and that's a great bother; in short I don't like being alone with the cat, when other people are around it is less embarrassing, but otherwise it's a considerable nuisance to undress in front of her, do one's exercises, go to bed" (*L* 170, trans. modified). Here again Kafka prefigures the situation of the burrower, who considers but ultimately rejects the presence of another creature in his burrow to help him guard against enemies. Indeed, the burrower can be considered the last in Kafka's series of bachelors, characters who wish to secure the conditions of solitary life but cannot renounce companionship altogether. The best example is Blumfeld, the eponymous antihero of Kafka's fragment "Blumfeld, an Elderly Bachelor" ("Blumfeld, ein älterer Junggeselle," 1915), who wants to enjoy the pleasures of life unimpeded by the preferences and demands of another person, but nevertheless longs for someone to observe his fixed daily routines. This wish for minimal companionship seems completely unrealistic, until Blumfeld comes home to find a pair of blue and white celluloid balls bouncing around his apartment. These two disembodied "eyeballs" are the independent and inorganic optical prosthesis he has been fantasizing about, the least common denominator of companionship.[40]

Unlike Blumfeld, Kafka's burrower does not consciously desire companionship, but he seems unable to verify the security of the burrow without the presence of another. He considers recruiting a guard or assistant (*Vertrauensmann*) to help him, but quickly dismisses the idea, as he could only trust someone who could be watched over (*NSF II* 597). The irony of this statement comes from the fact that the word *Vertrauensmann* contains the word *Vertrauen* (trust), and the burrower is patently unwilling or unable to trust this hypothetical figure. Indeed, he would be brought in as a helper but would prove to be a burden. Kafka describes this burden in terms that recall the cat in his mice letter. First, the *Vertrauensmann* would demand something in return for his help, just as the cat wants to sit in Kafka's lap and be caressed. Second, his presence in the burrower's private space would be "embarrassing [*peinlich*]," just as Kafka feels ashamed to perform his daily routine in front of the cat. Finally, the burrower could only trust him if he could "watch over" him (*überwachen*), just as Kafka feels he must keep a close eye on the cat (*NSF II* 597). Ultimately these bachelors (Kafka, Blumfeld, the burrower) are incapable of trust and unable to conceive of security and comfort as a collective project. The helpers they imagine taking in would not only fail to eliminate the disturbances in their homes, but their presence would raise feelings of suspicion and worry in the bachelors, which would distract them from work.

Kafka's description of the cat is consistent with his reflections on the benefits and drawbacks of animal companionship. It also returns us, quite literally, to the question of embodiment. Kafka's burrower narrative is propelled by a drive to embody a noise that cannot be embodied, or what I have called the relentless compulsion to deacousmatize. As noted, the "mice letter" lacks this particular dynamic, since the cause of the disturbance is known. Nevertheless, the mice's visual absence generates considerable excitement and agitation. Even if it has named its cause, the text withholds visual confirmation of the auditory disturbance—that is, unless we consider a particular form of indirect "embodiment":

> My sense of hearing has become a thousand times sharper and has become more uncertain by the same proportion [*Mein Gehör hat sich tausendmal verfeinert und ist ebensoviel unsicherer geworden*]—if I rub my finger over the sheet, I no longer know for certain whether I am hearing a mouse. But the mice are not fantasies of mine, for the cat comes to me in the evening thin and is taken out in the morning fat. (*L* 171; *B* 369)

Here as in "The Burrow," an increased sensitivity to sound is actually disorienting and destabilizing; the more he hears, the less he seems to understand. Unlike the creature in that story, however, Kafka here seems to have indirect visual evidence for the noise he has heard: though he does not see the mouse itself, he sees the bulging belly of the cat that has eaten it. It is significant that Kafka does not rely on the absence of noise to confirm that the mouse in his bedroom is dead. This would be impossible, according to his own description, considering that his hearing has become so overrefined as to be unreliable. Moreover, we know from "The Burrow" that negative confirmation (the absence of a sound) is not sufficient proof that an intruder is gone; Kafka needs a visual sign. This seems to support Chion's idea that determining the source of a disembodied sound requires visual confirmation. Yet the fat-bellied cat is both an acquiescence to this notion and a playfully morbid rejection of it: it is physical, visible proof of embodiment that still withholds the sounding body. The sight of the mouse is both given and denied, revealed and concealed.

The second letter on noise to Felix Weltsch lacks the deacousmatizing impulse that characterizes both "The Burrow" and the two 1917 letters on murine disturbances. That is, it does not present noise as something to be located, seen, and counteracted. In this letter from early July 1922, written in the village of Planá in the Bohemian forest, Kafka is preoccupied both with the problem of noise in the abstract and with a particular instance of it: the buzz saw. At first, perhaps in response to Weltsch's reflections on noise from a previous letter, Kafka announces that he will give up on the idea of erecting a barricade that would protect him against all noise: "Because of the density of the world, each noise that has been overcome is replaced in endless succession by a new one that has still to be overcome" (*L* 336). The cycle of noise is inevitable; one escapes from one disturbance only to fall victim to the next.

> The noise also has something fascinating and narcotic about it [*Der Lärm hat etwas Fascinierend-Betäubendes*]. If I sit in one room—I

am fortunate in sometimes having two rooms to choose from—and, just as for you, there is a sawmill across the road, which is bearable for short intervals, but when the circular saw takes over, as has been happening continually of late, it makes one curse life, if I sit in this ill-fated room, I cannot leave it, even though I am free to go into the adjoining room and must do so, for the sound of the saw is unbearable, but I cannot change rooms, only go back and forth and perhaps observe that the second room isn't quiet either, and children are playing in front of its window. (L 337, trans. modified; B 388)

Unlike the other texts examined here, this letter expresses the desire to escape from the noise, rather than approach, locate, and identify it. Kafka easily names the source of the sound, and implies that nothing is to be gained by visual confirmation. Here the problem of noise is not a cognitive challenge, but simply an irritant: it is ever present and unavoidable. Kafka nevertheless describes himself as constantly moving back and forth between noisy alternatives. Even when he is trying to escape noise rather than confront it, his actions and thoughts are thoroughly determined by it. Noise exerts a kind of dirty magnetism.

In all of these letters, the problem of noise is closely aligned with the issue of work. In the first mice letter (the one addressed to Weltsch), Kafka figures the noise of the intruding animals as "the work of an oppressed proletarian people."[41] Noise represents an exchange of labor between Kafka and the mice: it is not just that their noise-making prevents him from working, but that by representing it as a kind of work Kafka finds a substitute for the work he is himself unable to do. Here too, in the 1922 letter, the noise of the saw prevents Kafka from writing, yet it is associated with the work of another. He imagines telling the bookkeeper at the sawmill that the noise of the saw is disrupting his work, but decides it would be unreasonable to request that operations cease, considering there is work to be done. The workers at the sawmill are simply doing their jobs, fulfilling the duties of their occupations. Thus, the undesired sounds that intrude on Kafka's workspace is rationalized in terms of an exchange of labor. It is worth noting, too, that the sawmill is necessary for the production of paper, which links it to the material conditions of Kafka's and all writing.

The letter continues with an account of the conditions under which Gustav Mahler composed his musical works. Significantly, to present the ideal acoustic conditions of labor Kafka chooses a composer, someone who works to imagine and inscribe artistic configurations of sound:

Or else I think of Mahler, whose summertime life is described somewhere, how every day at five-thirty, he was very healthy in those days and slept so soundly, he would bathe out in the open and then walk into the woods, where he had a "composing hut" (he would find his

> breakfast prepared there) and he would work there until one in the
> afternoon, and the trees, which later would make so much noise in
> the sawmill, stood still in their host around him, deflecting the noise
> [*lärmabwehrend*]. (*L* 337, trans. modified; *B* 389)

Kafka figures the labor of musical composition as an exchange of music and
noise: the trees that will one day produce noise (on account of the saws that
will fell them) remain silent for the duration of Mahler's working hours;
indeed, they form a kind of acoustic shield that protects the composer and
guarantees his ability to work. These trees, in Kafka's idealized description,
are not only silent, but *deflect* noise, and thus actively work to secure a quiet
workspace for the composer. Kafka thereby adds another level to the labor
exchange: in addition to the silence required for the artist's work (writing,
composition) and the noise that inheres in proletarian work (operating the
saw), there is the music that results from achieving an ideal balance between
these kinds of work. Kafka does not imagine a world without noise, since
he realizes that certain kinds of noisy work are inevitable, but he does fan-
tasize about delaying or displacing those activities in order to protect the
acoustic workspace of the artist. To strike such a balance between silence
and noise, between the work of the artist and proletarian labor—to live as
Mahler, in Kafka's romanticized tale, was able to live—represents an ideal
configuration of sound for artistic ends, one in which musical sound and
disruptive noise are kept apart. But this model of acoustic separation does
not in fact work for Kafka and his characters. Work, noise, and writing are
inextricable and mutually dependent: there is no story without the noise
in the burrow, and presumably no literary oeuvre without all the noise in
Kafka's world.

Kafka's next letter to Brod, from July 12, 1922, not only summarizes these
links between noise, work, and writing, but in so doing prefigures "The Burrow": "Dearest Max, I have been dashing about or sitting as petrified as a
desperate animal in his burrow. Enemies everywhere. Children outside this
room and also outside the other" (*L* 338). The language is so evocative of
"The Burrow" that one wonders whether the noise in the burrow is not also
inspired by the noise of children who play around outside Kafka's window
and disturb his peace and concentration. He writes further on in the letter:

> But yesterday afternoon, for example, children were playing outside
> my window. Right under me there was a nasty group, while a bit
> off to the left there was a nice one, lovely-looking children, but the
> noise made by both was the same. It drives me from my bed, out of
> the house in despair, with throbbing temples through field and forest,
> devoid of all hope like a night owl. And when I lie down at night in
> peace and hope, I am awakened at half past three and don't fall asleep
> again. At the nearby railroad station, which however is not in itself

disturbing, timber is perpetually being loaded. This involves constant hammering, though it is usually gentle and intermittent. This morning, however, and I don't know whether it will be this way always, they began hammering very early and the noise rings through the quiet morning and the sleep-famished brain in quite another way than it does by day. . . . For the past few days some two hundred Prague schoolchildren have been quartered here. A hellish noise, a scourge of humanity. . . . I am also losing any taste for good noise [*guten Lärm*], and how people flock together in theaters merely for the sake of the noise will soon become incomprehensible to me. (*L* 338–39)[42]

In a way this remarkable description is an addendum to the 1912 sketch "Great Noise," where noise is irksome and disruptive without being acousmatic. The sounds in both texts have identifiable sources, and the fact that they can be located and named does little to reduce their irritating and disturbing qualities. These texts are reminders that even if Kafka's most famous noises—Gregor's squeaking voice, the Sirens' deadly silence, Josefine's acoustically indeterminate singing, and the noise in the burrow—are difficult to identify and describe, there are other noises in Kafka that are not cognitive and semiotic puzzles, but simply a nuisance.

Yet even a noise as straightforward as the loud bustle of children or the hammering sound of lumber being loaded onto train cars arouses complex and contradictory feelings in Kafka. Although the noise is maddening, it gives him a peculiar kind of energy; more fundamentally, it is an obstacle to writing but also serves as a reliable topic for his letters. This final point is supported by Kafka's introduction of the idea of "good noise." It is unclear what sort of real-world noise qualifies as good, since Kafka never expresses delight or pleasure in any of the noises he encounters. Presumably this concept belongs to the realm of literature. Though the noise in "The Burrow" is not good in any conventional sense, and certainly the burrower perceives it as altogether terrible, it gives Kafka an object or experience through which to articulate the limits of what a fictional character can hear and understand. Perhaps "good noise" describes sound that complicates a work of literature and simultaneously makes itself available for the theorization of that work. It is inaudible, unlocatable, and uncaused, but nevertheless helps define the limits of fictional consciousness.

The Telephonic Acousmêtre in *The Castle*

In 1922 Kafka was also thinking about noise and work in the context of his great unfinished novel, *The Castle,* which contains some of his most extensive and complex representations of disembodied sounds, and his only explicit literary treatment of their technological mediation. The letters that describe acoustic disruptions in relation to work provide a context for understanding the telephonic acousmêtre in *The Castle*.

As Michel Chion has argued, telephones played a major role in cinema even before the advent of sound film. "One might think that it is the talking cinema that gave birth to stories built around telephones. We have only to see old silent films . . . to dispel this notion. The telephone, and everything having to do with the circulation of sounds and voices, was as interesting to silent film as it was a challenge to depict."[43] Silent film can depict people engaged in telephone conversations and thereby evoke the experience of acousmatic sound, even if the contradictory reality is that "a telephone is the opposite of a silent movie, in that it gives us a voice without letting us see who is speaking"; silent film, by contrast, shows us speakers without letting us hear what they are saying.[44] But this neat inversion does not actually explain silent film's interest in the device. "Why is the telephone a favorite device of suspense narrative?" Chion asks. "Because it serves in separation and disjunction; the voice travels through space, bodies stay where they are."[45]

What Chion does not say is that one needs neither an acoustic medium nor a visual one to capture the suspense and confusion associated with the telephonic acousmêtre. The experience of "separation and disjunction" can be communicated as powerfully through literature as through film, silent or sound. One can hear a disembodied sound, or see or read about a character hearing a disembodied sound—all of these approaches communicate the unsettling yet titillating experience of hearing a voice on the line and not knowing where the source of that voice is located or to whom it belongs. In the case of Kafka, this uneasy interest is intensified by the fact that his characters often do not have direct access to the telephone (they merely watch others using one) or they do not understand what they are hearing on the line. Chion notes that the suspense provided by the telephone also helps structure film narrative:

> Just as the intervention of an acousmatic voice often makes the story into a quest whose goal is to anchor the voice in a body, the voice of a stranger on the phone poses the necessity of localizing the source of the call, i.e. the voice's point of origin, and thus assigning a place to the voice that doesn't yet have one—and then, putting a face to this voice. For when the voice is not yet localized, it tends to suffuse the whole filmic space, and to take on terrifying powers.[46]

The telephonic acousmêtre introduces such a quest in *The Castle*: the voice on the line represents an uncertain, unstable connection to the castle, but access nonetheless. It motivates K.'s search for a way in. In Kafka's novel, the effects of the telephonic acousmêtre are agitating and disruptive (as well as comedic), though not exactly "terrifying." If mysterious telephone calls frequently enhance horror in cinema, they enhance the sense of the uncanny and the absurd in Kafka's novel. Moreover, the telephonic voices in *The Castle* cannot be deacousmatized. They suffuse the literary space of Kafka's novel with the unfulfillable promise of contact with the castle.

There are three important scenes involving the telephone in *The Castle*. They represent a double movement, both toward an increasingly direct access to and engagement with telephonic sound and away from an understanding of the telephone as a medium of communication. The answer to the question implicitly posed in all of them—can one trust what one hears on the telephone?—is both yes and no. One cannot trust the content or message of the disembodied voice on the line, but there is a kind of truth in the inarticulate, incessant sound of telephonic activity that accompanies castle work: the technological acousmêtre communicates the noise of work.

The first encounter with a telephone comes early in the novel, soon after K. arrives in the village. He witnesses a telephone conversation taking place on his behalf between Schwarzer, a young man at the inn where K. has fallen asleep, and an undercastellan called Fritz. In this episode the disembodied voice coming from the castle is largely inaudible to K. and the reader. It has a negative presence, as K. only hears Schwarzer respond and react to Fritz's voice. K. seems to make out the name of the undercastellan and to detect when there is silence on the other end, but he must otherwise rely on Schwarzer's side of the conversation, which is first paraphrased and then cited directly. This places K., along with the narrator and reader, in a rather tenuous position vis-à-vis telephonic sound: its ringing disturbs his rest and the voices it transmits are largely inaccessible to him. K. is at the mercy of an apparatus to which he is not privy.

This starts to change toward the end of the scene. First, Schwarzer's words seem to echo Fritz's, which clues K. in to the content of their conversation: "'Just what I said! Not a trace of a land-surveyor. A common, lying vagabond, and probably worse'" (C 7, trans. modified). The opening exclamation suggests that Schwarzer is confirming what he has just heard, which is bad news for K. (the men are in agreement that K. is not who he claims to be) but notable in that K. has found a way into the conversation. Then the phone rings again, "with a special insistence, it seemed to K.," and his fate is suddenly reversed: "He listened to a fairly long statement, and then said in a low voice: 'A mistake, is it? I'm sorry to hear that. The head of the department himself said so? Very peculiar, very peculiar. How am I to explain it all to the Land-Surveyor?'" (C 7, trans. modified). It seems that Schwarzer is echoing back the precise words he has just heard, but turning Fritz's statements into questions. Taken aback by the castle's reversed judgment on K.'s status, Schwarzer finds himself unable to respond to the voice on the line. He simply repeats what he has heard, with mild incredulity.

These phone calls reflect a complex engagement with the phenomenon of disembodied sound. They simultaneously emphasize the challenge of writing about the multiple sounds of the apparatus and how unquestioningly we buy into its conditions and demands: the ringing of the phone, the disembodied voice on the line, and potential problems of hearing and communication. Since neither K. nor the narrator has his ear to the receiver, the narrator must describe a conversation of which he hears only one side. Kafka employs familiar techniques for representing the embodied voice (the one who speaks on the phone and is physically present), such as paraphrase and citation, but he must also develop novel ways to write about the disembodied, technologized, half-audible voice on the line. This voice is presented through echoing and modified repetition: its content is reflected and refracted through the embodied voice. This means that the voice on the line is not only disembodied and technologically mediated, but becomes accessible only when its contents are repeated by another.

All this seems to point to the tenuous and compromised status of the disembodied voice, yet this scene actually demonstrates an absolute trust in it. K. appears certain that the judgment passed on him—that he is a common vagrant, not a land surveyor—will hold. After the surprise second phone call, whose content is also transmitted in Schwarzer's echoed responses, K. is equally confident that the judgment will be reversed: "K. pricked up his ears. So the Castle had recognized him as the Land-Surveyor" (C 7). K.'s conclusion hardly jells with the multiple mediations of the content being delivered. The passage validates the telephone as a medium of accurate and trustworthy communication, even though access to voices on the line is limited and indirect.

This is the starting point of the telephonic imaginary in *The Castle*. In K.'s next encounter with the apparatus, he gets closer to the disembodied voice but begins to lose confidence in its communicative function. Once again, someone from the village is calling the castle on K.'s behalf, this time in an attempt to gain entry. Though K. himself is not holding the receiver, he hears the reply: "The 'no' of the answer was audible even to K. at his table. But the answer went on and was still more explicit; it ran as follows: 'neither tomorrow nor at any other time' " (C 26). K. seems to have gotten one step closer to the disembodied voice on the line, and the communicative act is entirely successful, though its result is disappointing.

At this point K. decides to take matters into his own hands and call the castle himself. He is hoping to get not only a positive response, but one as clear and comprehensible as the one the last phone caller elicited. K.'s plan arouses excitement and skepticism, but no one is prepared for his encounter with the telephonic acousmêtre:

> The receiver gave out a buzzing [*Summen*] of a kind that K. had never before heard on a telephone. It was like the humming [*Summen*] of countless children's voices—and yet it was not a humming [*Summen*], but rather the song [*Gesang*] of distant, very distant voices—blended in a virtually impossible manner into one high but resonant sound

that vibrated on the ear as if it were trying to penetrate beyond mere hearing. K. listened without attempting to telephone, leaned his left arm on the telephone shelf and listened like that. (C 27, trans. modified; S 36)

When K. finally gets the phone to his ear, he hears not a voice, but an indeterminate and "virtually impossible" sound. Is it "buzzing" or "singing"? Does it originate in a single voice or multiple voices? Is it made by a child or an adult? Does it come from near or far? Kafka packs all this ambiguity and confusion into a single sentence, and offers no answers. K. is stunned into silence, and the reader also shares in this confusion about the nature and effects of the voice on the line. At last K. has direct access to the disembodied telephonic voice, but finds himself so overwhelmed by its inner contradictions that he can muster no response. He turns into a passive listener, which is to say, he fails to make proper use of the communicative medium. This is what it means to "listen without telephoning."

K. seems to lose his voice temporarily. When he is addressed by the landlord, someone in his physical presence, K. yells at him, a speech act that draws K. back into the realm of vocal communication. The voice on the line responds to K.'s yelling, which was of course meant for someone else. This creates the feeling, once again, that a voice that is "present" (i.e., embodied) is required to complete the act of telephony, although the whole point of the apparatus is to dispense with embodiment. This time K. can understand and describe the voice on the line—" 'Oswald speaking; who's there?' " it states in a "severe, arrogant voice with a small defect in its speech"—but he still finds himself unable to respond: "K. hesitated to announce himself, for he was at the mercy of the telephone; the other could shout him down or hang up the receiver, and that might mean the blocking of a not unimportant way of access" (C 27). When he finally does respond, he claims to be the assistant to the land surveyor. He becomes increasingly entangled in this lie as he is asked to specify which land surveyor and which assistant; when he gives an answer, Josef, this only raises more questions, as the assistants are called Artur and Jeremias.[47] After the issue of his identity is sorted out (not correctly, but to the satisfaction of the voice at the other end of the line), K. finally brings himself to ask his question: " 'When can my master come to the Castle?' 'Never,' was the answer. 'Very well,' said K., and hung up the receiver' " (C 28).

At this point K. is no closer to his goal (access to the castle) than he was prior to the phone call, but he has successfully engaged in an act of telephonic communication, a meaningful exchange of disembodied voices. Ironically, this shows not only that even K.'s victories hardly advance his situation and cause, but also that the apparently successful exchange rests on a series of lies and obfuscations. Telephonic communication only succeeds when K. assumes a false name and position, which means that the interaction takes place between a disembodied voice and a liar. In the language of communication theory, messages are transmitted, but the status of both the sender and recipient is uncertain at best and false at worst. Voices are heard, information is exchanged, and meaningful responses are elicited, but the basic condition of this apparent exchange is deception and trickery.

K.'s second encounter with the telephone thus brings him into direct contact with the apparatus and allows him to hear and engage with the disembodied voice on the line, yet the value of the communicative act is undermined. Indeed, the closer K. gets to the telephone, the less it seems that the apparatus can aid communication. This passage also introduces another element that will prove central to K.'s final encounter with the telephone in *The Castle*: the inexplicable buzzing on the line. This telephonic noise, the ambiguous wordless humming that emanates from the receiver, is the essential acoustic dimension of the apparatus. Kafka's narrator does not invalidate the new medium as a whole, but he does undermine its communicative power. One cannot trust the content or tone of the disembodied voice on the line, but this does not mean there is no truth to telephonic sound. The precise nature of this truth, which emerges with alarming clarity in the third and final telephonic encounter, is noise.

In the earlier scene in which K. was exposed to the humming or buzzing (*Summen*) on the line, it was suggested that grasping this experience requires more than mere hearing: the disembodied voice on the line "vibrated on the ear as if it were trying to penetrate beyond mere hearing" (C 27). This "Summen" is not like other verbal messages. It is a disembodied sound that penetrates the listener's body, paralyzes him, and stuns him into silence. This effect is especially remarkable when one recalls that the sound K. hears resists embodiment (its source cannot be known) and defies attempts at characterization (it is full of contradictions: single/multiple, near/far, adult/childlike, buzzing/singing). Kafka has created a telephonic acousmachine, one whose source will always elude the searcher.

The third telephone scene in *The Castle* is not an encounter with the apparatus, but a discussion of it that takes place between K. and the director (*Vorsteher*). When K. tries to explain that his engagement as land surveyor was confirmed on the day of his arrival via a phone conversation between Schwarzer and Fritz, K. is promptly informed that these telephone calls do not constitute real contact: "'You haven't once up to now come into real contact [*Berührung*] with our authorities. All those contacts [*Berührungen*] of yours have been illusory, but because of your ignorance of the circumstances you take them to be real'" (C 93; S 115). Interestingly, K. is not accused of lying or presenting false information; he is simply told that there has been no actual "contact." It seems K. has misunderstood the nature of the telephone, which is a real and functioning apparatus, just not one that enables communication. K.'s error was to think that its purpose was to allow for verbal exchange between physically separate entities. As the director explains through an analogy, the telephone is a one-way entertainment machine: "'In inns and such places it may be of real use—as much use, say, as a penny in the music-box slot—but it's nothing more than that' " (*C* 93). This explains why K. mistook humming for song, as well as his silence and paralysis in the face of this sound: he was not so much having a phone conversation as engrossed in the low-fi playback of recorded music.[48]

Yet it would be wrong to dismiss the sound coming from the telephone receiver, this "humming of countless children's voices," this "song of distant, very distant voices," as frivolous entertainment, not least because it is associated with castle work.

> "In the Castle the telephone works beautifully of course; I've been told it's being used there all the time; that naturally speeds up the work a great deal. We can hear this continual telephoning in our telephones down here as a rustling and singing [*Rauschen und Gesang*], you must have heard it too. Now, this humming and singing transmitted by our telephones is the only real and reliable thing you'll hear, everything else is deceptive." (*C* 93–94, trans. modified; *S* 116)

At first the director's explanation seems simple: the buzzing, which is now referred to as "rustling and singing," is the acoustic accompaniment to or by-product of the work being done in the castle. When K. rings up the castle, he hears these sounds, whose purpose is not to communicate a message but to signal the constant activity of castle employees. But why does their labor involve the telephone? If this apparatus is not a communicative medium but an expressive one, what sort of work is being done? The novel does not answer this question. The status of the castle and the people and work associated with it remain indeterminate. Yet the director's assumption that constant phone conversations *clearly* enhance industriousness and efficiency reflects a naive and blind faith in technology.

Even if K. and the reader are unwilling to accept that the "rustling and singing" improve or accelerate the work of the castle, it is worth noting that Kafka again tries to account for acousmatic sound through the rhetoric of work. This humming is the single true, reliable, and honest sound that the telephone transmits. Notwithstanding the director's clichéd embrace of technological progress, the "rustling and singing" seem to stand in a proper relation to work. This aligns the disembodied sounds of telephony with Kafka's epistolary reflections on the scuttling mice, whose proletarian work keep Kafka from writing, and the circular saw, whose noisy buzzing signals the manual labor of the forester and once again prevents the work of the author. For K., as for Kafka, the work of others presents an acoustic disturbance that obstructs one's own work: a disembodied noise thwarts K.'s attempts to perform his duties at the same time as it indicates that in a distant, unspecified, inaccessible place—the castle—*work is being done*. This noise-induced exchange of labor is a fantasy, a mental construction that allows Kafka and

K. to rationalize their own failure to work as a necessary consequence of other people's productivity.

The telephone, this modern bearer of the acousmêtre, thus participates in the same logic of labor exchange that Kafka invoked in his 1917 and 1922 letters to Weltsch. Here it is helpful to remember that the second letter was written while Kafka was hard at work on *The Castle*, which makes it tempting to read K.'s encounters with the telephonic acousmêtre biographically: K. is prevented from his work by disembodied sounds, just as Kafka was; K. rationalizes this disruption according to an exchange of labor, just as Kafka did. Thus, Kafka projects the frustration of his own writing experience, which he figures as a kind of work (perhaps even more so at this point, since by 1922 it was clear that he would not be returning to his office job), onto a character whose work is also disturbed by disembodied noise. Moreover, neither K. nor Kafka can simply dismiss the sounds that interfere with his work, not just because they are an ineradicable acoustic presence over which he has little control, but because they point to seemingly legitimate forms of work. Kafka realizes that the forester is simply doing his job and he cannot interfere with this, and K. is made to recognize that the buzzing and singing transmitted over the telephone line is indicative of "the extremely important work up there that goes on furiously the whole time" (C 94). The work of the castle is not to be interrupted.

The letter from 1922 also helps explain why Kafka would characterize the disembodied sound on the line as "rustling and singing." This description points to the complexity and inconsistency of the sound transmitted from the castle: it is noise *and* music. What exactly this means is not clear, but these terms call up contrasting associations and reactions: cacophony and melody, irritation and pleasure, excess and measure. The double description is also reminiscent of Kafka's idealized account of Mahler's work space in this letter, in which "rustling [*Rauschen*]" and "song [*Gesang*]" were separate and perfectly compartmentalized: while Mahler was composing music, the trees deflected external sound and guaranteed silence; later the noisy work of sawing wood could proceed. In Kafka's imagination there is a neat exchange of manual and artistic labor in Mahler's world, but in his own and K.'s rather imperfect worlds these kinds of work exist in a tangled, insoluble mess. Telephonic sound in *The Castle* thus signals not the meaninglessness and futility of castle activity, but the indeterminate and unknowable status of the work being done. For there seems to be little doubt that *some* kind of work is taking place, and that the voices, noises, and music that K. and others perceive when they call are its acoustic effects, but whether this work is proletarian labor or office work, manual or mental, and mundane or artistic cannot be discerned.[49]

This is why K. cannot simply ignore the disembodied sounds on the telephone line. The conversation between K. and the director ends with a discussion about the "real meaning" of these castle phone calls (C 94). After hearing the director's claims that the telephone is not a medium of communication, that everything it seems to transmit other than inchoate buzzing is in fact illusory, and that one rarely if ever gets to speak to anyone with real power and influence, K. is ready to dismiss the telephone and disavow his earlier trust in it. The director stops him in his tracks:

> "These telephone replies certainly have a real meaning [*wirkliche Bedeutung*], why shouldn't they? . . . All these utterances have no official significance [*amtliche Bedeutung*]; when you attach official significance [*amtliche Bedeutung*] to them you go astray. On the other hand, their private significance [*private Bedeutung*] in a friendly or hostile sense is very great, generally greater than any official significance [*amtliche Bedeutung*] could ever be." (C 94–95, trans. modified; S 117)

The director insists on the importance of the phone calls to the castle, even if we cannot grasp the difference between "official" and "private" significance, or whether "real" significance is equal to the latter. Indeed, the proliferation of distinctions is less about specifying meanings than unsettling conclusions. Here the assertion of a difference prevents K. from dismissing the phone calls, but gets him no closer to understanding their importance. Though K. cannot trust the content of the disembodied voices on the line, the "rustling and singing" are genuine if mysterious indications of castle work. The technological acousmêtre has no message to communicate, but this does not render it meaningless or worthless. Rather, it expresses the fluid and unspecifiable acoustic dimension of work.

Like the noise in "The Burrow," telephonic sound in *The Castle* is perceptible but not localizable or identifiable. These voices on the line are another instance of the acousmachine, sounds that come from an elsewhere that is nowhere. They cannot be deacousmatized, for this process would imply direct access to the castle, and this is what Kafka's novel persistently withholds. The unreal, unknowable object at the novel's center cannot simply materialize, just as the source and nature of the noise in "The Burrow" cannot simply be discovered. Such resolutions would flatten the mysteries at the heart of these narratives, and thus make present the absent centers that structure Kafka's works. Deacousmatization would erase their liminal, indeterminate status, which is precisely what makes them troublesome and productive. The telephone must remain an acousmachine if the castle is to be both real and inaccessible, perceptible and unknowable.

Metalepsis as Species Transcendence:
Kafka's "Investigations of a Dog"

In 1922, the year he composed *The Castle*, Kafka also wrote "Investigations of a Dog," which presents the most powerful instance of global metalepsis in his oeuvre. In this story a narrating dog identifies various mysteries about "dogdom [*die Hundeschaft*]," which he formulates as research questions: for instance, where does canine nourishment come from, and why do some members of the species, the "air-dogs [*Lufthunde*]," practice a kind of levitation? These problems represent complex enigmas from the dog's perspective, and indeed for his entire species. They might initially present some confusion for the reader as well, until she realizes that humans are responsible for producing all the seemingly uncaused and inexplicable effects experienced by the dogs. The dogs can see and eat the food left out for them, but not the human hands that put it there. Likewise, they perceive their fellow lapdogs as floating "air-dogs" because they are blind to the human laps they sit on and the human arms that carry them. Thus, the topics that fuel the narrating dog's research are banal and mundane from the human perspective. The story's central lesson, it seems, is that we cannot see what we cannot see.

To belong to a species is to live with certain limitations on perception, experience, and cognition. Not only are Kafka's dogs incapable of removing these blinders; they are also in general unaware of their presence. These limits determine their capacity for self-understanding—that is, until one day the narrator dog begins to see what he cannot see. "Investigations of a Dog" introduces what I call "species transcendence": a single dog begins to grasp his circumscribed perspective on the world; he becomes aware of the perceptual and cognitive horizons that govern his understanding and, at times, cause him to misinterpret the world and give false explanations for its apparent mysteries and problems. Species transcendence names this moment of recognition—when an individual perceives something from a realm beyond, consciously or not, with or without attempting to explain it. In "Investigations of a Dog" this trace insight into a world beyond canine experience and comprehension is so minimal that it causes more confusion than insight. This has comic effects, since the narrating dog comes up with far-fetched and overly complicated explanations for basic phenomena. He does not know that there are simple solutions to all the "mysteries" of dogdom, which he is constitutionally incapable of grasping. His research program is fueled by his perceptual and cognitive blind spots.[50]

An allegorical reading is possible: the dogs symbolize the hubris of humans, who pose research questions that seem worthy of intensive study and reflection, but in response to which members of another species, whose powers of perception and cognition far surpass ours, could effortlessly give simple answers. Yet the allegory is more complicated than this, because Kafka produces fictions about creatures—mice, dogs, apes, and so on—that are neither fully animal nor fully human. Like humans, they are capable of experiencing and knowing certain things but not others, but because they are not human, the (human) reader can observe and consider their actions and beliefs from a position of (supposedly) greater insight or authority. Species transcendence occurs when an animal becomes aware of the limits of its perceptual and cognitive world, and it reaches a climax in those rare instances in which the animal accesses or intuits something that lies beyond those limits: it has an intimation of another world. By recognizing its limits, the animal relativizes its own existence and thereby begins to locate its place among higher and lower forms of consciousness.

"Investigations of a Dog" offers an instance of species transcendence, even if the dog's sense of a world beyond is never more than a faint intimation, and this constitutes a form of global metalepsis: transcending the limits of consciousness and experience functions analogously to transitioning between narrative worlds in fiction. One process is epistemological while the other is narratological, but they converge in fictional works that problematize the ability to make reports about knowledge. Fictions that narrativize the porousness of species worlds point to the porousness of story worlds. In these works, metalepsis takes the form of an account of species transcendence.

Dr. Seuss's children's book *Horton Hears a Who!* offers a simple yet illuminating example of species transcendence. In this story, the elephant Horton is so sensitive to sound that one day, splashing about in the Jungle of Nool, he hears "a very faint yelp / As if some tiny person were calling for help."[51] Horton, we discover, has heard a sound from another world, one located on a tiny speck of dust, inhabited by the *Whos* and appropriately called *Who-ville*. When the other animals in the jungle hear Horton talking to the clover on which he has placed the dust speck for protection, they think he has gone mad: they themselves cannot hear anything, and moreover they have no reason to believe that there is a world (and possibly millions of worlds) embedded within theirs. But it turns out that Horton really does hear a *Who*, and that the *Whos*, whose world has been put in disarray on account of Horton's incredulous and bullying jungle mates, need his help. It is only by enlisting every last *Who* to make a ruckus that they make enough noise for the other animals to hear them and believe Horton, at which point they also declare themselves willing to serve as the guardians of *Who-ville*, and the story ends.

Stories about the transcendence of species worlds have an inner/outer structure: either a member of a species becomes aware of a world outside and beyond its limits (such as the dog in Kafka's story, who gets an inkling of a higher human consciousness) or a member of a species becomes aware of a world embedded within its world, but previously imperceptible to it (such as Horton).[52] In both cases it can be hard—indeed, world-shattering—to accept this sudden new access to a realm of which one was previously unaware, and, as Horton discovers, even harder to convince others of it. Horton himself barely believes his ears at first, so it is unsurprising that his jungle friends remain incredulous until they can confirm the existence of the *Whos* with their own powers of hearing. There is one further connection between Dr. Seuss's story and Kafka's: they both involve metaleptic sound. In theory one could perceive something from a world beyond or within in multiple ways, but in both of these works this happens through hearing. Thus, it appears that what moves between the worlds in question is a sound—a rogue noise whose source lies in one world but whose effects extend into another, a trans-diegetic sound. As I discussed earlier, the transcendence of narrative worlds via sound also takes place in "The Burrow."

"Observed from a Distance," a story by the Italian writer Primo Levi, offers another instructive example of species transcendence and global meta-lepsis. It takes the form of a report on the state of humanity and the earth in 1967 from the perspective of a higher life form in outer space. The story belongs to the category of metaleptic fictions in which a creature discovers a world below or within its own, yet the structure is also slightly more complicated than this, because it also involves the recognition by the lower consciousness (humans) that it has been discovered by the higher consciousness (Selenites, the mythic native inhabitants of the moon). Thus, humans must reckon with being the objects of another species' scientific study. The Selenites' report has been translated into human language and delivered into human hands, and contains both insights into and misunderstandings about human existence.[53] If the misinterpretations in "Investigations of a Dog" have a comic and absurd quality, there is more pathos and wisdom to these errors in "Observed from a Distance."

The Selenites can only make out very large formations and structures, such as cities, skyscrapers, ships, and stadiums, though they can neither name them nor accurately describe their function. Since they have no inkling of intelligent life on earth, they interpret everything as a natural phenomenon. For instance, having observed the grid-like structure of cities and their expansion outward along spokes, the writer of the report concludes: "The analogy with crystalline growth is obvious and leads one to surmise that Cities are vast zones in which the Earth's surface is characterized by pronounced crystallinity."[54] Buildings and crop fields, which are described but not named, also seem to reflect a "crystalline organization."[55] To take another example, the author of the report offers the following hypothesis about ships, having monitored their "growth" and movement (which they characterize as periodic or aperiodic):

> A bold new theory deserving of attention asserts that they are aquatic animals, the periodic ones intelligent, the others less so (or less well-endowed with a sense of direction). The first group might feed on some material or living species found in Ports. The others, perhaps, feed on smaller ships (to us invisible) in the open sea.[56]

Though the Selenites are looking down on earth from above, a perspective that would seem to put them in the position of greater knowledge, they are actually in a similar position to Kafka's dogs: they can only see half of what is going on before their eyes, and they must account for the other half through (pseudo-)scientific theorization. In Levi's story, we do not know whether it is the distance and quality of their viewing instruments that prevent them from understanding more fully, or whether, like Kafka's dogs, they are constrained by their alien nature. But both stories give the reader the unmistakable advantage of knowing more than the narrators, and hence of being able to evaluate and correct the faulty hypotheses they offer. What is mysterious to them is everyday reality to us. Watching them fumble to explain these "mysteries" is both laughable and poignant—more laughable in Kafka's case, more poignant in Levi's, but a little bit of each in both.

The report in "Observed from a Distance" takes a sobering turn, unbeknownst to its authors, in section 5, "Anomalous Period," which "indicates the period 1939–45, which was characterized by numerous deviations from the Earth's norm":

> As previously mentioned, in the majority of the Cities the phenomenon of evening light (2.1) appeared disrupted or extinguished. Growth also appeared slowed or stopped altogether (2.2). The darkening of the SDE craters was less intense and regular (3.1); the same was true for the coastline darkening (3.2); the SDE luminosity of the urban filaments (3.2), the craters (2.3), and the periodic ships (4.1.1) disappeared.
>
> The pendular rhythm of the periodic ships (4.1.1) appeared seriously diminished; instead the number and mass of aperiodic ships increased, as if they had overpowered the periodic ships. The sudden disappearance of ships in the open sea, a phenomenon normally quite rare, occurred with great frequency. . . .
>
> . . . The end of the Anomalous Period was marked by two very bright explosions, occurring in Japan within 2 days of each other. Similar or stronger ones were observed afterward on various islands in the Pacific and in a confined area of central Asia; at the moment in which we are writing, the phenomenon appears to be extinct or dormant.[57]

Thus Levi gives an account of World War II from the perspective of an alien in outer space who knows nothing of human existence, much less human brutality and tragedy. The report describes a series of effects without causes—changes in patterns of illumination, shipping routes and frequencies, construction in cities, and so on. It says nothing of the human emotions and actions responsible for these changes, or the resulting devastation. The Selenites are unaware of human life, though they perceive the large-scale consequences of human activity.

Levi's story resonates powerfully with Kafka's metaleptic fictions. Here species transcendence is a two-way street, since the Selenite reporter gives his interpretation of earthly occurrences, but the report is also translated for human readers within the story. These readers know they are being observed from a distance by a foreign species. This suggests a peculiar kind of self-relativizing consciousness, an awareness that one can be viewed from beyond the limits of one's reality—or, to speak in narratological terms, that one person's reality can be another person's diegesis. The fact that this nondiegetic perspective, the view from another world, creates a situation of seemingly uncaused effects also resonates powerfully with "The Burrow" and "Investigations of a Dog," stories that present worlds in which effects—often but not always acoustic ones—are perceptible, but their causes are not. One can describe these perceived phenomena as uncaused, or one can say that their causes lie in other worlds. It depends on where one stands.

Much like "The Burrow," "Investigations of a Dog" is a story with a first-person, nonhuman narrator who experiences phenomena that are beyond his powers of understanding—sounds without sources, sights that appear senseless. The salient difference is that in "Investigations of a Dog," the canine narrator thinks (wrongly) that he can name and understand what he perceives. At other moments, he simply denies what he seems to see and hear. Unlike the burrower, who grows frustrated and despondent at his inability to locate the source of the noise, the dog is rather skilled at rationalizing the irrational, explaining the inexplicable. He has absolute faith in his powers of explanation: "In the course of a long life you will encounter many things that would be even more astonishing if taken out of context and seen through the eyes of a child. Furthermore, you can also, of course—as the apt expression goes—'rationalize [*verreden*]' it, as with everything else" (*KSS* 137; *NSF II* 433). Astonishing and extraordinary things, and maybe *everything*, can be "rationalized"—explained or explained away. *Verreden* is a tricky word: it does not exclude the possibility of a correct explanation, nor does it guarantee it. The dog seems to grasp that everything can be given an apparently reasonable explanation.

In fact, his explanations are frequently false, but these errors can lead the reader to truths unavailable to the narrating dog, for she can infer the true and often banal causes of his seemingly bizarre encounters. The narrator cannot access the source of sights and sounds located in the human world, but bits and pieces of this foreign realm come through: he perceives the effects but not the causes of human activity, and ultimately he cannot account for these fragmented and intermittent sensations.[58] Moreover, his powers of explanation are limited by his canine consciousness. "I am not a hair's breadth distant from my canine nature," Kafka's dog narrator insists (*KSS* 143). This is at once a recognition of the limits of his world and an ingenious way to relativize them: it suggests that there *is* actually an outside to dogdom, even if the narrator dwells entirely within it. At other times the narrating dog explicitly doubts the existence of a noncanine realm: "For what else is there besides dogs? Who else can you call upon in this vast, empty world? All knowledge, the totality of all questions and all answers, resides in dogs" (*KSS* 141). The invocation of this outside, even if in negative terms, has a powerful rhetorical effect: it posits a definite cognitive boundary to dogdom. The reader is thus able to perceive and understand the world as the dog does, and to grasp the limits of his consciousness—to see what he cannot see, and why. In fact, the narrator is constantly and unwittingly dropping hints about a world beyond his own. The story even begins with this intuition: "On closer scrutiny I soon find that something was not quite right from the very beginning, that a little fracture was in place" (*KSS* 132). The dog's report is an attempt to account for this fissure.

It is only natural that the dog thinks that dogdom contains all the questions and answers. As Ritchie Robertson argues, "Kafka . . . is satirizing the narrator by showing that the problems he investigates arise from the limitations of his consciousness. The dogs' ignorance of human beings seems to be as irremovable as the barrier between being and consciousness."[59] Though it is remarkable that "the reader is offered a perspective superior to that of the unreliable protagonist," the point of this narrative technique is not simply to allow the reader to laugh at canine folly and ignorance, nor to extend this critique to human scientific endeavors.[60] Beyond these satirical effects, Kafka's story raises the possibility of species transcendence: in other words, consciousness can arise between species, even if knowledge cannot be shared and communicated along these channels. The narrating dog never breaks out of dogdom, despite vague intimations of a world beyond, and the creature in "The Burrow" does not even consciously perceive a crack in his reality. In both works, inexplicable sensations have their causes in other worlds, but their animal narrators are for the most part cognitively blocked from seeing this truth. Each work shows the effects of this blockage—exasperation in "The Burrow" and self-deception in "Investigations of a Dog."

"Investigations of a Dog" thus presents auditory and visual perceptions whose causes cannot be located and named, disembodied sounds and sights. Before examining the acousmatic music and noise that play such a prominent role in the story, it is worth considering its presentation of a visual correlate to the acousmêtre: a disembodied image. How can something be both visible and disembodied? It can be an optical illusion (a hallucination, a projection, a ghost, virtual reality), or it can be real and uncaused. In the former, sense perception plays a trick: one appears to see something, whereas in truth one sees only the simulacrum of that thing. Kafka is not particularly interested in these sorts of illusions. His fantastical beings (Gregor Samsa, Odradek, Red Peter, Josefine, etc.) really are what they seem to be; they are not *trompes l'oeil*. Rather, the mystery of these works involves identifying what these creatures "really are," given the physical forms they assume. Thus the inexplicable sights in "Investigations of a Dog" are real *and* uncaused; their causes derive from an inaccessible beyond of which the perceiving and narrating consciousness can have no knowledge.

The phenomenon of "air dogs [*Lufthunde*]" serves as an example of a disembodied image. These small pets seem to float or drift in the air because they spend their days in the laps and arms of their owners, human beings who are invisible to dogs. The narrator can see his fellow canines, the lap-dogs, but not the cause of their hovering. He can either search endlessly for the cause of this perplexing sight, or he can simply accept and name it, and thereby treat the mystery as solved. He does make an earnest attempt to explain the phenomenon, the first step of which is to accept the inexplicable:

> I considered anything possible, no prejudices limited my conceptual powers; I tracked down the most senseless rumors and followed them as far as I could; in this senseless life the most senseless things seemed to me more probable than anything sensible and especially produc-tive for my research. (*KSS* 144)

This statement seems to preempt the objection that the dog simply rational-izes every inexplicable sight and sound he encounters. Indeed, he accepts the fact that precisely the most senseless phenomena—things that defy sense and sensation—are the most "probable." Thus he does not try to deny the reality of the air dogs; he does not simply explain them away. Though he has never seen one, he notes that he has "long been firmly convinced of their existence" (*KSS* 144, trans. modified). This is the first step of scientific research: to find an object worthy of study and validate its existence.

In order to solve the mystery of the air dogs, the narrator poses a series of questions about them, all of which are aimed at the task of *begründen*—justifying, explaining, motivating, or giving reasons for their strange existence, but also literally grounding them, that is, bringing them down to the ground. He begins by reflecting on the impossibility of this task.

> People begin to produce reasons [*begründen*], to piece together some sort of rational foundation [*Begründung*], they make a beginning, although they will not go beyond this beginning. But that is still some-thing. And in the process something comes to light that, while not the truth—we will never get this far—intimates the deep-rootedness of the lie. All the senseless phenomena of our life, and quite particularly the most senseless, can be rationalized [*begründen*] in this way. Not completely, of course—that is the devilish joke—but just enough to ward off awkward questions. (*KSS* 144; *NSF II* 448)

This is one of the narrator's deepest moments of insight. By admitting that the process of rationalization can never be completed, he acknowledges that the puzzle of the air dogs is insoluble. But the process is revealing—it exposes not the truth, but "the deep-rootedness of the lie." This "lie" derives from excessive confidence in canine powers of understanding; it is the illusion that everything can be adequately explained within the bounds of dogdom. The roots of this lie are deep because they are the foundation of canine self-understanding. The search for "grounding" thus has a further meaning: the truth floats in the air, astonishing and inexplicable, whereas attempts to ground this truth, to root it in the earth, represent potentially false rationalization. The claim that follows—that "all the senseless phenomena of our life, and quite particularly the most senseless, can be rationalized in this way"—demonstrates the degree to which the dog, despite this momentary insight into the limits of his species consciousness, rests content with the false or incomplete explanations he supplies. Canine understanding is not a matter of discovering the truth behind "senseless phenomena," but of avoiding potential embarrassment. The answers and explanations need not be true, so long as they are plausible and respectable.

The running joke in the discussion of the air dogs is that they cannot be "grounded" in two senses: their existence cannot be explained, and they cannot be brought down to the earth. To explain their existence would be to "explain them away": the peculiar phenomenon of air dogs would vanish, as they would descend to the ground, walk on all fours, and cease to present a mystery. Rather than air dogs, they would be ordinary ground dogs; the phenomenon would dissolve in its explanation. The metaphor of groundedness and rootedness thus has a further dimension: the air dogs are ontologically resistant to grounding, for they would disappear in the process.

In addition to the optical mystery of the air dogs, "Investigations of a Dog" contains two crucial scenes of musical mystery. In the first, the narrator encounters a troupe of dancing dogs. He is utterly baffled by their strange activity—the music, the noise, the unusual gestures and movements, the mélange of odors—because he cannot see the humans for whom these dogs are performing. The narrator describes these sights, sounds, and smells, but is unable to form these perceptions into a coherent whole. He cannot comprehend the scene because he can only perceive and cognize the activity of the dogs; he is blind to half of what is taking place. To make sense of the scene he would have to grasp the interplay of canine and human activity: a human orchestra is playing music, a troupe of seven humanly trained dogs is dancing to it, and an audience of humans is presumably clapping, speaking, smoking, and cheering in response. The perspective of the dog can be likened to overhearing one side of a telephone conversation—we can describe what is being said by one party, we can even speculate about what the other party is saying, but in the end it is hard to get a sense of the conversation as a whole. The key difference between these scenarios is that when we overhear one side of a phone conversation, we are at least aware that we are missing something; we know it is a two-sided interaction and grasp the incompleteness of our perception. The narrating dog is largely ignorant of what he does not know.

What he does not know and cannot know is the cause, the reason, the motivation—the *Begründung*—of the scene before him. What does it mean for the narrator dog not to be able to ground the existence of the dancing dogs? In what sense does their presence elude him? His encounter involves at least three modes of perception—sight, sound, and smell—and each of these requires it own justification. The last of these, the olfactory, plays a minor role: the only reference to smell is in the narrator's description of his initial encounter—"everything full of intoxicating smells swelling up in confusion"—and this phrase was inserted in Kafka's revision of the text (*KSS* 134). It adds to the feeling of sensory confusion and overload, but it is not unusual: we are often confronted with unidentifiable smells, though the canine version of this experience is arguably of greater significance than the human one.

The sense of visual mystery is more significant. The narrator describes the dancing dogs in exquisite and lengthy visual detail, only to undermine this perception with concise finality:

> The way they raised and set down their feet, certain turns of their heads, their running and their resting, the attitudes they assumed toward one another, the combinations they formed with one another like a round dance, as when, for example, one braced his front paws on the other's back and then they all positioned themselves so that the first dog, erect, bore the weight of all the others, or as when, their bodies slinking close to the ground, they formed intertwined figures and never made a mistake—not even the last one, who was a little unsure of himself, did not always immediately hook up with the others, staggered a little, as it were, when the melody struck up, but was unsure only by comparison with the magnificent certainty of the others, and even had he been much more unsure, indeed utterly unsure, he would not have ruined anything, since the others, great masters, were keeping time so steadily. And yet you hardly saw them, you hardly saw a single one of them. (*KSS* 134–35, trans. modified)

There is a stark discrepancy between the detail of the visual description, which includes subtle gestures, slight movements, and intricate bodily formations, and the denial of visibility at the end of the passage. With respect to the air dogs, one must affirm the perception even if one cannot explain it; one will find some sort of justification (*Begründung*), even if it is really just a matter of "explaining it away [*verreden*]." The dancing dogs present the opposite scenario: no matter how vivid the perception, if it cannot be "grounded" it must be considered unreal; the narrator would sooner doubt his perceptual abilities than validate inexplicable sights.

Thinking, wrongly, that he cannot trust his eyes, the narrator puts his faith in his ears instead. He seems to trust completely in the sounds he hears, though his initial descriptions of them are vague: he refers simply to "noise [*Lärm*]" and to "music [*Musik*]," using each term repeatedly and with little or no adornment, as if the qualities of these sounds were entirely self-evident. These are acousmatic sounds: the narrator cannot see or know where either the music or the noise is coming from. But they are also uncaused sounds, in the same sense that the noise in the burrow is uncaused—their source lies in an elsewhere that is nowhere, a world to which the perceiving subject has no access. But the narrating dog will not simply accept this mystery.

> Had I not seen that they were dogs and that they themselves brought this clamor [*Lärm*] with them—although I could not see how they produced it—I would have run away this minute, but as matters stood, I stayed. (*KSS* 134; *NSF II* 427)

> They did not speak, they did not sing, in general they held their tongue with almost a certain doggedness [*mit einer gewissen Verbissenheit*], but they conjured forth music out of that empty space. (*KSS* 134; *NSF II* 428)

Despite visual evidence to the contrary, the narrator confidently claims that the dancing dogs produce the music; this is a declaration of inexplicable but certain agency. He thinks all senseless phenomena can be rationalized, though, so he must assume that these mute dogs are engaged in a mysterious, magical, noncorporeal conjuring of music. They can make music without giving off a visual sign of making music. His use of canine metaphors reminds us that the joke is on him, the narrating dog, whose earnest scientific manner betrays no humor or self-doubt. For we must remember that the supposed mystery has a simple, even banal solution: human musicians are present, but the narrating dog is ontologically incapable of seeing them; their visibility, though not their audibility, lies beyond the realm of his sensory and cognitive faculties.

Later the narrating dog describes the music with great precision and passion, though these details hardly resolve the question of how it is produced. Indeed, he suggests that the auditory rush prevents him from seeing and thinking clearly:

> You observed them in the usual way, like dogs that you meet on the street; you wanted to go up to them, exchange greetings, for they were also very close—dogs, certainly much older than me and not of my long-haired woolly variety but also not too unusual in size and shape, really rather familiar; I knew many of such a breed, or a similar one, but while you were still caught up in such reflections, the music gradually took over, practically seized hold of you, swept you away from these real little dogs, and quite against your will, resisting with all your might, howling as if pain were being inflicted, you could attend to nothing but this music that came from all sides, from the

heights, from the depths, from everywhere, pulling the listener into
its midst, pouring over him, crushing him, and even after annihilat-
ing him, still blaring its fanfares at such close range that they turned
remote and barely audible. (*KSS* 135)

For someone who described himself as "unmusical," Kafka produced a
remarkably detailed account of the devastating impact of musical experience
on his narrating dog. It recalls the description of Gregor Samsa listening to
his sister Grete play the piano: "Was he an animal, that music could move
him so?" (*M* 54). Yet the primary cause of the narrator's cognitive destabilization is not the musical experience, or even the perplexing relationship
between music and noise, but the confusion and unease generated by its dis-
embodiment. As the narrator states, "Their secretive nature [*verschwiegenes
Wesen*] seemed to me more important than the music" (*KSS* 160; *NSF II*
481). The German word *verschwiegen* suggests not only secrecy, but silence,
even the quality of being closed-lipped. Taken together with the dogs' powerful musicality, this quality represents the heart of their mysterious existence:
they are simultaneously closed-lipped *and* musical. The visual appearance of
nonparticipation combined with the auditory perception of musical effects is
the problem of uncaused sound.

Perhaps the story's first clue that the narrating dog really has intimations
of a world beyond can be found in its title, even if it was not originally chosen
by Kafka. As Stanley Corngold argues, this title points to

> an overarching consciousness reading or registering this memoir. For,
> just as the narrator throughout the tale will reveal almost no trace
> whatsoever of the existence of a consciousness higher than that of
> the dog—in a word, no trace of human consciousness—we cannot
> imagine the dog narrator himself, or then again a dog administrator,
> or even a dog readership to whom this report was to be submitted,
> titling it the researches "of a dog"—of whom else would the prod-
> uct be? . . . This trace-presence in the title of "Forschungen eines
> Hundes"—the tailings of a higher, a human consciousness—alert us
> to the narrative duplicity that informs the entire memoir-report, an
> ontological duplicity mirroring the duplicity of genres. It is the omni-
> presence of the unremarked, invisible human order.[61]

My only disagreement with Corngold's reading is that there is "almost no
trace whatsoever" of a higher consciousness within the narrative. The narrator's numerous references to "the race of dogs [*das Hundegeschlecht*],"
"dogdom [*die Hundeschaft*]," and "the being of dogs [*das Hundewesen*]"
suggest the distinctiveness of dogs over and against other species; these references to caninity are continuous reminders of the "omnipresence of the
unremarked, invisible human order." One can read this psychologically (the

narrator has a subconscious inkling that dogs are not alone in the world) or as a kind of "blind insight": he consistently identifies the very thing he cannot see, and thereby pinpoints that which is incompatible with his view of the world. In any event, these textual elements indicate the presence of a higher, outside consciousness.

Throughout the fragment the narrator wrestles with these subconscious inklings or blind insights: should he acknowledge or suppress these faint suspicions of another world? The references to "senseless phenomena" and to things that are "astonishing," in addition to the discourse on "grounding" and the idea of "explaining away," are all part of this sensory and cognitive struggle. As someone engaged in "science [*Wissenschaft*]," a word that appears in the story several times, the dog wants to think of his work as guided by empirical evidence. He wants to trust his senses, to affirm the empirical, even if this forces him to embrace the incredible and to accept the possibility that there are causes, reasons, and explanations beyond his powers of understanding. The alternative is to question one's sensory powers—to say that there is nothing that is actually incredible or inexplicable, but rather only things that *appear* so. The narrator adopts this approach, at least to some extent, when trying to reckon with the dancing dogs: rather than fully admit that their musicality is incredible—that it represents a sound without a source—he insists that the dogs must be responsible for the music, even though they appear to his eyes not to be. But this process of "rationalization" or "grounding" is never entirely successful. The narrator finds himself unable to provide satisfactory answers to the puzzling phenomena he encounters: neither the air dogs nor the dancing dogs are fully explained, and other issues, such as the mystery of canine nutrition, likewise find no resolution.

The narrator associates complete openness to the ungraspable with a childish sensibility: children tend to harbor unconditional faith in their sensory powers, even if they cannot form this perceptual yield into a coherent whole. They are able to see and hear the world without feeling the need to rationalize and explain everything. Children see more, because they do not automatically filter out that which seems senseless and impossible; their notion of reality is more elastic than that of adults. Thus the narrator notes: "In the course of a long life you will encounter many things that would be even more astonishing if taken out of context and seen through the eyes of a child" (*KSS* 137). The child accepts a state of wonder, whereas the adult resorts to rationalization techniques, or simply fails to see what cannot be grasped. The struggle of the researcher, who seeks to penetrate the mysteries of the world, is to find a balance between amazement and rationalization.

There is a final musical encounter in "Investigations of a Dog" that draws together these two central concerns of the story, uncaused sound and the struggle of the researcher. The narrator, in a state of hunger-induced delirium (he has starved himself for his research on canine nutrition), has an out-of-body experience which raises the fleeting possibility of species transcendence. He encounters another singing dog—presumably a hunting dog, whose music comes from a huntsman's horn—and fully embraces a senseless, ungrounded perception. The effects of starvation have restored the perceptual and cognitive functions of a child, which allow him to perceive the world in a way that is open and unprejudiced, and dispenses with the constant impulse to "ground."[62]

The episode begins with a rather lengthy conversation between the starving dog and the hunting dog, in which each one makes a futile attempt to understand the other's motivations: the hunting dog cannot grasp why the starving dog will not leave the premises when asked, and the starving dog cannot comprehend why the hunting dog insists that he do this. All this is "self-evident" and "natural" to the hunting dog, but not to the more critical and probing narrator. As in the case of the air dogs and the dancing dogs, here too the narrator is confronted with canine effects that have human (and hence imperceptible and unknowable) causes. The hunting dog's final question—"'Don't you understand things that are self-evident [*das Selbstverständliche*]?'"—is a trigger for the narrator (*KSS* 159; *NSF II* 478). He suddenly grasps the paradox of not grasping the self-evident, of not understanding that which contains its own understanding (the German word *das Selbstverständliche* literally means that which can be understood by itself).

> I no longer answered, for I noticed—and at this, new life ran through me, such life as is conferred by terror—I noticed through intangible details, which perhaps no one besides me could have detected, that from the depths of his chest this dog was getting ready to sing. "You are going to sing," I said. "Yes, he said gravely, I am going to sing; soon, but not yet." "You are already beginning," I said. "No," he said, "not yet. But get ready." "I can hear your song in spite of your denials," I said, trembling. He was silent. And then I believe I perceived something that no dog had ever experienced before me; at any rate, cultural memory does not contain even the slightest hint of it; and in infinite anxiety and shame I hurriedly lowered my face into the puddle of blood in front of me. What I seemed to perceive was that the dog was already singing without his being aware of it—no more than that: that the melody, detached from him, was floating through the air and then past him according to its own laws, as if he no longer had any part in it, floating at me, aimed only at me. (*KSS* 159)

The narrator describes this moment as rejuvenating, which suggests his return to a childlike mode of perception, unconstrained by the laws of causality and rational justification. Indeed, he claims that he alone can perceive these "intangible details"; they are simply unavailable to the mature canine, who suppresses unreasonable sights and sounds, willfully or unconsciously.

What exactly does the narrator perceive here? What is this jarring, powerful, and ultimately unaccountable perception that he nevertheless acknowledges and affirms? It represents, once again, a disjunction between the auditory experience of music and the visual appearance of a singer. His experience is unprecedented in the canine world because it is an impossible perception: a song whose singer does not appear to be singing. There is a possible connection to ventriloquism—recall Moissi's recitational style—and to Kafka's silent Sirens: they appear to sing but (probably) emit no sound, whereas the dog appears not to be singing but produces a sound. This is also the problem of the acousmêtre (the source of the sound is elsewhere and invisible) or nondiegetic sound (the source of the sound is nowhere, i.e., in another world). According to the narrator, the dogs *must* be responsible for the sound, even if all visual evidence suggests otherwise. He is willing to contradict his own visual perception because he cannot conceive of a sound whose source derives from another world, an inaccessible and unknowable beyond. The narrator cannot "rationalize" this astonishing experience, nor can he transcend his own consciousness and speculate about a realm outside his grasp. He is left to conclude that there is in fact nothing "self-evident" about "that which is self-evident." He grasps that this term is a dead-end answer, a substitute designation for the apparently inexplicable. But he also displays a momentary understanding when he states that the music he hears was meant for him, that it detaches from the "singing" dog and aims straight for him, the listener. He is dimly aware that this is a metaleptic sound: it derives from another world and enters into his. There is a hint of species transcendence through sound.

In the end, this inkling of a world beyond is too much for the narrator to bear. Rather than affirm the impossible and embrace the incredible, he denies the perception, together with the nascent understanding of other worlds that it brought forth.

> Today, of course, I deny any such perceptions and attribute them to my overstimulation at the time, but even if it was an error, it nevertheless had a certain grandeur and is the sole reality, even if only an apparent reality, that I salvaged and brought back into this world from the time of my fast, and it shows, at least, how far we can go when we are completely out of our senses [*bei völligem Außer-sich-sein*]. And I really was completely out of my senses [*völlig außer mir*]. (*KSS* 159; *NSF II* 479)

Unable to rationalize the experience, the narrator rejects it outright as a product of hunger-induced delirium. He chooses denial and dismissal over insistence that he, a dog, has grasped that which is unfathomable to canines. It is easier to suppress a single sense experience than to overturn an entire perceptual and cognitive paradigm. But when he claims to have been "outside myself [*außer mir*]," he is not simply describing an odd feeling. He was not just out of sorts, but actually disembodied, in the sense of being removed from his body. The dog transcends his physical body—"I was truly completely outside myself," in another translation—which is why he can momentarily glimpse that which is otherwise inaccessible to his species. He must leave his own body to perceive a sound that is at once disembodied and embodied. This self-removal allows him to perceive as a child does, without the constraints of (canine) reason and logic. It allows him momentarily to understand that which is beyond his powers of understanding. This disembodied state is the precondition for his perception of the disembodied song of the hunting dog.

Having denied its validity, the dog refers to this experience as "only an apparent reality." Ultimately he is not able to transcend canine powers of perception and cognition in any real or lasting way, but the incident nonetheless introduces the possibility of species transcendence. Though the narrator immediately denies the experience—in the end, rationalization proves easier than confronting the ungraspable—it has tremendous explanatory potential for the reader. To be "outside oneself" is not only to be physically removed from one's body, but also to be outside one's species world. This is the perspective needed to understand the phenomenon of a sound without a source. In "The Burrow," this perspective is absent. In "Investigations of a Dog," it is offered up to the reader, and dangled enticingly in front of the canine narrator.

Both stories revolve around animals that are disturbed by intrusions from other worlds that they are unequipped to understand or combat. "Investigations of a Dog" is a less subtle though funnier story, since Kafka gives his reader numerous opportunities to see and understand what the narrating dog cannot, even though it is right before his eyes, and to laugh at him. Each mystery or "research question" leaves him metaphorically butting his head against the limits of dogdom. The convoluted and counterempirical "explanations" that he dreams up all point to the fact that his only real scientific principle is to ground everything in the canine—a dogged insistence on dogdom. The reader laughs at the narrator's folly, but this is not all: she becomes attuned to the false explanations that result from the limits of species consciousness combined with the inclination to rationalize. There is no parallel discourse in "The Burrow," yet it is governed by the same perceptual and cognitive constraints: the burrower cannot conceive of an outside to "burrowdom." He knows there is a physical space beyond his burrow, but not that there is a world beyond whose effects are perceptible to him but whose causes are inaccessible. Nor can the burrowing animal explain away dissonant experiences, as the investigating dog does. He tries, but right up until the end of the fragment he is wondering, guessing, speculating, and generating hypotheses that inevitably prove wrong. He exists in a permanent state of agitation and uncertainty. For the burrower uncaused sounds find no resolution, whereas the dog simply denies sense perceptions that do not mesh with his preconceptions of the world. The burrower suffers from inexplicable sensations, whereas the dog takes comfort in false rationalizations. They represent different attitudes toward the experience of uncaused sound and species transcendence.

Noise as a Figure of Metalepsis

In *The Voice in Cinema*, Michel Chion delineates what he sees as the four powers of the acousmêtre: "the ability to be everywhere, to see all, to know all, and to have complete power. In other words: ubiquity, panopticism, omniscience, and omnipotence."[63] For Chion, the filmic acousmêtre is a kind of God or Primal Mother associated with acts of origination and creation, which is why its powers seem "magical."[64] It is removed and inaccessible, but all-knowing, all-seeing, all-mighty. Indeed, its force derives from the authority it exercises in the absence of a physical body or location, which gives the acousmêtre the status of a first cause—that which is itself uncaused and hence the ultimate cause of all things.

While Chion's acousmêtre has metaphysical powers, Kafka's acousmêtre generally takes the form of a noisy disturbance. These sounds—the noise in the burrow, the buzzing on the telephone, the scuttling of mice, the music of the dancing dogs—lack the sovereignty and grace of a godlike acousmatic voice. They are annoying and unnerving, the unwanted side effect of a nonexistent main or desired effect. It is hard to accept the acousmatic sounds in Kafka's writings as truly uncaused because they seem to have no good reason to exist in the first place. An uncaused acousmatic voice that evokes creation and birth can be regarded as a first cause, whereas Kafka's acousmêtre exists only to disrupt.

The significance of Kafka's uncaused acousmatic noises lies precisely in their mundane character. They are the sounds encountered in everyday life, which disrupt work, sleep, and communication. They are unwanted sounds, acoustic refuse. Their meaning and purpose is to disturb and unsettle the act of making sense. Such sounds, persistent and inexplicable, cannot simply be silenced or ignored. They present an obstacle or barrier to understanding, which hints at the presence of other worlds. Uncaused (or nondiegetic) acousmatic sounds interest Kafka because they allow him to explore moments where sensory experience outstrips cognitive capacity. We see and hear more than we can understand. We perceive things for which there is no accounting.

There are three ways to respond to this imbalance between perceptual and cognitive ability. The first is recourse to the supernatural: we can explain the inexplicable by invoking miracles, magic, or divine intervention, but ultimately this is just a name for an inability to explain. Moreover, the instances of acousmatic sound in Kafka's writings are too base to make this sort of explanation plausible. In Kafka's world, ordinary things do not conceal extraordinary truths. On the contrary, seemingly magical things—a man transformed into an insect, a talking ape, a singing mouse—are stripped of their supernatural air; their strangeness lies in their ordinariness. For Kafka, noise is not a disguised form of divinity.

The second possibility is rationalization: we can explain the inexplicable through scientific study and reasoned analysis. According to this view, there is nothing within the realm of experience that eludes our powers of understanding, even if there are phenomena that have yet to be explained. This is the view of the narrating dog in "Investigations of a Dog," who Kafka uses to caricature the attitude of the scientist. The canine researcher may not claim to know everything, but he implicitly believes in the potential knowability of all things. This premise distorts his "discoveries," for every obstacle to understanding is rationalized and integrated into his explanations rather than recognized as a true limit. The scientist is blind to the compensatory mechanisms he develops as a response to his circumscribed ability to perceive and understand the world, which is determined by his membership in a given species. He cannot see that "research" and "knowledge" are functions of the limits imposed by his species consciousness.

The third possibility is to recognize that our knowledge has invisible walls: we are limited by our place in the world, which is determined by our species membership. We are mentally incapable of conceiving of a realm external to this, in which our modes of sensation and rules of understanding do not apply, yet we are periodically confronted with bits and pieces of information, fragmentary impressions, and perhaps even partial insights into other worlds. We have no way to order or understand these data; often we do not even sense them properly or fully. They are fundamentally inassimilable to human knowledge even as they exist at the margins of experience.

It should be clear by now that I think Kafka champions the third option. There is no character in Kafka who lives and reasons according to it, though the burrower comes closest in his resistance to both supernatural explanation and pat rationalization. He accepts that the torturous process of searching for the cause of the noise in the burrow is both necessary and endless. There will be no resolution to the mysterious disembodied sound, which is why there can be no end to the story. This acceptance takes the form, late in the story, of an abandonment of certainty. Once again reflecting on the possibility of digging an "investigation tunnel," he asks himself: "The tunnel is supposed to bring me certainty? I have reached the point where I do not even want certainty" (*KSS* 188). Though the burrower will never achieve certain knowledge about the noise, he must continue to seek it and to act as though he might. Given that the security and maintenance of his burrow is his reason for existence, he cannot simply renounce thinking and caring about it. In the sentences that follow his renunciation of certainty, the burrower proceeds to reflect on and speculate about the noise—is the noisemaker just passing through? is it building its own burrow? what sort of confrontation might they have?—until the story breaks off midsentence.

A good deal rests on how one interprets the burrower's renunciation of certainty. Within the bounds of one's species consciousness, certainty is a valid ideal, but it is unduly constraining when trying to account for the truly foreign, the otherworldly. To insist on certainty is not in truth to be certain about everything, but to force every encounter and experience into familiar explanatory models and thus to willfully deny the fact that some things must remain beyond one's grasp. The burrower's renunciation of certainty demonstrates an acceptance of the limits of knowability. He will never come to know the causes and reasons for the inexplicable phenomena he encounters, but he accepts that they belong to a world beyond his reach, a world of which he has only the faintest intimations.

By contrast, the investigating dog clings to the illusory ideals of scientific thinking. He too gets a glimpse of another world in the form of various interspecies interactions that he misinterprets, but he consistently subsumes these experiences under canine logic. He would rather explain things away than embrace the unfathomable. From the perspective of the reader, he opts for falsehood over uncertainty. The burrower is also tempted by illusory answers to the problem of uncaused acousmatic noise, which explains his desperate ongoing attempts to understand the sound—to name it, understand it, and rationalize its presence—but they are failed efforts and he always comes back to the impossibility of knowing. He accepts the fact that he has no answers. To give up on certainty is not to abandon the search for causes, but to let go of the idea that the search will yield results.

Certainty about other worlds requires multiple perspectives; otherwise it is too easy to dismiss the intimations as hallucinations, misunderstandings, or the consequences of paranoid thinking. For this reason, the burrower can never have certainty and neither can the reader of "The Burrow." As a first-person narrative, it cannot offer any perspective outside the burrower's; there is simply no space outside the narrator's thoughts. In Kafka's story, the burrower is both the sole auditor of the sound and the only source of information about it. Everything in the story is filtered through his consciousness, indeed is a product of his consciousness. With the possible exception of the title, there is no escape from the mind of the narrator in a first-person fiction that contains no verbal material deriving from other sources (direct speech, letters, newspaper reports, etc.). To put the matter in the narratological terms offered by Dorrit Cohn, "The Burrow" is an example of a story that not only uses the *technique* of interior monologue—presenting the character's mental discourse in the first person—it participates in "a narrative *genre* constituted in its entirety by the silent self-communion of a fictional mind."[65] This genre, which Cohn calls "autonomous interior monologue," is a touchstone for defining a particular narrative mode that lacks "narrative context."[66] It is impossible to speak of an "outside" to fictional consciousness in these works. Such a space could only be posited in a genre or medium capable of verifying this "outside" from other perspectives, such as omniscient literary narration or film. In first-person narratives, certain knowledge about other worlds cannot be attained, and musings about such things will be met with suspicion.

"The Burrow" is unique because it presents the contents of a tightly circumscribed consciousness, yet it permits the reader to grasp something that the burrower himself cannot: the existence of other worlds. The text thus produces a kind of knowledge that is purely literary—contingent on the medium of literature—since it derives from a narrative situation that is particular to the literary genre of the autonomous interior monologue. This knowledge emerges in that small space between what the narrator of such a monologue says and what its reader understands. This small space, I argue, is generated by the noise in the burrow, which is why I insist that we understand this instance of metaleptic sound as a literary figure, rather than a technique (which I associated with local metalepsis) or a theme (which I associated with global metalepsis).

Nor can we categorize the metaleptic function of the noise in "The Burrow" as simply "rhetorical" or "ontological," a distinction that some critics have espoused. According to Marie-Laure Ryan,

> Rhetorical metalepsis interrupts the representation of the current level through a voice that originates in or addresses a lower level. . . . [It] opens a small window that allows a quick glance across levels, but the window closes after a few sentences, and the operation ends up reasserting the existence of boundaries. This temporary breach of illusion does not threaten the basic structure of the narrative universe. In the rhetorical brand of metalepsis, the author may speak *about* her characters, presenting them as creations of her imagination rather than as autonomous human beings, but she doesn't speak *to* them, because they belong to another level of reality.[67]

By contrast, "ontological metalepsis opens a passage between levels that results in their interpenetration, or mutual contamination"; indeed, the levels become "hopelessly entangled."[68] Moreover, the awareness of this interpenetration or contamination extends to the fictional characters. As Ryan explains, "In a narrative work, ontological levels will become entangled when an existent belongs to two or more levels at the same time, or when an existent migrates from one level to the next, causing two separate environments to blend"—recall Cecilia from *The Purple Rose of Cairo*.[69] The characters themselves realize that their worlds have been transgressed, which leads to astonishment and confusion, and sometimes triggers a crisis of identity.

If for Ryan the essential difference between rhetorical and ontological metalepsis is character awareness, for Matthew Campora the distinction lies in whether bodies or voices transgress narrative levels: "The boundary crossing of rhetorical metalepsis, as the name suggests, is verbal: it is the voice of a narrator or character that crosses from one diegetic level to another."[70]

In contrast, ontological metalepsis "is a more destructive transgression of the boundaries that separate diegetic levels. . . . [Here] it is a corporeal being (rather than just a voice) that crosses the diegetic boundary, causing the previously distinct levels of the film [or other work] to bleed together."[71] Despite its neatness and accessibility—is it simply a voice that transgresses or a body?—Campora's distinction between rhetorical and ontological metalepsis does not hold. After all, a voice can have more radical effects than Campora acknowledges, and bodies that intrude from other worlds but go unnoticed can have no effect at all. Conversely, whether it is a voice or body that enters into one world from another, the metaleptic act can be described as ontological if the characters in the work must come to terms with the transgression. Thus, for instance, in Miguel de Unamuno's 1907 novel *Mist* the narrative transgressions are entirely verbal, yet the narrator speaks directly to his protagonist Augusto and tries to influence his actions—specifically, he tries to get him not to kill himself. This is rhetorical *and* ontological metalepsis, in Campora's understanding of the terms, since it is merely verbal and yet the narrative levels clearly bleed together.

And so we return to Ryan's argument: the distinction lies not in the agent of boundary crossing—voices or bodies—but in the extent to which the characters become aware of this transgression. She focuses not on the source of metalepsis but on if and how characters react to it. A character must feel that her world has been shattered in order to call the metaleptic act ontological; otherwise it is merely rhetorical. This argument is far more convincing, yet Kafka's metaleptic noises defy even this more sophisticated typology. Though the burrower and to a large extent the narrator-dog do not understand the implications of what they are perceiving, they nonetheless perceive and even describe a transgression of narrative worlds: they simply fail to recognize it for what it is. It is precisely their misunderstanding that allows us readers to grasp the metalepsis: their confusion is our insight. Moreover, the worlds of these narrators are in fact shattered, and they do in fact undergo existential crises, even if Ryan's criterion for ontological metalepsis has not been met, since they are not really conscious of the transgression. In short, their worlds have been shattered, but they do not know it.

This is why I call noise a *figure* of metalepsis and why I insist that the knowledge produced by this figure is purely literary: it emerges in that small space between the reader's understanding and the first-person narrator's self-description. It derives from information that the narrator relays without understanding he is relaying it, from things he says without knowing their meaning or implications. Thus we do not observe the character having an existential crisis, since he is only dimly aware that something is awry; instead, the horror and the crisis are fully ours. Kafka's story is about the persistent encounter with another world, and the inability to either dismiss it or recognize it as such. The burrower is forever on the verge of metaleptic awareness, whereas we possess it to a greater degree. Thus, metalepsis is absent from the discourse of "The Burrow," which is a product of the burrower's consciousness, at the same time as it fuels that very discourse. It can hardly be termed the central concern of the story, given that the burrower is unaware that the noise he hears constitutes access to another world. Yet he is thoroughly preoccupied by the noise, which means it is far more than a "small window" into another world that quickly gets closed.

In my reading, the story's central and most remarkable feature is the noise in the burrow, since it allows the burrower to unknowingly communicate an experience of metalepsis to the reader. This sound is a product of the burrower's autonomous interior monologue, yet its meaning for him is entirely different from its meaning for the reader. For him it is just a bothersome, meaningless disturbance, while for the reader it represents the porousness of narrative worlds. This functioning on different levels is what makes the noise a complex literary figure. The burrower cannot grasp its metaleptic function, which is why he must remain blind to the insight that his narration provides for the reader. Indeed, if he were aware of its status, its literary quality would dissolve and the reader would be confronted with a typical case of ontological metalepsis. The noise in "The Burrow" can function as a *figure* of metalepsis precisely because it means one thing for the burrower and another thing entirely for the reader. It is inseparable from the literary language of its medium and the narrative conditions that govern its expression.

I have arrived, then, at an answer to the question that motivated this chapter: what is the function of acousmatic nondiegetic noise? Given that it has no metaphysical significance, how can we account for Kafka's interest in it? I have tried to show that Kafka was looking for ways to depict the limits of understanding and the possibility of accessing other worlds. In "Investigations of a Dog," this takes the form of a confrontation with the perceptual and cognitive limits that define the canine species. In "The Burrow," the creature hears a sound from another world, yet he never realizes that this is what is happening. In both cases, whether the narrator reaches the limit of his world or actually goes beyond it, this metaleptic movement is discernible to the reader. Noise takes on great significance for Kafka, for it is the means through which this kind of double consciousness can take place. For him metalepsis is not just about the author's intrusion into the text or the crisis of identity that results from a conscious encounter with another world. Rather, for Kafka the key experience of metalepsis is the relentless, nagging, and inexplicable feeling of an otherwordly intrusion in everyday experience, and the figure for this is noise.

Conclusion: *Umwelt* and Narrative

To link the transgression of narrative worlds and species worlds is to connect Kafka to a contemporary discourse about horizons of experience and knowledge in the biological sciences. In his book *Are We Smart Enough to Know How Smart Animals Are?*, the primatologist and ethologist Frans de Waal argues that if we cease to apply human standards of intelligence to animals, we might discover that animals perceive, understand, and react to their worlds in ways that are neither better nor worse than humans, but simply different. Their ways of knowing the world are unavailable to researchers who insist on judging only whether animals meet or fail to meet human standards and expectations. It is absurd to evaluate an animal's intelligence on the basis of whether it can do basic arithmetic, since no animal needs this skill for survival. Squirrels, for example, have a remarkable ability to remember where they have stashed away thousands of acorns for the winter; humans would be regarded as rather stupid if we were charged with this memory task. Waal notes that Kafka's story "The Metamorphosis" is contemporaneous with the work of German biologist Jakob von Uexküll, who called an animal's point of view its *Umwelt* (environment, surroundings). "*Umwelt* stresses an organism's self-centered, subjective world, which represents only a small tranche of all available worlds. According to Uexküll, the various tranches are 'not comprehended and never discernible' to all the species that construct them."[72] Indeed, each species stands at the center of its own Umwelt, which is defined by its own needs, habits, and preferences. To grasp that there are distinct Umwelten is to grasp that there is a conceptual horizon to all species, including our own.

One of the most compelling analogies Uexküll offers for explaining this limit is the soap bubble:

> We must . . . imagine all the animals that animate Nature around us, be they beetles, butterflies, gnats, or dragonflies who populate a meadow, as having a soap bubble around them, closed on all sides, which closes off their visual space and in which everything visible for the subject is also enclosed. Each bubble shelters other places, and in each are also found the directional planes of effective space, which give a solid scaffolding to space. The birds that flutter about, the squirrels hopping from branch to branch, or the cows grazing in the meadow, all remain permanently enclosed in the bubble that encloses their space.[73]

According to Waal, Kafka and Uexküll not only seek to understand and depict how animals think and feel, but also attempt to adopt animal perspectives on the world. They try to inhabit the animal's Umwelt, and even guide their readers to do the same. This suggests another way to read "Investigations of a Dog": Kafka invokes animals not just to put humans in their place, but because he is actually interested in how animals view and understand the world we share with them.

In Kafka's stories, noise hints at the existence of other worlds, which in turn gives the reader, if not always the characters, a sense of the limits of a given species' perceptual and cognitive capacities, of the borders that define its Umwelt. The dog and the burrower hear sounds that have no source in the worlds they inhabit; they are acoustic effects whose causes lie in other worlds. This phenomenon shows that noise can travel between worlds, which is why it functions as a figure of both metalepsis, the transgression of narrative worlds, and what I have called species transcendence, which is akin to Uexküll's notion of inhabiting another species' Umwelt. Noise moves between both narrative levels and (fictionalized) species worlds, which is the basis of the analogy between these instances of transgression, yet it means quite different things as it passes over these borders. I am most interested in how it is perceived and understood at the moment it hovers over the threshold between worlds.

These spatial metaphors help designate narratological and biological boundaries, yet these worlds do not necessarily constitute discrete spaces. Uexküll's bubble metaphor is instructive: any number of animals can occupy the meadow, but each one has its own "bubble" that determines how and what it sees. These bubbles constitute perceptual, not physical boundaries. Among the numerous accounts of Umwelt that Uexküll gives is that of a pet dog. He describes the difference between human and canine Umwelten in the context of how a specific space, the living room of a house, is experienced: the dog's visibility is restricted to surfaces that it could sit on and items associated with food, whereas the human can also see cabinets, shelves, books, and other objects. Human visibility is naturally greater, since the space is designed by and primarily for them. Uexküll's point is that a single space can be experienced in different ways and thus contains multiple Umwelten. In other words, the term *Umwelt* delineates not a discrete space but a way of inhabiting space.[74]

Similarly, in "Investigations of a Dog" a single musical encounter is perceived in at least two different ways by listeners who belong to two different species but inhabit the same physical space. The dog is unable to see something that is manifestly present to the human eye, namely the musicians, though both species can hear the music. Two different species, the human and the canine, occupy the same space, and each Umwelt produces its own kind of visibility and, probably, audibility. Kafka's story allows the human reader to inhabit the dog's Umwelt, and thus to get a sense of the differences in perspective between species.[75] The central insight here is not simply that dogs and humans perceive the same things differently, but that something visible to humans might be entirely invisible to dogs, just as we know that certain high-frequency sounds are audible to dogs but simply "nonexistent" (i.e., imperceptible) to humans.

Noise is the name humans give to sounds that can be heard but have no meaning or value in our Umwelt. By giving them the sustained attention he does, and by telling stories that destabilize the narrative levels and species worlds in which these noises are made and heard, Kafka raises the possibility that noise is perceived and understood in entirely different ways by members of distinct species. More simply, perhaps noise is only noise from a human perspective. What is noise in our world might be sonorous music in another; what is meaningful speech in our world might be garbled nonsense in another. By placing noise at these thresholds between the human and animal and between the diegetic and nondiegetic, Kafka captures both experiences at once. He wants to see what it would mean to inhabit two Umwelten at the same time, and noise is the object that permits this experiment.[76]

I have perhaps conflated two different interpretive possibilities here. We can understand noise either as the way that certain sounds manifest themselves in the human Umwelt, or as the name for sounds that can cross over from one Umwelt to another. The first interpretation treats noise like any other perceptual experience, which is to say, contingent on the Umwelt in which it is produced and perceived; noise is subjective, it is a matter of perspective. The second interpretation attributes to noise a special power to travel between Umwelten. It cannot be contained in one world, whether a species world or narrative world, and thus a multiplicity of perspectives is required to grasp it. I think that Uexküll subscribes to the former view and Kafka to the latter. Even if Uexküll's own theory at times anthropocentrically privileges sight over the other senses—for example in the bubble metaphor, in which an animal's sense of its space is defined entirely by what and how it *sees*—he clearly does not think that Umwelt is defined by vision alone. Touch is also central to his account,[77] and hearing, smell, and taste play more minor roles. Uexküll does not conceive of sights or sounds or smells as "traveling" between Umwelten; he thinks instead that "each and every subject lives in a world in which there are only subjective realities and that environments [Umwelten] themselves represent only subjective realities."[78] Though he wants his readers to imagine what the world looks like from the perspective of other species, this is a heuristic activity. It is not a way of life.[79]

Kafka, however, is interested in sound because it allows him to think about its transgressive potential. Is it possible to enter into another species' Umwelt? If so, does one inhabit two Umwelten at once, or can one toggle between them? Uexküll was certainly interested in exploring how different species perceive the world, but it is unclear what he thinks happens to a human's own Umwelt while she is exploring that of an animal. In "Investigations of a Dog," the human perspective seems to be copresent with the dog's, which is what makes the story so confusing. It is told from a dog's perspective but for a human audience, and it adopts a human discourse on science and research. The friction between these Umwelten is unavoidable, as it is part of the story's basic narrative conceit.[80] Kafka seems to have grasped something that perhaps Uexküll did not, which is that we still inhabit our human Umwelt when we feel and think our way into others, and this creates interference. Admittedly, he also wanted us to imagine a situation that the biologist Uexküll would never have dreamed of, namely that a dog would consciously offer up its perspective on the world for the benefit of human readers. Nevertheless, Kafka still hits upon a central problem with Uexküll's theory: it is impossible to put aside our human perspective entirely, even if we can grasp certain aspects of how other species experience their worlds. We might learn to inhabit other Umwelten, but we can never escape our own.

In her essay "Kafka's Hybrids," Margot Norris complicates this issue further. Not only can the distinction between human and animal Umwelten not be maintained because the investigating individual always belongs to one or the other, but the presence of humans in animal worlds makes this task even more difficult:

> In his non-human animal stories, Kafka supplements the environmental challenges that confront his organisms by obliging them to cope not only with inexplicable phenomena and overwhelming instinctual and physical exigencies (like the creature in the burrow) but also with the effect of powerful and oppressive humans in their lives. Kafka therefore presents animal ethology as directed by an intelligent, speculative, quizzical consciousness that imagines for the animal a rich, complex, emotional, and affect-filled inner life. This inner life in several of his animal narrations must be responsive not only to a natural environment but also to a cultural environment, and finally to the effects of human beings upon the animal itself.[81]

To paraphrase, animals trying to grasp their worlds must deal with the fact that they have already been contaminated by the presence of humans. Consequently, humans trying to understand and depict animal consciousness must not only try to bracket our human perspective in order to fully feel and think our way into the animal's Umwelt (my point), but we must at the same time consider that these animals live in worlds that are thoroughly shaped by humans (Norris's point), which means we must adopt an animal perspective on ourselves that is divorced from our innate perspective, our natural Umwelt.

Noise is what enables Kafka to capture this exhilarating but messy out-of-species experience. Unlike other perceptual stimuli, noise disturbs and destabilizes listeners in ways that allow them to explore the possibility of other worlds while remaining grounded in their own. This does not solve all the problems and paradoxes of experiencing multiple Umwelten, but it suggests a way out of them. To grasp noise as sound that straddles perceptual worlds helps make sense of the peculiar circumstance, present in both "The Burrow" and "Investigations of a Dog," of a sound whose cause lies in one world but whose effect is perceptible in another. There is no such thing as absolute or certain noise; there are only sounds that are perceived as such from within a given Umwelt. For Kafka, then, the experience of noise inherently transgresses worlds. The very fact that one perceives the sound as disruptive, unintelligible, or unpleasant indicates that one is inhabiting the "wrong" Umwelt—wrong precisely because it has this acoustical effect. Noise is a name for the dissonance between Umwelten.

This point emerges most clearly in these stories, which are as much about narrative limits and possibilities as they are about animals, but noise is associated with thresholds in all the works discussed in this book: sleep/wakefulness in "The Metamorphosis," singing/whistling in "Josefine," sound/silence in "The Silence of the Sirens," and writing/orality in "A Report to an Academy." Noise is always implicated in these borderlands. It seems to contain more than one perspective within it, or at least the idea or possibility of multiple perspectives. This makes it an ideal object for thinking about and even experiencing multiple Umwelten. Kafka's animals are so often linked to noise not because animals and noise both offer an escape from meaning, an abdication of sense and purpose, but because they are both crucial to his project of exploring the perceptual, representational, and cognitive limits of literary expression. In Kafka's stories, animals give us access to the meaning of noise, and noise gives us access to the meaning of animals. Together they do not dissolve meaning; rather, they reveal new horizons for its discovery.

Epilogue

✦

A Modernist Epistemology of Literary Sound

Interpretations of modernism have typically focused on contexts (urban, industrial, technological), themes (fragmentation, marginalization, displacement), and aesthetic styles and linguistic practices (expressionism, abstraction, stream of consciousness). Increasingly scholars have shifted toward thinking about the ways in which modernist art and literature produce new modes of perception and knowledge. For instance, in *Deafening Modernism* (2015) Rebecca Sanchez applies a "deaf epistemology" to literary works in order to understand their visual poetics and embodied language.[1] Her concern is neither the treatment of deafness nor biographies of deaf authors, but how a theoretical understanding of this disability informs modes of perception and understanding that are also at work in modernist literature. To give another example, Rebecca Schuman's *Kafka and Wittgenstein* (2015) offers readings of Kafka's fictions that are informed by Wittgenstein's philosophy of language. Rather than try to discover specific meanings in Kafka's works (allegorical, historical, biographical, etc.), Schuman demonstrates how a series of key concepts from Wittgenstein's thought can be used to dissolve their motivating paradoxes. By focusing on the linguistic operations of Kafka's writing, she reveals a shared mode of cognition and expression that involves playing with, and being played by, language. The point is not to solve the mysteries that lie at the heart of Kafka's stories—for instance, what does Josefine's song *mean?*—but to understand the questions themselves as a product of modernist sensibilities and modes of thought. Schuman's "analytic modernism," which is informed by contemporaneous problems in philosophy, especially language skepticism, could be extended to other philosophers and literary writers of the period.

Kafka and Noise aligns with these recent attempts to define modernist epistemologies. The issue is not that sound and noise mean anything in particular, or anything at all, but rather that they reflect distinctly modernist ways of perceiving and knowing. Acoustic phenomena and auditory experiences in literary writing present linguistic and narrative challenges that form the basis of this modernist epistemology of noise. The persistent presence of sound in a silent medium creates an interpretive tension, which in turn generates new ways of thinking about sensation, representation, and knowledge itself. Noise allows Kafka to ask fundamental questions about how we hear, how we think about what we hear, and how we represent what we hear. Most significantly, he uses noise to probe the limits of literary expression.

In chapter 1, this takes the form of an analysis of the acoustic close-up in silent film and literature. By intensifying and prolonging noise, this technique allows Kafka to represent key scenes of transformation in fundamentally new ways. We are not, in the end, able to say what the squeaking in Gregor Samsa's voice means or even to describe precisely how it sounds, but we can grasp its role in his transformation. In chapter 2, the analysis of visualized voices and implied sounds yields the basic insight that not all sound is heard. The gestural, bodily, and visual manifestations of sound in silent film and literature reveal new modes of sensation and understanding. To see sound and to read about seeing sound—to grasp sound through nonaural means—is often less a matter of imagining the sounds in question through acts of mental hearing than understanding how these unheard sounds structure the narrative space in which they play a part. In chapter 3, the analogy between Kafka's reflections on recitation and the anxieties around the coming of sound in cinema reveals a shared skepticism toward the role of the voice in modernist aesthetic production, specifically in the sonification of previously silent art forms. This might not contribute directly to the acoustic epistemology: here sound does not reveal a new way of knowing, though it does validate the voice as a central and fraught object around which modernist literature, film, and performance orient themselves. Chapter 4 offers the most radical and original contribution to the epistemology of modernist sound. By arguing for the existence, in Kafka's literary imagination, of acousmatic nondiegetic sound, it posits a peculiar acoustic phenomenon through which to explore the limits and possible transcendence of narrative and species worlds. Noise allows us to see and maybe even *see through* the conditions and constraints that govern how we apprehend the world around us, whether these are determined by the narrative in which we find ourselves, the species to which we belong, or the reality we have been conditioned to accept. We thereby begin to understand the perceptual and cognitive limits of our species world and consciousness.

Kafka's focus on sound and noise is thus a paradigmatic chapter in the history of literary modernism, because it reveals the new modes of perception and understanding at work within it. *Kafka and Noise* explores this modernist epistemology of literary sound with the help of film theory and practice. Film produces sensations and knowledge in ways that can inform, converge with, or run parallel to literature—and in some cases oppose it. In the case of sound, these connections and divergences prove particularly illuminating. But how can Kafka's writings share in the knowledge of film sound, which was not invented during Kafka's lifetime? In his 1938 essay "A New Laocoön: Artistic Composites and the Talking Film," Rudolf Arnheim wrote: "The art of the moving image is as old as the other arts, it is as old as humanity itself, and the motion picture is but its most recent manifestation."[2] Arnheim mostly had silent film in mind here, but the point holds for sound film, too: the imaginaries of these media precede their technical realization, and the theorization of these media might require altogether different tools. As I have demonstrated, Odysseus's Sirens capture the experience of silent film spectatorship, and the noise in the burrow requires literary means for its representation but cinematic tools for its interpretation.

Arnheim's comments on the aesthetics of sound film help illustrate the acoustic epistemology of literary modernism, since he too describes sound film in relation to other arts:

> The writer is not tied to the physical concreteness of a given setting;
> therefore, he is free to connect one object with another even though
> in actuality the two may not be neighbors either in time or in space.
> And since he uses as his material not the actual percept but its con-
> ceptual name, he can compose his images of elements that are taken
> from disparate sensory sources. He does not have to worry whether
> the combinations he creates are possible or even imaginable in the
> physical world.[3]

For Arnheim, then, literature is the ultimate "composite" art form, which he defines as one that appeals to multiple sensory faculties (e.g., opera, sound film, theater), since it can conjure different kinds of sensations through language. (In another sense, literature defies this way of conceptualizing art altogether, since it does not offer any direct sensory stimuli, but rather appeals to our mental faculties through linguistic abstraction. Even if we see words on a page when we read, it is not the optical sensation that arouses thoughts and feelings in us, but their translation into mental content.) To return to Arn-heim's point, literature has a special power to invoke sensations that are not "possible or even imaginable in the physical world." Kafka's use of literary sound exemplifies this point. He creates new ways of knowing sound through literary language, ones that are not necessarily contingent on film sound but become articulable through it. This is why the modernist epistemology of sound he develops can be related to film sound on various levels—as direct influence, as historical parallel, and as conceptual construct—but remains a distinctly literary phenomenon.

Andreas Huyssen makes a related argument about the relationship between literature and new media in his book *Miniature Metropolis: Literature in the Age of Photography and Film* (2015), though for him the contemporaneity of the aesthetic forms under consideration is essential.

> As a major experimental mode of urban writing, the miniature articu-
> lated the aesthetic specificity of literary language in its relationship to

the new media of photography and film, both of which took the city
and urban life as their major subject. The miniature did not imitate
photography and film, but worked through both their deficiencies
and achievements in representing urban life. The goal was to make
these new media productive for the literary enterprise without resort-
ing to imitation.[4]

Huyssen shows that literature takes up and reckons with the changes wrought
by film and photography, much as I do for sound technologies: "There will
always be moments when an older medium reasserts itself by critically working through what the new medium does and doesn't do."[5] He calls this
process "remediation in reverse" and focuses exclusively on the visual. In
an endnote he explain why his study does not examine acoustic experience:
"Rilke, Kafka, and Musil are three of my authors who address the issue of
urban sound and noise time and again in their writings about the city. If it
remains by and large outside my readings, it is because prose miniature, photography, and early film are all silent media."[6] In my reasoning, it is precisely
because literature is a silent medium that it can, to use Huyssen's words, critically work through what both sonifying and nonsonifying new media do and
don't do with sound. The modernist epistemology of sound develops not only
by analyzing what the new medium can do that the old one cannot (remediation) and what the old medium could do that the new one cannot (reverse
remediation), but by considering the comparative struggle with sound and
the pressures it places on perception, representation, and knowledge. It is a
product of media friction.

   Kafka himself sensed that his relationship to sound was defined by limits—
not only the limits of the literary medium and the genre of prose narrative, but
the limits of his personal constitution. "I do possess a certain strength which
might be briefly and imprecisely described as being unmusical," he wrote in
a letter to his lover Milena Jesenská on July 20, 1917.[7] Maurice Blanchot
explains: "Kafka, who never ceases to acknowledge that he is deafer to music
than anyone else in the world, does not fail to discover in this weak point
one of his strengths."[8] It is precisely the discomfort with music, the inability
to grasp it, and the insecurities it triggered in Kafka that created a drive to
engage so persistently and deeply with silence and noise, the "other sides"
of music. From Arnheim to Blanchot to Huyssen, and to others in between
and beyond, critics and scholars have sought to define modernism in terms
of the limits and obstacles that create new possibilities for aesthetic expression. Kafka's focus on sound and noise is a central chapter in this modernist
literary epistemology.

   I have argued throughout *Kafka and Noise* that the best way to approach
the strange, disruptive noises in Kafka's writing is through film theory and
film analysis. The specific issues at play—the acoustic close-up, implied
sound, the status of the voice, and disembodied uncaused sound—can each

be articulated and interpreted with the conceptual apparatus of film sound, broadly understood. This includes such related phenomena as silent film aesthetics, precinematic sound technologies, short-lived experimental forms like the *Tonbild*, and the cinematic writing found in Pinthus's expressionist *Kinobuch*. The modernist epistemology of literary sound proposed here thus relies on a complex historical and conceptual apparatus, all of which is tied in one way or another to the reality, imagination, or theory of film sound. In the first chapter I referred to this as "vertical hybridity."

Notwithstanding this broad understanding of film sound, it would be possible to extend the modernist epistemology of literary sound beyond cinema history, theory, and practice. Countless ideas from the rich interdisciplinary field of sound studies could be brought to bear on literary works, including compression, transduction, fidelity, soundscapes, synthetic and digital sound, the signal/noise distinction in information and communication theory, and many more. To give one example, the French philosopher Michel Serres's theory of noise as parasite posits that by disturbing any system (of communication, thermodynamics, social relations, etc.), noise also becomes its condition of possibility. It might be productive to apply such a theory to Gregor Samsa or Odradek, the creature in "The Cares of the Family Man" ("Die Sorge des Hausvaters," 1917), who both disrupt and constitute the familial structures in which they participate. Another example comes from the sound theorist Jonathan Sterne and his influential book *The Audible Past* (2003). He argues that the defining feature of sound in modernity is not the separation of sound from its source, but transduction: the conversion of sound into something else—electricity, waves, zeros and ones—and then back again into sound.[9] While such a claim might only apply to technologized sound, it could still prove enormously useful as a conceptual tool for thinking about how sound gets "converted" into literary language. In sum, there are numerous concepts from the growing field of sound studies that could help us analyze sounds in Kafka and other modernist writers, and thereby expand and deepen our understanding of how sound informs perception, cognition, and acts of imagination in their works.

I have just outlined one way that the present study could be expanded, namely by exploring other concepts from sound studies that might shed light on modernist literature. Another way is to consider how this examination of noise in Kafka expands the horizons of sound studies itself, and how we might continue this endeavor. Though I draw my concepts and terms from film studies rather than directly from sound studies, *Kafka and Noise* contributes to this field by demonstrating the relevance of literary sound for it. Sound studies generally theorizes the production and reception of actual sounds, and more often than not their relation to the visual. It has, to a large extent, ignored literary sound: first, because as a silent medium literature has no means of producing acoustic and auditory experiences directly; and second, because literature seems capable only of describing or translating external sonic realities rather than creating new ones. In other words, the first reason relates to the fact that literature does not sonify, and the second to its mimetic function. This study, however, has shown that sound is a mental phenomenon as much as an acoustic one and that is has tremendous creative and not merely reproductive power. Thus, by exploring the theoretical significance and conceptual intricacies of literary sound in Kafka's works, this book carves out a space for the medium of literature in sound studies. It demonstrates that literature does not merely represent historical realities about acoustic experiences, most notably sound technologies, but is a complex medium with its own tools and techniques for grappling with sound and expanding acoustic worlds. In short, literature's relationship to sound is not merely derivative or mimetic.

Kafka and Noise shows that sound studies has much to gain from attending to literature. The modernist epistemology of literary sound promises not only to enhance how we read Kafka and, in turn, how we understand literary modernism, but to show that new modes of perception, knowledge, and representation can operate within traditional media, even media that are silent and nontechnological. Once we accept that there are rich acoustic worlds beyond what can be perceived by the ear, we open ourselves—and we open sound studies—to the tremendous potential of sound in modernity. This is the promise of Kafka's noises.

NOTES

Chapter 1

EPIGRAPH: Theodor W. Adorno and Walter Benjamin, *The Complete Correspondence, 1928–1940*, ed. Henri Lonitz, trans. Nicholas Walker (Cambridge, Mass.: Harvard University Press, 1999), 70.

1. The exception is Jürgen Daiber's recent book, which offers a historical reconstruction of Kafka's frustrations with noise. His thesis is simple: "Noise disturbs or prevents the only activity that the author deems existentially necessary: writing." *Kafka und der Lärm: Klanglandschaften der frühen Moderne* (Münster: mentis, 2015), 14, trans. mine.

2. Franz Kafka, "Great Noise," trans. Jack Deming, published April 27, 2010, https://settingover.wordpress.com/?s=great+noise. Even though Kafka published "Great Noise" during his lifetime, it rarely appears in English-language collections of his works.

3. Walter Benjamin, "Franz Kafka: On the Tenth Anniversary of His Death," trans. Harry Zohn, in *Selected Writings*, ed. Michael Jennings, Howard Eiland, and Gary Smith, vol. 2, part 2 (Cambridge, Mass.: Harvard University Press, 1999), 801.

4. Benjamin, "Franz Kafka," 801.

5. Adorno and Benjamin, *Complete Correspondence*, 70.

6. Adorno and Benjamin, *Complete Correspondence*, 70.

7. Kafka did not want an image of Gregor on the cover of the work, since this would make it too easy to visualize him as a bug or beetle. Gregor's bodily form must remain indeterminate, since a vermin (*Ungeziefer*) is not a specific species of pest, but that which is undesirable and unfit for the home—"a shifting social construction." Stanley Corngold, "Thirteen Ways of Looking at a Vermin: Metaphor and Chiasmus in Kafka's *Die Verwandlung*," *Literary Research/Recherche littéraire* 21, nos. 41–42 (2004): 59.

8. "The Metamorphosis" employs free indirect discourse, which means that Gregor's thoughts and feelings are described in the third person. This is a hybrid mode of narration (it mixes the intimacy of first-person interiority with the distance of third-person reference), in much the same way that Gregor is a hybrid creature (he combines the inner life of a human being with the exterior form of an insect).

9. Theodor W. Adorno, *Prisms*, trans. Samuel and Shierry Weber (Cambridge, Mass.: MIT Press, 1997), 254, trans. modified.

10. For an alternative reading of the alarm clock that explores its implications for the idea of time in "The Metamorphosis," see Galili Shahar, "The Alarm Clock: The Times of Gregor Samsa," in *Kafka and the Universal*, ed. Arthur Cools and Vivian Liska (Berlin: de Gruyter, 2016). Shahar argues that the creature Gregor

introduces a new regime of archaic time, "a slow time that cannot be measured by clocks," in a failed gesture of resistance to the dominant order (263). In general Kafka's stories employ alternative ideas of time (the too late, the not yet, the missed alarm bell) that do not conform to the time of work, travel, and trade.

11. The first awakening (*erwachen*) is something one does to oneself, whereas the second is something that happens to one (*erwecken*). They can both be translated as "to awaken," but the subject of the first verb is the one who awakens, whereas the subject of the second verb is the person or object that does the awakening.

12. The first direct indication of time is 6:30 a.m., and the last is 7:00 a.m. Time also elapses before and after these markers.

13. Robert Weninger argues that a logic of "dys-communication" governs the narrative of "The Metamorphosis," and indeed that Gregor's transformation highlights and makes visible the inability to communicate that governed family relations before and after the transformation. "Sounding Out the Silence of Gregor Samsa: Kafka's Rhetoric of Dys-Communication," *Studies in 20th Century Literature* 17, no. 2 (1993): 271–77. For him, Gregor's eventual silence enables him to employ a kind of ventriloquism, whereby other characters in the story (Grete, the father) unwittingly give voice to Gregor's thoughts and feelings (277–78).

14. Joel Morris, "Joseph K.'s (A+x) Problem: Kafka on the Moment of Awakening," *German Quarterly* 82, no. 4 (2009): 474–75.

15. Franz Kafka, *Der Process: Apparatband*, ed. Malcolm Pasley (Frankfurt am Main: Fischer, 2002), 168, trans. mine.

16. Morris, "Joseph K.'s (A+x) Problem," 478–80.

17. Michael Levine reads Gregor's transformation as a process of reorientation in space, specifically from a three-dimensional to a two-dimensional existence. *Writing through Repression: Literature, Censorship, Psychoanalysis* (Baltimore: Johns Hopkins University Press, 1994), 159–67. Gregor's flattening creates "Gregorian space, which might be defined as the *way* people move through space and the ways in which they posture and position themselves" (166). My focus on the temporal dimension of Gregor's transformed awakening complements Levine's reading of its spatial character.

18. See also Mladen Dolar's excellent reading of the "moment of awakening" in "The Burrow." "The Burrow of Sound," *Differences* 22, nos. 2–3 (2011): 125–30.

19. See chap. 3, "The Vocal Supplement," where I argue that Kafka's ambivalence toward the "addition" of the voice to literary texts (primarily in the form of recitation) can be compared to the debates around the "addition" of sound to the medium of silent film. Of the theorists and critics involved in that debate, Balázs is one of very few who is keen to explore and theorize the potential of sound film from the start.

20. This was the year of the first sound film in Germany. The medium was born in Hollywood with *The Jazz Singer* (1927), but it took a few years for the technology and experimental spirit to catch on in Germany.

21. Béla Balázs, *Early Film Theory: Visible Man and the Spirit of Film*, ed. Erica Carter, trans. Rodney Livingstone (New York: Berghahn, 2010), 194.

22. Balázs, *Early Film Theory*, 196. For more on Balázs's idea of the acoustic close-up, see Reinhardt Meyer-Kalkus, *Stimme und Sprechkünste im 20.*

Jahrhundert (Berlin: Akademie Verlag, 2001), 353–54. He explains that in a later work Balázs developed the idea of "sound gestures [*Tongesten*]," as a way of describing the subtle qualities and shifts in sound analogously to the body. Balázs was as committed to new ways of hearing as he had been to new ways of seeing. He was interested not in the words of sound film, but the "audible microphysiognomy of the human being" (Meyer-Kalkus, *Stimme und Sprechkünste*, 354, trans. mine).

23. Michel Hazanavicius, dir., *The Artist*, 2011 (Culver City, Calif.: Sony Pictures, 2012), DVD, scene 5.

24. "Of all the arts the sound film was also the first to discover how to represent silence. Silence, the deepest and most significant human experience, is something that hitherto none of the silent arts, neither painting nor sculpture, nor even the silent film, has succeeded in expressing. . . . Silence is significant, moreover, only where there is also the possibility of sound. Where silence is intended. Where silence falls abruptly, or where it is entered as if by a traveller in a foreign land. Silence here becomes a great dramatic event, a cry turned inwards, a screaming hush. Silence of this kind is no neutral stillness, but a negative detonation, a holding of breath" (Balázs, *Early Film Theory*, 190). Michel Chion makes a related point: "By endowing the film with a synchronized 'sound track' and bringing the voice to this added track, the talkies allowed us not only to *hear silence*. . . , but also to have truly silent, mute characters. The deaf cinema, having presented them among speaking but voiceless characters, wasn't able to *make their silence heard*." *The Voice in Cinema*, ed. and trans. Claudia Gorbman (New York: Columbia University Press, 1999), 95.

25. One could extend this reading to argue that the film as a whole is about George's acoustic awakening. Much as in Kafka's "Metamorphosis," this awakening is completed belatedly. After the film's final scene, a spirited dance number performed by George and Pepi, the two performers stand motionless and smiling before the camera, audibly panting. The film has, once again, transformed into a sound film, but this time it can register George's voice too, not simply his silence. When he utters a single phrase—the words "with pleasure," in response to the director's request for a second take—George's thick but charming French accent is audible for the first time (Hazanavicius, *The Artist*, scene 13). Not only has George now fully transformed into an actor with a voice, but this act of vocalization has suddenly introduced a new question into the film, namely the role of non-American actors in Hollywood during and after the transition to sound. This not only has implications for George and Pepi's personal and professional relationship, but is also a meaningful comment on the film's own production narrative. *The Artist* is a French/U.S./Belgian coproduction with French and American actors, but was filmed entirely in Hollywood and Los Angeles.

26. Dolar, "Burrow of Sound," 128.

27. The chapter on sound in Thomas Elsaesser and Malte Hagener's *Film Theory: An Introduction through the Senses* (New York: Routledge, 2010), testifies to the centrality of these techniques and problems for the analysis of cinematic sound (146–68). Indeed, this short chapter serves as an excellent introduction to the sound film ideas employed in this book, since it touches on all of them: visualized sound in silent film, acoustic accompaniments to silent film, the challenges and debates around the transition to sound film, dubbing, ventriloquy, onscreen

and offscreen sound, diegetic and nondiegetic sound, acousmatic sound, sound's metamorphosizing potential, the affective polysemy of sound, and, most broadly and importantly for Elsaesser and Hagener, the power of sound to separate and reconnect bodies and voices, which relates to how it participates in the three-dimensional space of cinematic experience as opposed to the two-dimensional space of onscreen images.

28. Two important works are Sam Halliday's *Sonic Modernity: Representing Sound in Literature, Culture and the Arts* (Edinburgh: Edinburgh University Press, 2013) and Josh Epstein's *Sublime Noise: Musical Culture and the Modernist Writer* (Baltimore: Johns Hopkins University Press, 2014). Halliday argues that "sound in modernism, in whatever art form, is irreducible to sound alone. Sound, instead, is best conceived as a configuration, with 'real' sound at its centre, to be sure, but other sense phenomena, such as touch and vision, rarely at more than one or two removes on its periphery" (3). He establishes a productive taxonomy of sound in modernist literature: sounds that astonish, disturb, and overwhelm listeners (the shock experience); sounds that reveal personal or collective, often primordial, truths (the depth experience); and sounds, especially music, whose essence lies in their ungraspability ("the musico-immaterial and -ineffable" experience) (30). This model allows him to catalogue sounds mostly in works of British, Irish, and American literary modernism. Epstein uses "noise to develop a cultural history of musical-literary interactions" in the twentieth century (xviii). He looks at music, musicology, and literature in order to demonstrate that music and noise are "interrelated categories of sound, art, and culture" (xv). Whether they stand in opposition or have a fluid relationship, for Epstein's modernists music and noise articulate a fundamental anxiety about the failed autonomy of the artwork. Epstein's focus on music and society, not to mention his exclusive engagement with English-language literature, sets his project at a considerable distance from mine, yet his treatment of music and noise across two media represents an important link.

29. In modernity, we understand literature as constituted by the medium of writing. Certainly Kafka subscribed to this idea. Even if in the ancient, medieval, and early modern periods literature was primarily an oral art form, by around 1700 the practice of silent, solitary reading was well-established.

30. A glance at two sourcebooks on sound studies corroborates this point: neither *The Sound Studies Reader*, ed. Jonathan Sterne (London: Routledge, 2012), nor *The Oxford Handbook of Sound Studies*, ed. Trevor Pinch and Karin Bijsterveld (Oxford: Oxford University Press, 2012), includes a single chapter on sound in literature.

31. One basic problem is that sounds are almost always referred to by their causes. This is a classic instance of metonymy—the replacement of cause by effect—which tends to go entirely unnoticed in accounts of literary sound. The metonymy inherent in nearly every instance of literary sound could also serve as a starting point for its analysis.

32. Petr Szczepanik, "Sonic Imagination; or, Film Sound as a Discursive Construct in Czech Culture of the Transitional Period," in *Lowering the Boom: Critical Studies in Film Sound*, ed. Jay Beck and Tony Grajeda (Urbana: University of Illinois Press, 2008), 88.

33. Elsaesser and Hagener, *Film Theory*, 129.

34. Franz Kafka, *Letters to Felice*, ed. Erich Heller and Jürgen Born, trans. James Stern and Elisabeth Duckworth (New York: Schocken, 1973), 70.

35. Kafka, *Letters to Felice*, 149.

36. Carolin Duttlinger, "Film und Fotografie," in *Kafka-Handbuch: Leben— Werk—Wirkung*, ed. Manfred Engel and Bernd Auerochs (Stuttgart: J. B. Metzler, 2010), 72, trans. mine.

37. Hanns Zischler, *Kafka geht ins Kino* (Reinbek bei Hamburg: Rowohlt, 1996). Zischler examines the few explicit references to film in Kafka's diaries and letters, as well as comments by Max Brod and other friends. He combines this with information about film releases and screenings in Prague and Berlin during Kafka's residency in each of these cities. His approach is documentary, not analytical. The book was translated into English in 2003.

38. Peter-André Alt, *Kafka und der Film: Über kinematographisches Erzählen* (Munich: C. H. Beck, 2009). According to Alt, actions and behaviors in Kafka's fictions often seem unmotivated and hence defy the law of cause and effect (77). The ordering of events seems arbitrary because film, like Kafka's writing, shows bodies and events from the outside; inner motivations and justifications remain hidden. Beginning with Adorno's and Benjamin's comments on Kafka and gesture, Alt suggests that Kafka uses movement and gesture to depict a kind of nonpsychological perception, which exposes surfaces rather than interiority, much as silent film does (144). In a later article, Alt emphasizes Kafka's interest in speed and movement, especially in connection with modern modes of transportation, and links this to cinematic viewing. "Kino und Stereoskop: Zu den medialen Bedingungen von Bewegungsästhetik und Wahrnehmungspsychologie im narrativen Verfahren Franz Kafkas," in *Literatur intermedial: Paradigmenbildung zwischen 1918 und 1968*, ed. Wolf Gerhard Schmidt and Thorsten Valk (Berlin: de Gruyter, 2009). By contrast, Benjamin Noys has suggested that Kafka's writing in fact constitutes "a form of counter-cinema," on the basis of Kafka's expressed preference for the Imperial Panorama (*Kaiserpanorama*), a precinematic device that allowed one to view still images in succession through a stereoscopic process that produced a three-dimensional effect. "Film-of-Life: Agamben's Profanation of the Image," in *Cinema and Agamben: Ethics, Biopolitics and the Moving Image*, ed. Henrik Gustafsson and Asbjørn Grønstad (New York: Bloomsbury, 2014). Other voices in this debate include Peter Beicken, who argues for a "visual method" in Kafka that derives from cinematic viewing, and Bianca Theisen, who suggests that Kafka's writing "simulates" the moviegoer's encounter with the silent film screen. See, respectively, Peter Beicken, "Kafka's Visual Method: The Gaze, the Cinematic, and the Intermedial," in *Kafka for the Twenty-First Century*, ed. Stanley Corngold and Ruth V. Gross (Rochester, N.Y.: Camden House, 2011), and Bianca Theisen, "Simultaneity of Media: Kafka's Literary Screen," *MLN* 121 (2006).

39. Shai Biderman and Ido Lewit, eds., *Mediamorphosis: Kafka and the Moving Image* (New York: Wallflower, 2016).

40. This has been done outside Kafka scholarship, especially with the concept of cinematic montage as a formal feature of modernist literature. See Michael Wood, "Modernism and Film," in *The Cambridge Companion to Modernism* (Cambridge: Cambridge University Press, 2011). David Trotter critiques this approach in *Cinema and Modernism* (Oxford: Blackwell, 2007).

41. Several essays in Richard Abel and Rick Altman's 2001 collection *The Sounds of Early Cinema* (Bloomington: Indiana University Press, 2001) offer a cinematic approach to literary sound. Tom Gunning examines literary works that "anticipate" the technology of cinematic sound. This is less about prediction than the fact that certain literary fantasies, technological innovations, and aesthetic conventions belong to the same moment, and are thus mutually constitutive. For Gunning, various artistic and scientific endeavors that imagine the joining of recorded sound and moving images are responding to the same anxiety, namely the "loss of reality" that results from splitting apart the human sensorium through technologies that isolate and reproduce either sound or vision alone, such as the kinetoscope and phonograph (Tom Gunning, "Doing for the Eye What the Phonograph Does for the Ear," 14, 28–29). Mats Björkin's essay in the same collection argues that August Strindberg, without directly thematizing technologized sound, reflects the experience of the modern subject's "perception of the separation of the senses, when telephony, phonography, and cinema had begun to have an impact on the human senses" (Mats Björkin, "Remarks on Writing and Technologies of Sound in Early Cinema," 33). For him, the central feature of modern auditory experience is contamination—of sound by other noises, by the medium itself, by the conditions of perception, etc.—which itself reflects "dreams of totality and transparency" (37). These anxieties and fantasies about the human sensorium are *more*, not less legible in literature and other "contexts with higher cultural status" (37). The essays in Abel and Altman's volume are methodologically linked to this study: all rest on the premise that there are multiple ways that film and literature can work upon one another, beyond direct thematization and adaptation.

42. Alexander Honold, "Der singende Text: Klanglichkeit als literarische Performanzqualität," in *Literatur intermedial: Paradigmenbildung zwischen 1918 und 1968*, ed. Wolf Gerhard Schmidt and Thorsten Valk (Berlin: de Gruyter, 2009), 187–207. Honold posits these alternatives. For him, intermedial analysis is most productive when there is an "interference" between expressivity and content, a tension between form and subject matter (189, trans. mine). Sound in literature provides a paradigmatic instance of this. Honold's central example is Alfred Döblin's 1929 novel *Berlin Alexanderplatz*, in which the multiplicity of voices and city noises can no longer be represented through traditional narration but "penetrates the very form of representation" (199, trans. mine). Through various narrative techniques such as montage and free indirect style, sound becomes palpable, if not quite audible in the novel. This challenging reading experience enables an unparalleled attunement to sound.

43. This is also a central premise of Honold's essay. He explicitly sets forth a model of intermedial interpretation grounded not only in the media conditions of expression but also in the content of that expression: the message is more than just the medium ("Der singende Text," 189). This is a post-Kittlerian framework, in which technological developments and media conditions are crucial, but not the ultimate determinant of a work's meaning.

44. Friedrich Kittler, *Discourse Networks 1800/1900*, trans. Michael Metteer, with Chris Cullens (Stanford, Calif.: Stanford University Press, 1992).

45. Friedrich Kittler, *Gramophone, Film, Typewriter*, trans. Geoffrey Winthrop-Young and Michael Wutz (Stanford, Calif.: Stanford University Press, 1999).

Here Kittler shows not only that the technological conditions of early film infuse the literature of its moment, but that they both register changes in mass warfare and the treatment of madness and psychic disorder (124–33, 140–49). Statements such as "the history of the movie camera thus coincides with the history of automatic weapons" and "this differentiation of media decides the fate of madness" are typical of Kittler's declarative style and methodological innovation (124, 143).

46. A number of scholars have recognized the shortcomings of Kittler's approach and have tried to offer alternatives. Trotter notes that the dominant mode of analyzing modernist literature's relationship to early film is to make an "argument by analogy," according to which the literary text is structured like a film and uses cinematic techniques (montage, close-ups, pans, tracks). This suggests that there was an "exchange of transferable narrative techniques" between literature and film, which Trotter finds implausible (*Cinema and Modernism*, 1). He suggests instead, following Garrett Stewart, that there is a "parallel history" between cinema and literary modernism. This approach allows Trotter to read each medium on its own terms rather than force convergences or assert direct influence (6). In *The Senses of Modernism: Technology, Perception, and Aesthetics* (Ithaca, N.Y.: Cornell University Press, 2002), Sara Danius offers yet another way out of the problematic argument by analogy by positing a crisis of the senses in the early twentieth century that is bound up with technological change. Rather than view literary modernism as a reaction to or reflection of these new devices that record and reproduce sense data—what Danius calls the "myth of the split," that modernism is inside and modernity outside— she proposes that the aesthetic form of high-modernist literary works (Joyce, Proust, Mann) itself articulates this transformation of modes of perception and knowledge (28).

47. One exception to this claim is the work of the musicologist Brian Kane. He gives a penetrating reading of "The Burrow" in his book-length study of acousmatic sound, *Sound Unseen: Acousmatic Sound in Theory and Practice* (Oxford: Oxford University Press, 2014). While Kane is most interested in the development of this concept in the context of a phenomenology of sound, Kafka's story is a crucial case study. It offers something that philosophers and musicologists are unwilling or unable to theorize, namely a sound that remains indefinitely acousmatic, and hence can never be "reduced" to its causal explanation. For him, Kafka is crucial to a phenomenological engagement with sound.

48. See Wolf Kittler, *Der Turmbau zu Babel und das Schweigen der Sirenen: Über das Reden, das Schweigen, die Stimme und die Schrift in vier Texten von Franz Kafka* (Erlangen: Palm & Enke, 1985). This book centers on problems of communication and transmission in Kafka, and deals specifically with sound in sections on orality and music. For Kittler, sound and silence are products of the voice and thus play a part in communication, though they never become the central object of analysis and there is no attempt to conceptualize or theorize sound in Kafka. A related discussion of sound can be found in Wolf Kittler, "Schreibmaschinen, Sprechmaschinen: Effekte technischer Medien im Werk Franz Kafkas," in *Franz Kafka: Schriftverkehr*, ed. Wolf Kittler and Gerhard Neumann (Freiburg: Rombach, 1990). There he writes about gramophones and parlographs in connection with the torture apparatus in "In the Penal Colony" ("In

der Strafkolonie," 1914), but focuses more on their technical features than their audio recording and playback functions (116–27).

49. Gerhard Kurz uses a single story to reflect more generally on the significance of sound in Kafka's writings. He argues that the dialectic between rustling and stillness forms the basis of an "aesthetic program" according to which artistic production emerges from inchoate sound and reaches its highest form in silence. "The Rustling of Stillness," in *Kafka's Selected Stories: New Translations, Backgrounds and Contexts, Criticism*, ed. and trans. Stanley Corngold (New York: W. W. Norton, 2007), 344. Gerhard Neumann has argued along similar lines in "Nachrichten vom 'Pontus': Das Problem der Kunst im Werk Franz Kafkas," in Kittler and Neumann, *Franz Kafka*.

50. Bettina Menke examines the act of giving voice in Romanticism and Kafka. She sees the problem of noise and disarticulation in Kafka as a distancing from the romantic idea of giving voice. Menke offers readings of a number of Kafka's most important works on sound—"The Burrow," "The Silence of the Sirens," and "Josefine"—in an attempt to offer a holistic interpretation of acoustic phenomena in Kafka. While she is attentive to the specificity of the medium of writing, she avoids comparisons with other contemporary media. *Prosopopoiia: Stimme und Text bei Brentano, Hoffmann, Kleist und Kafka* (Munich: Wilhelm Fink, 2000), 19.

51. Relatedly, Gerhard Neumann, Stanley Corngold, John Hargraves, and John T. Hamilton have written insightful essays the topic of music and (non) musicality in Kafka's writings. Gerhard Neumann, "Kafka und die Musik," in Kittler and Neumann, *Franz Kafka*, 391–98; Stanley Corngold, "Kafka and the Philosophy of Music; or: Des Kommas Fehl hilft," *Journal of the Kafka Society of America* 28 (2004): 4–16; John A. Hargraves, "Kafka and Silence: An Alternative View of Music," in *Kafka's Selected Stories: New Translations, Backgrounds and Contexts, Criticism*, ed. and trans. Stanley Corngold (New York: W. W. Norton, 2007), 321–33; John T. Hamilton, "'Ist das Spiel vielleicht unangenehm?': Musical Disturbances and Acoustic Space in Kafka," *Journal of the Kafka Society of America* 28 (2004): 23–26.

52. Mladen Dolar, *A Voice and Nothing More* (Cambridge, Mass.: MIT Press, 2006), 188.

53. Dolar, "Burrow of Sound," 112.

54. Dolar, "Burrow of Sound," 130.

55. Gilles Deleuze and Félix Guattari, *Kafka: Toward a Minor Literature*, trans. Dana Polan (Minneapolis: University of Minnesota Press, 1986), 4–5.

56. Deleuze and Guattari, *Kafka*, 6.

57. Deleuze and Guattari, *Kafka*, 6.

58. Stanley Corngold has shown that this is an inaccurate assessment of Kafka's German. Kafka was not writing in a minor dialect of German, nor did he think of his use of German in this way. Moreover, his references to minor literature refer not to "minor uses of a major language," as Deleuze and Guattari suggest, but to literature written in minor languages, such as Yiddish and Czech. "Kafka and the Dialect of Modern Literature," *College Literature* 21, no. 1 (1994): 89+, *Expanded Academic ASAP*.

59. The German title of Kafka's most famous novel, *Der Proceß* (*The Trial*), means both "trial" and "process."

60. Deleuze and Guattari, *Kafka*, 28.

61. It has found particular resonance in postcolonial theory, studies of global literature and culture, Marxist theory, and animal studies.

Chapter 2

1. By 1900, the convention of silent, solitary reading had been the norm for at least five hundred years, since the late Middle Ages. Paul Saenger, *Space between Words: The Origins of Silent Reading* (Stanford, Calif.: Stanford University Press, 1997), 1, 273–78. This is not to deny the importance of reading aloud—recitation, declamation, oration—which experienced a popular resurgence in this period. See Meyer-Kalkus, *Stimme und Sprechkünste*, part VI, ch. 2, 3, 7, and 8, and Lothar Müller, *Die zweite Stimme: Vortragskunst von Goethe bis Kafka* (Berlin: Wagenbach, 2007), 13–37. While the vocalization of literature will take center stage in the following chapter, the present chapter examines sounds that are evoked within, rather than added to, silent media.

2. There has been much research on actual sound in silent cinema—that is, on the use of live and recorded music as well as lecturers and barkers to accompany film screenings, as well as the presence of speech, noise, and other sounds in early cinema. See Rick Altman, *Silent Film Sound* (New York: Columbia University Press, 2004), and Tom Gunning's "The Scene of Speaking: Two Decades of Discovering the Film Lecturer," in "The State of Sound Studies," ed. Rick Altman, special issue, *iris* 27 (1999): 67–79. A number of essays in Abel and Altman, eds., *The Sounds of Early Cinema*, offer concepts through which to discuss silent film sound; they will be referenced in this chapter. Claus Tieber and Anna K. Windisch, eds., *The Sounds of Silent Films: New Perspectives on History, Theory and Practice* (London: Palgrave Macmillan, 2014), provides further case studies of sound in silent world cinema. Rick Altman's "Silence of the Silents," *Musical Quarterly* 80, no. 4 (1996), effectively delineates varieties of audience, theater, and environmental sound in the silent film era, although its main point is to overturn the thesis that all silent films were accompanied by some form of sound (671, 679, 690).

3. Walter Benjamin, *Gesammelte Schriften*, ed. Rolf Tiedemann and Hermann Schweppenhäuser, vol. 2, part 3 (Frankfurt am Main: Suhrkamp, 1991), 1256, trans. mine.

4. For more on the visual and philosophical affinities between Kafka and Chaplin, see Shai Biderman, "K., the Tramp, and the Cinematic Vision: The Kafkaesque Chaplin," in *Mediamorphosis: Kafka and the Moving Image*, ed. Shai Biderman and Ido Lewit (New York: Wallflower, 2016), 198–209. Erica Weitzman also argues for a link between Chaplin's and Kafka's slapstick, via Bergson's theories about the role of the mechanical and the living in inducing laughter. The link between Kafka and Chaplin is physical and gestural, but also tied to "silent film's 'inherent affinity' for coincidence." *Irony's Antics: Walser, Kafka, Roth, and the German Comic Tradition* (Evanston, Ill.: Northwestern University Press, 2015), 115.

5. Benjamin, "Franz Kafka," 801. Deleuze and Guattari's attempt to distinguish between straight and bent heads in Kafka is consistent with the idea of developing a typology without fixed meanings and implications: "It's curious how the intrusion of sound often occurs in Kafka in connection with the movement

to raise or straighten the head—Josephine the mouse, the young musical dogs" (*Kafka*, 4–5).

6. Michael Levine, "Of Big Ears and Bondage: Benjamin, Kafka, and the Static of the Sirens," *German Quarterly* 87, no. 2 (2014): 197.

7. Melinda Szaloky, "Sounding Images in Silent Film: Visual Acoustics in Murnau's *Sunrise*," *Cinema Journal* 41, no. 2 (2002): 109–31. Szaloky wants to understand how mental hearing functions—how visualized sound helps the viewer call up sounds in her mind (117)—whereas I focus on images and words that evoke sounds, rather than on the sounds they supposedly evoke. I want to disrupt rather than indulge the signifying process in which the implied sounds of silent film and literature ask us to participate.

8. Benjamin, "Franz Kafka," 801.

9. A number of scholars have explored gesture in Kafka, including Hartmut Binder, *Kafka in neuer Sicht: Mimik, Gestik, und Personengefüge als Darstellungsformen des Autobiographischen* (Stuttgart: Metzler, 1976), and Isolde Schiffermüller, *Franz Kafkas Gesten: Studien zur Entstellung der menschlichen Sprache* (Tübingen: Francke, 2011). Binder produces a typology of gestures in Kafka's works, especially the letters and *The Castle*, and Schiffermüller argues that Kafka's gestures are above all engaged in acts of violent disfiguration and the deformation of meaning.

10. Kurt Pinthus, ed., *Das Kinobuch* (Zurich: Die Arche, 1963).

11. David Toop, *Sinister Resonance: The Mediumship of the Listener* (New York: Continuum, 2010), viii.

12. Szaloky, "Sounding Images," 110.

13. Isabelle Raynauld, "Dialogue in Early Silent Screenplays: What Actors Really Said," in Abel and Altman, *The Sounds of Early Cinema*, 69.

14. Implied sounds and actual sounds can interfere with one another, especially when the supplemental sound is not realistic. For instance, a lively and compelling musical score could distract viewers from the process of mental audition triggered by the images on the screen. A number of early film theorists including Balázs and Eisenstein advocated nonmimetic uses of actual sound. See Szaloky, "Sounding Images," 112, and Des O'Rawe, "The Great Secret: Silence, Cinema, and Modernism," *Screen* 47, no. 4 (2006): 397–99.

15. Raynauld, "Dialogue in Early Silent Screenplays," 75.

16. Szaloky, "Sounding Images," 111.

17. Balázs, *Early Film Theory*, 25.

18. Given Kafka's interest in the Yiddish theater, a language he did not fully understand, one could argue, following Balázs, that the experience of attending a theatrical performance in a foreign language approaches that of silent film. The German-Jewish author and critic Soma Morgenstern, whom Benjamin briefly references in his essay on Kafka, suggests precisely this in a series of notes on Kafka. He explains that Kafka's limited knowledge of Yiddish would not have presented a serious obstacle to understanding: "Nevertheless he could understand very well what was happening onstage, since in such Yiddish popular theater gesticulation, vivid and visible in all its fullness, acts almost as a second language. These gestures made their way into Kafka's prose, which leaves a dramatic impression on the reader. . . . It is not unreasonable to assume that his intimate relationship with this gestural language seduced and helped him to write such masterpieces as

'Investigations of a Dog.' " Soma Morgenstern, *Kritiken—Berichte—Tagebücher*, ed. Ingolf Schulte (Lüneburg: zu Klampen, 2001), 461, trans. mine. Martin Puchner also draws a link between gesture in Kafka's fiction and his interest in the Yiddish theater in "Reading the Sirens' Gestures: Kafka between Silent Film and Epic Theater," *Journal of the Kafka Society of America* 21, nos. 1–2 (1997): 27.

19. See Martin Puchner, " "Kafka's Antitheatrical Gestures," *Germanic Review* 78, no. 3 (2010): 177–93. Even though theater is not a soundless medium, Puchner's argument is relevant. His analysis of the exaggerated, melodramatic acting style that appears in many of Kafka's works dovetails with my claims about silent film acting. If Kafka's late writing "decomposes" theater, as Puchner claims, then it might be that silent film "recomposes" it; that is, Kafka's "struggle *against* the theater" might also be read as a struggle *for* silent film (181, emphasis added).

20. Michel Chion, *Film, a Sound Art*, trans. Claudia Gorbman (New York: Columbia University Press, 2009), 3, 7.

21. Chion, *Film, a Sound Art*, 5.

22. Chion, *Film, a Sound Art*, 12–13.

23. Dominique Nasta, "Setting the Pace of a Heartbeat: The Use of Sound Elements in European Melodramas before 1915," in Abel and Altman, *The Sounds of Early Cinema*, 96.

24. Nasta, "Setting the Pace of a Heartbeat," 102.

25. Nasta, "Setting the Pace of a Heartbeat," 102.

26. Chion, *Film, a Sound Art*, 6–7. While this effect is still at play in viewing silent films, film historian Kevin Brownlow argues that it was all the more so in the early days of silent cinema: "The silent film, with music, had extraordinary powers to draw the audience into the story, and an equally potent capacity to make their imagination work. They had to supply the voices and the sound effects, and because their minds were engaged, they appreciated the experience all the more. The audience was the final creative contributor to the process of making a film." Qtd. in Paul Fryer, *The Opera Singer and the Silent Film* (Jefferson, N.C.: McFarland & Company, 2005), 55.

27. Benjamin, "Franz Kafka," 802.

28. Benjamin, "Franz Kafka," 809.

29. See Puchner's analysis of pantomime: "Purposeful movement is arrested halfway or otherwise deprived of its goal; what has been a means to an end— throwing a ball; hitting an opponent—becomes an end in itself. It is the elimination of purposes that turns pantomimic gestures into signs, signaling the suggestion of a ball game or a boxing match without it really occurring onstage" ("Kafka's Antitheatrical Gestures," 187).

30. Alt, *Kafka und der Film*, 190.

31. Another illustrative example of implied sound can be found in Chaplin's *City Lights* (1931). The tramp's first encounter with the blind flower girl takes place thanks to an implied sound, namely the "noise" of the car door closing. This implied sound is also the source of her misunderstanding (she mistakenly takes the tramp to be wealthy, whereas in fact he has just climbed through a stopped car in order to cross a busy street) and consequently of the film's entire narrative arc. Chaplin thus ingeniously makes the film hinge on a sound that is inaudible to us, but which we can be certain took place and was audible to characters in the film.

32. See also Anna Brabandt, *Franz Kafka und der Stummfilm: Eine intermediale Studie* (Munich: Martin Meidenbauer, 2009), 21–33.

33. Alt, *Kafka und der Film*, 128.

34. Alt, *Kafka und der Film*, 130, trans. mine.

35. Alt, *Kafka und der Film*, 144, trans. mine.

36. Chion, *Film, a Sound Art*, 4.

37. Alt, *Kafka und der Film*, 144, trans. mine.

38. Homer, *The Odyssey*, trans. Richmond Lattimore (New York: Harper Perennial, 1991), 189–90.

39. Nasta argues that visualized sounds and the acts of subception they inspire produce a more immediate and brutal emotional reaction than actual sounds, which is why she theorizes this phenomenon in a study about early film melodrama (Nasta, "Setting the Pace of a Heartbeat," 102–4).

40. Balázs, *Early Film Theory*, 25.

41. Puchner also relates the Sirens' gestures to theater, pantomime, and silent film, but argues that there is a fundamental difference between the first and second descriptions of the Sirens' gestures: in the first, the song is the absent content of the gestures, the musical signified of the gestural signifier, and hence comparable to pantomime, where gesture and props substitute for the spoken word; in the second, the gestures represent pure expressivity, with no specific verbal content, and are thus likened to the silent cinema ("Reading the Sirens' Gestures," 29, 32). Puchner's astute distinction reflects the belief of early film theorists such as Rudolf Arnheim and Kurt Pinthus in the intrinsic wholeness of silent film; its visual language is complete and self-sufficient, not compensatory. This ideal is not always realized in actual silent films, where gestures are often used as they are in pantomime, namely to communicate what cannot be said in the absence of sound.

42. Fryer, *The Opera Singer and the Silent Film*, 55.

43. The fact that the Sirens do not possess "consciousness [*Bewußtsein*]" consolidates this argument: they wish not to do anything (for example, seduce and kill passersby), but rather merely to become the objects of a human's gaze. While it is difficult to reconcile the absence of consciousness with the fact that they do seem to have desires or wishes (the verb attributed to them is *wollen*, "to want"), even this aspect of the text makes more sense when conceived cinematically. "If the sirens possessed consciousness, at that moment they would have been annihilated; as matters stood, they remained, it was only that Odysseus eluded them" (*KSS* 128; *NSF II* 41). They can escape destruction because their status as mere objects of someone else's gaze guarantees the absence of consciousness.

44. Qtd. in Martin Loiperdinger, "German *Tonbilder* of the 1900s: Advance Technology and National Brand," in *Film 1900: Technology, Perception, Culture*, ed. Annemone Ligensa and Klaur Kreimeier (Herts, U.K.: John Libbey, 2009), 196.

45. Loiperdinger, "German *Tonbilder* of the 1900s," 190, 194–95.

46. Franz Kafka, *The Transformation (Metamorphosis) and Other Stories*, ed. and trans. Malcolm Pasley (London: Penguin, 1992), 179, trans. modified.

47. Kafka, *Transformation*, 181.

48. Kafka, *Transformation*, 182.

49. Kafka, *Transformation*, 178–79.

50. Max Brod, *Franz Kafka: A Biography*, trans. G. Humphreys Roberts and Richard Winston (New York: Schocken, 1960), 140; J. M. S. Pasley, "Two Kafka Enigmas: 'Elf Söhne' and 'Die Sorge des Hausvaters,'" *Modern Language Review* 59, no. 1 (1964): 73.

51. Pasley, "Two Kafka Enigmas," 74.

52. Breon Mitchell, "Kafka's 'Elf Söhne': A New Look at the Puzzle," *German Quarterly* 47, no. 2 (1974): 194.

53. Mitchell, "Kafka's 'Elf Söhne,'" 194.

54. See Alt, *Kafka und der Film*, 139, esp. note 22.

55. Pinthus, *Kinobuch*, 20, trans. mine.

56. Pinthus, *Kinobuch*, 20, trans. mine.

57. Friedrich Kittler claims that the contributors to the *Kinobuch* "turned the handicaps of contemporary technology into aesthetics" (*Gramophone, Film, Typewriter*, 172). He sees a compensatory mechanism at work: "The new media link that excludes literature was nevertheless committed to paper: in the shape of a screenplay that was never filmed. Pinthus's *Movie Book* printed plain text on cinema, books, and typewriters" (175).

58. Pinthus, *Kinobuch*, 72, trans. mine.

59. Pinthus, *Kinobuch*, 72, trans. mine, emphasis added.

60. Pinthus, *Kinobuch*, 10, trans. mine.

61. Rudolf Arnheim makes the same distinction in his 1938 essay "A New Laocoön: Artistic Composites and the Talking Film": "The better the silent film, the more strictly it used to avoid showing people in the act of talking, important though talking is in real life. The actors expressed themselves by posture and facial expression. Additional meaning came from the way the figure was shown within the framework of the picture, by lighting, and additionally by the total context of sequence and plot. The visual counterpart of speech, that is, the monotonous motions of the mouth, yields little and, in fact, can only hamper the expressive movement of the body. The motions of the mouth convincingly demonstrate that the activity of talking compels the actor into visually monotonous, meaningless, and often ludicrous behavior." Rudolf Arnheim, *Film as Art* (Berkeley: University of California Press, 2006), 187.

62. My analysis moves rather quickly over the story's sequence of self-negating hypotheses about Josefine's song because this has been extensively examined by other critics, particularly Wolf Kittler, who provides a compelling and detailed argument about Josefine's song as an absent center: because it eludes the symbolical and representational orders, it signifies "pure orality," "a language that does not speak" (*Turmbau zu Babel*, 185, 225, trans. mine). No specific quality of the voice can be discerned because it is pure voice, the condition of all speech that is repressed in all speech (270). Bettina Menke gives a detailed examination of Josefine's music as an "empty spot" (*Prosopopoiia*, 729–65, trans. mine). Margot Norris calls this uncharacterizable element in Josefine's voice "the trace," referring to Derrida's idea of "différance." "Kafka's Josefine: The Animal as Negative Site of Narration," *Modern Language Notes* 98, no. 3 (1983): 379. Dolar refers to the "minimal gap," alluding to the Duchampian aesthetic of the *objet trouvé*, an object that is differentiated and elevated through no inherent or identifiable quality but through the act of being singled out (*A Voice and Nothing More*, 176).

63. Puchner makes a similar point: "The narrator thus questions and destabilizes Josephine's song, so that in the end, after a number of mutually exclusive notions of the song [have been presented], the only thing he can narrate with confidence about the song are the gestures of its production. . . . And this position and gesturing is all that the reader will ever know about her voice. Her song has to be read into her gestures and postures, if it is to appear as a point of reference at all" ("Reading the Sirens' Gestures," 34). It might seem surprising that so many perceptive readers of this story have failed to see this basic point—that the story only succeeds in defining Josefine's musical gift gesturally, not acoustically—yet the narrator's insistent descriptions of her song lead us to look for answers there. I discuss the narrator's role in misleading readers below.

64. See also Karl Sobibakke, "Stimme und Ritual: Zu Kafkas 'Josefine, die Sängerin oder das Volk der Mäuse,'" *Links: Rivista di letteratura e cultura tedesca* 6 (2006): 99–108. He presents Josefine's singing as an "audio-visual media event" (99, trans. mine). While his focus on ritual and aesthetic symbolism diverges from mine, his argument is also based on the idea that Josefine is distinguished not by a musical (i.e., acoustical) quality but rather by the visual effect of her body movements and gestures and the mood they create (103–4).

65. Mary Simonson gives a compelling account of the significance of silent singing divas in the mid-1910s in her article "Screening the Diva," in *The Arts of the Prima Donna in the Long Nineteenth Century*, ed. Rachel Cowgill and Hilary Poriss (New York: Oxford University Press, 2012). Though she focuses on a few films starring the opera singers Geraldine Farrar and Mary Garden, she also mentions Enrico Caruso, Feodor Chaliapin, Lina Cavalieri, and Hope Hampton as further examples of opera singers who made silent movies, some of which were adaptations of operas, such as *Carmen* (1915), directed by Cecil B. DeMille and starring Farrar, and *Thaïs* (1917), directed by Hugo Ballin and Frank Hall Crane and starring Garden.

66. I thank Mary Simonson and Jacqueline Waeber, both of whom have done extensive research on silent film singers, for their help in clarifying this point.

67. While Simonson does not address the bared throat in particular, her central thesis about the silent film diva is that these performances were a display of physicality and bodily skill: "Nearly all of these films highlight the bodies and physicality of the women carefully and extensively, through endless sequences of physical display and action, stunts, and moments of bodily risk, trauma, and recovery" ("Screening the Diva," 87). Following Simonson, I wish to move away from the "vococentric" view of these silent film divas, which focuses on their absent voices, and to focus instead on what *is* featured, quite prominently, namely their bodies (96).

68. Michal Grover-Friedlander, *Vocal Apparitions: The Attraction of Cinema to Opera* (Princeton, N.J.: Princeton University Press, 2005), 181.

69. Grover-Friedlander, *Vocal Apparitions*, 191–92. See also Sophie Andrée Herr's dissertation on voice in silent film: "Die Stimmen im Stummfilm" (Ph.D. diss., Freie Universität Berlin, in progress). In her chapter on opera, she makes an argument similar to Grover-Friedlander's, emphasizing the significance of the absent voice in silent film and how this absence enhances its operatic quality.

70. Hargraves, "Kafka and Silence," 331.

71. Nicola Gess argues that two contemporary models of collective musical experience are at work in the story: one about the power of music to unite a people, especially in times of war, and one that critiques and exposes the phenomenon of "musical fakes"—talentless charlatans who deceive their audiences into thinking their performances have aesthetic or ethical value. Though seemingly incompatible, Gess shows the presence of both models in Kafka's story. She discusses Josefine's "theatricality"—the "spectacle of making gestures and pulling faces"—but ultimately dismisses them as yet another form of "nothingness." "The Politics of Listening: The Power of Song in Kafka's 'Josefine, the Singer,'" in *Kafka's Selected Stories: New Translations, Backgrounds and Contexts, Criticism*, ed. Stanley Corngold (New York: W. W. Norton, 2007), 280.

72. The analysis of architectural narration in Kafka arguably begins with Deleuze and Guattari's work on Kafka, in which they characterize his work as "a rhizome, a burrow," and repeatedly use the metaphor of building and digging, of entrances and escape hatches, to discuss it (*Kafka*, 3). Gerhard Neumann argues that in Kafka's works architecture is more than an allegory for the process of writing; instead, architecture and subjectivity, both individual and collective, are mutually constitutive. He contends that in the encounter with architecture Kafka's characters struggle to find their place in the cultural order. "Chinesische Mauer und Schacht von Babel: Franz Kafkas Architekturen," *Deutsche Vierteljahrsschrift für Literaturwissenschaft und Geistesgeschichte* 83, no. 3 (2009): 469. I also discuss this mode of writing in "Hearing Spaces: Architecture and Acoustic Experience in Modernist German Literature," *Modernism/Modernity* 17, no. 4 (2010).

73. Kafka's oeuvre contains an even more overt example of animate architecture, the short story "The Bridge" ("Die Brücke," 1917). There the narrator describes his own body as an architectural structure, the duty he feels to continue to serve in this function, and his ultimate failure to do so. The piece begins: "I was stiff and cold, I was a bridge, I spanned an abyss; my toes were dug in on one side, my hands in the other; I had clamped myself in crumbling clay" (*KSS* 108). Neumann discusses this fragment in his article on architectural discourse in Kafka ("Chinesische Mauer und Schacht von Babel"), but he does not address how works that seem devoid of traditional architecture compensate with forms of improvised bodily architecture.

74. Hamilton, "'Ist das Spiel vielleicht unangenehm?,'" 23.

75. Raynauld, "Dialogue in Early Silent Screenplays," 70.

76. Hargraves makes a similar point, but comes to a different conclusion: that *none* of the mice hear Josefine's song. "It is not the sound but the sight of Josefine which makes her performance special" ("Kafka and Silence," 331). For him this invalidates Josefine's musicality.

77. Bernard Perron, "The First *Transi-Sounds* of Parallel Editing," in Abel and Altman, *The Sounds of Early Cinema*, 84.

78. Certain critics of the new sound film were incredulous about sound film's ability to unify space; they did not see the role of actual sound in constituting filmic space as an extension of and variation on the role of implied sound in constituting space in silent film. Most fundamentally, they understood that sound opened up the space of film beyond what was visible in a frame; sound created an

offscreen. (There is arguably an offscreen in silent film too, but they did not see this—and perhaps this is only visible in retrospect, from a time after the invention of sound film.) According to Rudolf Arnheim, for example, actual sounds disrupt the visual composition of scenes in ways that implied sounds do not. They pierce the edge of the frame and open up the filmic space to an outside, thereby compromising the unity and coherence of the visual space. *Film Essays and Criticism*, trans. Brenda Benthien (Madison: University of Wisconsin Press, 1997), 30. As Lutz Koepnick comments, "Insisting that film was meant to be a visual medium alone, Arnheim feared that the mobility and multidirectionality of the acoustical would pierce the frame of the image, blur the boundary between on- and off-screen space, and thus define cinema as both a heterogeneous medium and as a mere subordinate rather than a strong alternative to theatrical stage art." "June 1929: Lloyd Bacon's *The Singing Fool* Triggers Debate about Sound Film," in *A New History of German Cinema*, ed. Jennifer M. Kapczynski and Michael D. Richardson (Rochester, N.Y.: Camden House, 2012), 198.

79. Perron, "The First *Transi-Sounds*," 83.

80. It is remarkable how few other non-Germanic words there are in the story, and that of these many appear in the same paragraph that *Auditorium* does: *Opposition* (also twice), *Publikum*, and *Triumphpfeifen*, which is a mixed-origin word (*DzL* 354–55). This concentration of foreign-based vocabulary justifies the interpretive pressure I place on *Auditorium*. Others non-Germanic words that appear include *Prozessionen* (*DzL* 357), *Existenz* (*DzL* 362) and *Existenzkampfe* (*DzL* 363), *Tumult* (*DzL* 362), *Generation* (*DzL* 364), *profitieren* (*DzL* 365), *Musiktalente* (*DzL* 365), *Charakter* (*DzL* 365), *kapituliert* (*DzL* 368), *Koloraturen* (used eight times in one paragraph, *DzL* 373–74), *Konzert* (*DzL* 374), and of course *Josefine*, a name associated with the French language but of Hebrew origin, as it is the female version of the biblical name Joseph. This list of a dozen or so foreign-based words, even if it is incomplete, is astonishingly short considering that the story clocks in at over six thousand words. The fact that individual foreign-based words are frequently repeated indicates their special meaning.

81. The problem with this reading, Stanley Corngold has convincingly argued, is that we cannot actually know what a vermin is, since it can refer to numerous physical entities or simply to a theoretical aggregate entity with no material form, so what does it actually mean to say that Gregor turns into it? ("Thirteen Ways of Looking at a Vermin," 59). See also Rebecca Schuman, *Kafka and Wittgenstein: The Case for an Analytic Modernism* (Evanston, Ill.: Northwestern University Press, 2015), ch. 2.

82. Wolf Kittler makes this point as well: the "view of the mouse folk" does not exist, since it is an individual who speaks in the name of the mouse folk (*Turmbau zu Babel*, 245, trans. mine). Though he recognizes that the narrator could be fabricating the whole story about the collective, Kittler does not explore the possible consequences. He exposes the aporias of Josefine's singing from countless angles, but seems relatively uninterested in the comparable problems of narrative voice.

83. On the significance of speaking in the first-person plural and speaking for others in Kafka, see Vivian Liska, *When Kafka Says We: Uncommon Communities in German-Jewish Literature* (Bloomington: Indiana University Press, 2009), and Doreen Densky, "Literary Advocates: The Rhetorics and Poetics of

Speaking-For in Franz Kafka" (Ph.D. diss., Johns Hopkins University, 2013), Pro-Quest (AAT 3574941).

84. Michael Levine argues for the emancipatory potential of figures of suspension, in particular bodily positions and gestures: suspension allows for "a grasp that is not that of understanding, a grasp that instead dislocates understanding from within and makes of this creative *misunderstanding* a means by which to get a different hold on things." "'A Place So Insanely Enchanting': Kafka and the Poetics of Suspension," *MLN* 123 (2008): 1041.

85. Brabandt, *Franz Kafka und der Stummfilm*, 21–33, trans. mine.

86. Brabandt, *Franz Kafka und der Stummfilm*, 33, trans. mine.

87. Brabandt, *Franz Kafka und der Stummfilm*, 33, trans. mine.

88. Gerhard Neumann's argument about "unmusicality" in Kafka would seem to pick up where Brabandt's argument leaves off, though in reality his essay precedes hers by almost twenty years. Neumann argues that music, for Kafka, is a "force of nature" that "breaks into this soiled and stained everyday world, intractable and semantically empty." "Kafka und die Musik," in Kittler and Neumann, *Franz Kafka*, 396, trans. mine. He is arguing against those who offer a redemptive reading of music in Kafka—as a pure and free sign, unburdened by semantic or aesthetic content—in order to suggest, instead, that music is in fact unmusicality, which is to say, the impossibility of culture and art (396–98).

89. See also Theodor Adorno's comments on the significance of gesture in his "Notes on Kafka," in *Prisms*, esp. sections 2 and 7. For Adorno, Kafka's gestures are sometimes a counterpoint to words; they point to a prelinguistic expressivity (248–49). His gestures are an effect of his visual storytelling: "Many decisive parts in Kafka read as though they had been written in imitation of expressionist paintings which should have been painted but never were. . . . This kind of transfer is at the heart of Kafka's picture-world. This world is built on the strict exclusion of everything musical, in the sense of being music-like" (264). The rejection of music in Kafka's visually expressive writing is, Adorno suggests, a rejection of typical ideas of music—rhythm, melody, etc. In fact, "this asceticism endows him with the most profound relation to music in passages such as the song of the telephone in *The Castle*, the musicology in the 'Investigations of a Dog,' and in one of the last completed stories, 'Josephine.' By avoiding all musical effects, his brittle prose functions like music. It breaks off its meaning like broken pillars of life in nineteenth-century cemeteries, and the lines which describe the break are its hieroglyphs" (264).

Chapter 3

1. Brod, *Franz Kafka*, 178.

2. This chapter derives partly from an earlier article, "Works Recited: Franz Kafka and the Art of Literary Recitation," *Germanic Review* 86, no. 2 (2011): 93–113. Reproduced with permission from Taylor & Francis. Recitation has been popular in the German context for centuries: an upsurge in the practice around 1800 had a didactic function that related to rhetoric, speech, and the standardization of the German language (Meyer-Kalkus, *Stimme und Sprechkünste*, 223–50). Another important period is 1890–1930, around when Kafka lived, which Meyer-Kalkus calls "a heyday of vocal experiments" (251, trans. mine). Here the interest in recitation intersected with various developments in physiology and psychology, as well as avant-garde movements in the arts (251–318).

3. It is not known how many times Kafka heard Hardt recite, but he definitely met him after a recitation on October 1, 1921, in the Mozarteum in Prague (Müller, *Die zweite Stimme*, 140–41). Indeed, as Kafka's biographer Reiner Stach explains in *Kafka: Die Jahre der Erkenntnis* (Frankfurt am Main: Fischer, 2008), this was the first time that Kafka heard his own works recited by a professional: "Eleven Sons" and two other works from the collection *A Country Doctor* (440). Stach also relates a story in which Kafka, very sick in Berlin and indeed only a few months from death, had to miss a reading by Hardt in one of Berlin's grandest halls, which included his "Report to an Academy." Afterward Hardt visited Kafka in his apartment and gave a private performance (582). Kafka heard Moissi at least once on February 28, 1912, the occasion about which he writes in the diary entry discussed below (*T 393–95*).

4. I use the somewhat awkward English word "reciter" for the German *Rezitator* (or, in Kafka's spelling, *Recitator*) because neither reader nor orator quite captures the activity of this figure. It is a testament to the relative marginalization of recitation in the Anglo-American context as compared with the German-speaking world that we have no word in common usage to describe this figure, though two antiquated terms, reciter and declaimer, exist. Because of its similarity to the German, I use the former.

5. Kafka criticized certain styles of recitation and praised others. As far as their recitational practices were concerned, he was an admirer of Ludwig Hardt, a detractor of Hugo von Hofmannsthal, and a skeptical supporter of Alexander Moissi (Müller, *Die zweite Stimme*, 62–72, 140–41).

6. Franz Kafka, *The Blue Octavo Notebooks*, ed. Max Brod, trans. Ernst Kaiser and Eithne Wilkins (Cambridge, Mass.: Exact Change, 1991), 14, trans. modified.

7. Philip Auslander, "Live and Technologically Mediated Performance," in *The Cambridge Companion to Performance Studies*, ed. Tracy C. Davis (Cambridge: Cambridge University Press, 2008), 115.

8. Robert Spadoni, *Uncanny Bodies: The Coming of Sound Film and the Origin of the Horror Genre* (Berkeley: University of California Press, 2007), 17.

9. Spadoni, *Uncanny Bodies*, 13.

10. Robert Spadoni, "The Uncanny Body of Early Sound Film," *Velvet Light Trap* 51 (2003): 8.

11. Anton Kaes, Nicholas Baer, and Michael Cowan, eds., *The Promise of Cinema: German Film Theory, 1907–1933* (Berkeley: University of California Press, 2016), 556.

12. Before the invention of surround sound techniques such as Dolby, all the sound in a movie came from one speaker placed somewhere behind the screen.

13. Béla Balázs, whose attitude toward the coming of sound film was more positive than many other film theorists and filmmakers in Germany, makes precisely this point:

> Sound is hard to localize. The emission of a sound will thus have to be visually indicated either with a striking gesture or with a close-up of its source. If, however, the intended effect is that of a sound heard in the distance, then the image has at least to indicate its direction. By heads turning towards it for instance, or by the direction of a look. Sound can begin to be localized, then, through visual gesture.

The contemporary technology of fixed loudspeakers does not, however, allow sound to "stick" to the moving image. If an actor begins to speak in the left-hand corner of the screen, the sound does not travel with him if he then continues talking while walking towards screen right. What becomes necessary here is to interrupt the actor's walk with cut-in of the space: a shot in which the speaker cannot be seen but in which his voice can be heard. If in the following shot the speaker has arrived at screen right and is now seen in close-up, the sound will once again appear located on his lips. (*Early Film Theory*, 196–97)

14. Spadoni, "Uncanny Body," 7.

15. This feeling is evident in an early American work that describes one of the first public sound film screenings in August 1926, a speech by William H. Hays, president of the Motion Picture Producers and Distributors of America. As one contemporary described it:

> Then, suddenly, the picture began to speak! The audience hung on its every word, half expecting something to happen . . . that the machinery would break down. . . .
>
> The phenomenon was like watching a man flying without wings. It was uncanny. The shadow of William H. Hays was true to life. His lips moved and sound came forth. His was a short speech; when it was done and he stood there, people found themselves clapping, unconsciously. As if he heard them, he bowed. He seemed to be present, and yet he did not seem to be present. No wonder a scientist next day called it: "The nearest thing to a resurrection!"

Fitzhugh Green, *The Film Finds Its Tongue* (New York: Knickerbocker, 1929), 11–12; first ellipsis in the original.

16. Arnheim, *Film Essays*, 30.

17. Arnheim, *Film Essays*, 32.

18. Kaes, Baer, and Cowan, *Promise of Cinema*, 564.

19. Kaes, Baer, and Cowan, *Promise of Cinema*, 559–60; Sergei Eisenstein, *Film Forum: Essays in Film Theory*, ed. and trans. Jay Leyda (New York: Harcourt, 1949), 257–59. Others hold the exact opposite view: for example, Lotte Eisner claimed that the first years of sound film were a time of experimentation, but once German filmmakers became accustomed to the "miracle of sound," they stopped using it in innovative and challenging ways. *The Haunted Screen: Expressionism in the German Cinema and the Influence of Max Reinhardt*, trans. Roger Greaves (Berkeley: University of California Press, 2008), 313.

20. Kaes, Baer, and Cowan, *Promise of Cinema*, 556.

21. Spadoni, "Uncanny Body," 8.

22. Arnheim, *Film Essays*, 42.

23. Kaes, Baer, and Cowan, *Promise of Cinema*, 564.

24. Kaes, Baer, and Cowan, *Promise of Cinema*, 564.

25. Kaes, Baer, and Cowan, *Promise of Cinema*, 564.

26. Béla Balázs, *Theory of the Film (Character and Growth of a New Art)*, trans. Edith Bone (London: Dennis Dobson, 1952), 197.

27. Balázs, *Theory of the Film*, 199.

28. Balázs, *Theory of the Film*, 198.

29. I take this term from contemporary research in sound studies, where it is generally used to refer to the translation of data or information into sound, in order to understand or use that data or information in new ways. Jonathan Sterne and Mitchell Akiyama, "The Recording That Never Wanted to Be Heard and Other Stories of Sonification," in Pinch and Bijsterveld, *The Oxford Handbook of Sound Studies*, 544–60. My use of the term draws on this impulse, though it is actually simpler: art forms can be said to sonify when they produce sound, making silent film a nonsonifying art form and sound film a sonifying one. Recitation makes literature into a sonifying art form.

30. A few critics have reflected on the possible link between Kafka and Karl Kraus. Leo Lensing argues for Josefine as a vocal performer who reflects Karl Kraus's recitational techniques and critical mode. Kafka's reading of Kraus—who not only wrote about Yiddish, theater, literature, and music, but also panned many prominent reciters and actors of the day—thus bears on Kafka's ideas about recitation and the character Josefine. "'Fackel'-Leser und Werfel-Verehrer: Anmerkungen zu Kafkas Briefen an Robert Klopstock," in *Kafkas letzter Freund: Der Nachlaß Robert Klopstock (1899–1972). Mit kommentierter Erstveröffentlichung von 38 teils ungedruckten Briefen Franz Kafkas*, ed. Hugo Wetscherek (Vienna: Inlibris, 2003), 283–84; "Kraus the Mouse? Kafka's Late Reading of *Die Fackel* and the Vagaries of Literary History," in *Nexus: Essays in German Jewish Studies*, ed. William C. Donahue and Martha B. Helfer, vol. 3 (Rochester, N.Y.: Camden House, 2017), 71–96. Pascale Casanova claims that Kafka had a circle around him in Prague akin to the one Kraus gathered around him in Vienna. *Kafka, Angry Poet*, trans. Chris Turner (London: Seagull Books, 2015), 180–83. She also argues that Kafka adopted Kraus's "model of intransigent radicalism," only rather than linguistic critique Kafka's main interests were political (184). Casanova's examples of Kafka's supposed political radicalism are unconvincing. She reads Josefine as an allegory not for Kraus but for Martin Buber, whose pro-Zionist position is satirized, as is the romantic appropriation of the Chassidic tradition through him (222–24). Kraus remains a model of biting critique and linguistic integrity, and thus an inspiration for Kafka's radicalism. There is a link between Kafka and Kraus, but it has to do less with Bundist politics than the practice of recitation.

31. Müller, *Die zweite Stimme*, 26.

32. Franz Kafka, *Dearest Father*, trans. Hannah and Richard Stokes (London: Oneworld Classics, 2008), 20.

33. Kafka, *Dearest Father*, 21.

34. Kafka, *Dearest Father*, 86, trans. modified.

35. Kafka, *Dearest Father*, 86; *NSF II* 216.

36. Franz Kafka, *Briefe, 1902–1924*, ed. Max Brod (New York: Schocken, 1958), 337.

37. James Spearing, "Now the Movies Go Back to Their School Days," *New York Times*, August 19, 1928.

38. Since this film was produced in two versions, one German and one English, I will refer to both titles, depending on which version I am talking about. In the early days of sound film, until around 1933, multiple language versions of films were a common way of preparing films for international distribution. They were

extremely labor-intensive, time-consuming, and costly, since films had to be acted and shot multiple times, with either the same or different actors, depending on their proficiency in foreign languages and their star power. Accents presented their own problems: they could require tweaks in the plot or that audiences suspend disbelief.

39. An earlier article serves as the basis for my current analysis of this film: "*Be/Ruf*: Sound Control and Vocal Training in *Der blaue Engel*," in "Weimar Sound Film," ed. Theodore Rippey and John Davidson, special issue, *Colloquia Germanica* 44, no. 3 (2011): 259–81. Reproduced with permission from *Colloquia Germanica*.

40. Marlene Dietrich, *Nehmt nur mein Leben . . . Reflexionen* (Munich: Wilhelm Goldmann, 1979), 72–73, trans. mine.

41. Dietrich, *Nehmt nur mein Leben*, 73.

42. I have written elsewhere on this fascinating but largely ignored diary narrative in an article that focuses on the mechanisms of conspiracy theory and scandal formation: "The Mass-Produced Word: Kafka's Scandals," *Journal of the Kafka Society of America* 29, nos. 1–2 (2005): 29–36. Other than my essay and Müller's brief but noteworthy introduction to his book (*Die zweite Stimme*, 7–10), I am not aware of any scholarly engagement with these passages.

43. Some of the most prominent reciters of the day were known for their humorous impersonations of other famous actors and reciters. Indeed, Karl Kraus even wrote a poem in which he caricatured Ludwig Hardt (Lensing, "Kraus the Mouse?," 78–79). In a charitable reading, Reichmann's vocal palimpsest could be understood as participating in this tradition.

44. See for example Robert Musil's remarkable review of Moissi: "Moissi" (1921), in *Prosa, Dramen, späte Briefe*, ed. Adolf Frisé (Hamburg: Rowohlt, 1957), 601–4. Numerous reviews of Moissi by contemporaries can be found in Hans Böhm, ed., *Moissi, der Mensch und der Künstler in Worten und Bildern* (Berlin: Eigenbrödler, 1927), including the authors Richard Beer-Hofmann (48–49), Hugo von Hofmannsthal (51), Franz Werfel (23), and Stefan Zweig (56–57). Unsurprisingly, Karl Kraus derides and deprecates Moissi, yet his unrelenting attention to him—a search for "Moissi" in the digitized version of Kraus's journal *The Torch* (*Die Fackel*) yields 176 hits—suggests a deep fascination. Karl Kraus, ed., *Die Fackel*, Austrian Academy Corpus—FACKEL Online Version, digital edition no. 1, http://www.aac.ac.at/fackel. See especially "Moissi," in which Kraus calls him a "Sopranistin": Kraus insults Moissi's literary opinions, but is evidently amused and excited by his performances (*Die Fackel* 622–31 [June 1923]: 130–31). I thank Leo Lensing for pointing me to Kraus's extensive commentary on Moissi in *The Torch*.

45. The compact disc that accompanies Müller's book contains recordings of live performances by Moissi, Kainz, and others. There are eight recordings of Moissi, including a reading of "Prometheus" from February 17, 1912, just eleven days before the Moissi performance Kafka attended. My comments above are based on these recordings.

46. Meyer-Kalkus, *Stimme und Sprechkünste*, 251, 260.

47. Meyer-Kalkus, *Stimme und Sprechkünste*, 251.

48. Meyer-Kalkus, *Stimme und Sprechkünste*, 225.

49. Meyer-Kalkus, *Stimme und Sprechkünste*, 257.

50. See the editorial notes on "Prometheus" in Johann Wolfgang von Goethe, *Gedichte: 1756–1799*, ed. Karl Eibl (Frankfurt am Main: Deutscher Klassiker Verlag, 1987), 922–27. Jacobi's secret publication of Goethe's poem sparked a controversial debate about pantheism. Goethe criticized Jacobi not for withholding Goethe's identity (though technically he did), but for making it too obvious: Jacobi's publication also contained the poem "The Divine" ("Das Göttliche"), attributed to Goethe, which made the authorship of "Prometheus" obvious to any attentive reader. Goethe wrote to Jacobi that it would have been best to publish *both* poems anonymously (923–24). Given Kafka's deep engagement with Goethe's work, we can assume that he grasped the irony that precisely the poem "Prometheus," which had become a staple of the recitational oeuvre of the period (Reichmann, Moissi, and Kainz all recited it), itself had a fraught publication history that involved unauthorized publications and literary scandal. Kafka was an avid reader of Goethe, especially in this period: there are about fifty references to Goethe in Kafka's diaries between September 1911 and December 1913. Indeed, the diary entries that cover the first months of 1912, where most of Kafka's remarks about recitation are found, also contain the highest concentration of references to Goethe. On Kafka's perceived affinity to Goethe and feeling of being hindered by his achievements, see Ritchie Robertson, *Kafka: Judaism, Politics, and Literature* (Oxford: Clarendon, 1985), 25–26.

51. Barbara Freedman, "Errors in Comedy: A Psychoanalytic Theory of Farce," *New York Literary Forum* 5 (1980): 236–38.

52. Weitzman, *Irony's Antics*, 97–98.

53. Albert Bermel, *A History of Farce from Aristophanes to Woody Allen* (New York: Simon and Schuster, 1982), 60.

54. Although we tend to think of dubbing in the context of international audiences, the technique was originally used to make musicals in which the actors could not sing. This is precisely the situation both in the fictional plot of *Singin' in the Rain* (in which Lina cannot sing) and in its production narrative (in which Debbie Reynolds cannot sing). The practice of dubbing thus blurs diegetic and extradiegetic conditions.

55. Peter Wollen gives a brilliant reading of the problem of sound, dubbing, and authenticity: "Thus the core issue in the film is that of the relationship between sound and image. Things can only end happily when, so to speak, a properly 'married print' is produced, in which voice and image are naturally joined together. The underlying theme is that of nature as truth and unity, versus artifice as falsehood and separation. Kathy's voice becomes a kind of ornament that can be subtracted from her and added to Lina in defiance of its natural origins. This privileging of the bond between essence, body and voice, as the *logos* on which truth must be founded, is precisely that which was later to be attacked by the philosopher Jacques Derrida as the illusory basis of all Western metaphysics, from the time of the Greeks on. He associated this theory of the *logos*, normalised philosophically to the point where it is scarcely noticed, with the persistent philosophical denigration of writing as a form of artifice, obeying the logic of a supplement or additional ornament, rather than an integral reality. Read in this way, *Singin' in the Rain* could be characterised as the purest example of the translation of such a metaphysics from the realm of language to that of cinema. Dubbing, here, represents the cinematic form of writing, through which sound is separated from its origin and becomes a potentially

free-floating, and thus radically unreliable, semantic element." *Singin' in the Rain*, 2nd ed. (London: Palgrave Macmillan/bfi, 2012), 67–68.

56. Wollen, *Singin' in the Rain*, 67.

57. Wollen, *Singin' in the Rain*, 68.

58. The opening word of this famous story signals that the act of community formation has been completed: "*Our* singer is named Josefine" (*KSS* 94, emphasis added). On Kafka's complex and ambivalent relationship to communities, see Liska, *When Kafka Says We*, 1–3, 15–43.

59. Specifically, Kafka does this by arguing that Yiddish is the youngest European language and explaining its emergence during the period when Middle High German was transforming into New High German (*NSF I* 189). He also explains that Yiddish, more than a language, is "word, Hassidic melody, and the very being of this Eastern Jewish actor himself" (qtd. in Liska, *When Kafka Says We*, 29). It thus requires more than intellectual understanding. Kafka tells his audience that they possess powers or abilities "which enable you to understand Yiddish empathetically" (29). These claims are aimed at producing a sense of community, a union of performers and listeners, on the basis of a particular mode of listening. (Martin Chalmers's translation of the "Lecture on Yiddish" was produced for Liska's book.)

60. Rüdiger Schaper, *Moissi: Triest, Berlin, New York. Eine Schauspielerlegende* (Berlin: Argon, 2000), 95, trans. mine.

61. Lensing reads Kafka's skepticism toward recitation through the lens of his "mousy" figures and various reflections on "mousiness": *Maus* (mouse), *Moissi*, and *Mauscheln* (mumbling, but also a derogatory word for a defective, Jewish-inflected German) all belong to this vocabulary ("Kraus the Mouse?," 79–80).

62. Kafka famously shied away from *Musikwissenschaft*, or the study of music. Even those scholars who explore Kafka's relationship to music would admit that there is nothing "strictly musical" in Kafka's writings. Hamilton, "'Ist das Spiel vielleicht unangenehm?,'" 23–26; Corngold, "Kafka and the Philosophy of Music," 4–16.

63. "Austrian" is of course not a distinct language from German, though there are some lexical varieties and the accent and intonation are distinctive. Stroheim's German is distinctly Austrian and his English is inflected by this distinctly Austrian German.

64. Spadoni, *Uncanny Bodies*, 39.

65. Spadoni, *Uncanny Bodies*, 39.

66. Mark Winokur, "*Modern Times* and the Comedy of Transformation," *Literature/Film Quarterly* 15, no. 4 (1987): 225–26.

67. Jean-Loup Bourget argues convincingly that one can detect not only a resistance to the talkies, but a distinct nostalgia for silent film that runs through Chaplin's late "silent" films, from *City Lights* (1931) to *Modern Times* (1936) and *The Great Dictator* (1940) and finally even *Limelight* (1952). "Chaplin and the Resistance to the 'Talkies,'" in *Charlie Chaplin: His Reflection in Modern Times*, ed. Adolphe Nysenholc (Berlin: Mouton de Gruyter, 1991), 3–10.

68. Winokur, "*Modern Times*," 225.

69. The early film theorist and filmmaker Lászlo Moholy-Nagy introduced the idea of "counterpoint" as a way of describing a certain filmic use of sound, which he connected to synthetic sound: "It will not be possible to develop the creative

possibilities of the talking film to the full until the acoustic alphabet of sound writing will have been mastered. Or, in other words, until we can write acoustic sequences on the sound track without having to record any real sound. Once this is achieved the sound-film composer will be able to create music from a counterpoint of unheard or even nonexistent sound values, merely by means of opto-acoustic notation." Qtd. in Thomas Y. Levin, "'Tones from out of Nowhere': Rudolph Pfenninger and the Archaeology of Synthetic Sound," *Grey Room* 12 (2003): 48.

70. Bourget, "Chaplin and the Resistance to the 'Talkies,'" 4.

71. The reverse situation was not unlikely at all, as Chaplin very well knew: the Nazis took Chaplin to be an American Jew, calling him a "disgusting Jewish acrobat," and used footage of his visit to Germany in 1931 to promote *City Lights* in the antisemitic propaganda film *The Eternal Jew* (*Der ewige Jude*) of 1940. Bilge Ebiri, "*The Interview* Has Renewed Interest in Chaplin's *The Great Dictator*, Which Is a Great Thing," *Vulture*, December 19, 2014, www.vulture.com. Chaplin was neither American nor Jewish, but his art was considered degenerate.

72. Adrian Daub, "'Hannah, Can You Hear Me?': Chaplin's Great Dictator, 'Schtonk,' and the Vicissitudes of Voice," *Criticism* 51, no. 3 (2009): 468.

73. Daub argues that the opposition in *The Great Dictator* is not between vision and speech, but between "two kinds of speech—embodied/parochial/voiced versus visual/universal" ("'Hannah, Can You Hear Me?,'" 454). The film tries to work out how to add the voice without compromising the universality of gesture and pantomime.

74. Franz Kafka, *Nachgelassene Schriften und Fragmente I: Apparatband*, ed. Malcolm Pasley (Frankfurt am Main: Fischer, 2002), 67.

75. Iris Bruce, *Kafka and Cultural Zionism: Dates in Palestine* (Madison: University of Wisconsin Press, 2007); David Suchoff, *Kafka's Jewish Languages: The Hidden Openness of Tradition* (Philadelphia: University of Pennsylvania Press, 2012); Dan Miron, *From Continuity to Contiguity: Toward a New Jewish Literary Thinking* (Stanford, Calif.: Stanford University Press, 2010); Liska, *When Kafka Says We*.

76. Müller also treats the lecture on Yiddish as an instance of vocal artistic performance. He emphasizes the significance of hearing—specifically, of "what Western Jewish ears hear when they hear Yiddish"—as I do (*Die zweite Stimme*, 128, trans. mine).

77. Evelyn Torton Beck, *Kafka and the Yiddish Theater: Its Impact on His Work* (Madison: University of Wisconsin Press, 1971), ch. 2; Noah Eisenberg, *Between Redemption and Doom: The Strains of German-Jewish Modernism* (Lincoln: University of Nebraska Press, 1999), ch. 1; Casanova, *Kafka, Angry Poet*, 120–23; Miron, *From Continuity to Contiguity*, 321–23.

78. The anonymous reviewer calls Kafka's lecture a "fine and genial presentation." "Ostjüdischer Rezitationsabend," *Selbstwehr* 8, February 23, 1912, 3.

79. Vivian Liska's reading of the "Speech on Yiddish" is attentive to its performative qualities, especially its combativeness: "Kafka's description of Yiddish, the function he ascribes to it, and the way he addresses his audience are evidence less of an inclusive embrace than a provocative assault on the complacency and composure of the public attending the reading, essentially composed of the German-speaking, assimilated Jewish establishment of Prague" (*When Kafka Says We*, 30). Her incisive reading of the intentions and affects that govern Kafka's

lecture—provocation, disruptiveness, discomfort—accounts for the medium of spoken performance.

80. Kafka gives another account of recitation in a letter to Felice Bauer on December 4–5, 1912, in which he expresses a good deal of satisfaction with his performance: "Frankly, dearest, I simply adore reading aloud [*ich lese nämlich höllisch gerne vor*]; bellowing into the audience's expectant and attentive ear warms the cockles of the poor heart. . . . Nothing, you know, gives the body greater satisfaction than ordering people about, or at least believing in one's ability to do so. . . . Whenever I have given a talk, and talking is even better than reading aloud (it's happened rarely enough). I have felt this elation, and this evening was no exception. It is—and therein lies my excuse—the only more or less public entertainment I have allowed myself in the past three months" (*Letters to Felice*, 86; *Briefe an Felice*, 155–56). This is one of the most positive accounts of recitation to be found in Kafka's writings—there are unmistakable signs of pleasure, even thrill—yet even here his feelings are mixed: "höllisch gerne" suggests tainted desire, and references to "regret [*bereuen*]" and "forgiveness [*Verzeihung*]" serve as reminders of Kafka's ambivalence toward the practice.

81. Wolf Kittler argues that Kafka's "Silence of the Sirens," discussed above in chapter 2, engages this debate between written and spoken literature. The story offers a "theory of oral storytelling," in which silence becomes the precondition of a new type of reading in which the law has replaced desire (*Turmbau zu Babel*, 143, trans. mine).

82. For a fuller account, see Wolf Kittler, "Schreibmaschinen, Sprechmaschinen," 155, and Neumann, "Kulturelle Mimikry: Zur Affenfigur bei Flaubert und Kafka," *Zeitschrift für deutsche Philologie* 126 (2007): 140.

83. Neumann, "Kulturelle Mimikry," 140, trans. mine.

84. Neumann, "Kulturelle Mimikry," 140, trans. mine.

85. Neumann, "Kulturelle Mimikry," 141, trans. mine.

86. Gerhard Neumann, "Werk oder Schrift? Vorüberlegungen zur Edition von Kafkas 'Bericht für eine Akademie,'" *Acta Germanica* 14 (1981): 4, trans. mine.

87. The article, entitled "Kafka in memoriam: An Evening with Ludwig Hardt in Vienna" ("Kafka zum Gedächtnis: Vortragsabend Ludwig Hardts in Wien"), was originally published in the *Berliner Tageblatt* on July 1, 1924, and is reproduced in Morgenstern, *Kritiken—Berichte—Tagebücher*, 9–10, 720.

88. Morgenstern, *Kritiken—Berichte—Tagebücher*, 453–54, trans. mine.

89. Ludwig Hardt, "Der Autor und sein Rezitator," in *"Als Kafka mir entgegenkam . . .": Erinnerungen an Franz Kafka*, ed. Hans-Gerd Koch (Berlin: Klaus Wagenbach, 2013), 216, trans. mine.

90. Morgenstern, *Kritiken—Berichte—Tagebücher*, 462, trans. mine.

91. Morgenstern, *Kritiken—Berichte—Tagebücher*, 462, trans. mine.

92. Morgenstern, *Kritiken—Berichte—Tagebücher*, 463, trans. mine.

93. Morgenstern, *Kritiken—Berichte—Tagebücher*, 464, trans. mine.

94. Morgenstern, *Kritiken—Berichte—Tagebücher*, 464, trans. mine.

Chapter 4

1. This chapter is adapted from "Noises Off: Cinematic Sound in Kafka's 'The Burrow,'" published in *Mediamorphosis: Kafka and the Moving Image* (New York: Wallflower, 2016), ed. Shai Biderman and Ido Lewit. Copyright © 2016

Shai Biderman and Ido Lewit. Reproduced with permission from Columbia University Press.

2. Gérard Genette, *Narrative Discourse: An Essay in Method*, trans. Jane E. Lewin (Ithaca, N.Y.: Cornell University Press, 1980), 235.

3. Alice Bell and Jan Alber, "Ontological Metalepsis and Unnatural Narratology," *Journal of Narrative Theory* 42, no. 2 (2012): 176–86.

4. Genette, *Narrative Discourse*, 236. Metalepsis plays a rather small role in this early book, but it is the central topic of Genette's *Metalepsis: From Figure to Fiction* (*Métalepse: De la figure à la fiction* [Paris: Seuil, 2004]). This later work, far less systematic and more speculative than what came before, slowly unfolds the idea that metalepsis is a basic principle of all fiction. Through numerous examples from literature of all periods and from film, Genette suggests that fictional representation always requires readers and viewers to negotiate the inside and outside of a work, and hence to enter into the diegesis. "Figures" of metalepsis (i.e., when a narrator addresses a reader) are concrete instances of this, but in fact metalepsis is a basic underlying principle of all fiction. (Genette uses the term "figure" in a different way than I will at the end of this chapter). It is a "manipulation . . . of the particular causal relationship that unites . . . the author with his work or more broadly the producer of a representation with this representation itself" (14). Examples include such standard occurrences as calling an image up in the reader's mind in a work of literary fiction (79–88), or the fact that the character in a film is always accompanied by the ineradicable presence of the actor (35). In short, the residue of the real in fiction is metaleptic: "This perpetual and reciprocal transfusion of the real diegesis to the fictional diegesis, and from one fiction to another, is the very soul of fiction. . . . All fictions are woven through with metalepsis. And all reality, when it is recognized in a fiction, and when it recognizes a fiction, in its own universe: 'That man there is a real Don Juan'" (131). I thank Tessa Nunn for her assistance with reading and translating sections of this book.

5. Jorge Luis Borges's essay "Partial Magic in the *Quixote*" prefigures Genette's statement about metalepsis: "Why does it disturb us that Don Quixote be a reader of the *Quixote* and Hamlet a spectator of *Hamlet*? I believe I have found the reason: these inversions suggest that if the characters of a fictional work can be readers or spectators, we, its readers or spectators, can be fictitious. In 1833, Carlyle observed that the history of the universe is an infinite sacred book that all men write and read and try to understand, and in which they are also written." In *Labyrinths: Selected Stories and Other Writings*, ed. Donald A. Yates and James E. Irby (New York: New Directions, 1964), 196.

6. *The Purple Rose of Cairo* dramatizes a situation that is present in all fiction film, namely the simultaneous presence of the character and the actor, which makes all fiction film metaleptic (see Genette, *Métalepse*, 35).

7. Pierre Schaeffer, "Acousmatics," in *Audio Culture: Readings in Modern Music*, ed. Christoph Cox and Daniel Warner (New York: Continuum, 2004), 76–77.

8. Schaeffer, "Acousmatics," 77.

9. Schaeffer, "Acousmatics," 78.

10. Schaeffer, "Acousmatics," 79. Another term for "pure listening" is "reduced listening." Michel Chion differentiates this from both "causal listening"

(identifying sound sources) and "semantic listening" (discovering meaning in sound). "Reduced listening" is the only mode of listening that "focuses on the traits of the sound itself, independent of its cause and its meaning." *Audio-Vision: Sound on Screen*, ed. and trans. Claudia Gorbman (New York: Columbia University Press, 1994), 29. Schaeffer assumed there was a privileged relationship between acousmatic listening and reduced listening, but Chion proposes the opposite view: not seeing the source is a distraction; intent on identifying the sound source, the listener cannot properly focus on the sounds (*Audio-Vision*, 32).

11. Historian of sound Jonathan Sterne rejects the separation of sound and source as the foundational idea for discussing sound reproduction technologies. This idea assumes the primacy of face-to-face communication and bodily presence, as well as the coherence and timelessness of such notions as "the body" and "sensation." *The Audible Past: Cultural Origins of Sound Reproduction* (Durham, N.C.: Duke University Press, 2003), 19–21. This is a valid critique for someone who, wanting to write a history of sound recording, is reluctant to accept the premise that all recorded sound is degraded and disrupted. He begins instead from the idea of "transduction": all recorded sound involves the transformation of sound into something else—electricity, grooves on a record, zeros and ones—and its retransformation back into sound (22). Transducers give Sterne a neutral and objective starting point from which to begin his historical study. Nevertheless, it is undeniable that countless works of modern art are concerned with the separation of sound and source. See for example Lutz Koepnick, "Rilke's Rumblings and Lang's Bang," *Monatshefte* 98, no. 2 (2006): 199–214, and Nora Alter and Lutz Koepnick's introduction to *Sound Matters: Essays on the Acoustics of Modern German Culture*, ed. Lutz Koepnick and Nora M. Alter (New York: Berghahn, 2004), 8–9.

12. Levin, "'Tones from out of Nowhere,'" 34. Schaeffer, who is perhaps best known for his prominent role in developing *musique concrète*, a form of electroacoustic music in which sounds are manipulated and created technologically, was clearly enthralled by this aspect of the soundscape of modernity. As early as the 1930s he was experimenting with recording everyday noises and manipulating and combining them through audio technologies in order to produce acousmatic effects.

13. Friedrich Kittler, *Discourse Networks*, 316.

14. Friedrich Kittler, *Discourse Networks*, 316.

15. Chion, *Voice in Cinema*, 4.

16. In his description of his childhood encounter with the telephone, Walter Benjamin associates the telephonic voice with the voice of the dead and speaking "from beyond [*von drüben*]" (*Berliner Kindheit um neunzehnhundert*, in *Gesammelte Schriften*, vol. 7, part 1, p. 391, trans. mine). Early on, it was believed that the phonograph liberated the voices of the dead, allowing them to speak from beyond the grave (Sterne, *Audible Past*, 288–90).

17. Dolar, "Burrow of Sound," 116.

18. In my reading, noise is Kafka's exemplary figure for disturbance. Vivian Liska notes that there are numerous "unsettling beings," or figures of disruption, in Kafka's oeuvre. They produce struggles that cannot be resolved, since they are not simple enemies or antagonists; they are instead associated with distortion, uncertainty, restlessness, endless deferral, and the impossibility of closure (*When*

Kafka Says We, 35–36). Hansjörg Bay also argues for a "poetics of the intruder" in Kafka's works. "Kafkas Tinnitus," in *Odradeks Lachen: Fremdheit bei Kafka*, ed. Hansjörg Bay and Christof Hamann (Freiburg: Rombach, 2006), 64.

19. Brian Kane's *Sound Unseen* describes the phenomenological underpinnings of theories of acousmatic sound and offers a reading of the noise in "The Burrow" as an acousmatic sound (15–41, 134–61). Kane presents Kafka as a "'counter-theorist' to Schaeffer": Kafka's burrowing animal shows that "the sound object is never quite autonomous; that this nearly-*but-not-quite* autonomous auditory effect *necessarily* underdetermines attributions of source and cause" (138, 148). "The Burrow" maintains "the anxiety inherent in acousmatic sound against any reduction" and thereby "touches the root of the acousmatic situation, free of any drive to theorize away the problems of acousmatic sound" (159). According to Kane, Kafka's literary situation allows him to explore and sustain a sound in this state of irresolvable anxiety and uncertainty. I will argue that the noise in "The Burrow" is not nearly autonomous but in fact completely autonomous, which is why we must think of it as nondiegetic. Its status as simultaneously acousmatic and nondiegetic is what makes it a purely literary phenomenon.

20. In Dolar's reading, too, the process of deacousmatization is also figured in predominantly visual terms: locating the sound in space is a matter of the gaze ("Burrow of Sound," 116–17, 131).

21. Chion, *Voice in Cinema*, 21.

22. Nicola Twilley, "Seeing with Your Tongue: Sensory-Substitution Devices Help Blind and Deaf People, but That's Just the Beginning," *New Yorker*, May 15, 2017, https://www.newyorker.com/magazine/2017/05/15/seeing-with-your-tongue.

23. "Sound symbolism" is the term that Roman Jakobson and Linda Waugh use to describe words that sound like the thing they represent. The theory of sound symbolism is a refutation of classical linguistics' claim of the arbitrariness of the linguistic signifier. They explain this view in chapter 4, section 1 of *Sound Shape of Language* (Berlin: Mouton de Gruyter, 2002).

24. Bettine Menke argues that the noise in the burrow represents a problem of "disarticulation" and insists on its unreadability (*Prosopopoiia*, 98–135). I propose the opposite: the noise invites reading; in fact, the burrower continually takes up this invitation. Readers follow in his exegetical footsteps: we too tend to assume that the noise can be embodied, that it has a cause, and that it can be explained—hence the numerous allegorical readings critics have performed. See for example Britta Maché, "The Noise in the Burrow: Kafka's Final Dilemma," *German Quarterly* 55, no. 4 (1982), and Wolf Kittler, "Grabenkrieg—Nervenkrieg—Medienkrieg: Franz Kafka und der 1. Weltkrieg," in *Armaturen der Sinne: Literarische und technische Medien 1870 bis 1920*, ed. Jochen Hörisch and Michael Wetzel (Munich: Wilhelm Fink, 1990).

25. J. M. Coetzee, "Time, Tense and Aspect in Kafka's 'The Burrow,'" *MLN* 96, no. 3 (1981): 575.

26. Dolar, "Burrow of Sound," 115, 120.

27. Dolar, "Burrow of Sound," 121.

28. Dolar, "Burrow of Sound," 133.

29. Both Kane (*Sound Unseen*, 159–61) and Dolar ("Burrow of Sound," 116, 133–34) consider this possibility.

30. Dolar, "Burrow of Sound," 116.

31. The burrower begins to hear the sound at the moment he awakens, much as Gregor Samsa of "The Metamorphosis" and Josef K. of *The Trial* awaken at the start of their respective narratives. The precariousness of this in-between state—"awakening is the riskiest moment [*der riskanteste Augenblick*], says Kafka"—interests Dolar, who wants to "dwell on the particular edge that is crucial for Kafka: the blurred line between sleep and wakefulness, the edge of awakening" ("Burrow of Sound," 127, 125).

32. Coetzee, "Time, Tense and Aspect," 564.

33. Chion, *Voice in Cinema*, 23.

34. Chion, *Voice in Cinema*, 35.

35. Chion, *Voice in Cinema*, 36.

36. Chion, *Voice in Cinema*, 36–37.

37. Thomas Y. Levin, "Rhetoric of the Temporal Index: Surveillant Narration and the Cinema of 'Real Time,'" in *CTRL Space: Rhetorics of Surveillance from Bentham to Big Brother*, ed. Thomas Y. Levin, Ursula Frohne, and Peter Weibel (Cambridge, Mass.: MIT Press, 2002), 585.

38. Levin, "Rhetoric of the Temporal Index," 582–83.

39. Genette, who comes to the conclusion that metalepsis is a structuring idea for all fiction, would likely argue that this movement between fiction and reality is not a prefiguration of metalepsis, but its essence (*Métalepse*, 131).

40. Clayton Koelb's ingenious reading of the *Bällen* (balls) as deriving directly from the *bellen* (barking) of the imagined dogs offers another explanation for the presence of these strange objects: the narrator fulfills Blumfeld's desire for companionship through paranomasia. *Kafka's Rhetoric: The Passion of Reading* (Ithaca, N.Y.: Cornell University Press, 1989), 36–37.

41. This exchange is reminiscent of Josefine, who wants to be excused from work on account of the power of her song. For her there is a clear exchange of music for work, which others fail to grasp (see KSS 104).

42. Kafka, *Briefe, 1902–1924*, 390–91.

43. Chion, *Voice in Cinema*, 62–63.

44. Chion, *Voice in Cinema*, 63.

45. Chion, *Voice in Cinema*, 63.

46. Chion, *Voice in Cinema*, 63.

47. In addition to being the name of the protagonist of Kafka's novel, *The Trial*, Josef—in fact, Josef K.—is also the name under which Kafka's reservation had mistakenly been put when he went to check in to the hotel at the mountain resort in Spindelmühle in January 1922, just as he began working on *The Castle*. Clayton Koelb, *Kafka: A Guide for the Perplexed* (New York: Continuum, 2010), 59. "Despite my having legibly written down my name, despite their having correctly written to me twice already, they have Joseph K. down in the directory. Shall I enlighten them, or shall I let them enlighten me?" *The Diaries of Franz Kafka, 1914–1923*, ed. Max Brod, trans. Martin Greenberg, with Hannah Arendt (New York: Schocken, 1968), 213. The episode in which K. gives a "false" name on the phone to Oswald might be playing on this autobiographical experience: Kafka, after all, both is and is not Josef K. Likewise, there are suggestions, but no definitive proof that K.'s first name is also Josef (Koelb, *Kafka*, 166 n. 54).

48. John Durham Peters explains that telephones and early wireless technologies (e.g., radio) were *not* originally distinguished by whether the medium enabled a single line of communication between two parties or was a one-way channel that diffused content to a general audience. These uses of the medium have solidified over decades of use, but they are not inherent to the technologies. For Peters, the telephonic uncanny in Kafka has to do with the indeterminacy of the medium and its messages. "The Telephonic Uncanny and the Problem of Communication," in *The Sound Studies Reader*, ed. Jonathan Sterne (London: Routledge, 2012), 363, 369.

49. Wilhelm Emrich offers one of the first readings of the telephone in *The Castle*: for him the noise on the line represents the failure of human utterances to capture the truth, and the accompanying idea that only wordless music can be trusted and believed. *Franz Kafka*, 3rd ed. (Frankfurt am Main: Athenäum, 1961), 154–55. This is consistent with the general thrust of Emrich's book, which moves away from interpreting Kafka's works according to fixed symbols and allegories and toward seeing them as parables that reflect the totality of human experience but lack transcendental value or meaning.

50. Marianne DeKoven also shows how Kafka's stories reflect on "crossing the human-animal divide," yet she is more insistent on the "goal of decentering anthropocentrism" than I am. "Kafka's Animal Stories: Modernist Form and Interspecies Narrative," in *Creatural Fictions: Human-Animal Relationships in Twentieth- and Twenty-First-Century Literature*, ed. David Herman (New York: Palgrave Macmillan, 2016), 19. I think that Kafka's animal stories are supposed to tell us something about humans, and thus view them less as earnest forays into animal consciousness than parodic takedowns of human consciousness.

51. Dr. Seuss (Theodor Geisl), *Horton Hears a Who!* (New York: Random House, 1954).

52. Genette calls embedded diegetic levels—e.g., the world of the Whos within the world of Horton and his jungle mates—metadiegetic levels (*Narrative Discourse*, 228–29).

53. Primo Levi, "Observed from a Distance," in *Flaw of Form*, 608–16, trans. Jenny McPhee, in *The Complete Works of Primo Levi*, ed. Ann Goldstein, vol. 1, 573–747 (New York: Liveright, 2015). Two brief introductory notes cement the story's self-reflexive, metaleptic quality. The first playfully pays homage to all the literary fantasies about life in outer space, since such speculation will have been rendered "vain and futile" once humans land on the moon (608). The second explains that an extensive process of translation was necessary to make this report legible to humans. Not only was it written in "Selenitic linear B characters," but various simplifications have been made for the human reader, which cover over just how mysterious and inexplicable the observed phenomena are for the Selenites (608–9).

54. Levi, "Observed from a Distance," 610.

55. Levi, "Observed from a Distance," 611.

56. Levi, "Observed from a Distance," 615.

57. Levi, "Observed from a Distance," 615–16.

58. Hargraves refers to passages that suggest the "narrator's presentiments of another world, of a higher order" ("Kafka and Silence," 325). Stanley Corngold also demonstrates how the dog narrator might begin to transcend canine

consciousness. "Musical Indirections in Kafka's 'Forschungen eines Hundes,'" in *Franz Kafka: Narration, Rhetoric and Reading*, ed. Jakob Lothe, Beatrice Sandberg, and Ronald Speirs (Columbus: Ohio State University Press, 2011).

59. Robertson, *Kafka*, 277.

60. Robertson, *Kafka*, 279.

61. Corngold, "Musical Indirections," 173.

62. This kind of open and unprejudiced perception can also take place in the moment of awakening, as discussed in chapter 1.

63. Chion, *Voice in Cinema*, 24.

64. Chion, *Voice in Cinema*, 27.

65. Dorrit Cohn, *Transparent Minds: Narrative Modes for Presenting Consciousness in Fiction* (Princeton, N.J.: Princeton University Press, 1978), 15.

66. Cohn, *Transparent Minds*, 16–17.

67. Marie-Laure Ryan, "Metaleptic Machines," *Semiotica* 150, nos. 1–4: 441–42.

68. Ryan, "Metaleptic Machines," 442, 443.

69. Ryan, "Metaleptic Machines," 442.

70. Matthew Campora, "Art Cinema and New Hollywood: Multiform Narrative and Sonic Metalepsis in *Eternal Sunshine of the Spotless Mind*," *New Review of Film and Television Studies* 7, no. 2 (2009): 125.

71. Campora, "Art Cinema and New Hollywood," 125–26.

72. Frans de Waal, *Are We Smart Enough to Know How Smart Animals Are?* (New York: W. W. Norton, 2016), 8.

73. Jakob von Uexküll, *A Foray into the Worlds of Animals and Humans; with, A Theory of Meaning*, trans. Joseph D. O'Neil (Minneapolis: University of Minnesota Press, 2010), 69.

74. Uexküll, *A Foray into the Worlds of Animals and Humans*, plates 2 and 3.

75. In an article on Kafka, Cavell, and Uexküll, Michael Uhall gives a compelling account of "Investigations of a Dog": it is "Kafka's attempt to portray what it must be like to be a dog." "Creaturely Conditions: Acknowledgment and Animality in Kafka, Cavell, and Uexküll," *Configurations* 24, no. 1 (2016): 3. Uhall wants to expand Cavell's notion of "acknowledgment" of other minds to the realm of animals, and he uses Uexküll's concept of Umwelt to argue why this is not only possible, but a necessary condition of acknowledgment in general.

76. Margot Norris makes a related point: "In spite of their imaginative reach into the realm of animal ontology, Kafka's animal fictions do expose limits in the human ability to 'think ourselves into the being of another.' And it is precisely the contours of those cognitive and representational limits that conjure a sense, if not a glimpse, of the animal unknown (and perhaps 'unknowable') that lies beyond the cultural human. At the same time, I believe that Kafka's fictions allowed him to participate in nineteenth- and early twentieth-century shifts from an anthropocentric toward a more biocentric philosophical orientation. This allowed him to conduct a creative imaginative exploration of the human-animal divide, one that gives his literary experiments, however imperfect, a historical significance in the realm of intellectual history." "Kafka's Hybrids: Thinking Animals and Mirrored Humans," in *Kafka's Creatures: Animals, Hybrids, and Other Fantastic Beings*, ed. Marc Lucht and Donna Yarri (Lanham, Md.: Rowman & Littlefield, 2010), 18.

77. For Uexküll's account of tactile space, see *A Foray into the Worlds of Animals and Humans*, 60–61.

78. Uexküll, *A Foray into the Worlds of Animals and Humans*, 125–26.

79. In a review article in the *New Yorker* that mentions Waal's book, as well as Kafka and Uexküll as important precursors, Joshua Rothman discusses two recent cases of individual humans who tried to live as animals for an extended period (one a goat, another a badger) and then wrote books about it. "The Metamorphosis: What Is It Like to Be an Animal?," *New Yorker*, May 30, 2016, 70–74.

80. Norris makes a similar point about "A Report to an Academy": "It is a story curiously told empirically from the inside but rhetorically from the outside, as though the ape were his own zoological specimen, expounding upon himself in the form of the treatise" ("Kafka's Hybrids," 22). It is not simply that the ape *is* a man, but that he is negotiating the fact of being at once both man and animal.

81. Norris, "Kafka's Hybrids," 30.

Epilogue

1. Rebecca Sanchez, *Deafening Modernism: Embodied Language and Visual Poetics in American Literature* (New York: NYU Press, 2015).

2. Arnheim, *Film as Art*, 213.

3. Arnheim, *Film as Art*, 206.

4. Andreas Huyssen, *Miniature Metropolis: Literature in the Age of Photography and Film* (Cambridge, Mass.: Harvard University Press, 2015), 7.

5. Huyssen, *Miniature Metropolis*, 8.

6. Huyssen, *Miniature Metropolis*, 300.

7. Franz Kafka, *Letters to Milena*, trans. Philip Boehm (New York: Schocken, 1990), 92.

8. Maurice Blanchot, *The Space of Literature*, trans. Ann Smock (Lincoln: University of Nebraska Press, 1982), 192.

9. Sterne, *Audible Past*, 22.

BIBLIOGRAPHY

Abel, Richard, and Rick Altman, eds. *The Sounds of Early Cinema*. Bloomington: Indiana University Press, 2001.

Adorno, Theodor W. *Prisms*. Translated by Samuel and Shierry Weber. Cambridge, Mass.: MIT Press, 1997.

Adorno, Theodor W., and Walter Benjamin. *The Complete Correspondence, 1928–1940*. Edited by Henri Lonitz; translated by Nicholas Walker. Cambridge, Mass.: Harvard University Press, 1999.

Alt, Peter-André. *Kafka und der Film: Über kinematographisches Erzählen*. Munich: C. H. Beck, 2009.

Alt, Peter-André. "Kino und Stereoskop: Zu den medialen Bedingungen von Bewegungsästhetik und Wahrnehmungspsychologie im narrativen Verfahren Franz Kafkas." In *Literatur intermedial: Paradigmenbildung zwischen 1918 und 1968*, edited by Wolf Gerhard Schmidt and Thorsten Valk, 11–47. Berlin: de Gruyter, 2009.

Alter, Nora M., and Lutz Koepnick. Introduction to *Sound Matters: Essays on the Acoustics of Modern German Culture*, edited by Lutz Koepnick and Nora M. Alter, 1–29. New York: Berghahn, 2004.

Altman, Rick. "The Silence of the Silents." *Musical Quarterly* 80, no. 4 (1996): 648–718.

Altman, Rick. *Silent Film Sound*. New York: Columbia University Press, 2004.

Anonymous. "Ostjüdischer Rezitationsabend." *Selbstwehr* 8, February 23, 1912, 3.

Arnheim, Rudolf. *Film as Art*. Berkeley: University of California Press, 2006.

Arnheim, Rudolf. *Film Essays and Criticism*. Translated by Brenda Benthien. Madison: University of Wisconsin Press, 1997.

Auslander, Philip. "Live and Technologically Mediated Performance." In *The Cambridge Companion to Performance Studies*, edited by Tracy C. Davis, 107–19. Cambridge: Cambridge University Press, 2008.

Balázs, Béla. *Early Film Theory: Visible Man and the Spirit of Film*. Edited by Erica Carter; translated by Rodney Livingstone. New York: Berghahn, 2010.

Balázs, Béla. *Theory of the Film (Character and Growth of a New Art)*. Translated by Edith Bone. London: Dennis Dobson, 1952.

Bay, Hansjörg. "Kafkas Tinnitus." In *Odradeks Lachen: Fremdheit bei Kafka*, edited by Hansjörg Bay and Christof Hamann, 41–68. Freiburg: Rombach, 2006.

Beck, Evelyn Torton. *Kafka and the Yiddish Theater: Its Impact on His Work*. Madison: University of Wisconsin Press, 1971.

Beicken, Peter. "Kafka's Visual Method: The Gaze, the Cinematic, and the Intermedial." In *Kafka for the Twenty-First Century*, edited by Stanley Corngold and Ruth V. Gross, 165–78. Rochester, N.Y.: Camden House, 2011.

Bell, Alice, and Jan Alber. "Ontological Metalepsis and Unnatural Narratology." *Journal of Narrative Theory* 42, no. 2 (2012): 166–92.

Benjamin, Walter. *Berliner Kindheit um neunzehnhundert*. In *Gesammelte Schriften*, edited by Rolf Tiedemann and Hermann Schweppenhäuser, vol. 7, part 1, 385–433. Frankfurt am Main: Suhrkamp, 1991.

Benjamin, Walter. "Franz Kafka: On the Tenth Anniversary of His Death." Translated by Harry Zohn. In *Selected Writings*, edited by Michael Jennings, Howard Eiland, and Gary Smith, vol. 2, part 2, 794–818. Cambridge, Mass.: Harvard University Press, 1999.

Benjamin, Walter. *Gesammelte Schriften*. Vol. 2, part 3. Edited by Rolf Tiedemann and Hermann Schweppenhäuser. Frankfurt am Main: Suhrkamp, 1991.

Bermel, Albert. *A History of Farce from Aristophanes to Woody Allen*. New York: Simon and Schuster, 1982.

Biderman, Shai. "K., the Tramp, and the Cinematic Vision: The Kafkaesque Chaplin." In Biderman and Lewit, *Mediamorphosis*, 198–209.

Biderman, Shai, and Ido Lewit, eds. *Mediamorphosis: Kafka and the Moving Image*. New York: Wallflower, 2016.

Binder, Hartmut. *Kafka in neuer Sicht: Mimik, Gestik und Personengefüge als Darstellungsformen des Autobiographischen*. Stuttgart: Metzler, 1976.

Björkin, Mats. "Remarks on Writing and Technologies of Sound in Early Cinema." In Abel and Altman, *The Sounds of Early Cinema*, 32–38.

Blanchot, Maurice. *The Space of Literature*. Translated by Ann Smock. Lincoln: University of Nebraska Press, 1982.

Böhm, Hans, ed. *Moissi, der Mensch und der Künstler in Worten und Bildern*. Berlin: Eigenbrödler, 1927.

Borges, Jorge Luis. "Partial Magic in the *Quixote*." In *Labyrinths: Selected Stories and Other Writings*, edited by Donald A. Yates and James E. Irby, 193–96. New York: New Directions, 1964.

Bourget, Jean-Loup. "Chaplin and the Resistance to the 'Talkies.'" In *Charlie Chaplin: His Reflection in Modern Times*, edited by Adolphe Nysenholc, 3–10. Berlin: Mouton de Gruyter, 1991.

Brabandt, Anna. *Franz Kafka und der Stummfilm: Eine intermediale Studie*. Munich: Martin Meidenbauer, 2009.

Brod, Max. *Franz Kafka: A Biography*. Translated by G. Humphreys Roberts and Richard Winston. New York: Schocken, 1960.

Bruce, Iris. *Kafka and Cultural Zionism: Dates in Palestine*. Madison: University of Wisconsin Press, 2007.

Campora, Matthew. "Art Cinema and New Hollywood: Multiform Narrative and Sonic Metalepsis in *Eternal Sunshine of the Spotless Mind*." *New Review of Film and Television Studies* 7, no. 2 (2009): 119–31.

Casanova, Pascale. *Kafka, Angry Poet*. Translated by Chris Turner. London: Seagull Books, 2015.

Chaplin, Charles, dir. *The Kid*. 1921; Burbank, Calif.: Warner Home Video, 2003. DVD.

Chion, Michel. *Audio-Vision: Sound on Screen*. Edited and translated by Claudia Gorbman. New York: Columbia University Press, 1994.

Chion, Michel. *Film, a Sound Art*. Translated by Claudia Gorbman. New York: Columbia University Press, 2009.

Chion, Michel. *The Voice in Cinema*. Edited and translated by Claudia Gorbman. New York: Columbia University Press, 1999.

Coetzee, J. M. "Time, Tense and Aspect in Kafka's 'The Burrow.'" *MLN* 96, no. 3 (1981): 556–79.

Cohn, Dorrit. *Transparent Minds: Narrative Modes for Presenting Consciousness in Fiction*. Princeton, N.J.: Princeton University Press, 1978.

Corngold, Stanley. "Kafka and the Dialect of Modern Literature." *College Literature* 21, no. 1 (1994): 89ff.

Corngold, Stanley. "Kafka and the Philosophy of Music; or: Des Kommas Fehl hilft." *Journal of the Kafka Society of America* 28 (2004): 4–16.

Corngold, Stanley. "Musical Indirections in Kafka's 'Forschungen eines Hundes.'" In *Franz Kafka: Narration, Rhetoric and Reading*, edited by Jakob Lothe, Beatrice Sandberg, and Ronald Speirs, 170–95. Columbus: Ohio State University Press, 2011.

Corngold, Stanley. "Thirteen Ways of Looking at a Vermin: Metaphor and Chiasmus in Kafka's *Die Verwandlung*." *Literary Research/Recherche littéraire* 21, nos. 41–42 (2004): 59–80.

Daiber, Jürgen. *Kafka und der Lärm: Klanglandschaften der frühen Moderne*. Münster: mentis, 2015.

Danius, Sara. *The Senses of Modernism: Technology, Perception, and Aesthetics*. Ithaca, N.Y.: Cornell University Press, 2002.

Daub, Adrian. "'Hannah, Can You Hear Me?': Chaplin's Great Dictator, 'Schtonk,' and the Vicissitudes of Voice." *Criticism* 51, no. 3 (2009): 451–82.

DeKoven, Marianne. "Kafka's Animal Stories: Modernist Form and Interspecies Narrative." In *Creatural Fictions: Human-Animal Relationships in Twentieth- and Twenty-First-Century Literature*, edited by David Herman, 19–40. New York: Palgrave Macmillan, 2016.

Deleuze, Gilles, and Félix Guattari. *Kafka: Toward a Minor Literature*. Translated by Dana Polan. Minneapolis: University of Minnesota Press, 1986.

Delpeut, Peter, dir. *Diva Dolorosa*. 1999; New York: Zeitgeist, 2008. DVD.

Denksy, Doreen. "Literary Advocates: The Rhetorics and Poetics of Speaking-For in Franz Kafka." Ph.D. diss., Johns Hopkins University, 2013. ProQuest (AAT 3574941).

Dietrich, Marlene. *Nehmt nur mein Leben . . . Reflexionen*. Munich: Wilhelm Goldmann, 1979.

Dolar, Mladen. "The Burrow of Sound." *Differences* 22, nos. 2–3 (2011): 112–39.

Dolar, Mladen. *A Voice and Nothing More*. Cambridge, Mass.: MIT Press, 2006.

Duttlinger, Carolin. "Film und Fotografie." In *Kafka-Handbuch: Leben—Werk— Wirkung*, edited by Manfred Engel and Bernd Auerochs, 72–79. Stuttgart: J. B. Metzler, 2010.

Ebiri, Bilge. "*The Interview* Has Renewed Interest in Chaplin's *The Great Dictator*, Which Is a Great Thing." *Vulture*, December 19, 2014, www.vulture.com.

Eisenberg, Noah. *Between Redemption and Doom: The Strains of German-Jewish Modernism*. Lincoln: University of Nebraska Press, 1999.

Eisenstein, Sergei. *Film Forum: Essays in Film Theory*. Edited and translated by Jay Leyda. New York: Harcourt, 1949.

Eisner, Lotte. *The Haunted Screen: Expressionism in the German Cinema and the Influence of Max Reinhardt*. Translated by Roger Greaves. Berkeley: University of California Press, 2008.

Elsaesser, Thomas, and Malte Hagener. *Film Theory: An Introduction through the Senses*. New York: Routledge, 2010.

Emrich, Wilhelm. *Franz Kafka*. 3rd ed. Frankfurt am Main: Athenäum, 1961.

Epstein, Josh. *Sublime Noise: Musical Culture and the Modernist Writer*. Baltimore: Johns Hopkins University Press, 2014.

Freedman, Barbara. "Errors in Comedy: A Psychoanalytic Theory of Farce." *New York Literary Forum* 5 (1980): 233–43.

Fryer, Paul. *The Opera Singer and the Silent Film*. Jefferson, N.C.: McFarland & Company, 2005.

Gellen, Kata. "*Be/Ruf*: Sound Control and Vocal Training in *Der blaue Engel*." In "Weimar Sound Film," edited by Theodore Rippey and John Davidson, special issue, *Colloquia Germanica* 44, no. 3 (2011): 259–81.

Gellen, Kata. "Hearing Spaces: Architecture and Acoustic Experience in Modernist German Literature." *Modernism/Modernity* 17, no. 4 (2010): 799–818.

Gellen, Kata. "The Mass-Produced Word: Kafka's Scandals." *Journal of the Kafka Society of America* 29, nos. 1–2 (2005): 29–36.

Gellen, Kata. "Noises Off: Cinematic Sound in Kafka's 'The Burrow.'" In Biderman and Lewit, *Mediamorphosis*, 111–29.

Gellen, Kata. "Works Recited: Franz Kafka and the Art of Literary Recitation." *Germanic Review* 86, no. 2 (2011): 93–113.

Genette, Gérard. *Métalepse: De la figure à la fiction*. Paris: Seuil, 2004.

Genette, Gérard. *Narrative Discourse: An Essay in Method*. Translated by Jane E. Lewin. Ithaca, N.Y.: Cornell University Press, 1980.

Gess, Nicola. "The Politics of Listening: The Power of Song in Kafka's 'Josefine, the Singer.'" In Corngold, *Kafka's Selected Stories*, 275–88.

Goethe, Johann Wolfgang von. *Gedichte: 1756–1799*. Edited by Karl Eibl. Frankfurt am Main: Deutscher Klassiker Verlag, 1987.

Green, Fitzhugh. *The Film Finds Its Tongue*. New York: Knickerbocker, 1929.

Grover-Friedlander, Michal. *Vocal Apparitions: The Attraction of Cinema to Opera*. Princeton, N.J.: Princeton University Press, 2005.

Gunning, Tom. "Doing for the Eye What the Phonograph Does for the Ear." In Abel and Altman, *The Sounds of Early Cinema*, 13–31.

Gunning, Tom. "The Scene of Speaking: Two Decades of Discovering the Film Lecturer." In "The State of Sound Studies," edited by Rick Altman, special issue, *iris* 27 (1999): 67–79.

Halliday, Sam. *Sonic Modernity: Representing Sound in Literature, Culture and the Arts*. Edinburgh: Edinburgh University Press, 2013.

Hamilton, John T. "'Ist das Spiel vielleicht unangenehm?': Musical Disturbances and Acoustic Space in Kafka." *Journal of the Kafka Society of America* 28 (2004): 23–26.

Hardt, Ludwig. "Der Autor und sein Rezitator." In *"Als Kafka mir entgegenkam . . .": Erinnerungen an Franz Kafka*, edited by Hans-Gerd Koch, 213–17. Berlin: Klaus Wagenbach, 2013.

Hargraves, John A. "Kafka and Silence: An Alternative View of Music." In Corngold, *Kafka's Selected Stories*, 321–33.

Hazanavicius, Michel, dir. *The Artist*. 2011; Culver City, Calif.: Sony Pictures, 2012. DVD.

Herr, Sophie Andrée. "Die Stimmen im Stummfilm." Ph.D. diss., Freie Universität Berlin, in progress.

Homer. *The Odyssey*. Translated by Richmond Lattimore. New York: Harper Perennial, 1991.

Honold, Alexander. "Der singende Text: Klanglichkeit als literarische Performanzqualität." In *Literatur intermedial: Paradigmenbildung zwischen 1918 und 1968*, edited by Wolf Gerhard Schmidt and Thorsten Valk, 187–207. Berlin: de Gruyter, 2009.

Huyssen, Andreas. *Miniature Metropolis: Literature in the Age of Photography and Film*. Cambridge, Mass.: Harvard University Press, 2015.

Isenberg, Noah. *Between Redemption and Doom: The Strains of German-Jewish Modernism*. Lincoln: University of Nebraska Press, 1999.

Jakobson, Roman, and Linda Waugh. *The Sound Shape of Language*. Berlin: Mouton de Gruyter, 2002.

Kaes, Anton, ed. *Kino-Debatte: Texte zum Verhältnis von Literatur und Film, 1909–1929*. Munich: Deutscher Taschenbuch Verlag, 1978.

Kaes, Anton, Nicholas Baer, and Michael Cowan, eds. *The Promise of Cinema: German Film Theory, 1907–1933*. Berkeley: University of California Press, 2016.

Kafka, Franz. *The Blue Octavo Notebooks*. Edited by Max Brod; translated by Ernst Kaiser and Eithne Wilkins. Cambridge, Mass.: Exact Change, 1991.

Kafka, Franz. *Briefe, 1902–1924*. Edited by Max Brod. New York: Schocken, 1958.

Kafka, Franz. *Briefe, 1914–1917*. Edited by Hans-Gerd Koch. Frankfurt am Main: Fischer, 2005.

Kafka, Franz. *The Castle*. Translated by Willa and Edwin Muir. New York: Schocken, 1995.

Kafka, Franz. *The Complete Stories*. Edited by Nahum Glatzer. New York: Schocken, 1983.

Kafka, Franz. *Dearest Father*. Translated by Hannah and Richard Stokes. London: Oneworld Classics, 2008.

Kafka, Franz. *The Diaries of Franz Kafka, 1910–1913*. Edited by Max Brod; translated by Joseph Kresh. New York: Schocken, 1968.

Kafka, Franz. *The Diaries of Franz Kafka, 1914–1923*. Edited by Max Brod; translated by Martin Greenberg, with Hannah Arendt. New York: Schocken, 1968.

Kafka, Franz. *Drucke zu Lebzeiten*. Edited by Wolf Kittler, Hans-Gerd Koch, and Gerhard Neumann. Frankfurt am Main: Fischer, 2002.

Kafka, Franz. "Great Noise." Translated by Jack Deming. Published April 27, 2010. https://settingover.wordpress.com/?s=great+noise.

Kafka, Franz. *Kafka's Selected Stories: New Translations, Backgrounds and Contexts, Criticism*. Edited and translated by Stanley Corngold. New York: W. W. Norton, 2007.

Kafka, Franz. *Letters to Felice*. Edited by Erich Heller and Jürgen Born; translated by James Stern and Elisabeth Duckworth. New York: Schocken, 1973.

Kafka, Franz. *Letters to Friends, Family, and Editors*. Translated by Richard and Clara Winston. New York: Schocken, 1977.

Kafka, Franz. *Letters to Milena*. Translated by Philip Boehm. New York: Schocken, 1990.

Kafka, Franz. *The Metamorphosis*. Edited and translated by Stanley Corngold. New York: Modern Library, 2013.

Kafka, Franz. *Nachgelassene Schriften und Fragmente I*. Edited by Malcolm Pasley. Frankfurt am Main: Fischer, 2002.

Kafka, Franz. *Nachgelassene Schriften und Fragmente I: Apparatband*. Edited by Malcolm Pasley. Frankfurt am Main: Fischer, 2002.

Kafka, Franz. *Nachgelassene Schriften und Fragmente II*. Edited by Jost Schillemeit. Frankfurt am Main: Fischer, 2002.

Kafka, Franz. *Der Proceß: Apparatband*. Edited by Malcolm Pasley. Frankfurt am Main: Fischer, 2002.

Kafka, Franz. *Das Schloß*. Edited by Malcolm Pasley. Frankfurt am Main: Fischer, 2002.

Kafka, Franz. *Tagebücher*. Edited by Hans-Gerd Koch, Michael Müller, and Malcolm Pasley. Frankfurt am Main: Fischer, 2002.

Kafka, Franz. *The Transformation (Metamorphosis) and Other Stories*. Edited and translated by Malcolm Pasley. London: Penguin, 1992.

Kane, Brian. *Sound Unseen: Acousmatic Sound in Theory and Practice*. Oxford: Oxford University Press, 2014.

Kittler, Friedrich. *Discourse Networks 1800/1900*. Translated by Michael Metteer, with Chris Cullens. Stanford, Calif.: Stanford University Press, 1992.

Kittler, Friedrich. *Gramophone, Film, Typewriter*. Translated by Geoffrey Winthrop-Young and Michael Wutz. Stanford, Calif.: Stanford University Press, 1999.

Kittler, Wolf. "Grabenkrieg—Nervenkrieg—Medienkrieg: Franz Kafka und der 1. Weltkrieg." In *Armaturen der Sinne: Literarische und technische Medien 1870 bis 1920*, edited by Jochen Hörisch and Michael Wetzel, 289–309. Munich: Wilhelm Fink, 1990.

Kittler, Wolf. "Schreibmaschinen, Sprechmaschinen: Effekte technischer Medien im Werk Franz Kafkas." In Kittler and Neumann, *Franz Kafka*, 75–163. Freiburg: Rombach, 1990.

Kittler, Wolf. *Der Turmbau zu Babel und das Schweigen der Sirenen: Über das Reden, das Schweigen, die Stimme und die Schrift in vier Texten von Franz Kafka*. Erlangen: Palm & Enke, 1985.

Kittler, Wolf, and Gerhard Neumann, eds. *Franz Kafka: Schriftverkehr*. Freiburg: Rombach, 1990.

Koelb, Clayton. *Kafka: A Guide for the Perplexed*. New York: Continuum, 2010.

Koelb, Clayton. *Kafka's Rhetoric: The Passion of Reading*. Ithaca, N.Y.: Cornell University Press, 1989.

Koepnick, Lutz. "June 1929: Lloyd Bacon's *The Singing Fool* Triggers Debate about Sound Film." In *A New History of German Cinema*, edited by Jennifer M. Kapczynski and Michael D. Richardson, 197–201. Rochester, N.Y.: Camden House, 2012.

Koepnick, Lutz. "Rilke's Rumblings and Lang's Bang." *Monatshefte* 98, no. 2 (2006): 199–214.

Kraus, Karl, ed. *Die Fackel*. Austrian Academy Corpus—FACKEL Online Version. Digital edition no 1. http://www.aac.ac.at/fackel.

Kurz, Gerhard. "The Rustling of Stillness: Approaches to Kafka's *The Burrow*." In Corngold, *Kafka's Selected Stories*, 333–55.

Lensing, Leo. "'Fackel'-Leser und Werfel-Verehrer: Anmerkungen zu Kafkas Briefen an Robert Klopstock." In *Kafkas letzter Freund: Der Nachlaß Robert Klopstock (1899–1972). Mit kommentierter Erstveröffentlichung von 38 teils ungedruckten Briefen Franz Kafkas*, edited by Hugo Wetscherek, 265–92. Vienna: Inlibris, 2003.

Lensing, Leo. "Kraus the Mouse? Kafka's Late Reading of *Die Fackel* and the Vagaries of Literary History." In *Nexus: Essays in German Jewish Studies*, edited by William C. Donahue and Martha B. Helfer, vol. 3, 71–95. Rochester, N.Y.: Camden House, 2017.

Levi, Primo. "Observed from a Distance." In *Flaw of Form*, 608–16. Translated by Jenny McPhee. In *The Complete Works of Primo Levi*, edited by Ann Goldstein, vol. 1, 573–747. New York: Liveright, 2015.

Levin, Thomas Y. "Rhetoric of the Temporal Index: Surveillant Narration and the Cinema of 'Real Time.'" In *CTRL Space: Rhetorics of Surveillance from Bentham to Big Brother*, edited by Thomas Y. Levin, Ursula Frohne, and Peter Weibel, 578–93. Cambridge, Mass.: MIT Press, 2002.

Levin, Thomas Y. "'Tones from out of Nowhere': Rudolph Pfenninger and the Archaeology of Synthetic Sound." *Grey Room* 12 (2003): 32–79.

Levine, Michael. "Of Big Ears and Bondage: Benjamin, Kafka, and the Static of the Sirens." *German Quarterly* 87, no. 2 (2014): 196–215.

Levine, Michael. "'A Place So Insanely Enchanting': Kafka and the Poetics of Suspension." *MLN* 123 (2008): 1039–67.

Levine, Michael. *Writing through Repression: Literature, Censorship, Psychoanalysis*. Baltimore: Johns Hopkins University Press, 1994.

Liska, Vivian. *When Kafka Says We: Uncommon Communities in German-Jewish Literature*. Bloomington: Indiana University Press, 2009.

Loiperdinger, Martin. "German *Tonbilder* of the 1900s: Advance Technology and National Brand." In *Film 1900: Technology, Perception, Culture*, 187–99. Edited by Annemone Ligensa and Klaur Kreimeier. Herts, U.K.: John Libbey, 2009.

Maché, Britta. "The Noise in the Burrow: Kafka's Final Dilemma." *German Quarterly* 55, no. 4 (1982): 526–40.

Menke, Bettina. *Prosopopoiia: Stimme und Text bei Brentano, Hoffmann, Kleist und Kafka*. Munich: Wilhelm Fink, 2000.

Meyer-Kalkus, Reinhardt. *Stimme und Sprechkünste im 20. Jahrhundert*. Berlin: Akademie Verlag, 2001.

Miron, Dan. *From Continuity to Contiguity: Toward a New Jewish Literary Thinking*. Stanford, Calif.: Stanford University Press, 2010.

Mitchell, Breon. "Kafka's 'Elf Söhne': A New Look at the Puzzle." *German Quarterly* 47, no. 2 (1974): 191–203.

Morgenstern, Soma. *Kritiken—Berichte—Tagebücher*. Edited by Ingolf Schulte. Lüneburg: zu Klampen, 2001.

Morlhon, Camille de, dir. *La broyeuse de coeurs*. 1913. In *Kafka Geht ins Kino / Kafka va au cinéma / Kafka Goes to the Movies*, DVD 2. Compiled by Hanns Zischler. Munich: Edition Filmmuseum, 2017. DVD.

Morris, Joel. "Joseph K.'s (A+x) Problem: Kafka on the Moment of Awakening." *German Quarterly* 82, no. 4 (2009): 469–82.

Müller, Lothar. *Die zweite Stimme: Vortragskunst von Goethe bis Kafka*. Berlin: Wagenbach, 2007.

Musil, Robert. "Moissi" (1921). In *Prosa, Dramen, späte Briefe*, edited by Adolf Frisé, 601–4. Hamburg: Rowohlt, 1957.

Nasta, Dominique. "Setting the Pace of a Heartbeat: The Use of Sound Elements in European Melodramas before 1915." In Abel and Altman, *The Sounds of Early Cinema*, 95–109.

Neumann, Gerhard. "Chinesische Mauer und Schacht von Babel: Franz Kafkas Architekturen." *Deutsche Vierteljahrsschrift für Literaturwissenschaft und Geistesgeschichte* 83, no. 3 (2009): 452–71.

Neumann, Gerhard. "Kafka und die Musik." In Kittler and Neumann, *Franz Kafka*, 391–98. Freiburg: Rombach, 1990.

Neumann, Gerhard. "Kulturelle Mimikry: Zur Affenfigur bei Flaubert und Kafka." *Zeitschrift für deutsche Philologie* 126 (2007): 126–42.

Neumann, Gerhard. "Nachrichten vom 'Pontus': Das Problem der Kunst im Werk Franz Kafkas." In Kittler and Neumann, *Franz Kafka*, 164–98. Freiburg: Rombach, 1990.

Neumann, Gerhard. "Werk oder Schrift? Vorüberlegungen zur Edition von Kafkas 'Bericht für eine Akademie.'" *Acta Germanica* 14 (1981): 1–21.

Norris, Margot. "Kafka's Hybrids: Thinking Animals and Mirrored Humans." In *Kafka's Creatures: Animals, Hybrids, and Other Fantastic Beings*, edited by Marc Lucht and Donna Yarri, 17–31. Lanham, Md.: Rowman & Littlefield, 2010.

Norris, Margot. "Kafka's Josefine: The Animal as Negative Site of Narration." *Modern Language Notes* 98, no. 3 (1983): 366–83.

Noys, Benjamin. "Film-of-Life: Agamben's Profanation of the Image." In *Cinema and Agamben: Ethics, Biopolitics and the Moving Image*, 89–101. Edited by Henrik Gustafsson and Asbjørn Grønstad. New York: Bloomsbury, 2014.

O'Rawe, Des. "The Great Secret: Silence, Cinema, and Modernism." *Screen* 47, no. 4 (2006): 395–405.

Pasley, J. M. S. "Two Kafka Enigmas: 'Elf Söhne' and 'Die Sorge des Hausvaters.'" *Modern Language Review* 59, no. 1 (1964): 73–81.

Perron, Bernard. "The First *Transi-Sounds* of Parallel Editing." In Abel and Altman, *The Sounds of Early Cinema*, 79–86.

Peters, John Durham. "The Telephonic Uncanny and the Problem of Communication." In Sterne, *The Sound Studies Reader*, 363–71.

Pinch, Trevor, and Karin Bijsterveld, eds. *The Oxford Handbook of Sound Studies*. Oxford: Oxford University Press, 2012.

Pinthus, Kurt, ed. *Das Kinobuch*. Zurich: Die Arche, 1963.

Puchner, Martin. "Kafka's Antitheatrical Gestures." *Germanic Review* 78, no. 3 (2010): 177–93.

Puchner, Martin. "Reading the Sirens' Gestures: Kafka between Silent Film and Epic Theater." *Journal of the Kafka Society of America* 21, nos. 1–2 (1997): 27–39.

Raynauld, Isabelle. "Dialogue in Early Silent Screenplays: What Actors Really Said." In Abel and Altman, *The Sounds of Early Cinema*, 69–78.

Robertson, Ritchie. *Kafka: Judaism, Politics, and Literature*. Oxford: Clarendon, 1985.

Rothman, Joshua. "The Metamorphosis: What Is It Like to Be an Animal?" *New Yorker*, May 30, 2016, 70–74.

Ryan, Marie-Laure. "Metaleptic Machines." *Semiotica* 150, nos. 1–4 (2004): 439–69.

Saenger, Paul. *Space between Words: The Origins of Silent Reading*. Stanford, Calif.: Stanford University Press, 1997.

Sanchez, Rebecca. *Deafening Modernism: Embodied Language and Visual Poetics in American Literature*. New York: NYU Press, 2015.

Schaeffer, Pierre. "Acousmatics." In *Audio Culture: Readings in Modern Music*, edited by Christoph Cox and Daniel Warner, 76–81. New York: Continuum, 2004.

Schaper, Rüdiger. *Moissi: Triest, Berlin, New York. Eine Schauspielerlegende*. Berlin: Argon, 2000.

Schiffermüller, Isolde. *Franz Kafkas Gesten: Studien zur Entstellung der menschlichen Sprache*. Tübingen: Francke, 2011. ·

Schuman, Rebecca. *Kafka and Wittgenstein: The Case for an Analytic Modernism*. Evanston, Ill.: Northwestern University Press, 2015.

Seuss, Dr. (Theodor Geisl). *Horton Hears a Who!* New York: Random House, 1954.

Shahar, Galili. "The Alarm Clock: The Times of Gregor Samsa." In *Kafka and the Universal*, edited by Arthur Cools and Vivian Liska, 257–69. Berlin: de Gruyter, 2016.

Simonson, Mary. "Screening the Diva." In *The Arts of the Prima Donna in the Long Nineteenth Century*, edited by Rachel Cowgill and Hilary Poriss, 83–100. New York: Oxford University Press, 2012.

Sobibakke, Karl. "Stimme und Ritual: Zu Kafkas 'Josefine, die Sängerin oder das Volk der Mäuse.'" *Links: Rivista di letteratura e cultura tedesca* 6 (2006): 99–108.

Spadoni, Robert. *Uncanny Bodies: The Coming of Sound Film and the Origin of the Horror Genre*. Berkeley: University of California Press, 2007.

Spadoni, Robert. "The Uncanny Body of Early Sound Film." *Velvet Light Trap* 51 (2003): 4–16.

Spearing, James. "Now the Movies Go Back to Their School Days." *New York Times*, August 19, 1928.

Stach, Reiner. *Kafka: Die Jahre der Erkenntnis*. Frankfurt am Main: Fischer, 2008.

Sternberg, Josef von. *Der blaue Engel*. UFA, 1930; New York: Kino on Video, 2001. DVD, disc 1.

Sterne, Jonathan. *The Audible Past: Cultural Origins of Sound Reproduction*. Durham, N.C.: Duke University Press, 2003.

Sterne, Jonathan, ed. *The Sound Studies Reader*. London: Routledge, 2012.

Sterne, Jonathan, and Mitchell Akiyama. "The Recording That Never Wanted to Be Heard and Other Stories of Sonification." In Pinch and Bijsterveld, *The Oxford Handbook of Sound Studies*, 544–60.

Suchoff, David. *Kafka's Jewish Languages: The Hidden Openness of Tradition*. Philadelphia: University of Pennsylvania Press, 2012.

Szaloky, Melinda. "Sounding Images in Silent Film: Visual Acoustics in Murnau's *Sunrise*." *Cinema Journal* 41, no. 2 (2002): 109–31.

Szczepanik, Petr. "Sonic Imagination; or, Film Sound as a Discursive Construct in Czech Culture of the Transitional Period." In *Lowering the Boom: Critical*

Studies in Film Sound, edited by Jay Beck and Tony Grajeda, 87–104. Urbana: University of Illinois Press, 2008.

Theisen, Bianca. "Simultaneity of Media: Kafka's Literary Screen." *MLN* 121 (2006): 543–50.

Tieber, Claus, and Anna K. Windisch. *The Sounds of Silent Films: New Perspectives on History, Theory and Practice*. London: Palgrave Macmillan, 2014.

Toop, David. *Sinister Resonance: The Mediumship of the Listener*. New York: Continuum, 2010.

Trotter, David. *Cinema and Modernism*. Oxford: Blackwell, 2007.

Twilley, Nicola. "Seeing with Your Tongue: Sensory-Substitution Devices Help Blind and Deaf People, but That's Just the Beginning." *New Yorker*, May 15, 2017. https://www.newyorker.com/magazine/2017/05/15/seeing-with-your-tongue.

Uexküll, Jakob von. *A Foray into the Worlds of Animals and Humans; with, A Theory of Meaning*. Translated by Joseph D. O'Neil. Minneapolis: University of Minnesota Press, 2010.

Uhall, Michael. "Creaturely Conditions: Acknowledgment and Animality in Kafka, Cavell, and Uexküll." *Configurations* 24, no. 1 (2016): 1–24.

Waal, Frans de. *Are We Smart Enough to Know How Smart Animals Are?* New York: W. W. Norton, 2016.

Weitzman, Erica. *Irony's Antics: Walser, Kafka, Roth, and the German Comic Tradition*. Evanston, Ill.: Northwestern University Press, 2015.

Weninger, Robert. "Sounding Out the Silence of Gregor Samsa: Kafka's Rhetoric of Dys-Communication." *Studies in 20th Century Literature* 17, no. 2 (1993): 263–86.

Winokur, Mark. "*Modern Times* and the Comedy of Transformation." *Literature/Film Quarterly* 15, no. 4 (1987): 219–26.

Wollen, Peter. *Singin' in the Rain*. 2nd ed. London: Palgrave Macmillan/bfi, 2012.

Wood, Michael. "Modernism and Film." In *The Cambridge Companion to Modernism*, 268–83. Cambridge: Cambridge University Press, 2011.

Zischler, Hanns. *Kafka geht ins Kino*. Reinbek bei Hamburg: Rowohlt, 1996.

INDEX

Page references in **boldface** refer to illustrations.